REAL WORLD FREEHAND 4

6-1-95

Read P. 77-107

Real World
FreeHand 4

by
Olav Martin Kvern

AN OPEN HOUSE BOOK

PEACHPIT PRESS

for Stanley Fleming Kvern & Cordelia Ellen Kvern

REAL WORLD FREEHAND 4
Olav Martin Kvern

PEACHPIT PRESS, INC.
2414 Sixth St.
Berkeley, CA 94710
(510) 548-4393
(510) 548-5991(fax)

Editor: Stephen F. Roth
Copy editor: Glenn Fleishman
Cover design: Ted Mader & Associates (TMA)
Cover illustration: Robert Dietz
Interior design, illustration, and production: Olav Martin Kvern

DISTRIBUTION
Peachpit Press books are distributed to the US book trade by Publishers Group West, 4065 Hollis, PO Box 8843, Emeryville, CA 94609, phone (800) 788-3123 or (510) 658-3453, fax (510) 658-1834. Peachpit books are also available from wholesalers throughout the US including Baker & Taylor Books, Golden-Lee Book Distributors, and Ingram Book Company. Resellers outside the book trade can contact Peachpit directly at (800) 980-8999.

ISBN 0-56609-103-9

9 8 7 6 5 4 3 2 1

Printed and bound in the United States of America

 Printed on recycled paper.

If I weren't one of the authors of Aldus FreeHand, I'd want this book to teach me how to use it. Actually, I'd want Ole to teach me, but he lives two thousand miles away. And he probably would get pretty tired of showing me the tricky parts over and over and over. With *Real World FreeHand* I have his advice and insight any time I need them.

When we started on FreeHand nearly five years ago, we had a vision of an easy–to–use, yet extraordinarily powerful graphics program. We wanted it to be usable by both novices and professional designers, and give results limited only by a person's artistic ability. It should be as intuitive as a pencil, but as powerful as a mind link to a hallucination machine. We've come a long way in those five years. Of course, we aren't quite up to the level of our vision yet. But it wouldn't have been much of a vision if we could achieve it in just five years of programming.

We had another vision too—one of talented artists working with computers, multiplying their abilities a hundredfold, and avoiding the dull, routine work of aligning things that simply refused to align; of specifying type, then setting the job aside while waiting for the galleys to come back from the typesetting house; of doing what our first ad agency did—cutting that type apart letter by letter and hand setting it with just the right spacing; of hearing the client ask to change a word in the middle of one of those blocks when the final extended deadline is tomorrow morning. With FreeHand, everything is malleable until the moment when a scanning laser beam starts to reveal the billions of pixels that make up your page on the drum of a laser printer or to the film of an imagesetter.

We also thought everybody ought to have a chance to undo their mistakes. Any mistakes. A bunch of mistakes. Imagine how much bolder you could be in real life if you had a chance to undo some of your blunders. Call your broker and tell him to undo that stock you sold last week. Go back two years and change your mind about marrying that bum who just passed out on the couch. You can't do it in real life, but you sure can with FreeHand. It is an underappreciated fact that FreeHand lets you undo more than just the easy things. FreeHand is the only program I have ever seen that lets you undo *every* editing operation, as many as 99 operations back.

I am really happy with what we finally achieved in FreeHand 4 (née Calvin). Our Calvin development team (thanks, Samantha, Rusty, Kevin, John, Bob, Dennis, Matt, Michael B., Jeff, Michael T., Bill, Alan, and Robbie) worked for months fixing bugs that companies who don't care as much about perfection as Altsys and Aldus would have shipped with. They kept improving it even after it was good enough, kept working on it until they were sick of it, in fact. I think there are three factors in our success: we really care about doing the best job we know how, we have several very smart software engineers working on it, and we have some awesomely talented users who continue to tell us how to make it even better.

Reading the drafts of this book is a lot like reading a biography of your own daughter. The writer talks about her accomplishments. Her beauty. Her charm. Her high-pitched whiny voice. Well, no writer is perfect. Fortunately, Ole laughs with us on those few occasions where the reality differs from the vision. And he goes on to explain those hard parts step by step in a way that almost anybody can understand.

I've reconsidered my first sentence. I do want this book, even though I did write a lot of FreeHand. *Real World FreeHand* is a great study guide: we'll continue to improve the parts of FreeHand Ole finds great, and we'll rework the parts Ole finds need lots of explaining. Reader, you've made two good choices. Crank up Free-Hand and get started with *Real World FreeHand*. I think you'll have fun with both.

Jim Von Ehr
President and CEO,
Altsys Corporation

Introduction

I don't read Finnish. But there it was, in the mail: a review of my book in a Finnish magazine. Did they like it? Hate it? I couldn't tell.

I wasn't thinking about it, much, right at that moment—I was busy throwing things into a bag to take to the hospital. Leslie, my wife, was in labor, and it was time to go.

The next night, as I was rocking my newborn son to sleep, our anesthetist, a friendly, interesting woman (who had, only a few hours before, been poking a big needle into Leslie's back), stopped by to see how we were doing. Business was slow at Ballard Hospital's birthing center—we were the only "customers," and it was the middle of the night. I rocked, we talked.

In the course of our conversation, she mentioned that she'd emigrated to the United States from Finland.

What could I do? I pulled the crumpled review out of my coat pocket, and asked if she'd glance at the it and tell me whether the reviewer liked the book or not. She insisted on doing a full translation of the text—in trade for a copy of the book for her son, a FreeHand user.

And the review? It was a rave.*

So here we are again. If you're a new reader, welcome. If you read the previous edition of this book, welcome back!

*"Vaikka FreeHandin tuntisi miten hyvin tahansa, löytyy tästä kirjasta silti uutta tietoa," which we quoted on the back of the book, means, more or less (according to my translator), "Even if you think you know everything about FreeHand, you'll learn something from this book."

Where I'm Coming From

Why should you listen to what I have to say about working with FreeHand? I've worked as a technical, medical, archaeological, and veterinary illustrator, as well as a general-purpose book and magazine illustrator. I've also worked as a designer, typesetter, paste-up slave, and art director.

More importantly, I bring my experience as a FreeHand user. I really have been through the long shifts (some of them longer than 40 hours) trying to get FreeHand files to print. On most of those late nights and early mornings, I could have been home in bed if I'd known just one key piece of information. But I didn't. There was no one to tell me.

I'm here to tell you.

If some piece of information in this book saves you one late night, one early morning, or gets your file to print on the first pass through the imagesetter instead of the second or third, I will have succeeded in my purpose.

Once, a janitor found me pounding on a Linotronic film processor (an ML-314, for you hardware tweaks) with a wastebasket. At 4:00 AM. I'd been up for more than 36 hours, and it'd just eaten a job that'd taken six hours to run on an imagesetter. I wrote this book in the hope that I could save others from repeating this scene.

Organization

This book's pretty simple: first, I'll show you how to get things into FreeHand; next, I'll talk about how to work with elements in FreeHand; and, finally, I'll tell you how to get your work out of FreeHand. Then, in Chapter 8, "PostScript," I'll show you how to extend FreeHand and make it do more than it could do when it came out of the box.

What's New in FreeHand 4. This is for people who've been using FreeHand 3 and want to know what's changed since then. The section works like an expanded table of contents: there's an overview of each new feature, followed by a page number where you can find further information.

Chapter 1: FreeHand Basics. This chapter is your orientation to the world of FreeHand. In it, I describe the publication window, selecting objects, moving objects, working with FreeHand's toolbox, and an overview of the way that you create and import elements into FreeHand (including basic path drawing).

Chapter 2: Drawing. This is all about using FreeHand's drawing tools—from creating and joining paths to applying lines and fills, creating styles, working with blends, creating charts and graphs, and drawing using perspective. This chapter expands on the discussion of drawing paths and adjusting curve handles that started in Chapter 1, "FreeHand Basics."

Chapter 3: Text and Type. This chapter deals with working with text in FreeHand—how to enter, edit, and format text. It covers wrapping text around graphics, specifying type, FreeHand's type effects, joining text to a path, and converting text into paths.

Chapter 4: Importing and Exporting. FreeHand doesn't exist in a vacuum. You need to be able to import images from scanners and color image-editing programs, or to be able to import EPS graphics from other PostScript drawing programs. You need to be able to import text from your word processor. This chapter shows you how, and where, FreeHand fits in with your other applications. Topics include working with TIFFs, importing PICTs, importing formatted and unformatted text, opening and importing EPS files created in other programs, and converting old FreeHand 3 EPS files to Illustrator 1.1 EPS format so that you can open them.

Chapter 5: Transforming. This chapter shows you how to manipulate FreeHand elements you've drawn, typed, or imported, and describes how to use the transformation (skewing, scaling, rotation, and reflection) tools.

Chapter 6: Color. In this chapter, I cover creating and applying colors in FreeHand. I also discuss color models, the history of color printing, creating duotones, and controlling the conditions under which you view and create color publications.

Chapter 7: Printing. It don't mean a thing if you can't get it on paper or film. Here's how to do that, plus a bunch of tips that'll save you money at your imagesetting service bureau and your commercial printer. In this chapter, I also talk about the various options contained in FreeHand's Print and Print Options dialog boxes and how they affect your publications.

Chapter 8: PostScript. In many ways, this chapter is the heart of the book. In it, I show you how to use PostScript when working with FreeHand, and how to add features to FreeHand. I wrote this chapter because I want to demythologize the process of adding PostScript strokes and fills to FreeHand. You don't have to have an engineering degree, or be a rocket scientist, to add unique touches to FreeHand that'll make it truly your own program. This chapter shows you how.

Conventions

I've always wanted to write a book that didn't have a section on "Conventions." I should be good enough at what I do that you don't have to do anything more than read the text and look at the figures to get the point. But I do have a few idiosyncracies of terminology I think need going over.

- ◆ Field. You know, a box in a dialog box or palette you type text in.

- ◆ Submenu. One of those annoying little menus that pops off the side of legitimate menu items.

- ◆ Popup menu. One of those annoying little menus that pops up from something that should be a field.

Disclaimer

Some of the techniques in this book involve modifying either FreeHand's subsidiary files (like PPDs) or modifying FreeHand itself. While I've tried to make the procedures (in these cases, anyway) as complete and accurate as possible, you need to be aware that you're proceeding entirely at your own risk. Given that, there are a few things you can do to make everything less risky.

Work on copies of files. If you don't keep your original files in their original state, how can you ever go back to where you started? Always back your files up before you try altering them.

Remember that not everyone will have your system. You can't expect your friends and your imagesetting service bureau to be absolutely up-to-date with your current modifications if you don't give them to them. Therefore, if your publication requires a custom page size you've written into a PPD, make sure that your imagesetting service bureau has the PPD.

Clean up after yourself. If you change any of FreeHand's PostScript printing routines in a printer's RAM, make sure that you change them back to their original state before anyone else sends a job to that printer or imagesetter. Nothing is more embarrassing for you or as much of a bother to everyone else as having your name and "DRAFT" print across all of the jobs printed on a particular printer because you forgot to change *showpage* back to its original definition. This, in fact, is a great way to provoke the villagers to come after you with torches and pitchforks.

Don't call Aldus technical support if something you read in this book doesn't work. They're the best in the business, but they didn't write this book and shouldn't be expected to support it. This book is not an Aldus product, and Aldus Corporation has no control over its content. Neither does Altsys Corporation (the people who write FreeHand). I'm not kidding. Write to me, instead. My mail addresses are listed in Appendix C, "Resources."

Acknowledgments

Congratulations to everyone at Aldus and Altsys for producing such an amazing, creativity-enhancing tool—especially to the FreeHand engineering team at Altsys: Steven Johnson (without his clues, I wouldn't have been able to start—let alone finish—Chapter 8, "PostScript"), Samantha Seals-Mason, Rusty Williams, Kevin Crowder,

John Ahlquist, Bob Sander-Cederlof, Dennis Griffin, Matt Bendiksen, Michael Froman, Jeff Ahlquist, Michael Thenhaus, Bill Fahle, Alan Sibley, and Robbie Harris. Special thanks to Brian Welter, Pete Mason, and, especially, to Jim Von Ehr for his inspiring foreword.

Thanks to Harry Edwards and Nick Allison at *Aldus Magazine* for making me a better writer. Some of the material in this book was lifted directly from my columns in the magazine.

Tracy Tobin and and I worked together on the FreeHand 2.0 documentation, and many of the tips and techniques in this book were outright stolen from her (all the rest were stolen from Conrad Chavez).

Thanks to the Seattle Gilbert and Sullivan Society, and their photographer, Ray O. Welch, for giving me permission to use some of their archival photographs as example images.

Thanks to Ted Nace for being a great publisher (and the only publisher I've ever had to loan money to so he could take me out to dinner), and to my editor and good buddy, Steve Roth, for all of his help whipping the manuscript into shape. Gaen Murphree and Glenn Fleishman did a fantastic job proofreading and copy editing (both made good suggestions on content that changed the book for the better, as well as removing all those nasty quotation marks), and carl juarez helped with last-minute text corrections in Page-Maker. Jan C. Wright, the Queen of Indexing, pulled together a great index in record time. Thanks to the other denizens of "the office"—David "did you borrow my hard drive?" Blatner, Don Sellers, John Cornicello, Marci Eversole, Steve "thumper" Broback, Michele Dione, and the occasional Kim Rush.

As usual, Chuck Cantellay, Neil S Kvern, and the rest of the staff of Seattle ImageSetting helped tremendously with the sections on imagesetting service bureaus (and they imageset some of the book).

Finally, thanks to my wonderful wife, Leslie Renée Simons, and to my son, Max Olav Kvern, for their encouragement, understanding, and support.

Olav Martin Kvern
Seattle, 1994

What's New in FreeHand 4?

What's new in FreeHand 4? What's not? When I started writing this book, I thought I'd be able to *revise* the previous edition (and thereby achieve an hourly pay rate approaching that of the minimum wage). Instead, I found I'd have to *rewrite* the book to keep up with all the changes in FreeHand. It was fun, though—I found I was frequently changing text from "you *can't* do that in FreeHand 3" to "you *can* do that in FreeHand 4."

Interface in Your Face

It's obvious from the time you start FreeHand 4: FreeHand has a new user interface. The new look is built around eleven palettes (seven of them are are new), which replace about 70 separate dialog boxes in FreeHand 3. See page 12.

Inspector Palette

The Inspector is the most important palette in FreeHand 4. You use the it to set paragraph formatting options, to specify fills and strokes, to create new pages, and to arrange pages on FreeHand's pasteboard. FreeHand 4's Inspector palette alone replaces more than 30 of FreeHand 3's modal dialog boxes. See page 13.

Color List

FreeHand 4's Color List replaces FreeHand 3's Colors palette. *What* the Color List does is pretty similar to the old palette, but *how* it does it is very different. See page 384.

Color Mixer   This is the place where you create and edit colors. It's a palette, so you don't have to take your eyes off your publication while you work with color, as you did in FreeHand 3's Colors dialog box. See page 386.

Tints Palette   Use the Tints palette to quickly generate a range of tints from any color. See page 386.

Type Specifications Palette   You use the Type Specifications palette to set the font, type style, and size of your text. See page 205. I sure wish leading were in this palette, but it's in the Character Inspector—see page 211 for more on the Character Inspector.

Align Palette   FreeHand's Align palette takes the functions of FreeHand 3's Align and Alignment dialog box and puts them in a palette. See page 367.

Transform Palette   The Transform Palette brings FreeHand's transformation features (move, scale, rotate, and skew) out on your screen—making them easier to reach than they were in FreeHand 3. Unfortunately, some commonly-used commands are a little harder to reach than they used to be—especially the controls for moving an object numerically. See page 331.

Halftone Palette   You use the Halftone palette to quickly set halftone type, screen angle, and screen frequency for a selected object. See page 13.

Styles Palette   The new Styles palette works differently—and, in my opinion, better—than FreeHand 3's version. You now define and edit styles by example—the quickest and easiest way to work with styles. See page 153.

Layers Palette   FreeHand 4's Layers palette is easier to use, though, in some ways, a little less capable than FreeHand 3's Layers palette (there's no longer a Multilayer shortcut for making the current layer the only active layer—you've got to turn layers on and off to accomplish the same thing). See page 65.

Minimizing and Maximizing Palettes

You can display palettes in a "minimized" form, where only the palette's title bar is visible, by clicking the zoom box in the palette's title bar. When you want to display the entire palette again, click the zoom box and the palette expands to its full size. See page 16.

Page Layout

In the previous edition of this book, in a description of the Pages control in the Print dialog box, I said, "Whenever I see this, my heart leaps up. Can you imagine a multipage FreeHand? Wouldn't that be great? Are you ready to start calling Aldus and Altsys?"

I guess enough of us called.

Multiple Pages, Multiple Sizes, Multiple Page Orientations

You can create as many pages, in as many different page sizes and orientations as you can fit on FreeHand's pasteboard. You can view and work on any single page, or any number of pages, at any time—making FreeHand an ideal choice when you have to work with multipage spreads, such as brochures. See page 30.

Larger Page Size

FreeHand's maximum page size is now 54 by 54 inches—up from FreeHand 3's 40-by-40-inch limit. See page 33.

Print Spreads Using Manual Tiling

Being able to position multiple pages on the pasteboard is great—but you really need a way to print more than one of those pages on a single sheet of paper or imagesetter film. Luckily, FreeHand includes this capability (though I can't tell if it does so by intention or accident). See page 439.

Drawing

All of FreeHand 3's drawing features are still with us in FreeHand 4—and some of the tools (like the Knife tool) have even gotten better. In addition, FreeHand adds some new drawing tools.

Point Tool   FreeHand 4's toolbox looks about the same as the toolbox in Free-Hand 3, with a few important differences. the biggest change is that the individual point-drawing tools from FreeHand 3 have been combined into the Point tool (known at Aldus as the "Bezigon" tool). When you're using this tool, a click produces a corner point. Hold down Option key as you click, and you place a curve point. Hold down Control as you click, and FreeHand places a connector point. See page 94.

Calligraphic Pen Tool   FreeHand 3's Variable Stroke tool gave FreeHand users a way to create paths shaped like brush strokes. FreeHand 4 builds on this feature, adding the Calligraphic Pen tool. With the Calligraphic Pen tool, you can create thick and thin strokes, angled like those you would draw with a calligraphic nib. See page 91.

Polygon tool   FreeHand 4's Polygon tool makes it easy to draw any equilateral polygon, such as pentagons, octagons, and hexagons. You can also use it to draw stars with any number of points. See page 47.

Improved Knife Tool   FreeHand 3's Knife tool could only cut paths one path at a time. In FreeHand 4, the Knife tool works like—well, like a knife would (or, really, more like a chain saw!). It cuts every selected path you drag it across. See page 50.

Editable Arrowheads   When you don't see the arrowhead you want on the Arrowhead menus in FreeHand's Stroke Inspector, you can create your own. See page 135.

Path Operations

Path operations make it easy to create shapes that would be difficult or impossible to draw by hand—you can draw basic shapes (rectangles, polygons, and ellipses) and use the path operations to turn these basic shapes into more complex paths. See page 114.

Punch   Select two closed, overlapping paths and choose Punch from the Path Operations submenu of the Arrange menu when you want to cut the shape of the frontmost path out of the path behind it. Punch uses the frontmost object as a "cookie cutter." See page 128.

Union   Choose Union when you want to join overlapping (closed) paths together while deleting the area(s) where the paths overlap. See page 128.

Intersect   When you select two closed, overlapping paths and choose Intersect from the Path Operations submenu of the Arrange menu, FreeHand deletes the original paths, leaving only the area defined by their intersection. See page 126.

Simplify   Simplify analyzes a path and removes extraneous points on the path. Autotracing, for example, sometimes generates more points than are strictly necessary to describe a path. See page 117.

Correct Direction   Choose Correct Direction when you want to set a selected path's direction of the current path to clockwise. This path operation, and its counterpart, Reverse Direction, are particularly handy when you want to change the way text joins to a path. See page 115.

Reverse Direction   Reverse Direction does just what it says—it changes the direction of a path from whatever it currently is to its opposite (from clockwise to counterclockwise, for example). See page 116.

Remove Overlap   Choose Remove Overlap to remove any areas of a single path where the path crosses over itself. This path operation comes in handy when you're cleaning up complex paths you've generated by autotracing. See page 117.

Expand Stroke   Expand Stroke converts a closed path into a composite path, or converts an open path into a closed path that follows the open path's shape. You can specify the width of the new path as you use Expand Stroke. See page 128.

Inset Path   Inset Path creates another version of the selected shape, a precise distance inside (or outside) the current shape. See page 129.

Text and Text Blocks

In FreeHand 4, you can edit your text just as you see it in your layout—no more trips to the dreaded Text dialog box.

You can even edit text that's been joined to a path this way—just select the Text tool and click it in some text that's joined to a path. The insertion point follows the baseline of the type as it shifts and slants around the path.

Creating and Editing Text Onscreen

To create a text block, select the Text tool and drag it on the page (you can also simply click the Text tool on the page, but drag-creating a text block gives you control over the width and height of the text block. To add text to your new text block, start typing. See page 184.

Sizing Text Blocks To Fit Text

After you've finished typing text in a text block, you might want to resize the text block to fit the text. If so, select the text box with the pointer tool, and double-click the link box (the box that appears outside the lower-right corner of the text block). FreeHand sizes the text block so that it's no larger than the text it contains. See page 193.

Specifying a Text Block's Inset

If you want, you can specify an inset for your text block—essentially, the inset is a margin inside the text block. See page 203.

Multicolumn and Multirow Text Blocks

A FreeHand text blocks can contain up to 100 rows and 100 columns—which, when combined with FreeHand's new tabs and paragraph formatting, makes FreeHand a great choice for creating tables. See page 198.

Creating Borders on Text Blocks

FreeHand's text blocks—and the rows and columns they contain—can be stroked and filled. The same fill and stroke apply to all of the cells and cell borders inside the text block. See page 201.

Linking Text Blocks

FreeHand's text blocks, like PageMaker's, can be linked together so that text can flow from one text block to another. By linking text blocks, you can create articles that flow over several magazine pages, for example. See page 197.

Typography

FreeHand is now equipped with a fairly complete set of paragraph formatting controls, including indents and tabs, space above and below, and controls for hyphenation and justification. In addition, FreeHand 4 adds range kerning and hanging punctuation.

Formatting Paragraphs

You use the Paragraph Inspector, Alignment Inspector, and Spacing Inspector to format paragraphs in your FreeHand text blocks. See page 225.

Paragraph Rules

You can attach up to two rules to paragraphs in FreeHand 4—one rule above the paragraph; one rule below the paragraph. These rules are vertically centered in the space above and below the paragraph, and flow with the text as you edit or reformat the text. See page 241.

Setting Tabs

FreeHand 4 text blocks can contain left, right, center, and decimal alignment, and wrapping tabs. Wrapping tabs create a column inside a column of your text block, and are unique to FreeHand—no other page-layout or illustration program that I know of has anything like them. They're great for creating columns within columns, or for creating columns of unequal widths inside a text block (columns set with the Column Inspector always divide a text block evenly). See page 234.

Hanging Indents

As in both Microsoft Word and PageMaker, you can create a hanging indent by dragging the left margin icon to the right of the first-line indent icon, and then setting a left tab at the same position as the left margin icon. See page 239.

Range Kerning

When you want to tighten or loosen the spaces between all of the characters in a selection, use FreeHand 4's Range Kern field—which you can see in the Character palette. Enter a kerning value here, and FreeHand tightens (or loosens) the space between the selected characters. See page 223.

Automatic Hanging Punctuation

Because we don't "see" punctuation when we're reading, a line beginning (or, in some cases ending) with punctuation (especially quotation marks) doesn't look like it aligns with other lines in the surrounding text. It's a kind of typographic optical illusion. To compensate, try FreeHand's hanging punctuation—which moves the punctuation slightly beyond the edge of the text column. See page 233.

Automatic Copyfitting

When you've got too much text (or too little text) to fill a column, you can direct FreeHand to squash (or expand) the leading and/or the type size to get the text to fit in the text blocks you've allocated for the story. See page 244.

Wrap Text Around Objects

When you want text to avoid a path on your page, use FreeHand's new Text Wrap feature. See page 253.

Flow Text Inside Objects

You can flow text inside any closed path—it's like the opposite of a text wrap. Use this effect when you want to create angled columns, or when you need nonrectangular text blocks. Text inside a path is always a single column and a single row, but you can still use tabs to create multiple columns if you need to. See page 252.

Importing and Exporting

FreeHand's always been strong in the area of import and export, and, with Version 4, it's gotten even stronger. See Chapter 4, "Importing and Exporting," on page 263.

Editable FreeHand EPS

When you export a FreeHand publication as an EPS, you can choose to embed the original FreeHand file in the EPS—which means that you can open and edit the EPS just as you would any FreeHand publication file. No more having to keep two versions of the file around (one in EPS format, one in FreeHand native file format). Layers, styles, colors, and other FreeHand features are all preserved when you create an editable EPS. See page 309.

Text File Import and Export

FreeHand 4 can import text files you've saved as text-only (ASCII) or Rich Text Format (RTF). RTF is an ASCII coding system that's supposed to be able to describe anything you can have in a Microsoft Word file. PageMaker, Microsoft Word, and other page layout and word-processing programs can save text files as RTF. See page 294.

The nice thing about RTF is that local formatting—typestyles, type sizes, and font changes—is retained when you place the document in FreeHand. Because FreeHand lacks paragraph styles, that information in the RTF file is ignored and discarded. The text formatting remains the same, but it's local formatting.

FreeHand can also save text files as RTF or ASCII. When you export, FreeHand exports all of the text in your document, not just the text you've selected. See page 305.

Color

FreeHand 4 builds on FreeHand 3's legacy of strong color production tools, and adds a new ease of use and immediacy to working with color.

Color Wells and Color Swatches

As you look at FreeHand's palettes, you'll see lots of little squares of color. These are color wells, and they're the key to working with color in FreeHand. See page 375.

When you position your cursor over a color well (in the Color List, the Color Mixer, the Inspector, or the Tints palette) and drag, a small square of color emerges from the color well and follows the cursor. We call the moving square of color a "color swatch." See page 375.

Drag-and-Drop Color

You can drag color swatches from any color well to any other color well, but you can also drop the color swatches directly on objects in your publication to apply the color to the object (or, in the case of a path, to the path's fill or stroke). See page 374.

Drag-and-Drop Graduated Fills

To create a graduated fill using drag-and-drop, hold down Option as you drop a color swatch onto a path. See page 146.

Drag-and-Drop Radial Fills   To create a radial fill using drag-and-drop, hold down Control as you drop a color swatch onto the path. See page 148.

Automatic Tint Generation   To quickly create tints based on the current color, drag a color swatch from the Color List (or from any other color well) and drop it into the base color well in the Tints palette. FreeHand creates tints in 10 percent increments. You can also use the Tints palette to create custom tint percentages. See page 386.

FreeHand Basics

1

Start FreeHand, and you enter another world— a software model of a graphic artist's studio. Most programs are based on some real-world model: PageMaker works like a layout board, Excel works like an accountant's worksheet, and Word works like a reasonably smart electric typewriter. Metaphors like these make computer software "user-friendly"—partly because they give us something we're familiar with, and partly because they give the program a logic of its own.

In this chapter, I'll show you around the virtual reality that is FreeHand. There'll be lots of definitions of terms (how can you know what I'm talking about unless we're using the same vocabulary?) and "maps" of FreeHand's screen (how can you tell where you're going unless you know the lay of the land?). Almost all of the concepts and practices covered here are covered in greater depth in other chapters. In those cases, I'll provide a cross reference to the more detailed explanation.

I'll also be going through some techniques for changing the way FreeHand looks and behaves, because I believe that the tools you use should fit your working habits. Someday, all of our software will be completely modular and completely customizable, but, until that day arrives, there's always ResEdit.

At the end of the chapter, I'll run through my list of rules for using FreeHand. You can take them or leave them; there are many different ways to approach FreeHand, and my methods are not necessarily the ones that'll work best for you. Some of my habits are rooted in the primordial past (giant ground sloths, woolly mammoths, and Linotronic L100s roamed the earth), and some, while true today, may not apply when this book reaches your hands. That's the thing about computer software—as soon as you really know something, it's obsolete.

The Publication Window

When you open or create a FreeHand publication, you view and work on the publication in the publication window (see Figure 1-1). FreeHand's publication window gives you a view on FreeHand's pasteboard—the place everything happens in FreeHand.

In addition to the standard Macintosh title bar, close box, and zoom box (click it to make your publication window the size of the screen; click it again to return the publication window to a smaller size), FreeHand 4's publication window holds several other controls and features.

FIGURE 1-1
The publication
window

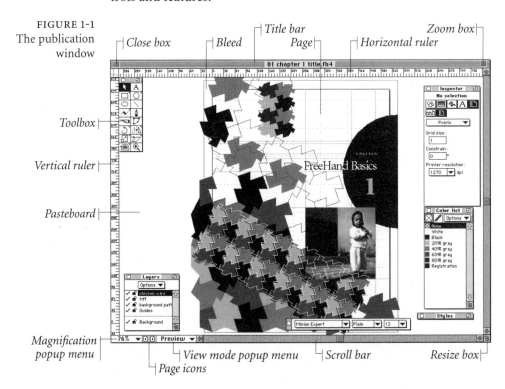

Info Bar. Immediately below the title bar, FreeHand's Info Bar displays information about the current state of the selected object and the position of the cursor or selected object (see Figure 1-2). You can display and hide the Info Bar by pressing Command-Shift-R, but you can't move it, as you could in FreeHand 3.

FIGURE 1-2
FreeHand's Info Bar

Info Bar showing that you've got nothing selected, and that your cursor is off the page. "h" shows the horizontal position of the cursor; "v" shows the vertical position of the cursor. FreeHand measures these coordinates from the publication's current zero point.

When you rotate an object, the Info Bar looks like this. "ch" shows the horizontal center of the object; "cv" shows the vertical center; "angle" shows you the angle of rotation.

Scroll bars. The most obvious, least convenient, and slowest ways to change your view of your publication are to click in a scroll bar, drag the scroll handles, or click the arrows on either end of the scroll bars. For more on better ways to get around, see "Moving Around in Your Publication," later in this chapter.

Page icons. Now that FreeHand publications can contain multiple pages, you need a way to move from one page to another. One way is to click the left page icon to move to the previous page in your publication, and click the right page icon to move to the next page. There's a better way to get from page to page, however: double-click the pages in the thumbnail view of FreeHand's pasteboard in the Document Inspector (for more on how to do this, see "Moving Around in Your Publication," later in this chapter).

View mode popup menu. Choose Preview or Keyline from this popup menu to switch between FreeHand's two view modes. You can also press Command-K to switch viewing modes.

In Preview mode, FreeHand renders the objects you've drawn as they'll be printed. In Keyline mode, FreeHand shows you only the outlines of the objects on the page (see Figure 1-3).

FIGURE 1-3
Preview and
Keyline views

 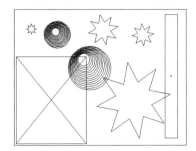

Preview mode shows you the objects in your publication as they'll be printed (more or less).

Keyline mode shows you only the outlines of the objects in your publication, and displays imported images as boxes with an "X" through them.

Both views have advantages and disadvantages. In Preview, you can see something resembling your printed publication, but it takes longer to display; Keyline view redraws quickly but doesn't usually resemble the printed publication. It's easier to select points in Keyline mode, and it's easier to select objects in Preview mode. You'll find yourself switching between Preview and Keyline often.

Magnification popup menu. Choose the magnification at which you want to view your publication from this popup menu, and FreeHand magnifies (or reduces) the view of the publication you see in the publication window. Again, there are several better ways to do this, as shown in "Moving Around in Your Publication," later in this chapter.

Inside the publication window, you'll see some, all, or none of the following items, depending on how you've set your defaults.

◆ The pasteboard

◆ A page or pages

◆ Rulers

◆ Ruler guides

◆ The grid

Page and Pasteboard

Like its sibling PageMaker, FreeHand is modeled around the concept of pages—areas on which you place graphic elements. Pages float on the pasteboard—a 56-inch square area. In FreeHand 4, you can create as many pages as you want, provided they all fit inside the pasteboard. You can use areas of the pasteboard that don't contain pages for temporary storage of the elements you're working with—just drag the elements off the page, and they'll stay on the pasteboard until you need them.

Bleed area, page size, and paper size. Objects can extend past the edge of the page, into an area of the pasteboard that's defined as the bleed. What's the point of having a "bleed?" Sometimes, you want to print objects that extend beyond the edge of your page (they'll be clipped off at the edge of the page when your commercial printer cuts your pages, but, sometimes, that's just the design effect you want).

Each page's bleed is shown in the publication window by line (a gray line on color and grayscale monitors, or a dotted line if you're working in black and white) surrounding the page. Different pages can have bleed areas of different sizes.

The size of the bleed, the page size, and the size of the paper in your printer affect each other. In FreeHand, the page size you define in the Document Inspector should be the same as the final size of the document's page after it's been printed by a commercial printer. You define the paper size—the physical size of the paper in your printer—in the Print Options dialog box. When you're printing to an imagesetter, the paper size is a defined area on the imagesetter's film roll (or sheet, for drum imagesetters).

If your publication's page size (without the bleed) is the same as the paper size you've chosen in the Print Options dialog box, you can expect FreeHand to neatly clip off the bleed area you've specified. Choose a larger paper size in the Print Options dialog box than your publication's page size when you want to print bleeds (choose Letter.Extra when you're printing a letter-size publication with a bleed, for example). If you're interested in creating new paper sizes for imagesetters (I don't know of any laser printer that can handle custom paper sizes), see "Rewriting PPDs" in Chapter 7, "Printing."

Multiple publications. You can have as many different publications open as FreeHand can fit into your machine's RAM. You move between open publications by choosing their file names from the Window menu, or by clicking on their windows, just as you'd switch between applications (see Figure 1-4).

FIGURE 1-4
Windows menu

List of open publications. FreeHand
displays a check beside the title of
the active publication.

Rulers

Command-R displays or hides FreeHand's rulers—handy measuring tools that appear along the top and left sides of your publication window (see Figure 1-5). They're marked off in the units of measurement specified in the Document Inspector. The actual increments shown on the rulers vary somewhat with the current page view; in general, you'll see more ruler tick marks and finer increments at 800% size than you'll see at 12% size.

As you move the cursor, lines in the rulers (called shadow cursors) display the cursor's position relative to the rulers (see Figure 1-6). When you select an object, FreeHand highlights areas on the rulers that correspond to the size and position of the object (I call this the "shadow selection").

FIGURE 1-5
FreeHand's rulers

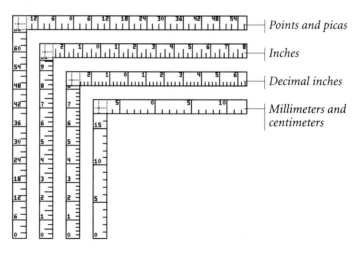

Points and picas

Inches

Decimal inches

Millimeters and
centimeters

FIGURE 1-6
Shadow cursors and
shadow selection

As you move the cursor, the shadow cursors follow.

As you move an object, the shadow selection shows the width and height of the object on the rulers.

Shadow cursors track your cursor's position in the rulers.

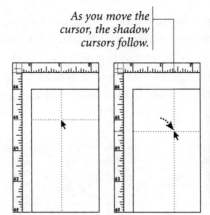
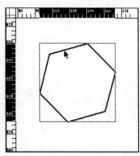

Zero point. The point where the rulers intersect is called the zero point. In FreeHand, you control the location of the zero point using the zero-point marker (see Figure 1-7), which you see at the upper-left corner of your screen (when you have the rulers displayed). You can think of it as the point where the two rulers intersect on the page, even though you can't see the point itself. You use the zero-point marker to reset the zero point (see Figure 1-8).

To move the zero point, drag the zero-point marker to a new position. As you drag, intersecting dotted lines show you the position of the zero point. When you've moved the zero point to the

FIGURE 1-7
Zero-point marker

Zero-point marker

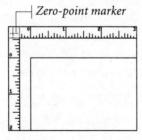

FIGURE 1-8
Repositioning
the zero point

Select the zero-point marker...   *...and drag it to a new location.*

FreeHand moves the zero point.

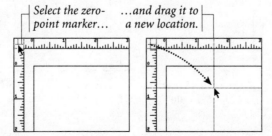

location you want, release the mouse button. The rulers now mark off their increments based on this new zero point.

If you need to reposition only the horizontal or vertical ruler's zero point, drag the zero-point marker along the other ruler—the one you don't want to change—until the zero point is where you want it (see Figure 1-9).

FIGURE 1-9
Repositioning only one
of the zero points

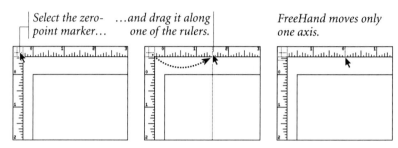

Select the zero-   ...and drag it along
point marker...   one of the rulers.

FreeHand moves only
one axis.

Tip:
Resetting the
Zero Point

To reset the zero point to the lower-left corner of the page, double-click the zero-point marker.

Ruler Guides

Ruler guides are nonprinting guidelines you use when you're aligning items on a page. To position a ruler guide, position the cursor over a ruler and drag the cursor onto the page or pasteboard. As you drag the cursor off the ruler, a line follows the cursor, showing you where your new ruler guide would fall. When you've got the line where you want it, release the mouse button. FreeHand positions a new ruler guide at this location (see Figure 1-10).

FIGURE 1-10
Positioning
a ruler guide

Position the
cursor over
a ruler...

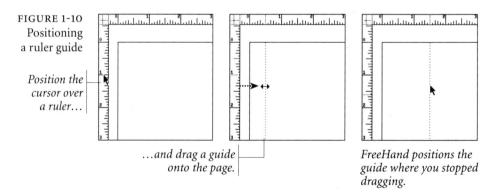

...and drag a guide
onto the page.

FreeHand positions the
guide where you stopped
dragging.

There's no limit to the number of ruler guides you can use in a publication.

When you want to remove a ruler guide, position the Pointer tool above the ruler guide, hold down the mouse button, and drag the ruler guide off the page (see Figure 1-11). If you can't select the ruler guide, you've probably got Lock Guides turned on. Turn it off by choosing Lock Guides from the View menu.

FIGURE 1-11
Removing a
ruler guide

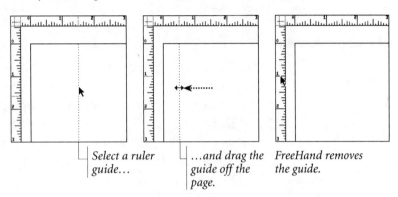

Select a ruler
guide…

…and drag the
guide off the
page.

FreeHand removes
the guide.

Snap to Guides Ruler guides are especially useful in conjunction with the Snap to Guides option (toggle this option on and off by pressing Command-;). When you've turned on Snap to Guides, objects within the distance (you've specified in the Preferences dialog box) automatically snap into alignment with the ruler guide (see Figure 1-12). For more on snapping in general, see "Snap Distance," later in this chapter.

FIGURE 1-12
Snap to Guides

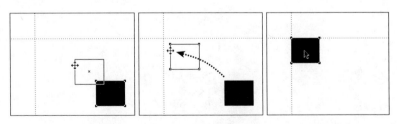

When you're dragging
an object with Snap to
Guides turned on,
nothing happens…

…until you drag the
object within a certain
distance of a ruler guide.
At this point, the guides
seem to pull the object
toward them…

…until the object snaps
to the guide (or guides).

To see how this works, turn on Snap to Guides, draw a box, position a ruler guide, and drag the box toward the guide. When the box gets within your specified distance of the guide, it snaps right to it. You can almost feel the magnetic pull of the guide in the mouse as you move the box closer to the guide. There's nothing actually affecting the movement of your mouse, of course, but it's a useful illusion.

FreeHand's Palettes

FreeHand's palettes work two ways—they display information about the publication (and about the object you've got selected), and they provide controls for changing the publication and the objects in it. The palettes are an integral part of FreeHand's new user interface, and are the key to doing almost everything in Free-Hand (see Figure 1-13).

- Toolbox
- Layers palette
- Styles palette
- Halftone palette
- Type Specifications palette
- Color List
- Color Mixer
- Tints palette
- Transform palette
- Align palette
- Inspector

You don't have to use the menus to display or hide the palettes—an action called "toggling." You can use keyboard shortcuts to save yourself lots of mouse movement (see Table 1-1).

FIGURE 1-13
FreeHand's palettes

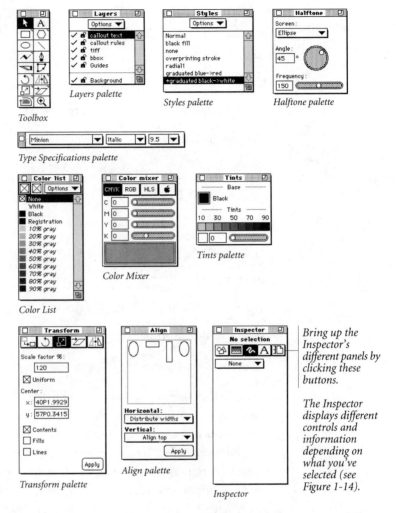

Toolbox

Layers palette

Styles palette

Halftone palette

Type Specifications palette

Color List

Color Mixer

Tints palette

Transform palette

Align palette

Inspector

Bring up the Inspector's different panels by clicking these buttons.

The Inspector displays different controls and information depending on what you've selected (see Figure 1-14).

The Inspector is the palette you'll use most when you work with FreeHand. I refer to each of the subpanels of the Inspector as an Inspector, such as the Paragraph Inspector, the Fill Inspector, and the Stroke Inspector (see Figure 1-14). This saves me from having to say things like "the Character subpanel of the Paragraph section of the Inspector."

Do you really have to click the different icon buttons in the Inspector to display the different sections of the Inspector? No— you can use keyboard shortcuts for almost all of the Inspectors. Take a look at Table 1-2 on page 16.

TABLE 1-1
Palette keyboard
shortcuts

Palette	To display or hide the palette, press
Align palette	Command-Shift-A
Color List	Command-9
Color Mixer	Command-Shift-C
Halftone palette	Command-H
Inspector	Command-I
Layers palette	Command-6
Styles palette	Command-3
Tints palette	Command-Shift-Z
Toolbox	Command-7
Transform palette	Command-M*
Type Specifications palette	Command-T

* If the palette's visible, pressing Command-M again won't make it go away.

Note that there is no keyboard shortcut for the Setup Inspector, where you set up the publication's grid and measurement system. This seems like an oversight to me.

The Align palette is an exception to the above rules. When you select different alignment and distribution options from the Align palette's popup menus, FreeHand doesn't immediately apply the alignment. To apply a setting you've made in the Align palette, you have to click the Apply button in the palette (pressing Return or Enter doesn't work).

Tip:
Applying
Palette
Changes

When you make a change in a palette using a button or a popup menu, that change takes effect immediately. When you make a change by entering a value in a field, however, you have to press Return to let FreeHand know you've finished entering text. In the Transform palette, you can click the Apply button or press Return to apply your changes. When you're through making changes in the Inspector, press Return to apply your changes (there's no Apply button).

FIGURE 1-14
The many faces
of the Inspector

The Object Inspector displays different options depending on what kind of element you've selected.

When you select a text block, the Object Inspector displays three panels full of options.

*Object Inspector
(path selected)*

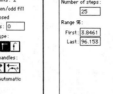

*Object Inspector
(blend selected)*

Object Inspector

Column Inspector

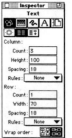

*Copyfit
Inspector*

Fill Inspector

Stroke Inspector

The Fill Inspector and the Stroke Inspector replace FreeHand 3's Fill and Line dialog box.

You'll find FreeHand's paragraph-formatting features in the four panels of the Text Inspector.

*Character
Inspector*

*Paragraph
Inspector*

*Spacing
Inspector*

*Alignment
Inspector*

*Document
Inspector*

*Setup
Inspector*

TABLE 1-2 Inspector keyboard shortcuts	**To display the**	**Press**
	Page Inspector	Command-Option-D
	Fill Inspector	Command-Option-F
	Column Inspector*	Command-Option-R**
	Copyfit Inspector*	Command-Option-C**
	Object Inspector	Command-Option-B**
	Stroke Inspector	Command-Option-L
	Alignment Inspector	Command-Option-A
	Character Inspector	Command-Option-T
	Paragraph Inspector	Command-Option-P
	Spacing Inspector	Command-Option-K

*   Only appears when a text block is selected

** Only appears if the Inspector is already visible (press Command-I first, to display the Inspector, and then press this keyboard shortcut).

Tip:
Moving
Through Fields

To move from one field to the next in a palette, press Tab. To move from one field to the previous, press Shift-Tab.

Tip:
Cycling
Through
Palettes

To cycle through all of the visible palettes containing fields, press Command-` (accent grave; it's just below the ~ or tilde symbol). Each press of Command-` takes you to the next available palette. Why only palettes containing text fields? Because there's not much point using a keyboard shortcut to move to a palette in which you have to use the mouse anyway. It's great, on the other hand, to be able to jump from the Size field in the Type Specifications palette to the Leading field in the Paragraph Inspector without moving the mouse.

Tip:
Now You
See 'Em...

With all these floating palettes, it's easy to run out of room on your screen to see anything but the palettes. While there are keyboard shortcuts to display or hide all of the palettes, you might like this better: you can shrink a palette down to just its title bar by clicking the zoom box at the right end of the title bar. The title bar stays on the screen (see Figure 1-15). When you want to display the entire palette, click the box again, and the palette expands to its full size.

FIGURE 1-15
Zooming palettes

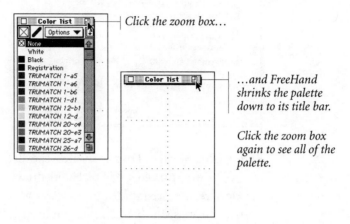

Click the zoom box...

...and FreeHand shrinks the palette down to its title bar.

Click the zoom box again to see all of the palette.

Preferences

FreeHand 3 had lots of different preference settings that people never understood or used, and FreeHand 4 has even more. It's worth learning what the different choices are, however, because the Preferences dialog boxes are one place inside FreeHand where you can truly fine-tune FreeHand's performance and behavior. Preference settings are so useful, in fact, that I'm hoping that Free-Hand 5 will have a Yet More Preferences dialog box, or a Son of More Preferences dialog box. The possibilities are endless.

When you choose Preferences from the File menu, FreeHand displays the Display panel of the Preferences dialog box. You use the popup menu at the top of the dialog box to view and change preferences for Editing, Exporting, and Sounds. From now on, I'll refer to each section of this dialog box as if it were a separate dialog box (as, in fact, each is).

Display
Preferences

The options in the Display Preferences dialog box control the way that FreeHand draws objects on your screen (see Figure 1-16). Many of these preferences can speed up—or slow down—the time it takes FreeHand to redraw the screen.

FIGURE 1-16
Display Preferences
dialog box

```
┌────────────────────────────────────────┐
│ ▒▒▒▒▒▒▒▒▒▒  Preferences  ▒▒▒▒▒▒▒▒▒▒    │
│        ┌──────────────┐                 │
│        │ Display    ▼ │                 │
│        └──────────────┘                 │
│                                         │
│   ☐ Better (but slower) display         │
│   ☒ Display text effects                │
│   ☐ Buffered drawing                    │
│   ☒ Convert PICT patterns to grays      │
│   ☐ Dither 8-bit colors                 │
│   ☐ Redraw while scrolling              │
│   ☒ Adjust display colors  [Calibrate…] │
│   ☐ High-resolution TIFF display        │
│   Greek type below [8      ] pixels     │
│                                         │
│   Guide color: [    ]  Grid color: [  ] │
│                                         │
│              [ Cancel ]  [   OK   ]     │
└────────────────────────────────────────┘
```

Better (But Slower) Display. When the Better (But Slower) Display option is turned off, FreeHand draws graduated and radial fills on screen more rapidly, using fewer gray steps to render them. Turn it on to see a better representation of your fills on screen. This option has no effect on the printing of the fills.

Display Text Effects. The Display Text Effects option displays any of FreeHand's text effects you've applied to text blocks in your publication. If you don't turn this option on, you'll see the text displayed at the correct size and leading, but without the effects. If the text effects extend beyond the text block (Zoom Text often does, for example), the selection rectangle shows the extent of the text and the effects when you move the text block. Turning this option on shows you your text effects, but slows down your screen display (see Figure 1-17).

FIGURE 1-17
Display Text
Effects option

*Zoom Text with Display
Text Effects on*

*Zoom Text with Display
Text Effects off*

Buffered Drawing. From your Macintosh's point of view, you're very slow. And you don't do very much work, either. FreeHand makes use of the spare time between your mouse clicks and keystrokes drawing all of the objects in your publication—off screen, where you can't see them. Then, when you do something that requires FreeHand to redraw the screen, it blasts them onto the screen at once. This results in faster screen display of your publication.

The only drawback to the off-screen drawing technique is that it consumes more memory than drawing each object individually when redrawing the screen. Therefore, any time RAM is limited, FreeHand draws object by object.

If you're running FreeHand with less than 1.5Mb of RAM allocated to it, uncheck this option.

Convert PICT Patterns to Grays. When you import object PICT files, such as those created by MacDraw or Canvas, FreeHand needs to know what to do with any PICT patterns used to represent shades of gray (like those you see when you choose Pattern from the popup menu in the Fill Inspector). In my opinion, you should turn this preference on—and leave it that way.

PICT patterns are no substitute for real gray shades, and they don't print reliably on imagesetters. If you've just got to have those PICT patterns, go ahead and leave this option unchecked, but don't say I didn't warn you (for more on patterned fills, see "Patterned Fills" in Chapter 2, "Drawing").

Note that this option has nothing to do with bitmap PICT files— bitmap PICT files are always converted to TIFF when you place or open them (for more on this conversion, see Chapter 4, "Importing and Exporting").

Dither 8-Bit Colors. If you're working with an eight-bit video system, you can check this box to make FreeHand dither colors (that is, use patterns of different-colored pixels) to represent the colors you're using in your publication. These dither patterns do not affect printing. Why does FreeHand need to use dithering? Because an eight-bit video system has only 256 colors available—which means it's easy to pick a color your system can't display.

Leave this box unchecked, and FreeHand will use the eight-bit color that's closest to the color you're working with.

This one's up to you—dithered colors more accurately represent the colors you've chosen, but you might not like the pixel patterns it creates. In any case, FreeHand always uses dithering to represent colors in graduated and radial fills.

Redraw While Scrolling. If you want FreeHand to redraw while you're scrolling, check this option. If you'd rather FreeHand waited to redraw the screen until you've finished scrolling, leave it unchecked. This option affects both scrolling using the scroll bars and scrolling using the Grabber Hand (for more on using the Grabber Hand to scroll, see "Moving Around in Your Publication," later in this chapter). FreeHand always redraws the screen when you scroll while you're dragging an object. Turning this option on makes scrolling slower.

Adjust Display Colors. When you click the Calibrate button in the Preferences dialog box, the Display Color Setup dialog box appears (see Figure 1-18).

Click the Cyan, Magenta, and Yellow buttons to select the colors you want from the Apple Color Picker dialog box. Which colors are correct? I use the settings shown in Table 1-3; you can type the numbers right into the fields in the Color Picker. You might want to use different settings, however, depending on your monitor and viewing environment.

You can also adjust the colors by holding a printed color sample next to your screen and modifying your display colors until they match the sample. Ideally, you'd only use printed process-color swatches from the commercial printer and press you intend to use to produce the publication, printed on the paper stock you've chosen for the job (though I confess I've never done this myself).

You don't need to adjust all of the colors—once you've changed Cyan, Yellow, and Magenta, FreeHand adjusts the other colors accordingly (though you won't see a difference in the dialog box display until you close and reopen the dialog box).

These adjustments are for screen display only and have nothing to do with the percentages of process colors FreeHand will print.

FIGURE 1-18
Adjusting your
color display

*Click one of the color wells in
the Display Color Setup
dialog box…*

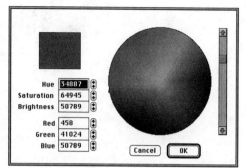

*…and FreeHand displays the Apple Color Picker,
where you can choose a color that matches (or
comes close to matching) a printed sample of the
color you want to use.*

TABLE 1-3
HSB and RGB color
settings for process
colors

Color	H	S	B	R	G	B
Cyan	32768	65535	65535	0	65535	65535
Magenta	54614	65535	65535	65535	0	65535
Yellow	10922	65535	65535	65535	65535	0
Black	65535	65535	65535	65535	65535	65535

Don't trust your monitor. The colors you see on your screen are only there to remind you of which color you've applied to different objects. Specify your colors by referring to printed samples of the spot or process colors you want to use. For more on specifying colors, or on calibrating your monitor to display colors more accurately, refer to Chapter 6, "Color."

High-Resolution TIFF Display. If you check this option, Free-Hand gets its information about how to render a TIFF from the original TIFF file that's linked to your FreeHand publication, which means that FreeHand renders the best possible display of the TIFF image for your current magnification level. With this option off, FreeHand constructs a low-resolution screen version of the image and uses it for display at all magnification levels (see Figure 1-19).

FIGURE 1-19
High- and low-
resolution TIFF
display options

Low-resolution TIFF display   *High-resolution TIFF display*

The tradeoff is the speed of screen redraw. High-resolution TIFF images can take forever to draw on your screen. Given this, it's a good idea to leave this option unchecked until those times when you absolutely must see all of the detail in the TIFF.

Greek Type Below N Pixels. This option displays type as a gray bar if it's shorter, in pixels, than the value you enter. As you zoom close to the text, you'll see the characters in the text block again (see Figure 1-20). This happens because the type's taller, in pixels, at larger magnifications.

The advantage of using this option is that greeked type redraws much faster than the actual characters, speeding up your screen display. This option applies to both Preview and Keyline views.

Tip:
Greek All (or
Almost All)

You can always choose to greek all (almost, anyway…) of the text in your document at most views by entering "200"—the largest value you can enter—in the Greek Type Below field. This will greek all type below 200 points at 100% view, and all type below 400 points at most Fit Page views (the exact magnification of the Fit Page view depends on the size of your page).

FIGURE 1-20
Greeked type

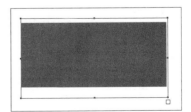

24-point type at 100% view; Greek Type Below set to six points.   *24-point type at 100% view; Greek Type Below set to 100 points.*

Guide Color. To change the color of FreeHand's ruler guides, click the color swatch. The Guide Color dialog box appears (I call this dialog box the Apple Color Picker). Click on the color in the color wheel you want to use for the nonprinting guides in your publication and press Return to close the dialog box. FreeHand uses the new color for displaying the ruler guides.

Grid Color. To change the color of FreeHand's grid, click on the color swatch to display the Grid Color dialog box, then choose a color in the Apple Color Picker's color wheel. After you press Return to close the dialog box, FreeHand displays the grid in the new color.

Editing Preferences

Choose Editing from the popup menu in any Preferences dialog box to display the Editing Preferences dialog box (see Figure 1-21).

Number of Undo's. This option sets the number of actions held in FreeHand's Undo queue. Enter smaller numbers here if you find you don't use that many levels of Undo or want to save memory. Enter larger numbers here if you change your mind a lot and don't like the idea of using Save As and Revert when you're experimenting with possibilities. Remember, however, that each level of Undo adds to the amount of RAM that FreeHand uses (the amount of RAM consumed depends on the action). You can enter any number from one to 99 in this field.

FIGURE 1-21
Editing Preferences
dialog box

```
┌─────────────────────────────────────────┐
│ ▒▒▒▒▒▒▒▒▒▒▒▒ Preferences ▒▒▒▒▒▒▒▒▒▒▒▒    │
│                                          │
│         ┌─ Editing    ▼─┐                │
│                                          │
│  Number of undo's:     │ 10 │            │
│                                          │
│  Preview drag:         │ 1  │   items    │
│                                          │
│  Pick distance:        │ 5  │   pixels   │
│                                          │
│  Cursor key distance:  │ 0P1│            │
│                                          │
│  Snap distance:        │ 3  │   pixels   │
│                                          │
│    ☒ Changing object changes defaults    │
│    ☒ Join non-touching paths             │
│    ☒ Remember layer info                 │
│    ☐ Groups transform as unit by default │
│    ☒ Dynamic scrollbar                   │
│                                          │
│           ┌────────┐  ┌─────────┐        │
│           │ Cancel │  │   OK    │        │
│           └────────┘  └─────────┘        │
└─────────────────────────────────────────┘
```

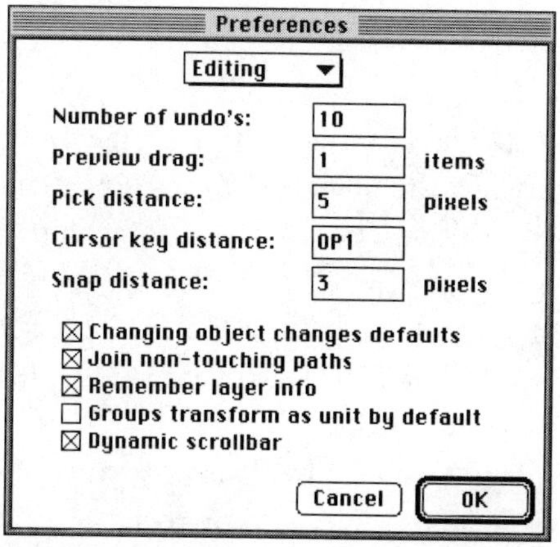

Preview Drag. When you drag an object quickly, FreeHand displays only a box showing the general dimensions of the object. If you pause slightly before you drag the object, however, FreeHand displays the object itself as you drag (see Figure 1-22). When the value in the Preview Drag field is one (FreeHand's default), Free-Hand always displays a box (that is, not the objects themselves) when you're dragging more than one object. Increase this value, and you'll be able to see more objects as you drag them, but the amount of time you'll have to wait before FreeHand redraws the objects increases commensurately. You can enter values from zero to 32,000 (don't even think about it!) in this field.

Tip:
Viewing
Objects as You
Drag Them

Hold down Option as you start to drag an object or objects, and FreeHand displays the objects as you drag them. It's a temporary way of turning on Preview Drag. So instead of increasing the value in the Preview Drag field, leave it at one—or even set it to zero—and hold down Option when you want to see objects as you drag them.

FIGURE 1-22
Preview Drag

 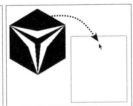 

Select the object you want to move.

Drag quickly, and FreeHand displays only the object's bounding box as you drag.

Wait for a second (or hold down Option), and FreeHand displays the object as you move it.

Pick Distance. How close to the edge of an object do you have to click to select the object? How does FreeHand "know" you want to select the object? The value you enter in the Pick Distance field determines how close, in pixels, you can click before FreeHand decides you're trying to select the object. You can enter a value from zero to five pixels in this field—the lower the value, the more accurate your clicks have to be.

The Pick Distance field also controls how close you have to get to an object to apply a color to it using drag-and-drop color. If you're having trouble dropping color swatches on paths, you might want to increase the value you've entered in the Pick Distance field (for more information, see "Drag-and-Drop Color" in Chapter 6, "Color").

Cursor Key Distance. Enter a number in the Cursor Key Distance field to set the distance a selected object moves when you press the arrow keys to "nudge" an object.

Snap Distance. FreeHand has lots of different "snaps" under the View menu. There's Snap to Guides, Snap to Point, and Snap to Grid. Snap to Point makes FreeHand points snap together when you drag them to within a specified distance of each other. Snap to Guides snaps objects to ruler guides when you drag objects within a specified distance of them. Snap to Grid makes objects snap to an underlying grid, which you define in the Setup Inspector.

The number you enter in the Snap Distance field in the Editing Preferences dialog box sets the distance (in screen pixels) that all of the Snap commands rely on. Set the Snap Distance option to five pixels, and the next time you drag an object within five pixels of an active snap point (point, ruler guide, or grid intersection), FreeHand snaps the object to that point.

If you just can't seem to get one point to land on top of another so that you can close a path or connect the end of one path to the end of another (see "Open and Closed Paths" in Chapter 2, "Drawing," for more on closing paths), try increasing the number in the Snap Distance field. If, on the other hand, you're having a hard time keeping points from snapping together, enter a smaller number in the Snap Distance field.

Changing Object Changes Defaults. If you check the Changing Object Changes Defaults box, any changes you make to a selected object's attributes (colors, type specifications, fills, and strokes) are carried over to the next object you create. For example, if you've created a stroke and set its width to six points and its color to 20-percent gray, the next path you create has the same stroke width and color.

When this option's unchecked, you set defaults for the entire document by making changes to object attributes (colors, fills, lines, type specifications, and so on) without having any object selected. In this case, each new object you create picks up the publication's default attributes regardless of what changes have been made to selected objects created or modified previously.

Join Non-Touching Paths. When Join Non-Touching Paths is on, FreeHand joins the endpoints of paths when you select the points and press Command-J (or choose Join Elements from the Arrange menu). With Join Non-Touching Paths turned off, FreeHand only joins the endpoints of paths that are within the distance in pixels you entered in the Pick Distance field.

Remember Layer Info. In FreeHand 3.0, you'd lose layer information when you cut, copied, or pasted objects, or when you grouped and ungrouped objects. This feature, which first appeared in Free-Hand 3.1, gives you the option of keeping that layer information. With Remember Layer Info on, you can cut and paste, group and ungroup, as much as you like, and the objects you're working with always appear on their original layers.

If you're copying objects into a publication that doesn't contain the layers, FreeHand adds those layers to the publication. If you've deleted layers, and ungroup a group containing objects originally assigned to those layers, FreeHand adds the layers to the Layers palette.

If, on the other hand, you want to paste objects from other layers into the current layer, turn off Remember Layer Info.

Groups Transform as Unit by Default. When you're transforming (moving, scaling, skewing, or rotating) objects, you can choose to have the transformation affect the line weights and fills of objects in the group. If you don't want this to happen, uncheck this box. For more on Groups Transform as a Unit by Default, see Chapter 5, "Transforming."

Dynamic Scrollbar. When this option is off, FreeHand doesn't re-draw the screen as you drag the slider in the scroll bars—it redraws when you stop dragging. If you want to see your publication as you scroll using the slider, check this box. Bear in mind, however, that turning this option on makes scrolling slower. Turn this option off if you're running low on RAM.

Note that both the Dynamic Scrollbar and the Redraw While Scrolling preferences sound like they address the same issue—they don't. The Redraw While Scrolling preference affects all scrolling methods; the Dynamic Scrollbar option applies only to scrolling by dragging the slider in the scroll bar.

Exporting Preferences

Choose Exporting from the popup menu in any of the Preferences dialog boxes to display the Exporting Preferences dialog box (see Figure 1-23).

FIGURE 1-23
Exporting Preferences
dialog box

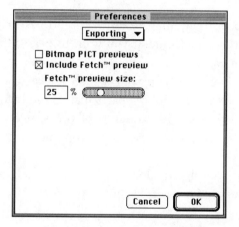

Bitmap PICT Previews. When this option is off, Macintosh EPS files you export from FreeHand contain object (or vector) PICT previews—almost like using a MacDraw file for a screen preview. Object PICT previews provide more accurate screen previews than bitmaps—but they also take substantially longer to draw on your screen, and can be larger than a TIFF preview of the same graphic.

Include Fetch Preview. If you plan to add exported FreeHand files to an Aldus Fetch image database, check this option. If you don't, leave it unchecked—the previews do make your exported files larger.

When you check this option, you can choose how large you want to make the preview. As you'd expect, larger previews are more accurate representations of your file, and they also take up more space on disk. As you do this, remember that most people look at previews in Fetch in Thumbnail view, so you can probably get by with a small (say, 25 percent) preview.

Sounds Preferences

Choose Sounds from the popup menu in any Preferences dialog box to display the Sounds Preferences dialog box (see Figure 1-24). When you check Snap Sounds Enabled, FreeHand plays a sound when a snap happens. When you're dragging an object toward a ruler guide, for example, you might want to hear it snap into position.

Snap to Grid, Snap to Point, Snap to H(orizontal)-Guide, Snap to V(ertical)-Guide. If you want to hear different sounds for different snaps, you can choose the sounds you want here—all of the sounds currently in your system appear in the popup menus. If you want to audition a particular sound before committing yourself to hearing it thousands of times, select the sound from the popup menu and press the appropriate Play button.

Snap Sounds Enabled. Turn on this checkbox to enable the snap sounds you've selected above.

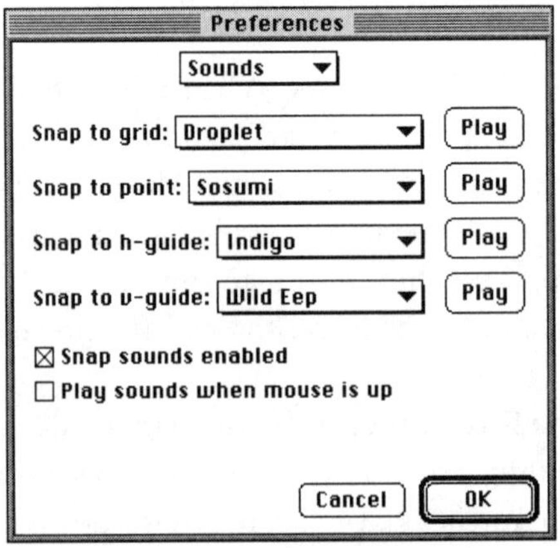

FIGURE 1-24
Sounds Preferences
dialog box

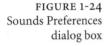

Play Sounds When Mouse Is Up. Turn on this option if you want to hear the snap sounds whenever your cursor crosses a snap point, regardless of whether you're moving or sizing an object. This is actually useful when you're trying to draw something on a grid—you'll hear a sound if you're in the right place to start drawing. Most of the time, however, this makes FreeHand sound like an out-of-control video game.

Setting FreeHand's Defaults

"Defaults" are the settings you start out with when you start Free-Hand. FreeHand has two kinds of defaults—application defaults (which, for the most part, correspond to the settings in the Preferences dialog boxes), and document defaults. FreeHand's defaults control page size, fill type and color, available styles, type specifications, and other details.

Changing Application Defaults

The FreeHand Preferences file is hidden in your Aldus folder in the System Folder and controls virtually everything about FreeHand 4—even things you didn't know needed controlling. Note that this file differs from your Aldus FreeHand Defaults template file in that this file controls the FreeHand application, while the template controls the documents you create (see "Changing Document Defaults," later in this chapter). Most of the items you see in the Preferences dialog box, can be found here.

What can you do with this file? Here's an example: If you want to add more predefined line weights to FreeHand's Stroke Widths submenu, open the FreeHand Preferences file using any text editor, then scroll to the line that reads:

```
(StockLineWeights) (0.25 0.5 1 1.5 2 4 6 8 12)
```

You can add line weights by typing numbers into this line. If you wanted to add a three-point and a ten-point line, for example, you'd change the line so it looked like this:

```
(StockLineWeights) (0.25 0.5 1 1.5 2 3 4 6 8 10 12)
```

The next time you start FreeHand, you'll see the line weights you entered on the Stroke Widths submenu.

Now if I could just figure out what this line means:

```
(ThrashOMeter) (No)
```

For more on what's in this file, and what you can do with it, see Appendix B, "Your FreeHand Installation."

Changing Document Defaults

When you create a new FreeHand document, do you immediately add a set of colors to the Colors List, change the default line weight, display the rulers, or add styles to the Style palette? If you do, you probably get tired of making those changes over and over again. Wouldn't it be great if you could tell FreeHand to create new documents using those settings?

You can. Open the file named Aldus FreeHand Defaults that's in the Aldus folder in your System Folder, make the changes you want using FreeHand's dialog boxes and palettes, and save the file (using the same file name) as a template. Make sure that the new file replaces the original file in your Aldus folder.

The next time you create a new FreeHand document (changing the "Aldus FreeHand Defaults" file has no effect on existing documents); it'll appear with the same defaults as you specified in the defaults file.

Tip: Reverting to FreeHand's Original Defaults

If you've gotten hopelessly away from FreeHand's original defaults and want to go back to them, move the Aldus FreeHand Defaults file out of the Aldus folder (or your FreeHand application folder) and put it somewhere else. Or rename the file. When FreeHand can't find the defaults file, it creates new documents using the original default settings (which are stored inside FreeHand).

Setting Up Pages

The first thing you do when creating a publication is to set up your publication's pages using the Document Inspector and the Setup Inspector. You can always make changes in these palettes, if you need to; changing the values here only changes the underlying pages and their associated settings, and won't change anything you've drawn or imported (objects might end up sitting on the pasteboard, but they won't disappear or change shape).

Using the Document Inspector

To display the Document Inspector, click the Document button in the Inspector palette, then click the Pages button (or, better, press Command-Option-D). The Document Inspector displays a window in the middle of the Inspector, showing you a miniaturized view of FreeHand's pasteboard (see Figure 1-25).

FIGURE 1-25
Document Inspector

The Document Inspector displays a thumbnail view of the pasteboard.

FreeHand highlights the current page.

The Document Inspector's popup menu is the key to working with pages in your publication.

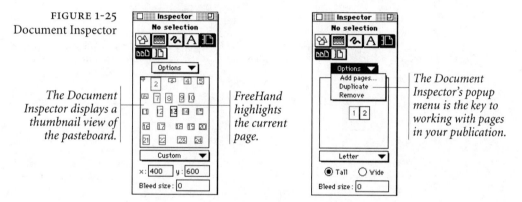

Adding pages. To add a new page, choose Add Pages from the popup menu at the top of the palette (see Figure 1-26). FreeHand displays the Add Pages dialog box. Choose a page size (the current page size is the default) and press Return. FreeHand adds a new page (or pages) to your file, and positions them on the pasteboard.

You can change your page setup at any time by clicking the page in the Document Inspector—its outline changes to black when it's the current selection—and choosing a new page size from the popup menu below the window.

Rearranging pages. To rearrange your pages on the pasteboard, drag the page icons around in the Document Inspector. FreeHand won't let you position one page on top of another, so it's easy to get pages to abut perfectly. Bleed areas, on the other hand, do overlap other pages, as they should (see Figure 1-27).

FIGURE 1-26
Adding pages

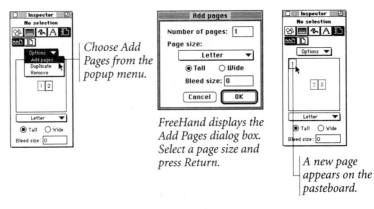

Choose Add Pages from the popup menu.

FreeHand displays the Add Pages dialog box. Select a page size and press Return.

A new page appears on the pasteboard.

FIGURE 1-27
Rearranging pages

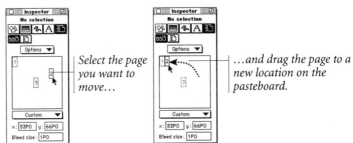

Select the page you want to move…

…and drag the page to a new location on the pasteboard.

As you move the pages around in the Document Inspector, note that their page numbers change. FreeHand numbers pages according to their position on the pasteboard—the page closest to the upper-left corner of the pasteboard is always the first page, the next closest is the second page, and so on.

Duplicating pages. To create a duplicate page of an existing page, click the page in the Document Inspector and choose Duplicate from the popup menu. FreeHand adds the duplicated page to your pasteboard, if there's room to add it.

Removing pages. To remove a page, click the page in the Document Inspector and choose Remove from the popup menu.

Page size. Generally, you'll want to enter the page size you want for your printed publication. I see far too many people (especially those who should know better) laying out single business cards in the middle of a 51-by-66-pica (that's 8.5-by-11-inch) page. Try not to do this; it wastes film and time when you go to your image-setting service bureau (if you operate the imagesetter yourself, it's even more important). If your design features elements that extend beyond the edge of the page, use the Bleed option, described later in this section.

You can specify any page size from six by six picas (one inch square) to 324 by 324 picas (54 inches square). However, as you specify your page size, remember the paper sizes available for the printer you'll be using for your final printing. Linotronic L300s, for example, print on a roll of film that, while very long, is just 11.7 inches (70 picas) wide. When you need the larger page sizes, you can always look for an imagesetter that uses wider film, or you can print tiles (selected parts) of your publication and paste them together (see Chapter 7, "Printing," for more on tiling).

Tiling is ugly, and I try to avoid it. There are often better ways to create large layouts (I tend to create them small, print them at high resolution, then enlarge them using a commercial printer's copy camera).

You can print multiple pages on a single sheet of paper or film using manual tiling to print "reader spreads" or "page spreads." For more on printing reader spreads and page spreads (imposition), see Chapter 7, "Printing."

Tip:
Getting That Big
Page to Fit

FreeHand sometimes refuses to create a page or change a page size—you'll enter a custom page size, and get the message "Could not complete the 'Set page info' command because an object would be placed off the pasteboard," or "Could not complete the 'Set page info' command because the page would overlap another page." You get these messages even when you know that there's plenty of room on the pasteboard (or between pages) to add the new page or change the page size. What gives?

Here's the deal: FreeHand calculates the space available for the new (or changed) page from that page's lower-left corner. If the page would extend within six picas (one inch) of the edge of the pasteboard, or over another page, in either dimension, measured from the current location of the lower-left corner of the page, FreeHand refuses to create (or change) your page.

The solution? Move the page farther left and/or down on the pasteboard, or move other pages to make room for the new page or new page size.

Page orientation. If you're using one of the preset page sizes, you can choose a Tall or Wide orientation. If you're creating a custom page size, the measurements you enter in the X and Y fields determine the page's height and width, respectively. If you want a Wide orientation page, enter a larger value in the X field than you've entered in the Y field. It's that simple.

Once again, try to keep the printer you'll be using for your final printing in mind. In some cases, you might find yourself laying things out sideways to get them onto a film roll's limited width (though you can flip the printing orientation of your publication by rewriting the PPD you're using—see "Rewriting PPDs" in Chapter 7, "Printing").

Bleed. Enter the amount of space you want to print that extends beyond the edge of the page. The value you enter here is added to all four sides of the page. Again, keep the page sizes of your final output device in mind as you enter the bleed area. If your publication's page size is 10 by 12 picas and your imagesetter's page size is 11 by 13 picas, the largest bleed area you'd be able to use is 6 points (though you could always rewrite the PPD file you're using to accommodate a larger bleed, provided the imagesetter you're printing to can handle it).

Using the Setup Inspector

Click the Document Setup button in the Document Inspector palette to display the Setup Inspector (see Figure 1-28).

Unit of measure. Choose your favorite unit of measure from the popup menu in the Setup Inspector. I prefer points and/or picas, because they're the measurement system of type, and type is the backbone of all of my designs, but I'll try not to be a fascist about it. You can always override the current unit of measure for setting your type in dialog boxes, as shown in Table 1-4.

FIGURE 1-28
Setup Inspector

TABLE 1-4
Overriding units of
measurement

If you want this value	Type this in the dialog box
7 inches	7i
22 points	p22
11 picas	11p*
6 picas, 6 points	6p6
23.4 millimeters	23.4m*

* There are approximately 236,220.4 picas in a kilometer.

Grid Size. The value you enter in this field controls the distance between intersections of a nonprinting grid on each page in your publication (see Figure 1-29). The grid starts at the zero point on the rulers and moves when you move the zero point.

When you choose Grid from the View menu, FreeHand displays the grid on your screen. The appearance of the grid varies,

FIGURE 1-29
The grid

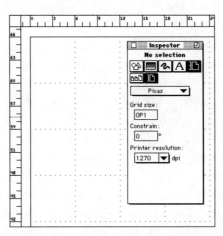

depending on the size of the grid, the current units of measurement, and the current magnification—at higher magnifications, you'll see a point at each grid intersection. When you choose Snap to Grid, objects you're creating, moving, or resizing snap to the grid. You can turn on Snap to Grid whether the grid's visible or not.

You can't enter a value smaller than one point in the Grid Size field.

Tip:
Avoiding
Annoying
Accuracy

Most of the time, when I'm working with a FreeHand publication, I don't want or need to know the location of an object (or my cursor, or a guide) with anything like the kind of accuracy that FreeHand, displays in the info bar by default. In fact, the extra decimal places become distracting. Here's an example: you want to position a rule 24 points from the bottom of the page, and no matter how hard you try to match the tick mark on the ruler, the info bar displays the rule's position as 24.21806. Why can't I get the object into the right position? What's happening?

There are only so many pixels on your screen. At certain views, it might not be possible to "hit" specific coordinates without some help, because that location is "between" two rows of pixels. Clearly, zooming in to a higher magnification will help, but the best thing to do is to set Grid to a small value, such as one point, and turn on Snap to Grid. Now, when you drag the rule into position, it'll snap to each point location, and the info bar will read in whole points—no more distracting decimals.

Constrain. The value you enter in the Constrain field controls the angle FreeHand uses when you constrain tools (see "Constraining Tools," later in this chapter).

The angle you enter here also affects how FreeHand draws rectangles and ellipses (see Figure 1-30). If you've entered "30" in the Constrain field, rectangles and ellipses you create are constrained to 30 and 120 degrees (rather than the default 90 and 180 degrees).

Printer Resolution. Type a value in the Printer Resolution field that corresponds to the resolution of the printer you intend to use for final output of your publication, or choose a value from the

FIGURE 1-30
Setting a
constraint angle

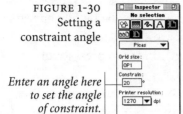

Enter an angle here
to set the angle
of constraint.

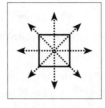

*When the constraint
angle is "0" (the default),
holding down Shift as
you drag an object
constrains its movement
to 45-degree angles.*

*If you change the angle,
the constraint axes are
based on the angle you
entered.*

The Constrain field also affects the way FreeHand draws basic shapes.

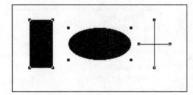

Constraint angle: 0

Constraint angle: 20

defaults listed in the popup menu. FreeHand uses this value to cal-culate the optimum number of steps to use in a graduated fill, a radial fill, or a blend (see Chapter 2, "Drawing"). FreeHand also uses this value for sizing bilevel bitmaps to the resolution of the output device ("magic stretching," to you PageMaker fans out there). For more on why you need to stretch bilevel bitmaps to your printer's resolution, see "Resizing Images to Your Printer's Resolution" in Chapter 4, "Importing and Exporting."

**What About
the Page Setup
Dialog Box?**

Choosing Page Setup from the File menu brings up the Apple Laser-Writer driver's dialog boxes and printing options. Almost every setting found in these dialog boxes is overridden by settings in FreeHand's Document Inspector and in the Print and Print Options dialog boxes.

There's still one important setting in these dialog boxes, how-ever. If you're having trouble printing a document containing multiple downloadable fonts, choose Page Setup from the File menu to bring up the LaserWriter Page Setup dialog box. Click the

Options button. The LaserWriter Options dialog box appears (see Figure 1-31). Turn on Unlimited Downloadable Fonts in a Document (if it's already on, leave it on), and then press Return twice to close the dialog boxes.

Many jobs that FreeHand would otherwise print have been canceled because this simple option was off. If your job isn't printing, try checking this option. Most of the time, however, you want to leave this option turned off, because it slows printing (it downloads fonts and flushes them from memory every time they're used—this makes more RAM available, but means you have to download fonts far more often).

FIGURE 1-31
LaserWriter Options
dialog box

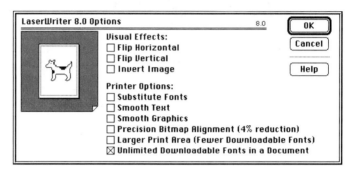

Moving Around in Your Publication

FreeHand offers three ways to change your view of the publication: zooming, scrolling, and moving from page to page. Zooming changes the magnification of your pages inside the publication window. Scrolling changes the view of the publication in the publication window without changing the magnification. Moving from page to page can be thought of as either automated scrolling or zooming, but I'm not sure which.

Zooming

Most of the time, I use zooming (that is, changing magnifications of the view of the publication) rather than scrolling (that is, changing my view of the publication without changing magnification) to move from one area of the page or pasteboard to another.

Zooming with the View menu. The View menu offers several different magnifications (that is, the size of your pages inside the publication window) and several keyboard shortcuts (see Table 1-5).

All of these commands except Fit Page center the any object you've selected in the publication window. If there's no object selected, these shortcuts zoom in or out based on the center of the current view. Fit Page centers the publication in the publication window. This makes Fit Page the perfect "zoom-out" shortcut.

TABLE 1-5
Magnification
keyboard shortcuts

To reach this magnification	Use these keyboard shortcuts
Fit Page	Command-W
Fit All	None
12%	None
25%	None
50%	Command-5
75%	Command-7
100%	Command-1
200%	Command-2
400%	Command-4
800%	Command-8

Zooming with the Magnifying Glass. Another zooming method: choose the Magnifying Glass, point at an area in your publication, and click. FreeHand zooms to the next larger view size (based on your current view—from 100% to 200%, for example), centering the area you clicked on in the publication window. Hold down Option and the Magnifying Glass tool changes to the Reducing Glass tool. Click the Reducing Glass tool and you'll zoom out to the next smaller view size.

Tip:
Switching to the
Magnifying Glass

Hold down Command-spacebar to temporarily change any tool into the Magnifying Glass to zoom in; or hold down Option-Command-spacebar to change any tool into the Reducing Glass to zoom out (see Figure 1-32).

FIGURE 1-32
Magnifying Glass

Press Command-spacebar…

…and the cursor turns into the Magnifying Glass.

Click the Magnifying Glass, and FreeHand zooms in to the next magnification level.

To zoom out, hold down Command-Option-spacebar to turn any tool into the Reducing Glass, and click again.

Tip:
The Best Way
to Zoom In

To zoom in, press Command and hold down the spacebar to turn the current tool (whatever it is) into the Magnifying Glass tool, then drag the Magnifying Glass in the publication window. As you drag a rectangle (like a selection rectangle) appears. Drag the rectangle around the area you want to zoom in on, and release the mouse button. FreeHand zooms in on the area, magnifying the area to the largest size that fits in the publication window (see Figure 1-33).

To zoom out, use one of the keyboard shortcuts—Command-W, for Fit Page, is especially handy.

Tip:
What's the Most
Accurate View in
FreeHand?

Lots of FreeHand users have noticed that elements seem to shift slightly as they zoom in and out, and have wondered which magnification is most accurate. It's simple: it's the 800% view. Interestingly, the Fit Page view is pretty good, too.

If something's a point off in the 800% view, it sometimes looks like it's about a mile away in the Fit Page view. Which is good. You

FIGURE 1-33
Drag magnification

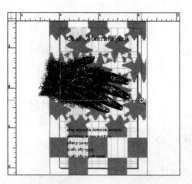 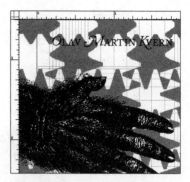

Drag the Magnifying Glass around the area you want to zoom in on and release the mouse button.

FreeHand zooms in on the area you selected.

want to know when lines aren't where you want them, so a little exaggeration is a good thing.

The final arbiters of accuracy are the numbers in the Object Inspector. If points don't seem to line up, select them by turn and look at their coordinates in the Object Inspector. By comparing their numeric positions, you'll know exactly where they are, and whether they're where you want them.

Scrolling

As I said earlier in this chapter, I rarely use the scroll bars to scroll. So how do I change my view of my publication? I use the Grabber Hand, or I let FreeHand do the scrolling for me as I move objects.

Scrolling with the Grabber Hand. You can also change your view of the publication using the Grabber Hand. If you hold down the spacebar and then hold down the mouse button, the cursor turns into the Grabber Hand. As long as you keep pressing the mouse button, you can slide the publication around in the publication window (see Figure 1-34).

Scrolling as you drag objects. Never forget that you can change your view by dragging objects off the screen (see Figure 1-35). If you know an object should be moved to some point below your current view, select the object and drag the cursor off the bottom of the publication window. The window scrolls as long as the cursor is off the bottom of the screen and the mouse button is down. Sometimes it's the best way to get something into position.

FIGURE 1-34
Grabber Hand

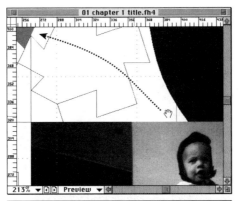

*Hold down the spacebar
with any tool selected to
turn the cursor into the
Grabber Hand.*

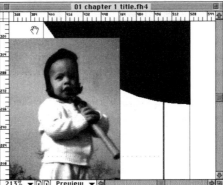

*Use the Grabber Hand
to drag your publication
around in the window.*

FIGURE 1-35
Scrolling by dragging

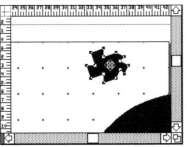
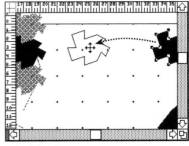

*As you drag an object, FreeHand
scrolls the current window to keep
up with your dragging.*

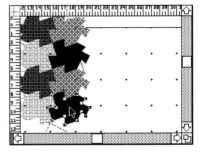

Moving from Page to Page

You move between pages in your FreeHand publication by scrolling (the slow way), or by clicking on the next page and previous page icons (the ones at the bottom of the publication window), but the best method is to display the Document Inspector (press Command-Option-D) and double-click the thumbnail of the page you want to move to. FreeHand moves to the page and displays it in Fit Page view.

Using FreeHand's Toolbox

If FreeHand is your workshop, and the menus and palettes are where you collect the wood, nails, and paint you use, the toolbox is where you keep your saws, hammers, and brushes.

Some of the following descriptions of the tool functions aren't going to make any sense unless you understand how FreeHand's points and paths work, and that discussion falls in "Points and Paths," later in this chapter. You can flip ahead and read that section, or you can plow through this section, get momentarily confused (remember that confusion is a great state for learning), and then become enlightened when you reach the descriptions of points and paths.

Or, you can flip ahead to Chapter 2, "Drawing" for even more on points and paths. It's your choice, and either method works. This is precisely the sort of nonlinear information gathering that hypertext gurus say can't be done in books.

You can break FreeHand's toolbox into four main conceptual sections (as shown in Figure 1-36).

◆ Tools for drawing basic shapes (the Rectangle, Polygon, Ellipse, and Line tools)

◆ Path-drawing tools (the Point, Freehand, and Pen tools, also known as the freeform drawing tools)

◆ Transformation tools (the Rotation, Reflection, Skewing, and Scaling tools)

◆ The Text tool

FIGURE 1-36
Tools in the toolbox

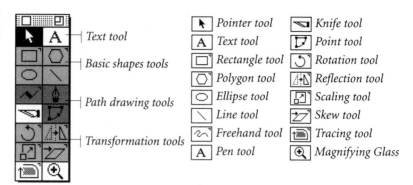

The basic shape tools draw complete paths containing specific numbers of points in specific positions on the path, while the path-drawing tools draw paths point by point. The transformation tools act on objects you've drawn, typed, or imported, and the Text tool is for entering text.

The remaining tools don't really fit into a single category—the Pointer tool is for selecting objects, the Knife tool is for splitting points and paths, and the Magnifying Glass tool is for changing your view of your publication.

The tool descriptions in the following section are brief and are only intended to give you a feeling for what the different tools are and what they do. For more on drawing objects with the drawing tools, see Chapter 2, "Drawing." To learn more about entering text with the Text tool, see Chapter 3, "Text and Type." For more on working with the Transformation tools, see Chapter 5, "Importing and Exporting."

Note: Talking about FreeHand's tools and their use can get a little confusing. When you select a tool in the toolbox (or press the keyboard shortcut to select a tool), what does the cursor become? In the previous edition of this book, I used the same wording as in FreeHand's documentation: "When you select a tool, the cursor turns into a crosshair." I didn't like that, because I think the cursor remains the cursor (and because we couldn't decide on "cross hair" or "crosshair"—either one sounds uncomfortable). Therefore, in this book, I'll use phrases like "select a tool and drag the cursor" or "select a tool and drag the tool."

**Toolbox
Keyboard
Shortcuts**

You can choose most of the tools in FreeHand's toolbox through keyboard shortcuts. This is usually faster than going back to the toolbox and clicking on the tool (see Table 1-6).

TABLE 1-6
Toolbox keyboard
shortcuts

Tool	Key
Pointer tool	Shift-F10
Pointer tool (temporary)	Hold down Command and the current tool turns into the Pointer tool. Release Command and the cursor changes back into the selected tool.
Text tool	A, or Shift-F9
Rectangle tool	1* or Shift-F1
Polygon tool	2* or Shift-F2
Ellipse tool	3* or Shift-F3
Line tool	4* or Shift-F4
Freehand tool	5* or Shift-F5
Pen tool	6* or Shift-F6
Knife tool	7* or Shift-F7
Point tool	8* or Shift-F8
Magnifying Glass	Hold down Command-spacebar and the current tool turns into the Magnifying Glass. Release Command-spacebar and the Magnifying Glass turns back into the selected tool. If your cursor is inside a text block, make sure you press Command slightly before you press spacebar, or you'll get a bunch of spaces in the text block.
Reducing Glass	Hold down Command-Option-spacebar and the current tool turns into the Reducing Glass. Release Command-Option-spacebar and the Reducing Glass turns back into the selected tool.

* The number keys on the numeric keypad work, too, if you've got one.

Pointer Tool   You use the Pointer tool to select and transform objects. You can press Shift-F10 to select the Pointer tool. You can use the Pointer tool temporarily by holding down Command when any other tool is selected.

Text Tool   You enter and edit text using the Text tool. To create a text block, select the Text tool and click on a point in the publication window; a text block appears with a flashing text-insertion point (or cursor) in the first line of the text block. To edit text, select the Text tool and click in a text block. For more on entering, editing, and formatting text, see Chapter 3, "Text and Type"). To select the Text tool, press A or F9.

Rectangle Tool   Use the Rectangle tool to draw rectangles. If you hold down Shift as you draw a rectangle, you can draw perfect squares.

Note that you can always draw rectangles and squares using the other drawing tools, but that the rectangles drawn using the Rectangle tool have some special capabilities (see Table 1-7, later in this chapter). Press 1 (on either the keyboard or on the numeric keypad) or F1 to select the Rectangle tool.

If you want to draw rectangles with rounded corners, double-click the Rectangle tool. FreeHand displays the Rectangle Tool dialog box. Drag the slider or enter a number to set the corner radius you want to use for your rounded corners (see Figure 1-37).

FIGURE 1-37
Specifying rounded corners

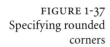

Double-click the Rectangle tool to display the Rectangle Tool dialog box. Enter a corner radius and press Return.

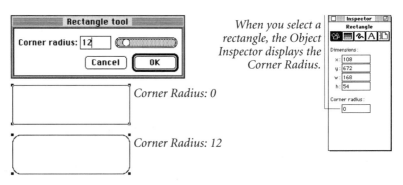

When you select a rectangle, the Object Inspector displays the Corner Radius.

Corner Radius: 0

Corner Radius: 12

If you draw a rectangle with square corners and then decide that you'd rather its corners were rounded, you can always change them using the Corner Radius field in the Object Inspector.

Polygon Tool

The Polygon tool makes it easy to draw equilateral polygons, such as pentagons, hexagons, and dodecagons. (Polygons are closed geometric objects that have at least three sides; they're equilateral if each side is the same length.) You can also use the Polygon tool to draw stars.

To change which polygon the Polygon tool draws, double-click the tool in the toolbox. FreeHand displays the Polygon Tool dialog box (see Figure 1-38), where you can specify the number of sides you want your star or polygon to have, and how acute (or obtuse) you want the star's interior angles to be. You can drag a slider for polygons or stars from three to 20 sides or points, or enter a larger number.

Clicking the slider after entering a larger number resets the number to 20. The preview is dynamically updated as you drag the slider or enter a number. For stars, there's another slider for changing the interior angles of the star from acute to obtuse.

Press 2 (on either the keyboard or on the numeric keypad) or F2 to select the polygon tool.

FIGURE 1-38
Polygon tool controls

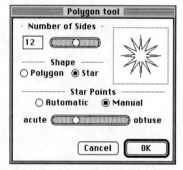

Double-click the Polygon tool to define what kind of polygons the Polygon tool draws.

Drag the slider to set the number of sides in the polygon, or enter a number.

Click Star, and options appear for drawing star-shaped polygons. Enter a number to specify the number of points you want for the star, then drag the Star Points slider to set the sharpness of the star's points.

Ellipse Tool
Use the Ellipse tool to draw ellipses. If you hold down Shift as you draw an ellipse, you can draw circles. Note that you can always draw ellipses and circles using the other drawing tools, but that the ellipses drawn using the Ellipse tool offer some special capabilities (see Table 1-7, later in this chapter). If you ungroup these ellipses, you lose those capabilities.

Press 3 (on either the keyboard or on the numeric keypad) or F3 to select the Ellipse tool.

Line Tool
Use the Line tool to draw straight lines. If you hold down Shift as you drag the Line tool, the lines you draw will be constrained to 45-degree angles.

Press 4 (on either the keyboard or on the numeric keypad) or F4 to select the Line tool.

Freehand Tool
Select the Freehand tool (it's not the FreeHand tool), hold down the mouse button, and scribble. The Freehand tool creates a path that follows your mouse movements, adding points according to its settings.

If you double-click the Freehand tool, the Freehand Tool dialog box appears. This dialog box, lets you customize the way the Freehand tool works. The Freehand tool is really three tools—the Freehand, Variable Stroke, and Calligraphic Pen tools. To change from one tool to another, choose the appropriate option from the popup menu in the Freehand Tool dialog box. The options you see in the dialog box depend on which tool you've selected. Note that the paths you draw using the Freehand tool are open paths (unless you intentionally close them), while the paths drawn using the variable stroke and calligraphic pen tools are closed paths.

Press 5 (on either the keyboard or on the numeric keypad) or F5 to select the Freehand tool.

Freehand tool. The Tight Fit option draws more points along the path as you draw, and the Draw Dotted Line option controls the way your path appears as you draw it. With Draw Dotted Line on, the Freehand tool simply places a series of dots as you draw and waits until you stop drawing to connect the dots and display the path you've drawn (see Figure 1-39).

FIGURE 1-39
Freehand tool options

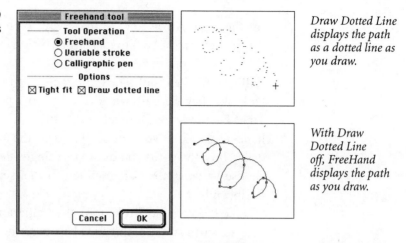

Draw Dotted Line
displays the path
as a dotted line as
you draw.

With Draw
Dotted Line
off, FreeHand
displays the path
as you draw.

Variable Stroke tool. The Variable Stroke tool (also known as the "variable blob tool") is good for creating paths that look like brush strokes (see Figure 1-40). Tight Fit and Draw Dotted Line are the same as those for the Freehand tool. In the Minimum and Maximum fields, enter the minimum and maximum widths you want for paths you create using the Variable Stroke tool.

If you have a pressure-sensitive drawing tablet (such as those made by Wacom and Kurta), you can use pressure to control the width of paths you draw using the Variable Stroke tool. If you don't have a pressure-sensitive tablet, however, you can get similar effects. As you drag the Variable Stroke tool on your page, press 2

FIGURE 1-40
Variable Stroke
tool options

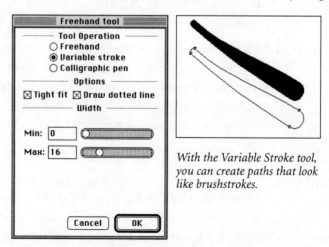

With the Variable Stroke tool,
you can create paths that look
like brushstrokes.

(or the Right Arrow key) to make your path get wider, or press 1 (or the Left Arrow key) to make your path narrower.

Calligraphic Pen tool. The Calligraphic Pen tool draws paths that look like they were drawn with a lettering pen (see Figure 1-41). Tight Fit and Draw Dotted Line are the same as those for the Free-hand tool. When you choose Fixed in the Width section of the dialog box, the paths you draw are a single, fixed width. When you choose Variable, the Calligraphic Pen tool simulates a pen with a flexible nib.

Like the Variable Stroke tool, the Calligraphic Pen tool is pressure-sensitive and uses the same keyboard shortcuts.

FIGURE 1-41
Calligraphic Pen
tool options

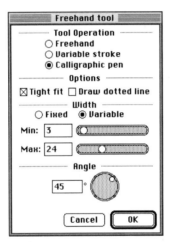

Drag the Calligraphic Pen tool to create paths that look like hand lettering.

Pen Tool

Use the Pen tool to create paths containing both curves and straight line segments (that is, both curve an dcorner points). Illustrator users will recognize the Pen tool immediately, because it works the same as Illustrator's Pen tool. Click the Pen tool to create a corner point, drag to create a curve point.

Knife Tool

The Knife tool splits paths or points. Just select a path or point, choose the Knife tool, and point at a path or point, and click, and FreeHand splits the path or point into separate paths where you clicked. You can also drag the Knife tool, and it cuts each selected path it encounters as you drag it.

Press 7 (on the keyboard or on the numeric keypad) or F7 to select the Knife tool. For more on splitting paths, see "Splitting Paths" in Chapter 2, "Drawing."

Point Tool

Use the Point tool to place points on your page (the FreeHand manuals call this tool the "Bezigon" tool, but I find I can't—I just can't—type the word). You can create curve points, corner points, or connector points. To add a corner point, all you need to do is click. To create a curve point, hold down Option and click. Add a connector point by holding down Control and clicking. As you position points, bear in mind that you can always change any kind of point into any other kind of point, and that you can always change the curve of line segments attached to points.

For more on corner points, curve points, and connector points, see "Points and Paths," later in this chapter.

Rotation Tool

To rotate an object, select the Rotation tool from the toolbox, select the object, and drag the Rotation tool on your page. The point at which you start dragging specifies the center of rotation. If you want to rotate an object around its center, hold down Control as you drag.

Reflection Tool

The Reflection tool creates a mirror image of an object around the object's vertical or horizontal axis (or both), around an angled axis, or around a fixed location on your page or pasteboard. To reflect an object, select the object, select the Reflection tool, then drag the Reflection tool on the page to flip the object. The point at which you start dragging determines the axis about which you're reflecting the object. Hold down Control as you drag if you want to reflect the object around its center point.

Scaling Tool

To scale (or resize) an object, select the object, select the Scaling tool, and drag the Scaling tool to size the selected object. The point at which you start dragging determines the center point around which you're sizing the object. Hold down Shift as you drag to retain the object's proportions as you scale it. If you want to scale the object around its center point, hold down Control as you drag.

Skewing Tool

Skewing alters the vertical or horizontal axes (or both) of objects, which makes them appear as though they're on a plane that's been slanted relative to the plane of the publication. To skew a selected object, select the Skewing tool from the toolbox and drag it on your page. As you drag, FreeHand skews the object. The point at which you start dragging sets the point around which the object skews (this means that the object will move, unless you've started dragging in precisely the center of the object). To skew the object around its center point, hold down Control as you drag.

Tracing Tool

To automatically trace objects in your publication, select the Tracing tool and drag a selection rectangle around the objects you want to trace. Many people have the idea that the Tracing tool is only for tracing bitmaps, which isn't true—it'll trace anything you can have on a FreeHand page.

If you double-click the Tracing tool, the Tracing Tool dialog box appears (see Figure 1-42). The Tight option adds more points to the paths generated by the tracing process. Trace Background and Trace Foreground are pretty straightforward. Choose Trace Background if you want to trace anything on a background layer; choose Trace Foreground if you want to trace things in the foreground layer(s).

FIGURE 1-42
Tracing tool settings

Magnifying Glass

Use the Magnifying Glass to change your view of the publication. Holding down Option changes the Magnifying Glass tool (which zooms in) into the Reducing Glass (which zooms out). To temporarily switch to the Magnifying Glass, hold down Command-spacebar, and then click the area you want to magnify, or drag a selection rectangle around it. To temporarily switch to the Reducing Glass, hold down Command-Option-spacebar, and then click or drag to zoom out.

For more on using the Magnifying Glass, see "Zooming," earlier in this chapter.

Constraining Tools

Most Macintosh drawing programs (beginning with MacPaint) have the concept of constraint: that holding down some key (usually Shift) makes tools behave differently. Usually, constraint limits movement to vertical and horizontal axes, relative to the sides of your Macintosh screen (though some applications limit movement to 45-degree increments). Table 1-7 shows how constraint works in FreeHand.

Additionally, you should note that constraint (holding down Shift) is affected by the angle you entered in the Constrain field of the Setup Inspector. All constraint, including drawing, is based on the angle you enter (see "Constrain," earlier in this chapter).

TABLE 1-7
Effect of constraint
on tools

Tool	Constraint
Pointer tool	If you're moving an object, holding down Shift limits the movement of the object to 45-degree tangents from the point at which you started dragging. You can hold down Shift at any time as you drag the object to get this effect.
	If you're selecting objects, holding down Shift extends the selection to include the next object or set of objects you click.
Polygon tool	Hold down Shift to constrain the rotation of the polygon's axis to 15-degree increments as you draw it.
Rectangle tool	Hold down Shift to draw squares.
Ellipse tool	Hold down Shift to draw circles.

	Tool	Constraint
TABLE 1-7 Effect of constraint on tools (continued)	Line tool	Hold down Shift to constrain the Line tool to draw lines in 45-degree increments (that is, 0, 45, and 90 degrees, where 0 degrees is horizontal and 90 degrees is vertical, relative to your publication).
	Freehand tool	Hold down Option to constrain line segments to straight lines (from the point you held down the key); hold down Option-Shift to constrain line segments to 45-degree angles.
	Pen tool	Shift constrains the next point placed to a 45-degree tangent from the previous point on the path.
	Knife tool	Same as Line tool.
	Point tool	Same as Pen tool.
	Magnifying Glass	None
	Reducing Glass	None

What's on My Page?

A FreeHand page can contain four kinds of objects: paths, basic shapes, text blocks, and imported graphics.

Points and Paths

So much of working with FreeHand depends on understanding the concept of points and paths that I've written about it several times in this book. The following section is an overview of the topic. For more (much more) on points and paths, see "Points and Paths" in Chapter 2, "Drawing."

In FreeHand, continuous lines are called paths. Paths are made up of several points and the line segments drawn between those points. A point can have curve control handles attached to it which control the curve of the line segments associated with the point (see Figure 1-43).

Many people call these handles "Bezier control points" (which is the technical, mathematical term for them). I find it confusing

FIGURE 1-43
Paths, points, and
control handles

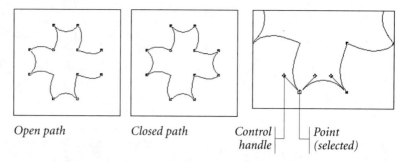

Open path   Closed path   Control   Point
                                     handle   (selected)

talking about two different kinds of "points," so I always call them "control handles" or "curve handles," and use "point" to refer to the point on the path. It's simple: there are points, and those points might have control handles.

Points come in three different flavors—curve points, corner points, and connector points—each with its own special properties.

◆ A curve point adds a curved line segment between the preceding and following points along the path. Curve points are shown onscreen as small circles and have curve control handles placed along a straight line from the curve point itself (see Figure 1-44).

The curve handle following the point controls the curve of the line segment following the curve point on the path; the curve handle preceding the point controls the curve of the line segment preceding the curve point on the path. Curve points are typically used for adding smooth curves to a path (see Figure 1-45).

◆ A corner point adds a straight line segment between the current point and the preceding point on the path (see Figure 1-46). Corner points are typically used to create paths containing straight line segments.

◆ A connector point adds a curved line segment following the point on the path. A connector point is something like a curve or corner point with one curve control handle extended and connects corner points and curve points (see Figure 1-47). I've been using FreeHand for years, and I have yet to use a connector point.

FIGURE 1-44
Curve points

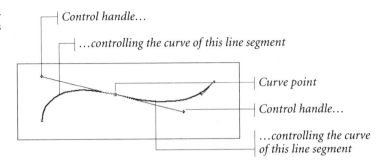

Control handle...

...controlling the curve of this line segment

Curve point

Control handle...

...controlling the curve of this line segment

FIGURE 1-45
Adjusting handles on
curve points

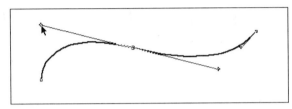

Select one of the curve handles...

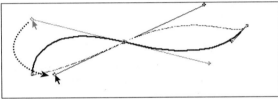

...and drag it to a new position.

When you drag one handle of a curve point, the other handle moves, too.

FreeHand displays the new curve.

FIGURE 1-46
Corner points

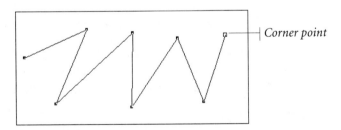

Corner point

FIGURE 1-47
Connector points

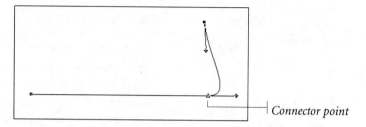

Connector point

You can always drag curve control handles out of corner and connector points. Select the point, hold down Option, and drag a curve control point out of the point. The first curve handle controls the curve of the line segment following the point along the path; the second curve handle controls the curve of the line segment preceding the point along the path.

What points should you use? Any type of point can be turned into any other type of point, and anything you can do with one kind of point can be done with any other kind of point. Given these two points (so to speak), you can use the kinds of points and drawing tools you're happiest with and achieve exactly the results you want. There is no "best way" to draw with FreeHand's free-form drawing tools, but it helps to understand how the particular method you choose works.

I always use the Point tool, and place corner points to draw straight line segments. I add curves later, once I've placed points where I want them along the path. This seems easiest to me; what you like may be different. Experiment until you find what method of drawing suits you best. For more on working with points and paths, see Chapter 2, "Drawing."

Basic Shapes

The Rectangle, Polygon, Ellipse, and Line tools draw basic shapes (that's what I call them, anyway). The Line tool draws a straight line segment between two points, which then behaves exactly as if you'd drawn it by placing two corner points. The other three tools draw paths with specific properties and points in specific places. It's as you'd expect: the Rectangle tool draws rectangles, the Ellipse tool draws ellipses, and the Polygon tool draws polygons. Objects drawn with the basic shapes tools act like grouped paths, but have certain special properties, as shown in Table 1-8.

	Shape	Special properties
TABLE 1-8 Special properties of basic shapes	Rectangle	The Object Inspector for rectangles contains fields specifying the object's X and Y (horizontal and vertical) coordinates, W and H (width and height), as well as a field for specifying the rectangle's corner radius. (If you ungroup the rectangle, you won't be able to change its corner radius using the Object Inspector). If you hold down Option as you draw a rectangle, FreeHand positions the center of the rectangle at the point where you started dragging, drawing the rectangle out from that point.
	Ellipse	The Object Inspector for ellipses contains fields specifying the object's X and Y (horizontal and vertical) coordinates, W and H (width and height). If you hold down Option as you draw an ellipse, FreeHand positions the center of the ellipse at the point where you started dragging, drawing the ellipse out from that point.
	Polygon	When you select a polygon, the Object Inspector displays the same information as it would if you selected a freeform path. If you hold down Option as you draw a polygon, FreeHand positions the center of the polygon at the point where you started dragging.

Text Blocks

FreeHand's text blocks can contain any number of typefaces, paragraph formats, colors, and sizes of type. Text blocks can also be linked to each other (so text flows between them as you edit the copy, reshape text blocks, or change formatting), and can be linked across pages. Text can flow along a path (that is, have its baseline follow a path), and can be flowed inside a path (see Figure 1-48).

FIGURE 1-48
Text blocks

For more on FreeHand's text-handling capabilities, see Chapter 3, "Text and Type."

Imported Graphics

FreeHand can import graphics saved in the PICT, EPS, paint-type (MacPaint, SuperPaint, etc.), and TIFF (including color TIFF) formats. PICT object graphics are disassembled into their component objects on import and are converted into FreeHand elements you can edit just as if you'd drawn them in FreeHand. EPS graphics you've opened (as opposed to placed) are also converted into FreeHand elements. TIFF, paint, and EPS files you've placed are imported and are handled very much like a FreeHand group, except that they cannot be ungrouped. You can use all of Free-Hand's transformation tools (for scaling, rotation, reflection, and skewing) to manipulate imported graphics (see Figure 1-49).

For more on working with imported graphics, see Chapter 4, "Importing and Exporting."

FIGURE 1-49
Imported graphics

Thinking Objectively

FreeHand's world is made up of objects (also called elements)—points, line segments, paths, basic shapes, text blocks, groups, and imported graphics. Each class of object has certain attributes that you can view and edit by selecting the object and looking at the Object Inspector.

The Object Inspector provides an extremely powerful way of looking at objects in your publication—by the numbers. If you want a rectangle to occupy exactly a certain space in your publication, you can always type the numbers right into the palette. Can I prove it to you? To position a six-by-six-pica rectangle three picas from the top and three picas from the left edge of your publication, follow these steps.

1. Reset the zero point to the upper-left corner of the publication (see "Rulers," earlier in this chapter).

2. Draw a rectangle with the Rectangle tool. Anywhere. Any size. I don't care.

3. Without deselecting the rectangle or selecting anything else, press Command-Option-R, then press Command-` to select the text in the X field in the Inspector.

4. In the X field, type "3p" (that's three picas from the left edge of the page). Press Tab to move to the Y field. Type "-3p" (that's three picas down from the top of the page) in the Y field, and press Tab to move to the W(idth) field. Enter "6p" and press Tab to move to the H(eight) field. In the H field, enter "6p".

5. Press Return.

The rectangle snaps into the position specified in the Object Inspector. You could have drawn it using the shadow cursors, Snap to Guides, or ruler guides—it's true. But, in this case, all you had to do was some typing, and the rectangle is positioned perfectly, exactly where you want it. If you know where something has to go, try using the Object Inspector to get it there. It can beat dragging, measuring, and waiting for the screen to redraw.

Selecting and Deselecting Elements

Before you can act on an object, you have to select it. You select objects with the Pointer tool by clicking them, dragging a selection rectangle over them, or by Shift-selecting (select one object, hold down Shift, and select another object). You can also choose Select All from the Edit menu.

When you select an object, FreeHand displays the object's selection handles. FreeHand displays selected objects a little bit differently depending on the method you've used to select them and the type of object you've selected. Figure 1-50 shows you the differences.

To deselect objects, click an uninhabited area of the page or pasteboard, or press Command-Tab.

FIGURE 1-50
Selecting objects

Shift-selecting

Click on one object to select it.   *Hold down Shift, and click on another object.*   *You've selected both objects.*

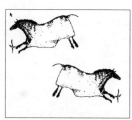 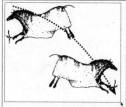 

Drag-selecting

Position the cursor outside the group of objects you want to select...   *...and drag a selection rectangle over the objects.*   *You've selected all of the objects inside the rectangle.*

Tip:
Deselect All

Pressing Command-Tab deselects all selected objects. This is particularly handy when you're having trouble deselecting an object at a high magnification—you can't see the currently selected object's selection handles because the object is larger than your page view. Pressing Command-Tab is easy, fast, and guaranteed to deselect all objects. Actually, if you're not entering text in a text block, you can just press Tab to deselect all objects. If your cursor is inside a text block, of course, you'll enter a tab character in the text block.

Tip:
Selecting Parts
of Paths

Sometimes, you only want to work on specific points in a path, rather than working on the path as a whole. To do this, drag a selection rectangle over only the points you want to select. If you want to select several points but can't reach them all with one selection rectangle, select some of the points by dragging a selection rectangle, then hold down Shift and drag more selection rectangles until you've selected all of the points you want.

Tip:
Selecting Paths
Instead of Points

If you've selected a path by dragging a selection rectangle over part of it, you've probably got some points specifically selected. While you sometimes want to do this, it can cause problems—when you drag the path, it's likely that the unselected points on the path stays put while the selected points move. To select the path as a whole when you've got some specific points selected, press ` (accent grave), located on the upper left of your keyboard underneath the ~ or tilde—see Figure 1-51).

FIGURE 1-51
Selecting paths only

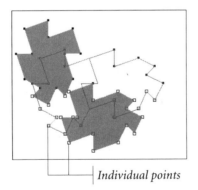

Individual points

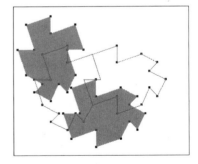

Press ` (accent grave) and FreeHand selects the paths as paths, rather than as individual points.

Tip:
Select Through
Objects

To select an object that's behind another object (or objects), hold down the Control key and click through the stack of objects until the selection handles of the individual object you want to select appear (see Figure 1-52).

FIGURE 1-52
Selecting through
stacks of objects

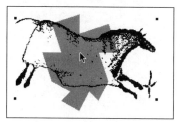

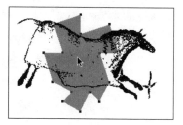

Control-click once to select the
object on top of the stack.

Control-click again to select
the next object in the stack.

Tip:
Subselecting
Items in a Group

You don't have to ungroup a group of objects to edit the objects in the group—you can select them and work with them just as if they were outside the group. Hold down Option and click on the element that you want to edit inside a group. While it's selected, you can change its attributes, text, shape, or position. When you deselect the subselected item, it goes back to being part of the group (see Figure 1-53).

If you're trying to select an object in a group that's behind other objects, hold down Option and Control as you click through the stack of elements. You can also select multiple buried objects this way by holding down Control-Option-Shift as you click through the stack of objects.

This set of features is flexible enough that you can select any number of groups or individual objects through a stack of items containing groups or individual elements.

When you have an object inside a group selected, and you want to select and act on the group, press ` (accent grave). FreeHand selects the group. When you're working with groups nested inside other groups, each press of ` selects the next encompassing group.

FIGURE 1-53
Subselecting items
inside groups

Point at an object inside
a group.

Hold down Option
and click to select the
object.

You can move or edit
the object, but it
remains inside the
group (in this example,
I've changed an object's
color and position).

Moving Elements

You can move individual points, sets of points, paths, groups or imported graphics, or sets of selected points, paths, or objects. Moving any single object is simple: just position the Pointer tool over the object (but not over a point in the path), hold down the mouse button, and drag the object to wherever you want it (Figure 1-54).

To move more than one object at once, hold down Shift and click on the objects you want to move. When you reach the last object you want to select, position the Pointer tool over the object, and, while still holding down Shift, press the mouse button. If you want to constrain the objects movement, continue holding down Shift, if not, release the Shift key, and drag all of the selected objects to where you want them.

FIGURE 1-54
Moving by dragging

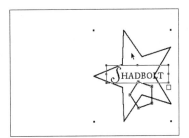

Select the objects you want to move...

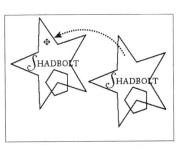

...and drag them to a new position.

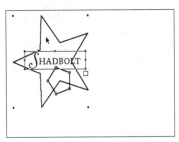

When the objects are where you want them, drop them (that is, stop dragging and release the mouse button).

Okay, I admit that this is pretty basic—but I do get asked, honest.

Alternatively, you can move objects using the Move palette. Select an object (or group of objects) and press Command-M to display the Transform palette (then click the Move icon at the top of the palette if the Move palette's not visible). Type the horizontal and vertical distance you want the selection to move in the fields, and press Return. FreeHand moves the object the distance you specified (see Figure 1-55). For more on moving, see "Moving," in Chapter 5, "Transforming."

FIGURE 1-55
Moving objects using
the Move palette

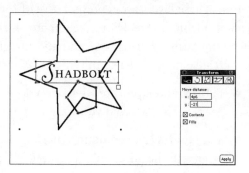

Select the objects you want to move and press Command-M to display the Transform palette (if it's not already visible). Click the Move icon to display the Move palette, type the distance you want to move the objects in the X and Y fields, and press Return (or click the Apply button).

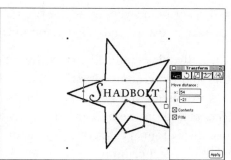

FreeHand moves the objects as you specified.

Working with Layers

Many authors would save the intricacies of working with the Layers palette for later in the book. Sorry. The Layers palette is one of the most important tools at your disposal for speeding up the process of creating publications with FreeHand.

Like many CAD programs, FreeHand uses the concept of layers—transparent planes on which you create and place elements. Once you've gone beyond creating very simple publications, you'll find layers indispensable because they help you organize and control the elements in your publication.

Layers give you control over which parts of your publication redraw while you're working on the file. If, for example, you're correcting text in a publication containing large TIFF images, put the TIFFs on their own layer and make it invisible while you work on the text. Don't spend time displaying things you're not working on and don't need to see.

Default Layers   FreeHand has three default layers: Foreground, Guides, and Background. These layers are representative of the three major types of layers available in FreeHand (see Figure 1-56). You can create or delete any number of background and foreground layers, but you can't create a new, or delete the existing, Guides layer.

◆ Foreground layers are where you do your drawing. In general, they're what you want to print, when you print.

◆ The Guides layer contains FreeHand's guides. Move the layer, and the guides move with it.

◆ Background layers are where you put objects you want to trace or use as guides. Background layers don't print.

The dotted line on the Layers palette defines the boundary background and foreground layers. Layers above the dotted line in the palette are foreground layers; layers below are background layers. Objects placed on the background layers are screened to 50 percent of their original color (this is intended to make tracing easier and doesn't affect printing).

FIGURE 1-56
Default layers

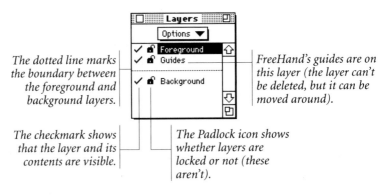

The dotted line marks the boundary between the foreground and background layers.

FreeHand's guides are on this layer (the layer can't be deleted, but it can be moved around).

The checkmark shows that the layer and its contents are visible.

The Padlock icon shows whether layers are locked or not (these aren't).

Using the Layers Palette

Here are some of the things you can do using the Layers palette.

- ◆ Make the Layers palette visible or invisible
- ◆ Move objects from one layer to another
- ◆ Create new layers
- ◆ Remove layers (and their contents)
- ◆ Make layers visible or invisible
- ◆ Change the stacking order of layers
- ◆ Make layers foreground or background
- ◆ Make layers printing or nonprinting
- ◆ Copy the contents of entire layers to other layers
- ◆ Lock layers (objects on locked layers cannot be selected)
- ◆ Rename layers

Toggling the Layers palette. You can display and hide the Layers palette by pressing Command-6. If it's currently displayed, Command-6 hides it, and vice-versa.

Moving objects from one layer to another. To send an object or objects to a specific layer, select the objects and click the name of the layer in the Layers palette. FreeHand moves the selected objects to that layer (see Figure 1-57).

FIGURE 1-57
Moving objects from
one layer to another

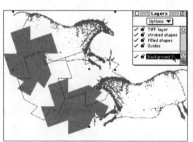

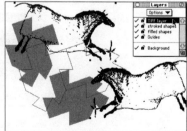

Select the objects you want to move (in this example, the objects are on the background layer).

Click on the layer name in the Layers palette. FreeHand moves the objects to the layer.

Creating new layers. To create a new layer choose New from the popup menu at the top of the Layers palette. FreeHand adds a new layer to the Layers palette. If you want to change the default name FreeHand's assigned to the new layer, double-click on the layer's name in the Layers palette, type a new name for the layer, and press Return (see Figure 1-58).

FIGURE 1-58
Creating and
naming a new layer

Select New from the Layers palette popup menu.

Double-click on the new layer's name and type the name you want for the layer.

Press Return, and FreeHand adds the new layer's name to the Layers palette.

Removing layers. To remove a layer, select the layer name in the Layers palette and choose Remove from the popup menu at the top of the palette. If there are objects on that layer, FreeHand asks if you want to remove those objects (see Figure 1-59). If that's what you want to do, click OK and all of the objects on that layer will be deleted along with the layer. If you don't want the objects removed, click Cancel, and move the objects to other layers. Then try removing the layer again.

FIGURE 1-59
Removing layers

Select the layer you want to remove and choose Remove from the Layers palette popup menu.

If there's anything on the layer, FreeHand displays this message. Click OK (or press Return) if you want to remove the objects on the layer. Otherwise, click Cancel and move the objects to other layers.

Making layers visible or invisible. If you want to make all of the objects on a layer invisible, click the checkmark to the left of the layer's name in the Layers palette. Everything that's on that layer disappears (see Figure 1-60). Don't worry. It's not gone; it's just not visible and can't be selected. To make the layer visible again, click the space to the left of the layer's name. The checkmark re-appears, and the objects on the layer become visible.

You can make all layers visible by choosing All On from the popup menu at the top of the Layers palette, or make all layers invisible by choosing All Off. When you want to work on just one layer, choose All Off and then make that one layer visible.

FIGURE 1-60
Making layers visible
or invisible

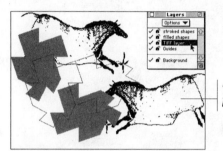

This figure is on the layer "TIFF layer".

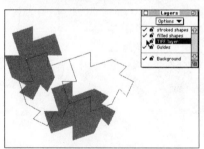

Click the checkmark to the left of the layer's name to make the layer invisible.

Changing the stacking order of layers. The stacking order of the layers you use is determined by the order in which they appear in the Layers palette. Layers closer to the top of the Layers palette are farther to the front in your publication. If you want to move the contents of a specific layer closer to the front, drag the layer name closer to the top of the Layers palette (see Figure 1-61).

Tip:
Moving the
Guides Layer

PageMaker users working with FreeHand used to complain that FreeHand's ruler guides got in the way of selecting and moving objects because there wasn't a way to send the guides to the back, like there is in PageMaker. With FreeHand 4, they'll have to start complaining that PageMaker's guides don't work like FreeHand's.

To send the guides all the way to the back, drag the Guides layer below the dotted line on the Layers palette. The Guides layer is now behind every foreground layer. If you want to move the Guides layer behind every background layer, drag the Guides layer to the bottom of the list in the Layers palette.

You could also move the Guides layer so that it fell behind one or more foreground layers.

FIGURE 1-61
Changing the stacking
order of layers

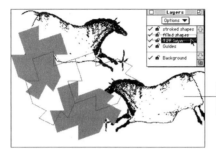

Drag the layer name up or down in the Layers palette.

This image is on the layer named "TIFF layer".

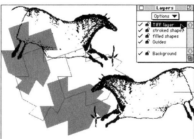

Drop the layer when it's where you want it.

The image comes to the front, along with any other objects on the same layer.

Making layers foreground or background. To make a layer a background layer, drag it below the dotted line in the Layers palette. To make a background layer into a foreground layer, drag it above the dotted line in the Layers palette. You can also drag the dotted line up and down in the palette, making whole ranges of layers foreground or background.

Making layers printing or nonprinting. If you want to print only the visible foreground layers (the layers above the dotted line in the palette with a checkmark to the left of their names), click All Visible Foreground Layers in the Print Options dialog box. If you want to print all foreground layers, whether they're visible or not, click All Foreground Layers.

Alternatively, you can make foreground layers into background layers to make them nonprinting, and vice versa.

The default Guides layer cannot be printed.

Copying layers. To copy all of the objects on a particular layer to a new layer, select the layer and choose Duplicate from the Layers palette's popup menu. FreeHand creates a new layer containing copies of all of the objects on the original layer. Your page won't look any different, of course, because the copied objects are exactly on top of the original objects.

Locking and unlocking layers. When you're working on a complex publication, it's too easy to select something you'd rather leave alone—or, worse, delete it. Instead of losing time "undoing" your mistakes, why not put the things you're done with (or, at least, not currently working on) on a layer of their own, and then keep them safe by locking the layer.

To lock a layer, click the Padlock icon to the left of the layer's name in the Layers palette (see Figure 1-62). The objects on the layer remain visible, but you can't select them. You can still change the layer's position in the stacking order when it's locked.

To unlock a layer, click the Padlock icon to the left of the layer's name. When the padlock's open, the layer is unlocked.

FIGURE 1-62
Locking and
unlocking layers

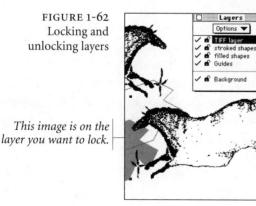

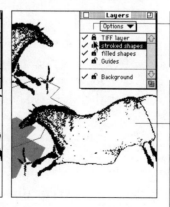

This image is on the layer you want to lock.

Click the Padlock to lock the layer.

Any objects you had selected on the locked layer become deselected. You won't be able to select this object again until you unlock the layer.

Renaming layers. You can rename a layer at any time. Double-click on the layer name in the Layers palette, type a new name for the layer and press Return.

Functionally, renaming layers makes not a bit of difference to FreeHand, but it might help you remember which layer contains which objects.

FreeHand and the Edit Menu

FreeHand works a little bit differently than other Macintosh applications, particularly in that you don't have to go through the Clipboard to copy items in your publication. Instead, you'll typically use Clone and Duplicate (which you'll find on FreeHand's Edit menu) inside a publication (you'll still need to use Cut and Copy to move items from publication to publication). Not only are Clone and Duplicate faster, they use less memory and have some useful features of their own.

Clone

The Clone command, Command-= (that's the equals sign at the upper right of the keyboard), creates a copy of the selected object, exactly on top of the original (see Figure 1-63). This can be a little confusing at first, because the cloned object's selection handles look just the same as the selection handles of the original object. New FreeHand users sometimes end up with stacks of identical objects in their publications.

Placing the object in the same position, however, offers distinct advantages. If, for example, you know that you want a copy of a specific object two picas to the right and two picas down from the location of the original object, just clone the object, then display the Move palette, and move the object numerically. If you hadn't started in exactly the same position as the original object, you'd have to do a bunch of measuring to figure out where the copied object was supposed to go.

Duplicate

The Duplicate command (Command-D) creates a copy of the object at a slight offset from the selected object (see Figure 1-64), or copies the object and repeats the last series of transformations (uses of

FIGURE 1-63
Cloning

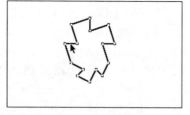

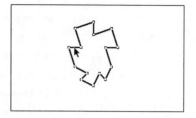

Select an object and press Command-= to clone it.

FreeHand places an exact copy of the object on top of the object. It doesn't look like a new object, but it's there.

FIGURE 1-64
Duplicating

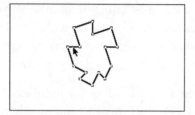

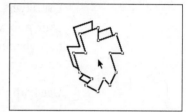

Select an object and press Command-D to duplicate it.

FreeHand places an exact copy of the object on the page.

the Move, Scaling, Rotation, Skewing, or Reflection tools). I'll cover more of the complex uses of the Duplicate command in Chapter 5, "Transforming."

The Tao of FreeHand

Here are those rules I promised at the beginning of the chapter.

Keep it simple. I don't mean that you shouldn't create complex publications. I mean create publications with an understanding of what's difficult for PostScript printers (especially imagesetters) to do, and do those things sparingly. You can probably just fill a complex path with a tiled fill, for example, rather than drawing a rectangle, filling it with the tiled fill, and pasting it inside the path. If you've got to use Paste Inside, avoid having more than around 50 (and certainly fewer than 100 in all cases!) points on the containing path. If you don't, you'll get a PostScript error. Understand that adding color TIFFs or "colorizing" grayscale TIFFs dramatically increases imagesetter processing time and makes it more likely you'll get a "VMerror" instead of a set of separations.

Use styles. Use styles. I haven't really mentioned styles yet, but I will in Chapter 2, "Drawing." Unless you work for people who never change their minds, and you never change your mind yourself, you need the ability to change things quickly and systematically—and that's where styles really shine. If you work for people who never change their minds, and you never change your mind yourself, please give me a call. (I've never met anyone like you.)

Use layers. And use them systematically. Not only will you find your publications easier to work with if you've spread the publication elements over several logical layers, but you'll be able to speed up your screen display, as well. Layers can speed printing, too.

Use trapping. I can't think of the number of color jobs I've ruined because of failing to think of trapping elements—especially type. See "Trapping" in Chapter 6, "Color."

Use color proofs. If you're working with process colors, it's an absolute necessity to make Cromalins (or MatchPrints, or the equivalent) from the same negatives you intend to use to print the publication. They're expensive, but they're cheaper than thousands of publications printed the wrong way because the film was wrong.

Talk to your commercial printer. This can often save you lots of time and money. The thing to remember when you're talking with your printer is that they're the experts. Don't be a jerk. Don't assume you know their job better than they do (you might, but don't assume you do). If possible, work out a printing contract for your job that spells out in exact terms what you expect of them and what they expect of you.

Talk to your imagesetting service bureau. First, ask them how to make PostScript files from FreeHand. If they don't know, start looking for another service bureau. Once you've found a service bureau that can answer that question, approach them very much the way you'd approach your commercial printer. A good working relationship with an imagesetting service bureau or inhouse imagesetter operator is essential.

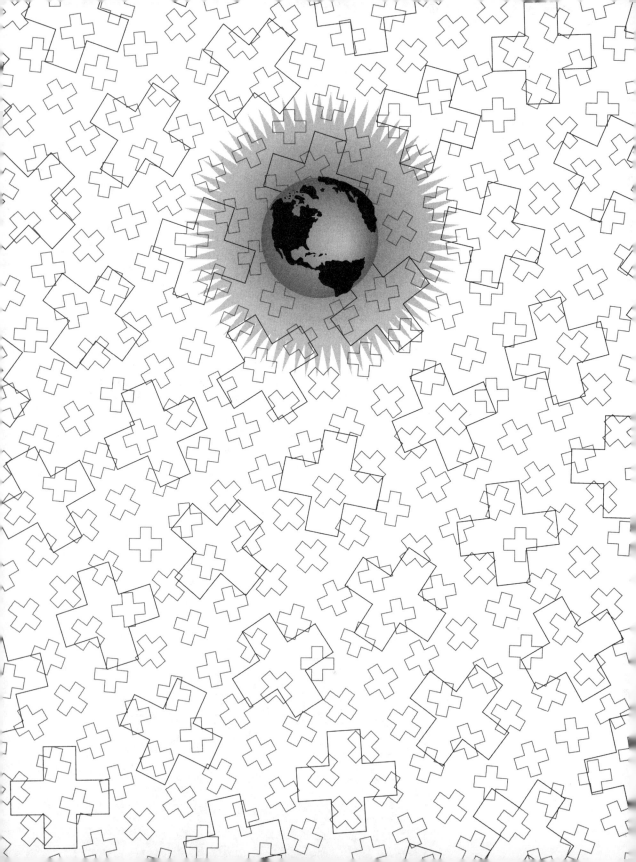

Human

beings draw pictures. The walls of caves inhabited since pre-historic times, the interiors of the tombs of the Pharaohs, and the development of desktop publishing all show that we're a kind of animal that likes to make marks on things. Drawing is at the center of us; it's one of the unique attributes that makes us human.

Drawing is also at the heart of FreeHand. Seven of the 16 tools in the FreeHand toolbox are drawing tools. Using these tools, you can draw almost anything—from straight lines and boxes to incredibly complex freeform paths.

As I explained in Chapter 1, "FreeHand Basics," the lines you draw in FreeHand are made up of points, and the points are connected by line segments. A FreeHand line is just like a connect-the-dots puzzle. Connect all the dots in the right order, and you've made a picture, or part of a picture. Because points along a line have an order, or winding, we call the lines "paths," and you can think of each point as a milepost along the path. Or as a sign saying, "Now go this way."

The drawing tools can be divided into two types: the Rectangle, Polygon, Ellipse, and Line tools are for drawing basic shapes; the Freehand, Pen, and Point tools draw more complex, or "freeform," paths (see Figure 2-1).

Which tools should you use? Don't worry too much about the distinction. The basic shapes drawn with the basic shapes tools can be converted into freeform paths, and the freeform drawing tools

FIGURE 2-1
Drawing tools

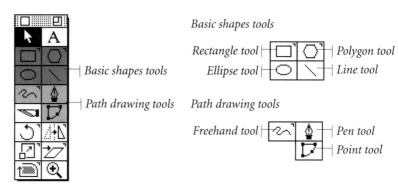

can be used to draw the same basic shapes. You can draw any path with any of the drawing tools (I was once stranded on a desert island with nothing but the Polygon tool, and survived), but some tools are better at some tasks, as I'll show you in the next few sections.

Basic Shapes

The basic shape tools (the Rectangle, Polygon, Ellipse, and Line tools) don't draw anything you couldn't draw using the freeform drawing tools (discussed later in this chapter); they just make drawing certain types of paths easier. They're shortcuts.

The operation of the basic shapes tools is straightforward, but there are a few details you need to know about. FreeHand aces may want to skip the next few paragraphs. It isn't that I'm getting paid by the word to write this (I'm not), but that I'm trying to cover all of the bases. It's amazing, too, what people can miss when they're learning a software product; I've seen FreeHand gurus who could write their own PostScript fills but weren't aware that you could turn a rectangle drawn with the Rectangle tool into a rounded-corner rectangle.

You can think of the paths drawn by the Rectangle and Ellipse tools as grouped paths. These paths have a few other special properties, as well, that you can't get by grouping a path drawn with the freeform drawing tools.

◆ You can edit the corner radius of rectangles drawn using the Rectangle tool.

◆ Basic shapes have a special constraint key you can use when you resize them, as described in the section, "Resizing Rectangles and Ellipses," below.

These magical properties disappear when you convert rectangles and ellipses into freeform paths (see "Converting Rectangles and Ellipses into Paths," below), and there's no way to convert the converted path back to its original state (apart from using "Undo").

To draw a rectangle, ellipse, or polygon, follow these steps (see Figure 2-2).

1. Select the appropriate tool from the toolbox (press 1 for the rectangle tool, 2 for the Polygon tool, or 3 for the Ellipse tool).

   If you want to draw a rectangle with round (rather than square) corners, double-click the Rectangle tool and set the corner radius you want in the Rectangle Tool dialog box before you start drawing.

   To specify what type of polygon you'll be drawing, double-click the Polygon tool and specify the polygon you want in the Polygon Tool dialog box before you start drawing.

2. Position the cursor where you want one corner of the shape. Or position the cursor where you want the center of the shape, and hold down Option. When you use the first method, you draw from one corner of the shape. When you use the second method, you draw out from the center of the shape.

3. Press down the mouse button and drag the mouse. FreeHand draws a path, starting where you clicked the mouse button.

   If you hold down Shift as you draw with the Rectangle tool, you draw squares. Hold down Shift as you drag the Ellipse tool, and you draw circles. Holding down Shift as you drag the Polygon tool constrains the rotation of the polygon (you can rotate the polygon as you draw) to 15-degree increments.

FIGURE 2-2
Drawing basic shapes

 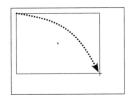 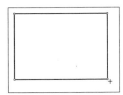

Select the basic shape tool (Rectangle, Polygon, or Ellipse)...

...and drag the tool in the publication window. When the basic shape looks the way you want it to...

...stop dragging and release the mouse button.

 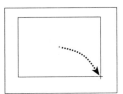 

If you want to draw from the center of the basic shape (rather than from the corner)...

...hold down Option as you drag the tool. Polygons are always drawn from their center point.

Stop dragging when the basic shape looks the way you want it to.

4. When the rectangle is the size and shape you want it to be, stop dragging and release the mouse button.

Drawing Lines

To draw a path as a single line segment between two corner points, follow these steps (see Figure 2-3).

1. Select the Line tool from the toolbox (or press 2).

2. Position the cursor where you want one end of the line to fall.

3. Press down the mouse button and drag the mouse. FreeHand draws a line, starting where you clicked the mouse button. If you want to constrain your line to 45-degree increments (based on the angle you specified in the Constrain field), hold down Shift as you draw the line.

4. When the line is the length you want, stop dragging the mouse, and release the mouse button.

FIGURE 2-2
Drawing basic shapes

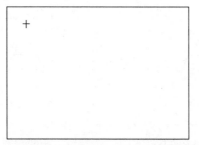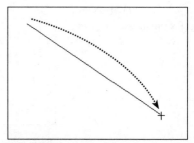

Position the line tool where you want one end of the line to start.

Drag the line tool across the page. Hold down Shift as you drag to constrain the line to 45-degree angles.

Resizing Rectangles and Ellipses

To resize any of the basic shapes, use the Pointer tool to select the rectangle or ellipse you want to resize and then drag any corner handle.

If you hold down Option as you drag a corner handle, Free-Hand uses a special type of constraint that only works with groups (FreeHand thinks of rectangles and ellipses as groups), and resizes the object around its center point (see Figure 2-4). This is a very handy feature when you need to enlarge an object while leaving its center in the same place.

FIGURE 2-4
Special constraint for
basic shapes

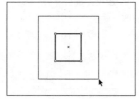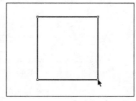

When you hold down Option as you resize a basic shape, FreeHand resizes the basic shape from its center.

Proportionally Resizing Rectangles and Ellipses

If you want to resize a rectangle or ellipse proportionally, you'd expect that you could just hold down Shift and drag a corner handle, but you can't—unless you're resizing a circle or a square—because holding down Shift and dragging a corner handle turns the object into a circle or square.

To resize a rectangle or ellipse proportionally, select the shape using the Pointer tool, and then press Command-G to group the shape. Position the Pointer tool over any corner handle. Hold down Shift and drag the corner handle to resize the shape (see Figure 2-5). Ungroup the shape after you finish resizing it.

FIGURE 2-5
Proportionally resizing
rectangles and ellipses

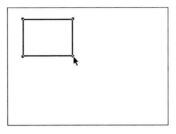
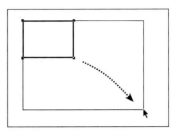

*Select a basic shape, press
Command-G, hold down Shift...*

*...and then drag the corner handle to
proportionally resize the basic shape.*

Changing a Rectangle's Corner Radius

To change a rectangle with square corners into a rectangle with rounded corners, select the rectangle with the Pointer tool and Press Command-Option-B to display the Object Inspector (if it's not already visible). Press Command-` to move your cursor to the Inspector, then tab to the Corner Radius field. After you enter the corner radius you want, press Return to apply your change. FreeHand converts the rectangle into a rectangle with rounded corners (see Figure 2-6).

To change rectangle with rounded corners into one with square corners, enter "0" in the Corner Radius field.

FIGURE 2-6
Rounding corners

*Select a rectangle and
press Command-
Option-B to display the
Object Inspector.*

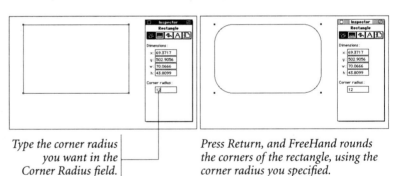

*Type the corner radius
you want in the
Corner Radius field.*

*Press Return, and FreeHand rounds
the corners of the rectangle, using the
corner radius you specified.*

Converting Rectangles and Ellipses into Paths

Why would you want to convert a rectangle or an ellipse into a freeform path? Sometimes you want only part of a basic shape to connect to a path (see "Adding Round Corners to a Path," later in this chapter, for an example).

To turn rectangle or an ellipse into a normal path, select the shape, and then press Command-U to ungroup it. The rectangle or ellipse becomes a freeform path, and can be manipulated as you'd manipulate any other freeform path (see Figure 2-7).

FIGURE 2-7
Converting basic
shapes into paths

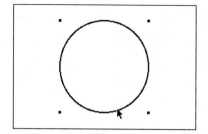 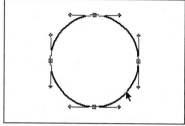

Select a rectangle or an ellipse and
press Command-U.

FreeHand converts the shape into a
freeform path, which you can edit as
you would any freeform path.

Tip:
Adding Round
Corners to a Path

When you're drawing paths with the freeform path-drawing tools, it can be difficult to draw an arc with a specific corner radius. To do that, follow these steps (see Figure 2-8).

1. Double-click the Rectangle tool and set the corner radius you want in the Rectangle Tool dialog box.

2. Draw a rectangle.

FIGURE 2-8
Adding a round
corner to a path

To add an arc with a
corner radius of 24 points
between these two lines...

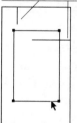

...draw a rectangle
and press Command-
Option-B to display
the Object Inspector
(if the Inspector's not
already visible, press
Command-I, first).

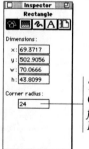

Type "24" in the
Corner Radius
field and press
Return.

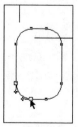 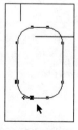 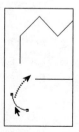 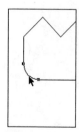

Select the points
on either side of
the arc you want.

Choose Split
Element from the
Element menu.

Drag the arc
into position.

Join the arc to
the path.

3. Without deselecting the rectangle, press Command-U to convert it to a path.

4. Select the points on the path on either side of the corner you want to add to your path and choose Split Element from the Arrange menu.

5. Select the corner you want and move it into position (you can delete the rest of the rectangle).

9. Join the round corner to the path (for more on joining paths, see "Joining Paths," later in this chapter).

Why don't we draw, ungroup, and split a circle to accomplish this same task? Because there's no way to specify the radius of the circle, short of drawing the circle to an exact size. It's far easier to enter a value for the corner radius in the Object Inspector.

Points and Paths

I briefly covered points and paths in Chapter 1, "FreeHand Basics," but there's still more to explain. Why is it that the most important things are often the ones that are the most difficult to learn?

When I first approached FreeHand and Illustrator, drawing by positioning points, constructing paths, and manipulating curve handles struck me as alien, as nothing like drawing at all. Then I started to catch on.

In many ways, when I used pens and rulers to draw, I was drawing lines from the point of view of everything *but* the line; in Free-Hand, I draw lines from the point of view of the line itself. This is neither better nor worse; it's just different and takes time to get used to. If you've just glanced at the toolbox and are feeling confused, I urge you to stick with it. Start thinking like a line.

Thinking Like a Line   Imagine that, through some mysterious potion or errant cosmic ray, you've been reduced in size so that you're a little smaller than one of the dots in a connect-the-dots puzzle. For detail and color, imagine the puzzles in a *Highlights* magazine in a dentist's office.

The only way out is to complete the puzzle. As you walk, a line extends behind you. As you reach each dot in the puzzle, a sign tells you where you are in the puzzle, and how to get to the next dot ("walk this way…").

Get the idea? The dots in the puzzle are points. The route you walk from one dot to another, as instructed by the signs at each point, is a line segment. Each series of connected dots is a path. As you walk from one dot to another, you're thinking like a line.

Each point—from the first point in the path to the last—carries with it some information about the line segments that attach it to the previous and next points along the path.

Paths are made up of two or more points, connected by line segments, as shown in Figure 2-9. Even if the line attribute applied to the path is None, (and the line doesn't print or show up in Preview mode) there's still a line segment there.

FIGURE 2-9
A path

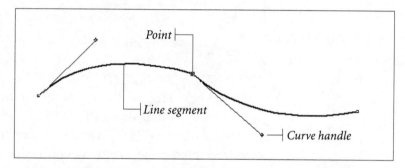

Winding

PostScript paths have a direction, also known as "winding" (as in "winding a clock"—nothing to do with the weather) that generally corresponds to the order and direction in which you place their points (see Figure 2-10). In our connect-the-dots puzzle, winding tells us the order in which we connect the dots.

When you create objects using the basic shapes drawing tools, FreeHand assumes a particular winding (see Figure 2-11). This is a useful thing to know, particularly when you're joining text to a path and want to control where that text begins on the path (Free-Hand always positions the first character of the text block at the path's starting point, unless you're joining text to an object you've drawn with the basic shape tools, in which case it behaves differently; see "Joining Text to a Path," in Chapter 3, "Text and Type").

FIGURE 2-10
The direction of a path

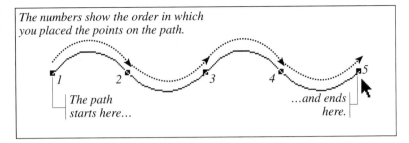

The numbers show the order in which you placed the points on the path.

The path starts here...

...and ends here.

FIGURE 2-11
Winding for
basic shapes

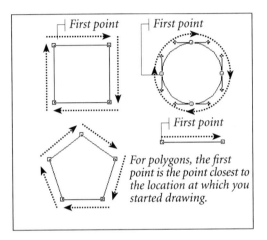

First point

First point

First point

For polygons, the first point is the point closest to the location at which you started drawing.

You can use FreeHand's new path operation Reverse Direction to reverse the winding of a path. Select the path and choose Reverse Direction from the Path Operations submenu of the Arrange menu. FreeHand reverses the direction of the path.

Reflecting paths can also change their direction. You can use Reverse Direction to restore the original winding of the path.

Curve Handles

You control the curvature of the line segments before and after each point using curve handles (see Figure 2-12). Points can have up to two attached curve handles. Typically, corner points have none, connector points have one, and curve points have two (for more on the different types of points, see "Types of Points" in Chapter 1, "FreeHand Basics").

The first curve handle you pull out of a point controls the curvature of the next line segment in the path along the direction (or winding) of the path. The second curve handle controls the curvature of the line segment before the point.

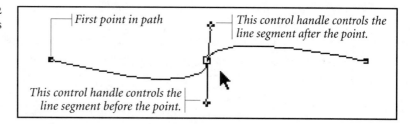

First point in path

This control handle controls the line segment after the point.

This control handle controls the line segment before the point.

Flatness

Besides winding, paths also have another property, flatness. Flatness is a PostScript setting which controls how accurately curves are rendered on a PostScript printer. What? Can't the printer just print a curve? No; laser printers, even PostScript laser printers, print by filling in pixels in a grid—just like MacPaint. Practically, this means that they only print straight lines. If you make the straight lines small enough, or short enough, however, they look like smooth curves. Flatness is PostScript's way of asking "How close is close enough?"

You can think of flatness this way: a flatness setting of one on a 300-dpi printer is equal to an inaccuracy in drawing curves of $\frac{1}{300}$ of an inch, or $\frac{1}{2540}$ of an inch on a Linotronic 300 at its highest resolution. The first is acceptable accuracy for proofing; the second is acceptable resolution for most publications. In fact, I've even gone to flatness settings of three without any problems when I knew I was going to be printing color separations at 2,540 dpi. You can enter flatness values from zero to 1,000. Figure 2-13 shows the effect of increased flatness setting at 1,200 dpi.

If you increase the Flatness setting to a high value—100, for example—you can see that smooth curves start to look like series of line segments. A flatness setting of zero ensures that the path prints at the highest level of accuracy possible, given the printer's resolution.

FIGURE 2-13
Flatness

Flatness of 0   *Flatness of 3*   *Flatness of 100*

Lower flatness settings take longer to print and use more of your printer's RAM (which is precious, unless you like PostScript error messages), because the printer has to draw more tiny line segments to render the path's curves. Setting flatness higher sometimes eliminates PostScript errors that prevent pages from printing, especially if there are a lot of points in the illustration you're trying to print.

To see the flatness setting for a path, select a path and press Command-Option-B to bring up the Object Inspector.

Path-Drawing Tools

You use the freeform drawing tools—the Freehand tool, the Pen tool, and the Point tool—to create paths. The following sections discuss each freeform drawing tool. These tools have already been discussed, briefly, in Chapter 1, "FreeHand Basics," but this section gives you more detailed descriptions of their uses.

Freehand Tool   The Freehand tool in the toolbox is actually three different tools: the Freehand tool, the Variable Stroke tool, and the Calligraphic Pen tool. You can switch between these tools by double-clicking the tool in the toolbox.

◆ The Freehand tool draws a single, open path that follows your cursor.

◆ The Variable Stroke tool draws closed paths that look like brushstrokes.

◆ The Calligraphic Pen tools draw closed paths that look like they were drawn with a flat-nib lettering pen.

Freehand tool. The simplest, quickest way to create a path on a FreeHand publication page is to use the Freehand tool. Just select the tool and scribble. As you drag the tool across the page, FreeHand creates a path that follows your mouse motion (see Figure 2-14).

FIGURE 2-14
Using the
Freehand tool

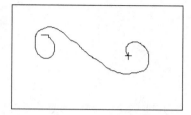 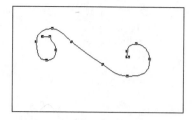

Select the Freehand tool and
drag it across the page.

FreeHand creates a path that
follows your mouse movements.

As you drag, FreeHand places corner and curve points along the path. To control how and where FreeHand positions these points, double-click the Freehand tool to bring up the Freehand Tool dialog box (see Figure 2-15).

The Tight Fit option controls the number of points FreeHand creates to construct the path. Turn off Tight Fit to create a simpler path, but bear in mind that the simplified path follows your mouse movements less accurately.

Draw Dotted Line displays the path you're drawing as a dotted line as you drag the Freehand tool. Turn Draw Dotted Line off to show the path as you draw it. Why would you want to do this? Drawing is a little faster with Draw Dotted Line turned on. I always leave it off. Note that when you've got Draw Dotted Line turned on, the path is drawn about the same way as it's always drawn in Illustrator.

If you need to back up along the path while you're drawing with the Freehand tool, hold down Command, and drag back along the path. To continue drawing the path, let go of Command and continue dragging the tool (see Figure 2-16).

FIGURE 2-15
Freehand Tool
dialog box

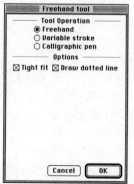

To set options for the Freehand
tool's behavior, double-click
the Freehand tool.

FIGURE 2-16
Erasing part of a
freeform path

FIGURE 2-16
Erasing part of a
freeform path

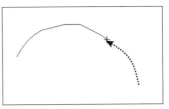

If you don't like what you've
drawn with the Freehand tool...

...hold down Command and
drag back along the path.

If you need to create a straight line segment while you're drawing a path using the Freehand tool, hold down Option as you're dragging: each line segment you add forms a straight line from the last point on the path. If you want to constrain the angle of the straight line segment to 45-degree angles (from the angle set in the Constrain field in the Document Setup Inspector), hold down Option-Shift as you drag the Freehand tool (see Figure 2-17).

Though the Freehand tool is the easiest way to create paths in FreeHand, I've always found it to be one of the least useful. Why? Mice are wonderful things, and they're probably the best way we currently have of getting positioning information into computers (I've tried trackballs and pens, too), but they're far better for placing points and manipulating curve handles than they are for drawing smooth lines.

FIGURE 2-17
Constraint and the
Freehand tool

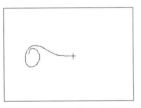
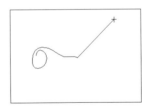

Hold down Option-Shift as you
drag the Freehand tool...

...and you constrain the lines you
draw to 45-degree angles.

Variable Stroke tool. The introduction of the wacky "variable blob tool" (known to serious persons as the Variable Stroke tool) in FreeHand 3.1 gave FreeHand users a way to create paths shaped like brush strokes. To see the Variable Stroke tool's controls, double-click the Freehand tool in the toolbox, then click the Variable Stroke option at the top of the Freehand Tool dialog box (see Figure 2-18).

FIGURE 2-18
Variable
Stroke tool

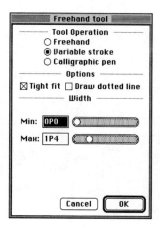

To set options for the Variable Stroke tool's behavior, double-click the Freehand tool and click the Variable Stroke option.

Variable strokes

If you have a pressure-sensitive tablet (such at those manufactured by Wacom, Calcomp, and Kurta), you can use the pressure of your stylus to change the widths of the path you draw with the Variable Stroke tool.

Tip:
If You Don't
Have a Tablet

What if you don't have a pressure-sensitive tablet? You can still use the tool's pressure-sensitivity. As you draw a path, press 2 (or Right Arrow) to increase the width of the path, or press 1 (or Left Arrow) to decrease its width. This technique takes a little practice, but you'll soon be drawing variable blobs as well as your friends and with their fancypants tablets (see Figure 2-19).

FIGURE 2-19
Pressure without
a tablet

Key presses

As you drag the Variable Stroke tool, press the Right Arrow key to increase the width of the stroke; press the Left Arrow key to decrease the width.

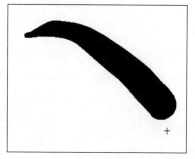

Calligraphic Pen tool. With the Calligraphic Pen tool, you can create paths that resemble lines drawn with a pen. To see the Calligraphic Pen tool's controls, double-click the Freehand tool in the toolbox, then click the Calligraphic Pen option in the Freehand Tool dialog box (see Figure 2-20).

FIGURE 2-20
Calligraphic Pen tool

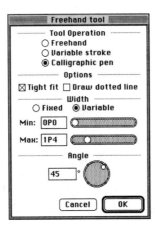

To set options for the Calligraphic Pen tool's behavior, double-click the Freehand tool and click Calligraphic Pen.

Calligraphic Pen strokes

As with the Variable Stroke tool, you can use the Calligraphic Pen tool's pressure-sensitivity even if you don't have a pressure-sensitive tablet—as you draw a path, press 2 (or Right Arrow) to increase the width of the calligraphic stroke, or press 1 (or Left Arrow) to decrease its width.

Pen Tool

When you click with the Pen tool in the publication window, Free-Hand places corner points. If you drag the Pen tool, and FreeHand places a curve point where you first started dragging—you determine the length of the curve handles (and, therefore, the shape of the curve) by the distance you drag (see Figure 2-21). If you're an Illustrator user, the Pen tool works the same way as the Pen tool in Illustrator.

To curve the line segment following a corner point, hold down Option as you place a corner point and drag. The curve handle doesn't appear until you place the next point. Once you place the next point, the curve handle appears and can be adjusted as you like (see Figure 2-22).

FIGURE 2-21
The Pen tool

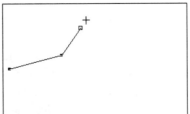

Click to create a corner point.

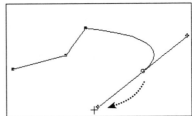

Drag to create a curve point.

FIGURE 2-22
Dragging a curve
handle out of a
corner point

 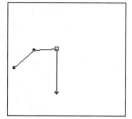 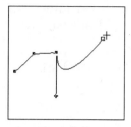

*Hold down Option as
you drag...*

*...and FreeHand
creates a corner point
with a single curve
handle.*

*This curve handle
applies to the line
segment following the
corner point.*

The trickiest thing about using the Pen tool this way is that you often don't see the effect of the curve manipulation until you've placed the next point. This makes sense in that you don't need a curve handle for a line segment that doesn't yet exist, but it can be quite a brain-twister.

To convert a curve point you've just placed to a corner point, hold down Option after you've finished dragging control handles out of the curve point (see Figure 2-23). This creates a corner point with two control handles extended.

FIGURE 2-23
Converting a curve
point to a corner
point (with two
control handles)

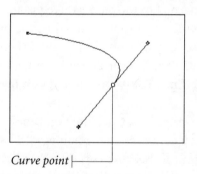 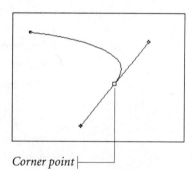

Curve point ⊢———

Corner point ⊢———

*Drag out the curve point's handles
as you would normally...*

*...then hold down Option and stop
dragging. FreeHand converts the
curve point to a corner point.*

To convert a curve point you've just placed to a corner point with one control handle extended, hold down Option and click on the point. Just to make life interesting, this control handle applies to the line segment *before* the corner point along the path. Ordinarily, the first curve handle dragged out of a corner point applies to the line segment *after* the point (see Figure 2-24).

FIGURE 2-24
Converting a curve
point to a corner
point (with one
control handle)

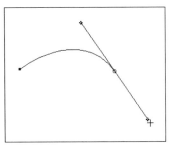

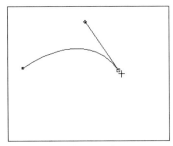

*Position a curve point, hold
down Option…*

*…and then click on the point to
convert it into a corner point.*

You can change the position of points, as you'd expect, by holding down Command (which, as you'll recall, chooses the Pointer tool without deselecting the current tool), selecting the point, and dragging the point to a new location.

Using the Point Tool

Use the Point tool when you want to create paths point-by-point. Dragging the Point tool as you place a point moves the point—unlike the Pen tool, where dragging adjusts the curve of the line segments attached to the point you're placing. In general, you place points with the Point tool, then adjust the points' control handles to get the curves you want. Which tool is better—the Point tool or the Pen tool? Your answer depends on who you are and how you like to work. I'm a Point-tool kind of guy, myself.

Placing corner points. Click the Point tool on the page, and Free-Hand places a corner point—a points with have no control handles extended from it. Because corner points have no control handles extended from them (initially—you can extend them later), line segments between corner points are straight (see Figure 2-25). Free-Hand displays corner points as small squares.

You can drag curve levers out of corner points: place the corner point as you normally would, then hold down Command (to turn the cursor into the Pointer tool) and Option, and drag a control handle out of the corner point (see Figure 2-26).

Note that you can also drag a control handle out of a corner point any time by selecting the point with the Pointer tool, then holding down Option, and dragging a control handle out of it.

FIGURE 2-25
Corner points

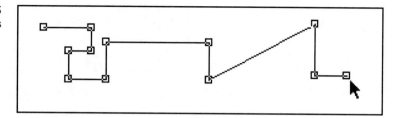

FIGURE 2-26
Dragging curve
handles out of
corner points

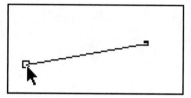

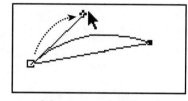

Select a corner point,
hold down Option...

...and drag a curve handle
out of the corner point.

Corner points are more
⁶exible than curve
points, because you can
adjust their control
handles independently.

Adjusting control handles on corner points

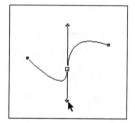

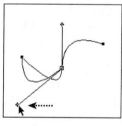

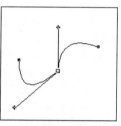

Point at a curve
handle...

...and drag.

The curve handle moves
independently of the
other curve handle.

The most significant difference between corner points and curve points is that the angle of control handles pulled out of corner points can be adjusted independently, while changing the angle of one control handle of a curve point changes the angle of the other control handle. This difference, in my opinion, makes corner points much more useful than curve points—especially given that you can do anything with a corner point you could do with a curve point or a connector point.

You can turn corner points into curve points by selecting the corner point, pressing Command-Option-B to display the Object Inspector, clicking the curve point button in the Inspector, and pressing Return to apply your change. The selected corner point becomes a curve point.

Placing curve points. Hold down Option as you click the Point tool, and you're placing curve points—points with two control handles pulled out of them. Curve points look like small circles. When you click to place a curve point, two control handles are extended from the point. How far FreeHand extends the control handles depends on the curve point's location on the path (see Figure 2-27).

You can increase or decrease the distance from one control handle to the curve point it's attached to without moving the other control handle, but both handles move if you change the angle one of them presents to the curve point—they always move along the same axis. This makes them somewhat less flexible than corner points (see Figure 2-28).

You can turn curve points into corner points by selecting the curve point, pressing Command-Option-B (to display the Object Inspector), clicking the Corner Point button in the Inspector, and pressing Return to apply your change.

FIGURE 2-27
Curve points

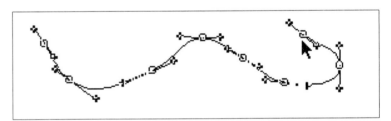

FIGURE 2-28
Manipulating
control handles
on curve points

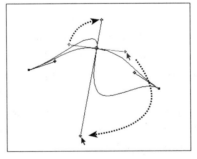
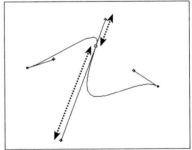

As you drag a control handle attached to a curve point, note that both curve handles move as you drag.

Control handles attached to curve points always move along the same axis.

Placing connector points. If you hold down Control and click the Point tool, you create connector points—points which may or may not have control handles pulled out of them depending on where they're placed in the path (and, I suspect, depending on their own whim). I never really have figured out connector points. Anyway, they look like little triangles.

If you place a curve point immediately after a connector point, the control handle for the line segment from the connector point to the curve point is extended from the connector point. This control handle is positioned along the axis formed by the connector point and the point preceding the connector point on the path, and is placed at the same distance from the connector point as the preceding point along this axis. When you drag the control handle, it moves along this axis (see Figure 2-29). If you want to change the curve, you'll have to convert the connector point into another type of point.

What's the use of connector points? They create smooth transitions between straight and curved line segments. I think of them as a sort of "half" curve point. They never seem to give me the curve I'm looking for, but you should experiment with them. In spite of my bias, they might be just what you're looking for.

FIGURE 2-29
Connector points

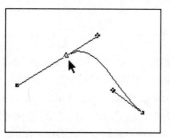

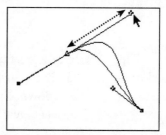

Connector points look like little triangles.

The control handle on a connector point can only move along its original axis.

Manipulating Control Handles

The aspect of drawing in FreeHand that's most difficult to understand and master is the care, feeding, and manipulation of control handles. These handles are fundamental to drawing curved lines in FreeHand, so you'd better learn how to work with them.

To adjust the curve of a line segment, use the Pointer tool to select a point attached to the line segment. The control handles attached to that point appear. If you don't see any control handles, the curve of the line segment is controlled by the point at the other end of the line segment. Select that point, and you'll see the control handle (or handles) you're looking for. Position the cursor over one of the control handles and drag. The curve of the line segment associated with that control handle changes as you drag the handle. When the curve looks the way you want, stop dragging (see Figure 2-31).

To retract a curve handle, drag the handle inside the point it's attached to, or select the point and use the Object Inspector, as described in "Issuing a Retraction," on the next page.

FIGURE 2-31
Manipulating a
curve handle

When you drag a
control handle, the
curve of the line
segment associated
with that control
handle changes.

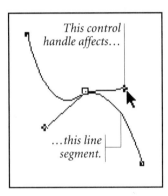
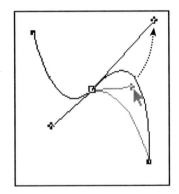

This control handle affects…

…this line segment.

Tip:
The Quick Way
to Make a Curve

Here's a great new FreeHand 4 feature (which I call "bend-o-matic") that might change the way you draw paths. Select the Pointer tool, hold down Option, and drag a line segment (any line segment between any two points). As you drag, FreeHand changes the position of the two control handles (one from either point) defining the curve of the line segment (see Figure 2-32).

FIGURE 2-32
Changing a curve
by dragging a
line segment

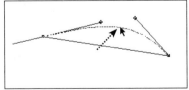

Point at the line segment you want to curve…

…hold down Option, and drag. FreeHand curves the path.

Tip:
Selecting
Multiple
Points

You can select several points at once by dragging a selection marquee over them. Once you have selected the points, their control handles appear. You can adjust any of the control handles without deselecting the other control handles, which means you can adjust control handles on a path while looking at the position of the path's other control handles (see Figure 2-33).

FIGURE 2-33
Selecting multiple
points and adjusting
curve control handles

*Drag a selection
rectangle over a path to
select all of the points
on the path...*

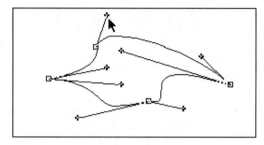

*...and you can adjust
curve handles while
looking at the positions of
all of the curve handles
on the path.*

Automatic Curvature

As you place curve or connector points along a path, FreeHand adds and adjusts curve control points where it thinks you'd like them. It's actually quite good at guessing. This is FreeHand's automatic curvature feature, which you can turn on or off for any point in your publication.

To turn automatic curvature on, select a point and press Command-Option-B to display the Object Inspector for that point. Check the Automatic checkbox, and FreeHand automatically decides how to extend curve handles from the point, based on the point's position in the path.

When you adjust a curve control handle, it turns automatic curvature off for that point. If you decide you've made an error, and would like to return to FreeHand's automatic curvature, you can display the Object Inspector and turn on the Automatic curvature option (see Figure 2-34).

Issuing a Retraction

Click one of the Retract buttons in the Object Inspector and the associated control handle is pulled back into the point. No more not quite being sure if you'd dragged the handle inside the point! Anything you'd ordinarily do by dragging a curve control handle inside a point, you can do using the Retract buttons in the Object Inspector (see Figure 2-35).

FIGURE 2-34
Automatic curvature

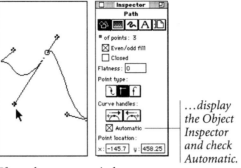
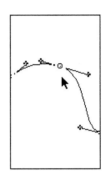

...display the Object Inspector and check Automatic.

If you change your mind about an adjustment you've made to a curve handle...

FreeHand returns the point's curve handles to their default position.

FIGURE 2-35
Retracting
control handles

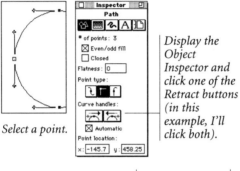
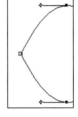

Display the Object Inspector and click one of the Retract buttons (in this example, I'll click both).

Select a point.

FreeHand retracts the point's curve handles.

This Retract button affects the curve of the line segment following the point.

This Retract button affects the curve of the line segment preceding the point.

Drawing Techniques

Now that you know all about the elements that make up paths, let's talk about how you actually use them.

Ways to Draw Paths

When you're drawing paths, don't forget that you can change the path after you've drawn it. I've often seen people delete whole paths and start over because they misplaced the last point on the path. Go ahead and place points in the wrong places; you can always change the position of any point on the path. Also, keep the following facts in mind.

◆ You can always split the path.

◆ You can always add points to or subtract points from the path.

◆ You can always change tools while drawing a path.

It's also best to create paths using as few points as you can—but it's not required (after all, you can always use the Simplify Path operation). Create paths in whatever way you find works best for you—there's no "right" way to do it. I've talked with dozens of FreeHand users, and each one uses a slightly different method for putting points on a page.

The classical method. Use the Point tool to place curve, corner, and connector points, and place points one at a time. I call this the "classical" method, because it's how people were taught to place points in FreeHand 1.0. To construct a path using this method, you use the Point tool, holding down Option as you click to produce a curve point, or Option-Shift to produce a connector point (see Figure 2-36).

People who use this method of constructing paths keep one hand on the mouse and one hand hovering around the keyboard,

FIGURE 2-36
The classical method

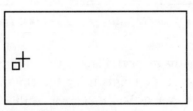

Choose the Point tool and click to place a corner point.

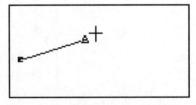

Hold down Control and click to place a connector point.

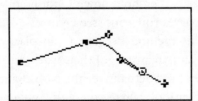

Hold down Option and click to place a curve point.

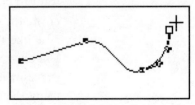

Continue placing points until you've drawn the path you want.

because they'll change point type by pressing keys (as described in "Using the Point tool," earlier in this chapter).

The "Illustrator" Method. Use the Pen tool only. I call this method the "Illustrator" method, because I've found that this set of users generally learned to use Illustrator before they started using Free-Hand. In this method, you click and drag the Pen tool to create paths containing only curve and corner points (see Figure 2-37).

FIGURE 2-37
The "Illustrator"
method

Choose the Pen tool and click to place a corner point.

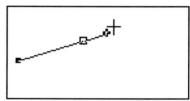

Option-drag a curve handle out of the next corner point.

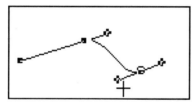

Drag out a curve point.

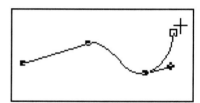

Click to place a corner point.

Drawing paths my way. Place corner points only, then pull curve handles out of the points using the Option-Drag technique (see "The Quick Way to Make a Curve," earlier in this chapter). I call this method "my way," because it's how I do it. In this method, you use the Point tool to place corner points defining the path you want to create, then hold down Option and drag line segments to create the curves you want (see Figure 2-38).

I like this method because I can place points quickly where I know I want them to go, then work on the fine details of the curves when I can actually see the path changing as I drag—unlike using the Pen tool, where you're dragging curve handles control-ling a line segment you haven't yet placed. The disadvantage of this method is that you need to know where you're going to place

FIGURE 2-38
My way

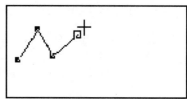

*Choose the Corner tool
and place a point.*

*Click to place three
more corner points.*

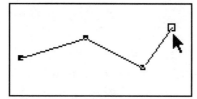

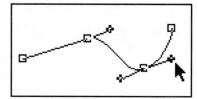

Drag the points into position.

*Drag out and adjust curve handles,
or hold down Option and bend line
segments (see "The Quick Way to
Make a Curve," earlier in this
chapter).*

points ahead of time, a skill you acquire by using the program a lot (see also "Keeping Paths Simple," below).

All three methods work well, and there's no reason not to mix and match methods in different situations. There's also no reason not to mix these methods with the use of the Freehand tool, the basic shapes tools, autotracing, or blending.

Keeping Paths Simple

People who've just started working with FreeHand tend to use more points than they need to describe paths. Over time, they learn one of FreeHand's basic rules: Any curve can be described by two points and their associated curve handles. No more, no less (see Figure 2-39). FreeHand's new Simplify Paths path operator makes a great path-drawing instructor—draw a path and then run Simplify Paths on it (select the path, then select Simplify Paths from the Path operations submenu of the Arrange menu). Notice where FreeHand deletes and removes points on the path you've drawn, and you'll get a good lesson in path drawing. Note, however, that Simplify Paths is not perfect, and may sometimes change the shape of your path (you can always undo the action).

FIGURE 2-39
Any curve can be
described by two
points

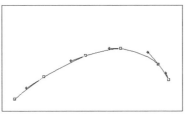

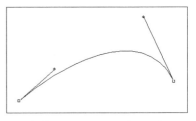

This path uses too many points.

Here's the same curve, using only two points.

Selecting and Moving Points

If you've gotten this far, you probably know how to select points, but here are a few rules to keep in mind.

◆ You select a point by clicking on the point with the Pointer tool.

◆ You can select more than one point at a time by holding down Shift as you click on each point with the Pointer tool, or you can drag a marquee around a number of points to select them all.

◆ When you move a point, the control handles associated with that point also move, maintaining their same position relative to the point. Note that this means that the curves of the line segments attached to the point change, unless you're also moving the points on the other end of the incoming and outgoing line segments (see Figure 2-40).

Flipping and Flopping

I hate drawing objects from scratch when I don't have to, so I use flipping and flopping to create most of the objects I use in a Free-Hand publication. What's flipping and flopping? It's the process of cloning an object and then selecting and moving some—not all—of the points on the cloned object. Look at Figure 2-41. Flipping and flopping depends on FreeHand's ability to select several points on a path without selecting the entire path.

Flipping and flopping comes in handy when you need to create two paths—even paths of different shapes—which share a common boundary. Redrawing the boundary between two paths is not

FIGURE 2-40
Effect of moving a
point on its attached
line segments

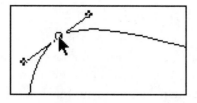

When you select and move a point...   *...the point's attached control handles move with the point.*

FIGURE 2-41
Fipping and flopping

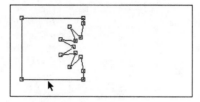
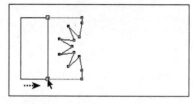

Clone the original object.   *Select individual points on the clone and drag them...*

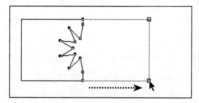
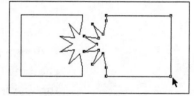

...until they're where you want them.   *You now have two objects with an identical border.*

just boring, but can be quite difficult if the boundary is complex enough. I'm not averse to tackling difficult tasks; I just hate to make something more difficult than it has to be, so I use flipping and flopping even when the shapes sharing a boundary are very different.

Open and Closed Paths

You can think of an open path as a line and a closed path as a shape. Open paths can't be filled, have objects pasted inside them, or be manipulated using the path operations Union, Punch, and Intersect. You can, always join the end points of an open path to create a closed path, or split a closed path to create an open path.

To use FreeHand's Object Inspector to close a path, select the path, press Command-Option-B to display the Object Inspector (if it's not already visible), and then check the Closed checkbox in the Inspector. Press Return to apply your changes, and FreeHand creates a straight line segment which joins the first point in the path to the last point in the path (see Figure 2-42).

FIGURE 2-42
Changing an open
path into a closed path

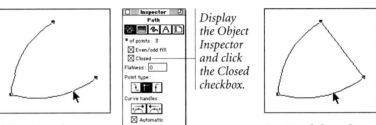

Select the path you want to close.

Display the Object Inspector and click the Closed checkbox.

FreeHand closes the path with a straight line segment.

Similarly, you can use the Object Inspector to change a closed path into an open path by following the above procedure but unchecking the Closed option. When you do this, FreeHand removes the line segment which joins the first point in the path to the last point in the path. When you convert a closed path into an open path, any clipped (pasted-inside) objects or fills disappear. They haven't really vanished; if you then convert the open path into a closed path, the clipped objects and/or fills reappear.

Closing a path using the Object Inspector is great, but what if you've got a curved path you want to close but don't want to close with a straight line segment (see Figure 2-43)?

1. Select the path.

2. Press Command-= to clone the path. A copy of the path appears on top of the path.

3. Drag a marquee over two of the end points (they'll be right on top of each other, so it won't look like anything's selected).

4. Press Command-J to join the end points. FreeHand joins the two points into one point.

FIGURE 2-43
Closing an
irregular path

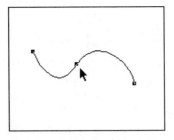

*Select the path you want to
make a closed path and clone it.*

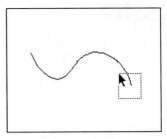

*Drag a selection marquee over the
end points and press Command-J.*

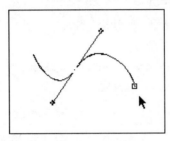

*Display the Object Inspector
and check Closed. FreeHand
closes the path.*

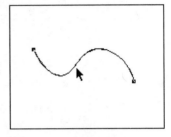

*Now you can work with the
path as you would with any
closed path.*

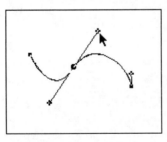

*When you adjust the curve
handles on a closed path created
with the above technique...*

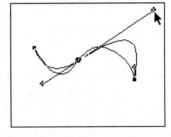

*...you're only changing the curve of
the lines on top. This may or may not
be what you want.*

5. Press Command-Option-B to display the Object Inspector.

6. Check Closed and press Return. FreeHand closes the path.

At this point, you've got a closed path that's the same shape as the original, open path. Now you can join it to other closed paths to create compound paths.

Splitting and Joining Paths

You can always add points to or subtract points from a path in FreeHand. You can also split an open or closed path into separate paths, connect paths to each other, create a composite path, or make a single path a closed path.

Splitting Paths

You can split a path in one of three ways.

◆ Select a point (or points) on the path with the Pointer tool, and then choose Split Object (Command-Shift-J) from the Arrange menu.

◆ Select the path, then click the Knife tool on the path (or on a selected point on the path).

◆ Select the path, then drag the Knife tool over the path.

When you split a path by splitting a point, FreeHand creates a new point on top of the point you selected. This new point is connected to the line segment going to the next point along the path's winding (see Figure 2-44).

When you split a path using the Knife tool, two new points are created (see Figure 2-45).

To select one or the other of the two paths you've created by splitting the path, press Tab (to deselect everything), and then select the path you want, or press ` (to select both paths), and Shift-click the path you don't want selected.

When you split a path and create two new points, it can be very difficult figuring out which end point belongs to which path. It's simple, actually. The point closest to the start of the path (following the path's winding) is farthest to the back, and the point farthest from the start of the path is on top of it (see Figure 2-46). You can always use Bring to Front and Send to Back to change which point's on top.

You can use the Split element command to split any number of points. Drag a marquee over all of the points you want to split, choose Split Object from the Arrange menu, and FreeHand splits all of the points (see Figure 2-47).

FIGURE 2-44
Splitting a path by
splitting points

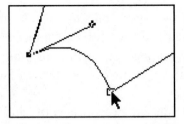 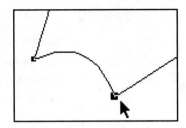

Select a point and choose Split Object
from the Element menu.

FreeHand splits the path at the point
you selected.

FIGURE 2-45
Splitting a path by
splitting a line segment

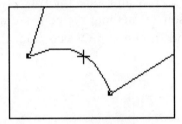 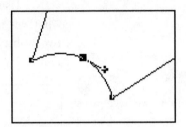

Select a path, select the Knife tool,
and then click on the path (or drag
the Knife tool across the path).

FreeHand splits the path
where you clicked.

FIGURE 2-46
Which point is on top?

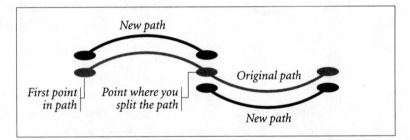

FIGURE 2-47
Splitting several
points at once

Drag a selection marquee over the
points you want to split.

Choose Split Object from the Element
menu. FreeHand splits all of the
selected points.

Joining Paths   You can join two open paths to create a single path, or you can join two closed paths to create a composite path. In this section, I'll talk about joining open paths. For more information on joining closed paths to create composite paths, see "Composite Paths," on the next page.

To join points on two open paths and create a single path, drag the end points of the two open paths over each other. It's easier to do this when Snap to Point (on the View menu) is active. Usually, FreeHand joins the two points. If FreeHand—for whatever reason—won't join the points, drag a marquee over the two points and choose Join Objects from the Arrange menu (see Figure 2-48).

FIGURE 2-48
Joining two open paths

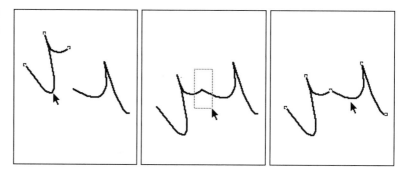

Drag the end points of two open paths over each other and select Join Objects to create a single, open path.

Tip:
If Join
Objects is
Grayed Out

If the Join Objects menu item is grayed out, one or both of the paths containing the points you've selected is probably a closed path, or both paths are open paths and you haven't selected a pair of points. If you're not sure if a path is closed or open, select the path and look at the Closed checkbox in the Object Inspector—if it's checked, the path is closed.

Tip:
If Join
Objects Doesn't
Do Anything

You can't join open paths without having two overlapping (or nearly overlapping) points selected. Move the paths or points so that two end points overlap, drag a marquee over the two points (it might not look like you've selected anything), and choose Join Objects from the Arrange menu (or press Command-J) to join the paths.

Composite Paths

In the old days, not only did I have to walk miles to school in freezing weather, but I also had to perform an impossibly difficult series of tasks just to create holes inside closed paths. While these rituals were kind of fascinating, they did nothing to help me hit my deadlines.

These days, creating holes in paths is easier—just make them into composite paths. Composite paths are made of two or more paths (which must be unlocked, ungrouped, and closed) which have been joined with Join Objects. Areas between the two paths, or areas where the paths overlap, are transparent (see Figure 2-49).

1. Select the Ellipse tool from the toolbox.

2. Draw two ellipses, one on top of the other.

3. Fill the ellipses with some basic fill.

4. Select both ellipses.

FIGURE 2-49
Creating
composite paths

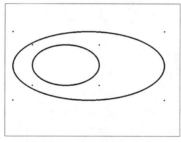

Create two ellipses using the
Ellipse tool.

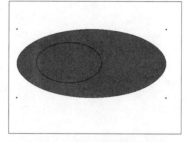

Apply the stroke and fill you want to
the ellipses.

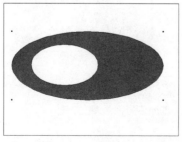

Press Command-J to join the
ellipses.

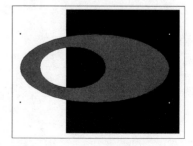

You've just created a composite
path. The inside of the shape is
transparent.

5. Press Command-J to join the two ellipses.

What if you don't want transparent areas where the paths overlap? Select the composite path. Press Command-I to display the Inspector (if it's not already visible), and press Command-Option-B to display the Object Inspector. Uncheck the Even/Odd Fill option. This fills all of the objects in the composite path with the same fill (see Figure 2-50).

FIGURE 2-50
Even/Odd Fill and
composite paths

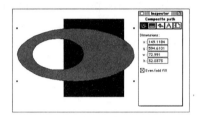 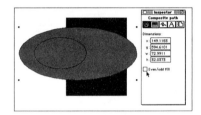

Even/Odd Fill on   *Even/Odd Fill off*

If you decide you don't want the paths to be composite paths anymore, you can change them back into individual paths. To do this, select the paths and press Command-Shift-J (or choose Split Object from the Arrange menu).

Composite paths can be transformed just as you'd transform any other path.

When you convert characters to paths, FreeHand automatically converts the characters as composite paths (see Figure 2-51). This is great, because you can paste things inside composite paths.

FIGURE 2-51
Characters converted
to paths are
composite paths

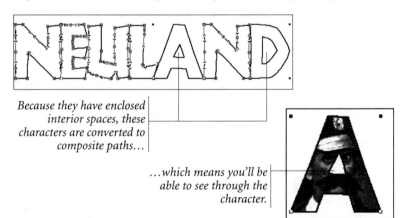

*Because they have enclosed
interior spaces, these
characters are converted to
composite paths...*

*...which means you'll be
able to see through the
character.*

Composite paths work much like groups of objects, in that you can continue joining paths to the composite paths, just as you can group objects together with groups.

When you join new paths to a composite path, each new path is added to the path in order. When you split the composite path, the first time you choose Split Object removes the most recently appended subpath; the next Split Object removes the next most recently appended subpath; and so on.

Editing Composite Paths

You can subselect the individual subpaths that make up a composite path in the same way that you subselect objects inside a group—hold down Option and click on the object. Once the object's selected, you can alter the position of the path's points, move or otherwise transform the path, delete points, delete the entire path, or clone the path (see Figure 2-52).

FIGURE 2-52
Subselecting
individual paths inside
composite paths

For clarity, these
two illustrations are
shown in Keyline view.

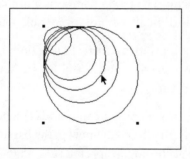

Select a composite path.

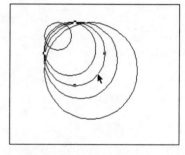

Hold down Option and click to
select a subpath.

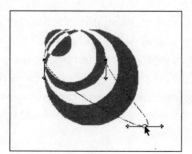

Modify the subpath.

The subpath remains part of the
composite path.

You can subselect multiple subpaths inside a composite path by holding down Shift as you select the subpaths. You can also select through overlapping subpaths or objects by holding down Control and Option as you click on the subpaths, just as you can Control-click your way through stacks of objects. You can apply any of Free-Hand's transformations to the subselected subpath.

When you join paths with different lines and fills, the composite path takes on the stroke and fill attributes of the path that's the farthest to the back.

Path Operations

FreeHand's new path operations (the commands you see on the Path Operations submenu of the Arrange menu) fall into three conceptual groups, which don't necessarily match their grouping on the submenu. The path operations automate path-drawing tasks that would be difficult—if not impossible—to do manually.

◆ The path utilities (Correct Direction, Reverse Direction, Remove Overlap, and Simplify) are handy commands for cleaning up paths.

◆ The path-generating commands (Blend, Expand Stroke, and Inset Path) create new paths based on existing, selected paths, according to specific rules that differ from command to command.

◆ Intersection operations (Intersect, Punch, and Union) give you ways of manipulating the areas of intersection between two (or more) overlapping closed paths. You can remove the overlapping area from one of the paths using Punch, or join the two paths together while deleting the overlapping area using Union, or you can delete both of the original paths, leaving only the area defined by their intersection using Intersect.

In my opinion, these are the most significant new features in FreeHand 4. Why? First, the path operators make it easy for new users to create shapes they could never draw by hand: they can draw basic shapes (rectangles, polygons, and ellipses) and use the path operations to turn these basic shapes into the shapes they want. Second, illustrators and graphic artists benefit, because they can draw more accurately. I can't count the number of times I've seen FreeHand illustrations ruined because of paths that didn't quite meet, or paths that were too complex to print.

The path operation features can save you lots of time, regardless of whether you're an amateur or a pro.

Correcting Path Direction

Most of the time, you could call Correct Path Direction, "make clockwise"—because that's what it does. You've probably noticed that you don't always get what you'd expect when you join paths to create a composite path. Sometimes, interior areas which you'd expect would be filled. You fix it by selecting the composite path and choosing Correct Path Direction (see Figure 2-53). Using Correct Path Direction has no effect on the shape of your path.

FIGURE 2-53
Correcting path
direction

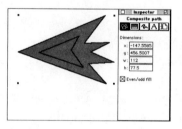

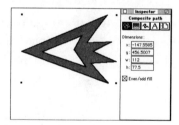

Before choosing Correct Path Direction—path doesn't fill properly.

After Correct Path Direction

Reversing Path Direction

When you want to change a path's direction (for example, when you want an arrowhead to appear on the other end of an open path), choose Reverse Path Direction from the Path Operations submenu. FreeHand reverses the direction of the path (see Figure 2-54). Reverse Path Direction has no effect on the shape of your path.

FIGURE 2-54
Reversing path
direction

Before Reverse Path Direction

After Reverse Path Direction

Removing Overlap

When a single FreeHand path crosses over itself, it becomes more difficult to print (and, to a certain extent, more difficult to edit). It's easy to create self-crossing paths when you're working with the Freehand tool, the Calligraphic Pen tool, or the Variable Stroke tool. It's also easy (it's practically unavoidable) to create composite paths which cross over themselves. Remove Overlap simplifies your paths by turning them into composite paths containing separate, closed paths (see Figure 2-55). It's kind of like a combination of Punch and Union, but works on a single path.

FIGURE 2-55
Removing overlap

Before Remove Overlap   *After Remove Overlap*

Simplifying Paths

Okay, confess—here's something we've all done (at least once): we place a bilevel TIFF in FreeHand, trace it with the tracing tool—thereby generating a single path containing billions and billions of points—and then express surprise when the publication won't print. These days, we don't have to give up our sloppy habits (not that it'd be a bad idea…), provided we remember to select the path and run Simplify on it before we try to print (see Figure 2-56).

Simplify is also a great tool for new users who haven't quite gotten the hang of FreeHand's drawing tools—they can draw a path (new users typically use too many points when drawing), and then see how FreeHand thinks the path should be drawn.

FIGURE 2-56
Simplifying a path

 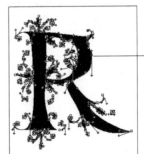

This part of the path went from 177 to 127 points after simplification.

Remember: fewer points = easier printing.

Before Simplify   *After Simplify*

Blending

Blending is a way of creating a number of paths, automatically, between two existing paths. Blending is one of FreeHand's most useful tools, especially for creating shaded objects. When Illustrator first introduced the world to blending, all of the marketing materials stressed this great new feature's ability to turn an "S" into a swan, or a "V" into a violin. That's pretty cool, *but how often do you actually need to do that?* Blending's actually a much less glamorous, much more useful tool (see Figure 2-57).

FIGURE 2-57
Blending

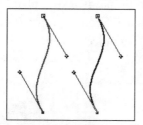

Select two points on two paths and choose Blend from the Path Operations submenu of the Arrange menu.

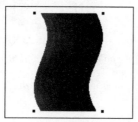

FreeHand fills in the intermediate blend objects.

Shading with blends

Blending: the rules of the road. FreeHand doesn't impose very many limitations on what, when, and how you can blend Free-Hand objects. The following are a few things you've got to keep in mind when as you create a blend.

You can blend any two ungrouped paths having like attributes. What do I mean by "like attributes?" I mean that you can blend a path containing a radial fill into a path containing another radial fill, but you can't blend a path containing a radial fill into a path containing a graduated fill.

When you try to blend paths having different stroke patterns, or patterned fills, the shapes of the objects blend, but the strokes or fills will flip from one to the other at the halfway point of the blend (see Figure 2-58).

FIGURE 2-58
Blending paths with
differing dashed
strokes

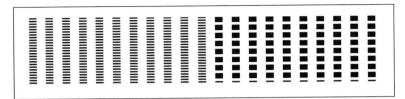

Blending relies on reference points. When you're blending, you have the option of selecting a "reference point" when you're working with open paths, and you *must* select a reference point on the starting and ending paths in the blend when you're blending closed paths. What's a reference point? It's a way of telling Free-Hand, "Blend these two objects; from this point to that point" (see Figure 2-59).

FIGURE 2-59
Reference points

The position of the reference points has a great effect on the blend. Select two reference points—one on either end of two paths…

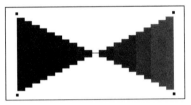

…and blend. In this example, the reference points make the blend flip over at its midpoint.

How many steps do you need? After picking reference points, the next most important part of creating a blend is the number you enter in the Number of Steps field in the Object Inspector (see Figure 2-60).

◆ The number you enter in the Number of Steps field is the number of steps you want in your blend, not including the original, selected objects.

◆ The number you enter in the First Blend field is the percentage of the distance between the original paths where you want to place the first blended path.

◆ The number you enter in the Last Blend field is the percentage of the distance between the original paths where you want to place the last blended path.

FIGURE 2-60
Blend controls in the
Object Inspector

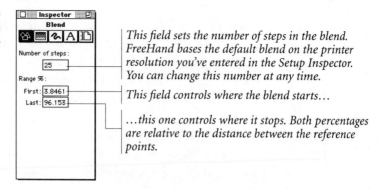

This field sets the number of steps in the blend. FreeHand bases the default blend on the printer resolution you've entered in the Setup Inspector. You can change this number at any time.

This field controls where the blend starts...

...this one controls where it stops. Both percentages are relative to the distance between the reference points.

◆ Most of the time, you'll just type a number in the Number of Steps field and press Return. You can enter numbers in the other fields to create special blend effects (see Figure 2-61).

When you're working with blends, you can determine the best number of blend steps to use, based on the length of the blend and the properties of your printer, by solving the following equation.

$$\text{number of steps} = (dpi/lpi)^2 * \% \text{ change in color}$$

In this equation, *dpi* is the resolution of your final output device in dots per inch; *lpi* is the screen frequency you'll be using, in lines per inch. The value *% change in color* is just that, and it's easy to figure out if you're using spot colors.

If you're using process colors, figure out which component process color goes through the largest percentage change from one end of the blend to the other, and use that value for the *% change in color* part of the equation.

FIGURE 2-61
Special blend effects

Normal blend: 19 blend steps; first blend step 5 percent; last blend step 95 percent.

Special blend: 19 blend steps; first blend step 20 percent; last blend step 80 percent.

The purpose of this equation is to tell you the minimum number of steps you should use. Below this number of steps, you'll start losing gray levels and bands of gray (or color) will appear in your blend. You can always use more blend steps than this, but you don't gain anything, and each additional blend step increases the complexity of your publication, and therefore increases the time your publication takes to print.

Also be aware that you never need more than 256 steps in a blend (unless you have to fill the gaps inside the blend), because that's the maximum number of gray levels that a PostScript printer can render.

What if using the optimum number of blend steps means that gaps appear in your blend? This happens when your original blend objects aren't big enough to cover the distance from one blend step to the next. When this happens, you can either increase the number of blend steps you're using, or you can figure out how much larger you'll have to make your blend objects using the following equation.

distance blend has to cover/number of steps = size of original object

Okay smart guy, you're saying, these equations work great for blending simple rectangles which happen to be running vertically or horizontally, but what about a diagonal blend between two like paths shaped like a camel's back (see Figure 2-62)? Huh? Huh?

It's easy—select the Line tool and draw a line from one point to another, then read the distance from the Info Bar.

You can also blend between intermediate objects to obtain an even higher degree of control over your graduated or radial fills.

FIGURE 2-62
Camel's hump blend

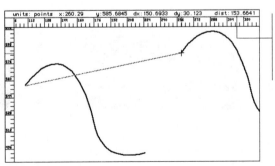

As you drag the Line tool, you'll see the distance between the two points in the Info Bar.

Blends and spot colors. Unlike FreeHand 3, FreeHand 4 lets you blend two spot-colored objects. Unfortunately, when you do this, FreeHand colors all of the intermediate objects using process colors—which is almost certainly not what you want. Does this mean you're out of luck if you want to crate tint builds by blending two spot colors? You're not—you can stack up two blends and set each spot color to overprint (see "Creating Tint Builds" in Chapter 6, "Color").

Alternatively, you can substitute one of the process colors (cyan, magenta, yellow, or black) for each spot color in your publication, and blend away. For more on how to do this, and how to make the process color look like your spot color onscreen, see "Substituting Process Colors for Spot Colors" in Chapter 6, "Color."

Creating a blend. Now that you know the rules, let's create a blend (see Figure 2-63).

1. Select two ungrouped paths (with matching or compatible attributes).

2. Choose Blend from the Path operations submenu of the Arrange menu (or press Command-Shift-E).

    Is Blend grayed out? If it is, your paths might not be of the same type (that is, you might have one open path and one closed path). If both of the paths are closed, you have to select a reference point. If one of the paths is closed, you have to make it an open path, or make the other path closed.

FreeHand blends the paths you've selected. The original objects and the newly created paths are grouped together following the blend.

If the attributes of the paths you're trying to blend are incompatible, FreeHand displays an alert (shown in Figure 2-64). Sorry, no blend. You'll have to track down what's different between the two paths, make changes, and try again.

You can enter negative numbers (to -100 percent) in the First and Last fields. You can use this to extend the blend past the original objects by up to the distance between them. Of what possible use is this? I haven't found one yet.

FIGURE 2-66
Creating a blend

Select two reference points and choose Blend from the Path Operations submenu of the Arrange menu.

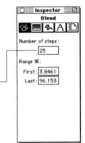

FreeHand creates your blend.

Enter the number of blend steps you want in the Object Inspector and press Return.

The blended objects are grouped.

Okay, this example's no more typical of the uses of blending than the swan or violin I mentioned earlier.

But it sure is fun!

FIGURE 2-67
What happens when you try blending incompatible objects

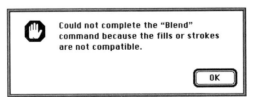

Editing blends. If you want to change the number of steps in your blend, select the blended objects and press Command-Option-B to display the Object Inspector. Change the blend by entering new values in the Number of Steps, First or Last fields, and press Return. FreeHand creates a new blend from the original objects (see Figure 2-68).

FIGURE 2-68
Editing blends

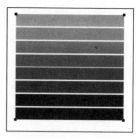

Select a blend. Press Command-Option-B to display the Object Inspector (if it's not already visible).

Enter a number in the Number of Steps field and Press Return.

FreeHand redraws your blend.

Changing the shape of the entire blend. You can change the shape and attributes of blended objects to a certain extent by changing the shape and attributes of the original shapes in the blend. Subselect the original path (or both original paths) by holding down Option as you click on the path (you are subselecting an element in a group). Next, change the path's attributes and/or shape. As you change the path's shape and attributes, FreeHand recreates the blend on the fly based on the current shape and/or attributes (see Figure 2-69).

FIGURE 2-69
Changing the shape
and attributes of
blended objects

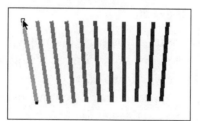

Hold down Option and click on the first or last object in the blend to subselect it.

Reshape the object. FreeHand alters the blend based on the new shape.

Editing an intermediate path in a blend. To edit one or more of the intermediate paths in the blend, ungroup the blend, select the path, and edit away. There's no way to get the changes you make to this intermediate point to ripple through the blend, however. If you want to do that, consider reblending between intermediate objects (see Figure 2-70).

FIGURE 2-70
Editing intermediate
paths in a blend

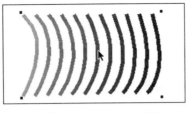 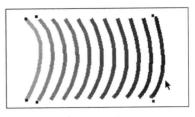

Select the blend you want to edit...   *...and press Command-U
to ungroup it.*

 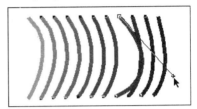

*Press Command-U to ungroup the
intermediate blend objects.*   *Now you can edit the intermediate
blend objects.*

Creating colors based on blend steps. When you create a blend, the colors applied to the intermediate paths in the blend are not automatically added to FreeHand's Color List. If you want to add one or more of the colors created by the blend to your Color List, this is the procedure (see Figure 2-71).

1. Select the blend.

2. Press Command-U twice to completely ungroup the blend (when you first press Command-U, FreeHand ungroups the original objects, but leaves the objects generated by the blend grouped; pressing Command-U again ungroups all of the objects in the blend).

3. Select one of the objects you created by blending.

4. In the Color List, choose New from the popup menu. FreeHand adds a new color to the Color List. The new color is based on the color of the object you selected.

Using Blend to create graduated and radial fills. If you want total control over the creation of graduated or radial fills in FreeHand, use Blend, rather than the Graduated or Radial fill types. If you use Blend, you accrue several significant advantages.

FIGURE 2-71
Adding colors based
on blended elements

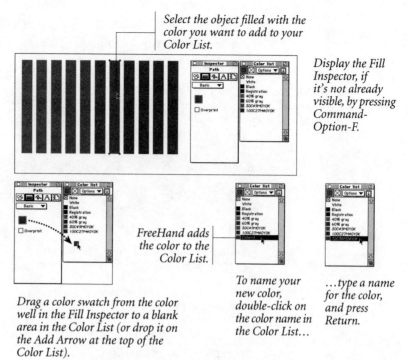

Select the object filled with the
color you want to add to your
Color List.

Display the Fill
Inspector, if
it's not already
visible, by pressing
Command-
Option-F.

FreeHand adds
the color to the
Color List.

Drag a color swatch from the color
well in the Fill Inspector to a blank
area in the Color List (or drop it on
the Add Arrow at the top of the
Color List).

To name your
new color,
double-click on
the color name in
the Color List...

...type a name
for the color,
and press
Return.

◆ Control over the graduation. FreeHand's Graduated fill type
offers you the choice between Linear and Logarithmic fill
progressions, but blending can give you more control. By
blending objects, you can make the blend go as rapidly or
slowly from color to color as you choose.

◆ Control over trapping. See Chapter 7, "Printing," for more
information on trapping graduated and radial fills.

◆ Optimization of your fill for printing on your final output
device (printer or imagesetter).

◆ Superior screen display of fills.

The only disadvantage I can think of is that you've got many
more objects on a page to worry about. Unless you ungroup them,
however, they'll be treated as a single group.

Blends also produce very different-looking results. I find that
I mix blends and graduated fills inside a publication to get the
effects I want. If I want a graduated fill that doesn't follow the

shape of an object, I'll often use a graduated fill. But if I want a graduated fill that does follow the shape of an object, I'll use a blend. Figure 2-72 shows the difference.

FIGURE 2-72
Blends and
graduated fills

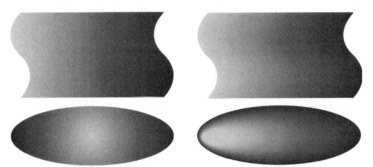

Graduated fills don't follow the shape of the object.

Blends follow the shape of the object.

To create a graduated fill using Blend, follow these steps.

1. Create a path that has the fill attributes you want for one end of the graduation.

2. Create a path that has the fill attributes you want for the other end of the graduation.

3. Select one point from the first path, and then select a point from the second path.

4. Choose Blend from the Path Operations submenu of the Arrange menu.

5. Display the Object Inspector, if it's not already visible, by pressing Command-Option-B. Type a number in the Number of Steps field and press Return.

Intersect   What do you do when you want to create a path that's defined by the intersection of two (or more) overlapping paths? Select the overlapping objects and choose Intersect from the Path Operations submenu, and FreeHand creates the path for you. It's that simple (see Figure 2-73).

The following are a few things to keep in mind when you use Intersect.

FIGURE 2-73
Using Intersect

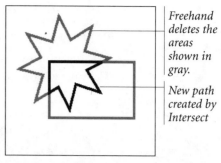

Freehand deletes the areas shown in gray.

New path created by Intersect

Select two or more closed paths (in this example, the star shape is on top).

Choose Intersect from the Path Operations submenu of the Arrange menu. FreeHand creates a new path based on the intersection of the shapes, and deletes the original paths.

◆ The path FreeHand generates when you choose Intersect takes on the formatting of the original path that's farthest to the back.

◆ If you run Intersect on a set of paths that don't intersect, FreeHand deletes all the paths.

◆ When you choose Intersect, FreeHand deletes the original paths as it creates the new path. If you want to keep the original paths, clone them before using Intersect.

Tip:
Simulating
the Effect of
Transparency
with Intersect

Here's a great "hidden" FreeHand feature—hold down Option as you choose Intersect from the Path Operations submenu, and FreeHand displays the Transparency dialog box. Choose a percentage ("0" equals complete transparency, "100" equals complete opacity—the same color as the topmost path) and press Return, and FreeHand colors the new path with a process color based on the colors of the intersecting objects (see Figure 2-74).

FIGURE 2-74
Transparency
dialog box

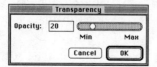

Transparency creates a new shape and colors it with a new color based on the colors of the original shapes.

Hold down Option as you choose Intersect, and FreeHand displays the Transparency dialog box.

When you use the Transparency dialog box, FreeHand retains the original objects, rather than deleting them, as it normally would after an Intersect. This means you don't have to clone objects you want to keep beforehand.

Punch When you want to use one closed path to cut a hole in another closed path, use Punch. Position the path you want to use as the "cookie cutter" above the path you want to use as "cookie dough," and choose Punch from the Path Operations submenu. FreeHand deletes the area where the two paths overlap from the path that's farthest to the back (see Figure 2-75). When the topmost path is entirely within the path behind it, FreeHand turns the paths into a single composite path.

FIGURE 2-75
Using Punch

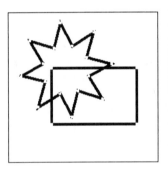
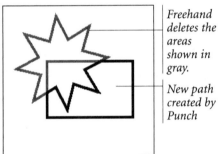

Freehand deletes the areas shown in gray.

New path created by Punch

Select two or more closed paths (in this example, the star shape is on top).

Choose Punch from the Path Operations submenu of the Arrange menu. FreeHand creates a new path by cutting the topmost path out of the paths behind it.

Union Often, I want to create a single path from two or more overlapping closed paths, but I don't want the path to have holes in it, as it would if I made it a composite path using Join Elements. Union does just what I want—it combines two paths while removing any areas where they overlap from the new path (see Figure 2-76). If the paths I've selected don't overlap, FreeHand creates a composite path.

Union is great for creating complex paths from simple paths, such as rectangles and ellipses.

Expand Stroke Because I do lots of illustrations featuring geometric grids and lattices, I've often wanted a command that would take an open path

FIGURE 2-76
Using Union

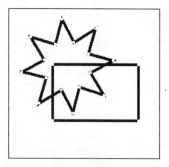

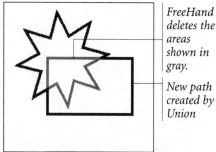

FreeHand deletes the areas shown in gray.

New path created by Union

Select two or more closed paths (in this example, the star shape is on top).

Choose Union from the Path Operations submenu of the Arrange menu. FreeHand creates a new path by merging the original paths and removing their areas of intersection.

I'd drawn and convert it into a closed path that I could fill or use as a clipping path. Expand Stroke creates two new paths, where each new path is a specific distance from the center of the original path. One of the generated paths is a specific distance *outside* the original path; the other is a the same distance *inside* the original path. Once FreeHand's created the paths, it joins them into a single, compound path. This is kind of hard to explain with words, so take a look at Figure 2-77.

FIGURE 2-77
Using Expand Stroke

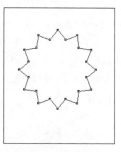

Select a path and choose Expand Stroke from the Path Operations submenu of the Arrange menu.

FreeHand displays the Expand Stroke dialog box. Enter the distance you want between the selected path and the new path in the Width field, and press Return.

FreeHand creates a new path, placing each new point a precise distance from each original point.

Inset Path Inset Path works like Expand Stroke—only Inset Path only creates one new path, a specific distance inside the original path (Figure 2-78). Note that scaling a path and using Inset Path produce (in most cases) very different results.

FIGURE 2-78
Using Inset Path

Select a path and choose Inset Path from the Path Operations submenu of the Arrange menu.

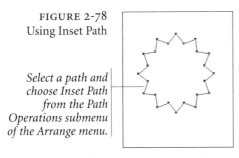

Clone the path first, if you want to keep it in its original shape—Inset Path operates on the current path.

FreeHand displays the Inset Path dialog box. Enter the distance you want between the selected path and the new path in the Width field, and press Return. Enter a negative distance to make the generated path larger than the original path.

FreeHand creates a new path, placing each new point a precise distance from each original point.

Tracing

When Illustrator 1.0 first appeared, tracing scanned artwork or MacPaint images was seen as the major use for the product. People just couldn't imagine creating entire pieces of artwork using a point-and-path drawing program. While times have changed—I think more people now use FreeHand and Illustrator to create illustrations without tracing—tracing is still a powerful option you can use in creating your FreeHand publication.

You can trace any object in FreeHand, and you can trace the object manually or use the Tracing tool.

Manual Tracing

To manually trace a TIFF, follow these steps (see Figure 2-79).

1. Import an image. Make sure you've got High-Resolution TIFF Display turned on in the Preferences dialog box; this way, you'll see the high-resolution display of your imported image rather than a 72-dpi rendition.

2. Without deselecting the TIFF, click on any background layer in the Layers palette to send the image to the background. This grays the image and makes it easier to trace. You can

FIGURE 2-79
Manually tracing an
imported image

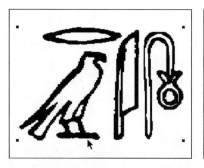

Import the image you want to trace.

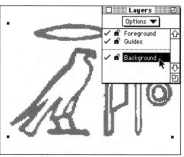

Send the image to a background layer.

Place points and paths until…

…you've traced the image.

also color the image some color (I like coloring it cyan, because I'm used to tracing things drawn in nonreproducing blue pen) and send it to some other layer—just make sure you're doing the tracing on a layer that's in front of the layer you send the image to.

3. Lock the background layer by clicking on the padlock icon next to the layer's name in the Layers palette.

4. Zoom in on some portion of the image and start placing points.

5. When you're through tracing the image, delete the image from your illustration, or send it to some nonprinting layer.

Why not use the Tracing tool? The Tracing tool is great, but you're smarter than it is. Often, you can trace an image more quickly than you can autotrace it, given the amount of time it can take to clean up an autotraced image.

When you're tracing—particularly when you're tracing objects other than bitmaps—the larger the object is, the more accurate your tracing will be. I often copy objects I want to trace to a new document or a new page, trace them there, and then bring the resulting paths back into my publication.

Autotracing

First, I have to clear something up. In spite of what you might have heard elsewhere, you can autotrace *anything* on a FreeHand page. I have to mention this because many people have the impression that you can only autotrace bitmapped images. In fact, you can autotrace text, paths, imported images—and even imported EPS graphics. Autotracing is a fast and fun way to create new paths from other FreeHand objects.

To autotrace an object, follow these steps (see Figure 2-80).

1. Select the Tracing tool from the toolbox. If you want to change the Tracing tool's settings, double-click the Tracing tool and make the changes you want in the Tracing Tool dialog box.

2. Drag the cursor around the area you want to trace. Keep this area as small as you can—autotracing can take a long time and can generate paths containing lots of points. It's sometimes a little easier to autotrace a complex or large object in several passes, and then join the resultant paths. If you run out of memory while you're autotracing, select a smaller area to trace or quit FreeHand, increase FreeHand's RAM allocation in the Finder, and then try tracing again.

After you release the mouse button, FreeHand autotraces the object or objects you dragged a rectangle around. It's a good idea to move the paths you've created to a new layer. Without deselecting the paths, choose New from the popup menu in the Layers palette. FreeHand creates a new layer and adds it to the top of the Layers palette. Click on the layer's name in the Layers palette to move the selected objects to that layer.

The current magnification has no effect on autotracing.

FIGURE 2-80
Autotracing

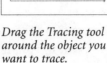

*Drag the Tracing tool
around the object you
want to trace.*

*FreeHand traces
the object.*

Strokes

Once you've created a path, you'll probably want to give the path some specific line weight, color, or other property. The process of applying formatting to a path is often called "stroking a path," and we refer to a path's appearance as its "stroke." Strokes specify what the outside of the paths looks like.

To apply a stroke to a path, you can choose one of FreeHand's default stroke widths from the Attributes menu, or you can specify a stroke using either the Stroke Inspector or the Styles palette.

Note that you can choose a number of predefined line weights from the Stroke Widths submenu of the Arrange menu. These are great, as far as they go, but you'll be doing most of your serious work using the Stroke Inspector. To display the Stroke Inspector, press Command-Option-L (you can think of "L" as Line).

Use the Stroke Type popup menu (the popup menu directly below the Inspector buttons) in the Stroke Inspector to choose the type of stroke you want to use.

Basic Strokes

Select Basic from the Stroke Type popup menu, the Stroke Inspector shows you the Basic stroke attributes. Most of the time, you'll be working with basic strokes. Though they're not flashy, there are a few interesting tricks to using them, and a couple of things to look out for.

Color. Drag a color swatch from the Color List (or the Color Mixer, or the Tint Palette) into the color well in the Stroke Inspector to apply a color to your path. If you're working with a named color (or a tint of a named color), that color's name appears next to the color well in the Stroke Inspector.

Overprint. Checking this option makes the stroke overprint, rather than knock out of, whatever's behind it. This setting overrides any ink-level overprinting settings in the Print Options dialog box (see Figure 2-82). This might not seem like much, but if trapping is important to you, it's one of the most important features in Free-Hand (see Chapter 6, "Color," for more about trapping).

FIGURE 2-82
Overprinting strokes

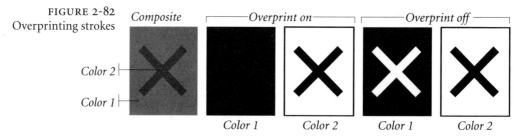

You won't see the effect of overprinting until you print separations of your publication. When you do that, you'll see something like these thumbnails.

Width. Enter a number to specify the width of your stroke. Don't type zero, even if it works to produce the finest stroke available on your 300-dpi printer, because a stroke weight of zero on an imagesetter produces an almost invisible line. If you want a hairline, use a .25-point stroke.

Cap. Select one of the Cap options to determine the shape of the end of the stroke (see Figure 2-83). The Cap option you choose has no visible effect on a closed path.

FIGURE 2-83
Line caps

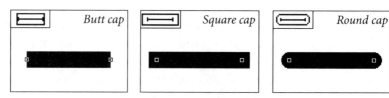

Join. The Join option determines how FreeHand renders corners—the places on a path where two line segments meet in a point (see Figure 2-84).

FIGURE 2-84
Line joins

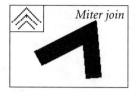 *Miter join*  *Round join*  *Beveled join*

Miter Limit. The number you enter in the Miter Limit field (from two to 180 degrees) sets the smallest angle for which FreeHand will use a mitered join. If the angle of the line join is less than the number you enter in the Miter Limit field, FreeHand renders the corner as a beveled line join (see Figure 2-85).

FIGURE 2-85
Miter limit

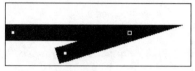 

Miter limit of two   *Miter limit of 30*

Dash. If you want a dashed line, choose one of the dash patterns from the Dash popup menu—that's the popup menu directly below the Miter Limit field (see Figure 2-86).

Tip:
Creating Your
Own Dash
Patterns

If you've looked at the Dash popup menu for a while and still don't see the dash pattern you're looking for, hold down Option and click the popup menu. The Dash Editor appears. In the Dash Editor, you can create a wide variety of dashed line patterns by entering different values in the Segment Lengths fields.

If you still can't find the dashed line style you want, you can create one using PostScript. See Chapter 8, "PostScript" for more on creating custom dashed lines.

Arrowheads. You can add arrowheads or (I guess) tailfeathers to any line you want by choosing an arrowhead style from the popup menus at the bottom of the Stroke Inspector. The leftmost popup menu applies to the first point in the path (according to the direction of the path); the rightmost popup menu applies to the last point in the path. You don't have to make choices from both of the popup menus (see Figure 2-87).

What if you can't find the arrowhead you need? You can make your own.

FIGURE 2-86
Dash patterns

Choose a dash pattern from the popup menu.

If you don't see the dash pattern you want, hold down Option and choose any pattern...

...FreeHand displays the Dash Editor dialog box, where you can create your own dash pattern.

FIGURE 2-87
Arrowheads

Choose an arrowhead from either of the popup menus.

If you want to create your own arrowhead, choose New from the popup menu.

FreeHand displays the Arrowhead Editor dialog box.

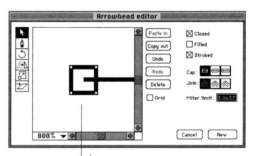

In the Arrowhead Editor dialog box, you can draw your new arrowhead, or you can paste in an arrowhead that you drew in the publication window.

1. Draw the shape you want for your custom arrowhead using any of FreeHand's drawing tools. The shape can be anything you want, but it must be a single path.

2. Select the path you've drawn and press Command-C to copy it to the Clipboard.

3. If the Stroke Inspector isn't already visible, display it by pressing Command-L.

4. Choose New from one of the Arrowhead popup menus at the bottom of the Stroke Inspector. FreeHand displays the Arrowhead Editor.

5. Click the Paste In button. The path you copied to the Clipboard appears in the Arrowhead Editor. Scale it, or change its shape if you want. When the arrowhead looks the way you want it to, click the New button to create a new arrowhead style. FreeHand adds your arrowhead to the popup menus at the bottom of the Stroke Inspector, and you can apply it to any open path in your publication.

You can also draw the arrowhead in the Arrowhead Editor, but I find it easier to draw it on a FreeHand page (where more drawing tools are available).

Custom Strokes

FreeHand's Custom stroke styles are something like the "graphic tapes" from Chartpak and Letraset (for those of you who remember what graphic production was like before computers). Like the graphic tapes, they come in handy when you need to do a custom border for a coupon or flyer (for a client who doesn't know any better).

When you choose a custom stroke from FreeHand's Effect popup menu, you'll see a preview of the stroke at the bottom of the Stroke Inspector. The color and width settings for custom strokes all work exactly as described in "Basic Strokes," above.

Enter different values in the Length and Spacing fields, and you can vary the custom stroke's appearance (see Figure 2-88, on the next page). The appearance of the Stroke Inspector for the Neon custom stroke is a little different—it doesn't have fields for Length and Spacing (they're irrelevant to the effect).

These stroke effects are PostScript, so they won't print on a non-PostScript printer.

Patterned Strokes

When you select Patterned from the Stroke Type popup menu, the Stroke Inspector fills in with a variety of patterns you can apply to your path (see Figure 2-89). The color and width settings for patterned strokes work exactly as described in "Basic Strokes," above.

You choose a pattern by clicking on the swatch of the pattern you want in the bottom of the Stroke Inspector (to display other patterns, drag the slider at the bottom of the Inspector). If you

FIGURE 2-88
Custom strokes

Here's an example of FreeHand's stock custom strokes. I printed each path using a pattern length of eight, a pattern width of eight, and a spacing of zero (except for "Rectangle," which I printed using a spacing of three).

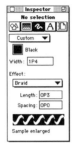

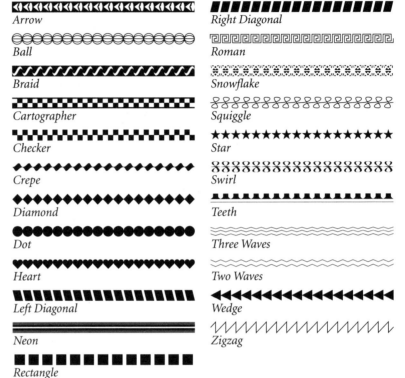

Arrow

Ball

Braid

Cartographer

Checker

Crepe

Diamond

Dot

Heart

Left Diagonal

Neon

Rectangle

Right Diagonal

Roman

Snowflake

Squiggle

Star

Swirl

Teeth

Three Waves

Two Waves

Wedge

Zigzag

The appearance of custom strokes can vary a great deal, depending on what variables you enter in the Inspector.

Here's what the parameters control.

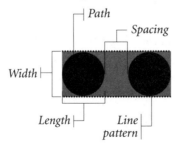

Example settings for the Braid custom stroke

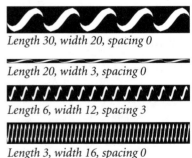

Length 30, width 20, spacing 0

Length 20, width 3, spacing 0

Length 6, width 12, spacing 3

Length 3, width 16, spacing 0

FIGURE 2-89
Patterned strokes

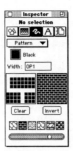

Choose a pattern from the scrolling display at the bottom of the dialog box, or click Clear to clear the current pattern and draw your own. Click Invert to invert the current pattern.

want to edit the pattern you've chosen, click inside the cell containing the enlarged view of the pattern. It's like a miniature paint program—click on a black pixel and it turns white; click on a white pixel and it turns black. If you want to create a pattern entirely from scratch, click the Clear button to set all of the pixels in the cell to white. Click the Invert button to invert the pattern shown in the cell. As you make changes, the preview of the pattern changes to show you what you've done.

Patterned strokes have several significant limitations.

◆ The pattern in a patterned stroke is always the same size—72 dots per inch—regardless of the weight of the stroke.

◆ Patterned strokes won't separate into process colors unless you're printing to a PostScript Level 2 printer.

◆ Patterned strokes can take a long time to print.

◆ Patterned strokes have an opaque background, so the pattern won't knock out of whatever's behind them. The entire path will, instead.

◆ You can't apply a halftone screen to patterned strokes.

◆ Patterned strokes are kinda ugly.

Patterned strokes are really intended to provide compatibility for imported PICTs drawn in MacDraw II. Some people feel more comfortable working with the patterned strokes than with the PostScript or custom stroke types, which is (in my opinion) unfortunate. If you're trying to make a stroke gray, apply a tint of black to the stroke. If you want to apply a stroke with a pattern to a path, use a custom stroke.

PostScript Strokes

When you choose PostScript from the Stroke Type popup menu in the Stroke Inspector, a large field appears at the bottom of the Inspector. In this field, you can enter up to 255 characters of PostScript code (you can also paste text into the field).

Don't press Return to break lines—FreeHand will think you're trying to apply the effect to the path (and won't enter a carriage return in the field, in any case). Separate your entries with spaces instead; PostScript doesn't need carriage returns to understand the code (see Figure 2-90).

Similarly, don't include the character "%" in your code—PostScript uses this character to denote comments, and will ignore any text following it (if you enter this character in the middle of your code, you'll probably cause a PostScript error).

PostScript strokes display on screen as a basic stroke of the width and color you specify. Your PostScript code can, of course, change the width or color of the stroke, if that's what you want.

While you can enter complete descriptions of PostScript strokes in this dialog box, you'll usually use it to call PostScript routines in external UserPrep files. See Chapter 8, "PostScript," for more on passing values to external routines.

FIGURE 2-90
PostScript strokes

FreeHand enters this code by default; delete it before you type your code.

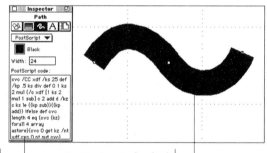

Type up to 255 characters of PostScript code in this field.

PostScript strokes look like this on your screen...

...but print according to the code you enter.

You can't see the complete code for this PostScript stroke in this screen shot (some of it has scrolled out of the field). For a complete code listing, see Chapter 8, "PostScript."

Editing Strokes

Once you've applied a stroke to a particular path, you can change the line using any of the following methods. As usual (in FreeHand), there's no "right" way to edit a stroke—which method is best and quickest depends on how you work and which palettes you have open at the time you want to change the stroke.

◆ Press Command-Option-L to display the Stroke Inspector, then make changes to the path's appearance in the Inspector.

◆ Choose one of the preset strokes from the Stroke Weights submenu of the Arrange menu.

◆ Choose Thicker or Thinner from the Stroke Weights submenu of the Arrange menu.

◆ Use the Color List to apply a color to the path (see Chapter 6, "Color," for more on applying colors using the Color List).

◆ Drag and drop a color swatch (from the Color List, the Color Mixer, the Tint palette, or the Inspector) onto the path (see Chapter 6, "Color," for more on drag-and-drop color).

◆ Click on a style name in the Styles palette.

Removing Strokes

To quickly remove a stroke from a path, use one of the following techniques.

◆ Select the path, then click on None in the Color List (when Line is selected at the top of the Color List).

◆ Drag a color swatch from None in the Color List and drop it on the Line button at the top of the Color List.

◆ Drag a color swatch from None in the Color List and drop it on the path (for more on drag-and-drop color, see Chapter 6, "Color").

◆ Select the path, then display the Stroke Inspector and choose None from the Stroke Type popup menu.

Fills

Just as strokes determine what the *outside* of a path looks like, fills specify the appearance of the *inside* of a path. Fills can make the inside of a path a solid color, or a graduated fill, or a pattern of tiny faces. Any closed (or composite) path you create can be filled.

You specify fills using the Fill Inspector. To display the Fill Inspector, press Command-Option-F. FreeHand features eight different fill types, which you can choose from the Fill Type popup menu—the popup menu at the top of the Fill Inspector.

Basic fills. Choose Basic from the Fill Type popup menu when you want to fill an object with a specific color (see Figure 2-91). Apply the color to your path by dragging a color swatch from the Color List (or the Color Mixer, or the Tint palette) into the color well in the Stroke Inspector (for more on applying colors to objects, see Chapter 6, "Color").

Check the Overprint checkbox to specify that this fill overprints any underlying objects. If you don't check Overprint, the object will be knocked out of any underlying objects unless its ink color has been set to overprint. Depending on the colors you're using in your publication and the printing process you intend to use, this might not be what you want (see Figure 2-92).

Tip:
Dragging and
Dropping
Basic Fills

To change any fill to a basic fill, hold down Shift as you drop a color swatch onto a path. FreeHand fills the path with a basic fill of the color you dropped on the path (see Figure 2-93).

Custom fills. Choose Custom from the Fill menu to use one of FreeHand's special fills, such as Bricks, Noise, or Tiger Teeth. These fills are PostScript, so you can't expect them to print on a non-PostScript printer.

To apply a custom fill, follow these steps (see Figure 2-94).

1. Select the path you want to apply the custom fill to.

2. Press Command-Option-F to display the Fill Inspector, if it's not already visible. Choose Custom from the Fill Type popup menu.

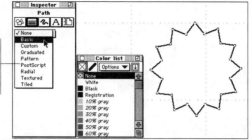

FIGURE 2-91
Applying Basic fills

Select the path you want to fill, then choose Basic from the Fill Type popup menu.

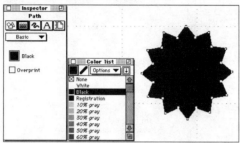

FreeHand fills the path with a basic fill of the current default color (in this example, "Black").

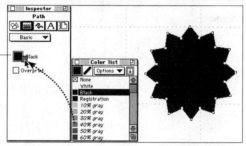

To change the color of the fill, drag a color swatch from one of the color wells in the Color List (or from the Color Mixer or the Tints palette) and drop it in the color well in the Fill Inspector.

Alternatively, you could click on the color name in the Color List, or drag a color swatch onto the Fill button at the top of the Color List.

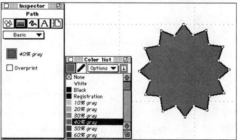

FreeHand applies the fill to the selected path.

FIGURE 2-92
Overprinting fills

Color 2

Color 1

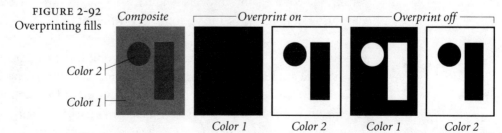

Composite   *Overprint on*   *Overprint off*

Color 1   Color 2   Color 1   Color 2

FIGURE 2-93
Drag-and-drop
basic fills

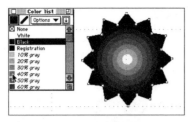

*Position the cursor over
the color you want to
use and press the mouse
button.*

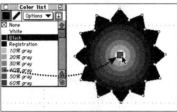

*Drag the color swatch
over the path you want
to apply it to, hold down
Shift, and drop the color
swatch into the path.*

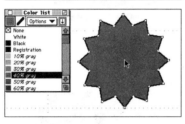

*FreeHand applies a
basic fill to the path.*

3. Choose a fill from the Effect popup menu in the Fill Inspector. Options for the specific fill you've chosen appear in the Fill Inspector. The number of parameters you can specify varies from fill to fill.

4. Specify the way you want the fill to appear and press Return to apply your changes.

Custom fills appear on screen as patterns of little Cs.

You can vary the appearance of the custom fills to a tremendous degree. For the Bricks fill, for example, you can specify the color, width, height, and angle of the "bricks" in the fill, as well as setting the color of the "mortar." Figure 2-95 shows how different variables can make the same fill look very different.

Graduated fills. Choose Graduated to fill an object with a linear or logarithmic graduation from one color to another—also known as a "fountain." You can set the beginning and ending colors, and you can specify the type of graduation (Linear or Logarithmic) and the angle the graduation is to follow (see Figure 2-96).

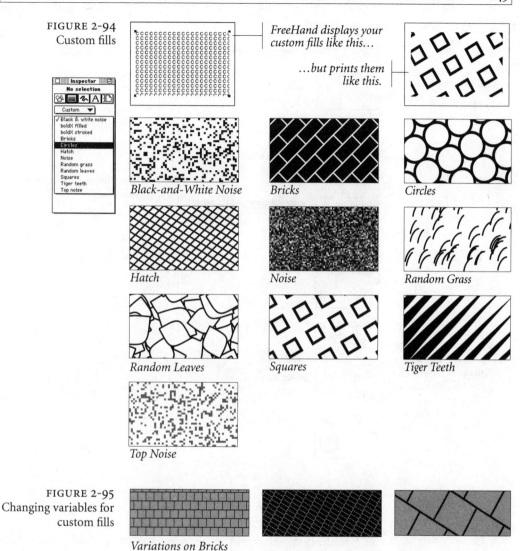

FIGURE 2-94
Custom fills

FreeHand displays your custom fills like this…

…but prints them like this.

Black-and-White Noise

Bricks

Circles

Hatch

Noise

Random Grass

Random Leaves

Squares

Tiger Teeth

Top Noise

FIGURE 2-95
Changing variables for custom fills

Variations on Bricks

Note that you can't specify graduations between two spot colors (though you can specify graduations between two tints of the same spot color, or between a spot color and FreeHand's default color "White"). There's a way around this limitation, however, as explained in "Substituting Process Colors for Spot Colors" in Chapter 6, "Color."

A far more serious problem is that you can't set graduated fills to overprint, which makes it harder (maybe harder than it should

FIGURE 2-96
Graduated fills

Select a path and choose Graduated from the Fill Type popup menu.

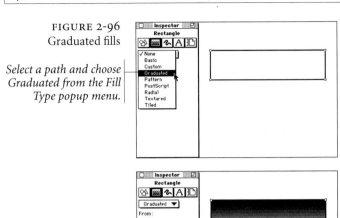

FreeHand applies a graduated fill to the path.

To change the appearance of your graduated fill, drag color swatches into the color wells in the Fill Inspector...

...or choose a different graduated fill type...

...or change the angle of the fill.

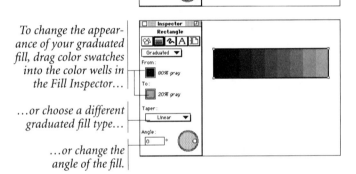

be) to trap abutting graduated fills. To see how to do that, see "Trapping," in Chapter 6, "Color."

Finally, if you're considering using a graduated fill, you should take a look at "Blending," earlier in this chapter.

Tip:
Dragging and
Dropping
Graduated Fills

To change any fill to a graduated fill, hold down Control as you drop a color swatch into a closed path. FreeHand fills the path with a graduated fill, and sets the To color to the color of the swatch you dropped on the path. FreeHand sets the From color to the original color applied to the path. FreeHand determines the angle of the graduation from the point at which you drop the color swatch (see Figure 2-97).

FIGURE 2-97
Drag-and-drop
graduated fills

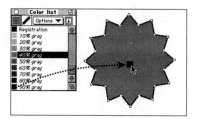 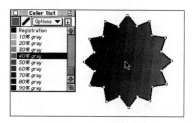

Hold down Control as you drop a color swatch into a path...

...and FreeHand applies a graduated fill to the path, using the color you dropped to set the fill's To color.

Patterned fills. Patterned fills have the same problems and limitations as patterned lines, discussed in "Patterned Lines," earlier in this chapter. I recommend that you don't use them.

Postscript fills. When you choose PostScript from the Fill menu, a large field appears at the bottom of the Fill Inspector (see Figure 2-98). PostScript fills work just like PostScript lines, described earlier in this chapter.

PostScript fills display on screen as a pattern of little PSs.

FIGURE 2-98
PostScript fills

FreeHand enters this code by default; delete it before you type your code.

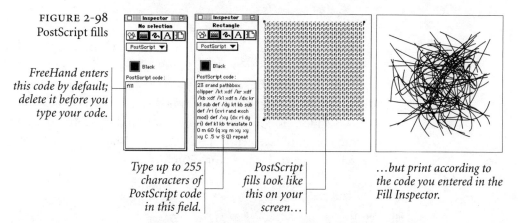

Type up to 255 characters of PostScript code in this field.

PostScript fills look like this on your screen...

...but print according to the code you entered in the Fill Inspector.

Radial fills. A radial fill creates a concentric graduated fill from the center of an object to the outside of the object. By default, the center of a radial fill is placed at the center of the two most distant points in the object (see Figure 2-99). You can control the location of the center of a radial fill using the Locate Center control in the Fill Inspector—drag the handle around, and FreeHand repositions the center of the radial fill. Radial fills are subject to the same limitations as graduated fills.

FIGURE 2-99
Radial fills

Select a path and choose
Radial from the Fill
Type popup menu.

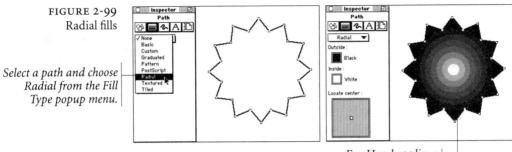

FreeHand applies a
radial fill to the path.

To change the colors
used in a radial fill,
drag color swatches
into the color wells in
the Fill Inspector.

Change the location of
the center point of the
radial fill by dragging
this control around.

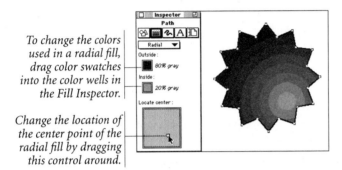

Tip:
Dragging
and Dropping
Radial Fills

To change any fill to a radial fill, hold down Option as you drop a color swatch onto the path containing the fill. FreeHand fills the path with a radial fill, and sets the Inside color of the radial fill to the color of the swatch you dropped on the path. FreeHand sets the Outside color to the original color applied to the path. FreeHand positions the center point of the radial fill at the point at which you dropped the color swatch (see Figure 2-100).

FIGURE 2-100
Drag-and-drop
radial fills

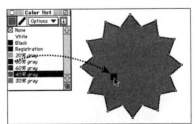

Hold down Option as you drop a color
swatch into a path…

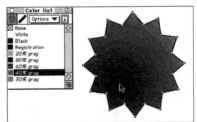

…and FreeHand applies a radial fill
to the path, using the color you dropped
to set the fill's Inside color. The point
at which you dropped the color swatch
sets the center point of the fill.

Tiled fills. Tiled fills repeat a pattern of FreeHand objects inside a path; they're like the tiles you see in your kitchen or bathroom. Here's how to create a tiled fill (see Figure 2-101).

1. Create the objects you want to have repeated inside a path. You're creating one of the tiles you'll have in your tiled fill.

2. Copy the FreeHand objects to the Clipboard.

3. Select the path you want to apply the tiled fill to.

4. Press Command-Option-F to display the Fill Inspector. Choose Tiled from the Fill Type popup menu. The tiled fill attributes appear in the Fill Inspector.

5. Click the Paste In button in the Fill Inspector. This pastes the objects you copied to the Clipboard into the window next to the button.

6. Adjust the scale, offset, and angle of the tiles. If you want the fill to be rotated, skewed, scaled, or otherwise transformed when you transform the path, check the appropriate options in the Transform palette.

7. Press Return to close the dialog box.

FIGURE 2-101
Creating a tiled fill

Create the objects you want to use in your tiled fill and copy them to the Clipboard by pressing Command-C.

Select a path and press Command-Option-F to display the Fill Inspector. Choose Tiled from the popup menu.

Click the Paste In button, and FreeHand pastes the objects you copied into the Inspector.

Change the scale, angle, and offset as you want, and Press Return.

Press Return, and FreeHand applies the tiled fill.

Offset doesn't change the distance between tiles in a tiled fill—it changes the position at which FreeHand starts drawing the tiles (ordinarily, FreeHand calculates tile positions based on the lower-left corner of a page). Values you enter in the X field move the horizontal starting point of the tiled fill (positive numbers move the starting point to the right; negative values move it to the right); values you enter in the Y field move the vertical starting point up (positive numbers) or down (negative numbers).

Tip:
Adding an offset
between tiles

To add more space between tiles in a tiled fill, follow these steps (see Figure 2-102).

1. Draw a square around the original tile. Apply a fill and line of None to the square.

2. Select the square and the original tile and press Command-C to copy the objects to the Clipboard.

3. Display the Fill Inspector by pressing Command-Option-F, if it's not already visible.

FIGURE 2-102
Increasing the
distance between tiles

*Click the Copy Out
button to copy the
original tile to the
Clipboard.*

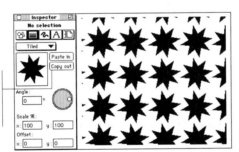 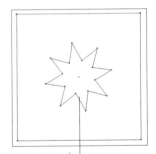

*Paste the object into a publication and draw a box around it.
Apply a fill and stroke of None to the box (shown here in
keyline view). Copy the new tile to the Clipboard…*

*…select the original
path, and click the Paste
In button. FreeHand
updates the tiled fill.*

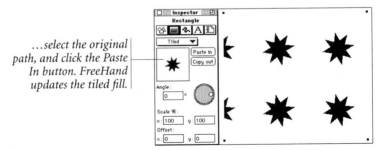

4. Choose Tiled from the Fill Type popup menu (if the Tiled Fill options aren't already visible in the Fill Inspector).

5. Click Paste In.

The objects you copied to the Clipboard appear in the Fill Inspector. You'll see that the square you drew adds a margin around the object you're tiling, but doesn't print or obscure objects behind the tiled fill. Make the square larger or smaller to control the distance between tiles.

Tip:
Moving
Paths Without
Moving Tiles

Using the X and Y Offset fields to move a fill inside a path can be frustrating. Can't you just drag the path over the part of the tiled fill you want to see? Sure—here's how you do it (see Figure 2-103).

1. Press Command-M to display the Transform palette, if it's not already visible.

2. Click the Move button in the Transform palette.

3. Uncheck the Fills checkbox.

4. Drag the path to a new location.

FIGURE 2-103
Moving paths
without moving fills

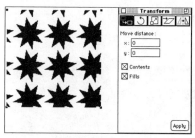

When you move a path with the Fills option checked...

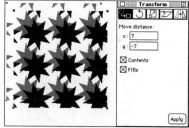

...the fill moves along with the path (original tiles shown in gray).

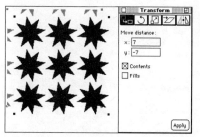

If you want the fill to stay where it is while the path moves, uncheck Fills (original path position shown in gray).

FreeHand moves the path, but doesn't change the starting location of the tiled fill. You can also accomplish this task using the Transform palette (see Chapter 5, "Transforming," for more on moving a path without changing the appearance of its fills or contents).

Textured fills. Choose Textured from the Fill menu to use one of FreeHand's textured fills, such as Denim, Burlap, or Coquille (as shown in Figure 2-104). The textured fills are actually small bitmap images that FreeHand repeats inside a path—in older versions of FreeHand, you could see an obvious pattern in paths filled with the textured fills. These days, the pattern is a little less apparent, because FreeHand randomly rotates and flips the bitmaps as it creates the tiles.

Textured fills print with an opaque background—as if you'd drawn a shape behind the fill and colored it white. If you want textured fills to print with a transparent background, take a look at "Making Textured Fills Transparent," in Chapter 8, PostScript.

FIGURE 2-104
Textured fills

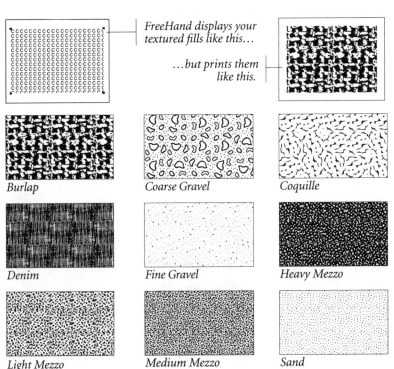

FreeHand displays your textured fills like this…

…but prints them like this.

Burlap

Coarse Gravel

Coquille

Denim

Fine Gravel

Heavy Mezzo

Light Mezzo

Medium Mezzo

Sand

Editing Fills Once you've applied a fill to a particular path, you can change the fill using any of the following methods.

- ◆ Press Command-Option-F to display the Fill Inspector, then change the path's appearance in the Inspector.

- ◆ Use the Color List to apply a color to the path (see Chapter 6, "Color," for more on applying colors using the Color List).

- ◆ Drag and drop a color swatch (from the Color List, the Color Mixer, the Tint palette, or the Inspector) inside the path (see Chapter 6, "Color," for more on drag-and-drop color).

- ◆ Click on a style name in the Styles palette.

Removing Fills To quickly remove a fill from a path, click None in the Color List when the Fill icon at the top of the Color List is selected, or drag a color swatch from None in the Color List and drop it on the Fill icon.

Working with Styles

Styles are named collections of graphic formatting attributes. If you're using a two-point line that's colored 60-percent gray, you can create a style with those attributes (you can even name it "2-point 60% gray line") and apply it to every path you want to have those attributes, rather than going to the Fill or Stroke Inspectors or the Color List every time.

When you format a path using the Stroke Widths submenu, or by choosing colors from the Color List, or by making changes in the Fill or Stroke Inspectors or the Halftone palette, or by dragging and dropping color swatches, you're formatting the path locally. We call this local formatting because the formatting applies to the selected path only, and is not explicitly shared with any other paths in your publication.

While styles are one of the most useful features of FreeHand, in my experience, as soon as you mention the word "styles," people start to panic.

There's no need to be scared—you're already thinking of the elements in your FreeHand publications as having styles. You think of each path as having a particular set of formatting attributes, and you think of groups of paths as having the same set of attributes ("These are all 12-point gray lines"). FreeHand's graphic styles give you the ability to work with FreeHand the way you already think about your publications.

Use styles. Any time you find yourself choosing the same formatting attributes over and over again, you can create a style and speed up the process of creating your publication. More importantly, you can use more of your brain for doing your creative work, rather than trying to remember that this sort of path has this sort of a line, this sort of a fill, this color, this line width, and this halftone screen. Forget that! Set up a style and let FreeHand do that kind of thinking for you.

While styles encourage you to think ahead, they're also flexible; you can change all of the paths tagged with a particular style at any time by simply editing the style's definition.

The Styles palette (see Figure 2-105) is the key to working with and applying styles. If the Styles palette is not visible on your screen, press Command-3 to display it. If the Styles palette is visible and you want to put it away, press Command-3.

FIGURE 2-105
Styles palette

Creating Styles

In FreeHand, you create styles by example. It's easy—once you've applied a set of attributes to a path using local formatting, you can turn that formatting into a style, which you can then apply to any other paths (see Figure 2-106).

1. Select the path with the attributes you want.

FIGURE 2-106
Defining a new style

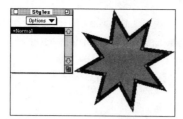

*Select a path that has the
formatting attributes you want.*

*Choose New from the Styles
palette's popup menu.*

*FreeHand creates a new style,
applying the style to the selected
path as it does so.*

*What's in a style? All of the settings for
all of the controls in the Halftone
palette, the Stroke Inspector, and the Fill
Inspector—all stored under one name in
the Styles palette.*

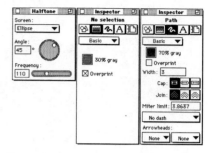

*FreeHand's default style names aren't
very descriptive, so you might want to
change them.*

*Double-click on the
style name in the
Styles palette.*

*Type a new name
for the style.*

*Press Return. FreeHand
changes the name of the
style in the Styles palette.*

2. Choose New from the popup menu at the top of the Styles
   palette (if the Styles palette isn't currently visible, press
   Command-3 to display it). FreeHand adds a new style name
   to the Styles palette.

3. To give the style another name (FreeHand's default
   names—"Style 1", "Style 2", etc.—aren't very descriptive),
   double-click on the style name in the Styles palette and type
   a new name. When you're through, press Return.

That's all there is to it. You've just created a style with the fill,
line, color, and halftone attributes of the path you selected.

Applying Styles

To apply a style, select the path you want to tag with the style, and then click on the style in the Styles palette. The path takes on all of the formatting attributes of the style (see Figure 2-107). The path is now "tagged" with the style.

FIGURE 2-107
Applying styles

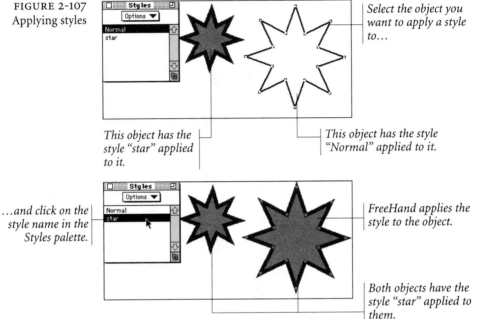

Select the object you want to apply a style to...

This object has the style "star" applied to it.

This object has the style "Normal" applied to it.

...and click on the style name in the Styles palette.

FreeHand applies the style to the object.

Both objects have the style "star" applied to them.

Redefining Styles

To redefine a style, create or select a path with the style applied to it. Make local changes using the Fill and Stroke Inspectors and the Halftone palette. When the path looks the way you want it to, choose Redefine from the popup menu on the Styles palette. All of the paths formatted using that style change to reflect the changes you've just made (see Figure 2-108).

Basing One Style on Another

Styles can inherit attributes from other styles. You can create a style that's just like an existing style except for some small difference, or create a style that's linked to any changes you make to an original style (color is a good example).

I call the original style the "parent" style and the inheriting styles "child" styles. When you change the properties of the parent style, the changes you make ripple through the child styles. Child styles inherit changes only in the properties they share with their parent

FIGURE 2-108
Editing styles

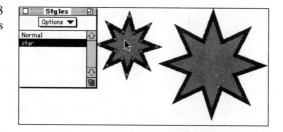

Select a path that's tagged with the style you want to redefine.

When you apply local formatting (that is, formatting independent of styles) to an object, FreeHand displays a "+" to the left of the style's name in the Styles palette.

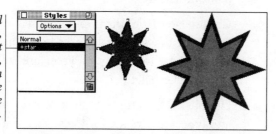

Change the path's fomatting (using any of the formatting techniques discussed earlier in this chapter).

Choose Redefine from the Styles palette's popup menu.

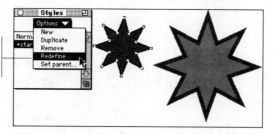

FreeHand displays the Redefine Style dialog box. Select the style you want to redefine (usually, it's the one applied to the current path) and press Return.

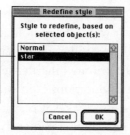
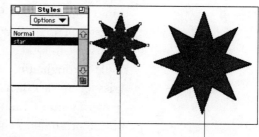

The formatting changes ripple through all of the paths tagged with the style you just redefined—even if they're not selected.

style. The attributes which differ between the parent and child styles remain the same.

People sometimes have difficulty understanding the use and worth of parent and child styles—even to the point of calling attribute inheritance a bug. It's not a bug, it's a feature.

To create a new style that's based on the existing style, follow these steps (see Figure 2-109).

1. Select a path tagged with the style you want to base the new style on.

2. Make a change to the path's formatting (its fill, stroke, or halftone setting).

3. Choose New from the popup menu at the top of the Styles palette (if the Styles palette isn't currently visible, press Command-3 to display it). FreeHand adds a new style name to the Styles palette.

4. Double-click on the default style name in the Styles palette and type a new name for the style, if you want. When you're done, press Return.

5. Choose Set Parent from the popup menu in the Styles palette. FreeHand displays the Set Parent dialog box.

6. Choose the parent style in the Set Parent dialog box and press Return to close the dialog box.

If you know what you're doing, you can use attribute inheritance to experiment—to try out new ideas quickly and easily. What would happen if all of those red lines (of whatever line width and pattern) were blue? What would happen if all of the paths you've filled with this tiled fill were filled with that graduated fill? The ripple-through effect of attribute inheritance from parent to child styles lets me ask "what if" questions quickly and easily.

Attribute inheritance also makes it easier for me to make last-minute production changes almost painlessly (there are no totally painless last-minute production changes). These are usually color changes. (Does anyone have a client/boss/whatever who never changes their mind about color after seeing the chromes? If so, could you please loan them to me?).

Duplicating Styles   If you want to base one style on another, select the style you want to copy and choose Duplicate from the Styles palette popup menu. FreeHand creates a new style with the same formatting attributes as the style you selected.

FIGURE 2-109
Basing one style
on another

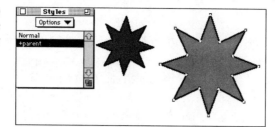

Select a path that's
tagged with parent
style and change its
formatting.

Choose New from the
Styles palette's popup
menu to create a new
style.

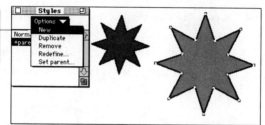

Choose Set Parent from
the Styles palette's
popup menu.

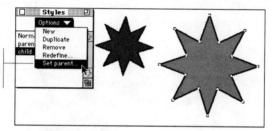

FreeHand displays the
Set Parent dialog box.
Select the style you want
to base your new style
on and press Return.

Once you've established a link
between styles, change to the
parent style apply to any
identical formatting attributes of
the child style.

In this example, the
strokes of the styles are
the same, so FreeHand
applies changes to the
stroke of the parent to
any paths tagged with
the child style.

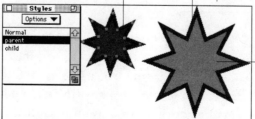

The child style's fill
differs, and is
unaffected by changes
to the fill of the parent
style.

Styles and Local Formatting

You can always override the formatting for a styled path by selecting the path and making changes locally using the selections on the Attributes menu. When you've changed a styled path locally, the style name in the Styles palette appears with a "+" before it when you have the path selected. The "+" indicates that the path's style has been overridden by some sort of local formatting.

Attribute inheritance for paths which are both styled and have local formatting works like this: child styles still inherit changes in the properties they share with their parent style; the attributes which differ between the parent and child styles (including local formatting) stay the same when you change the parent style.

If you've overridden the formatting of a styled path with local formatting, and you want to reassert the path's original style, select the path and click on the style name in the Styles palette. The style overrides (wipes out) the local formatting, and the "+" disappears from the style name in the Styles palette (see Figure 2-110).

FIGURE 2-110
Overriding local
formatting

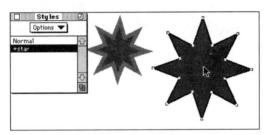

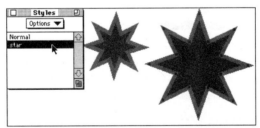

You can select more than one path with more than one sort of local formatting override and reassert the original style—select the paths and click on the style name in the Styles palette.

If you've locally formatted several paths with the same local formatting attributes and want to clear the formatting for each of the paths without having to select each one and reassert the style, try this.

1. Select one of the locally formatted paths and choose Redefine from the popup menu in the Styles palette. This incorporates the local formatting into the style's definition.

2. Use local formatting to change the selected path to match the original style's definition. As you change the path's formatting, a "+" appears next to the style's name in the Styles palette.

3. Choose Redefine from the Styles palette's popup menu.

After you choose Redefine, all of the paths—even those that had local overrides before you started this process—change back to the formatting specified by the style.

Note that you might have to go through this process several times if you have paths with different local formatting overrides.

Moving Styles from One Publication to Another

When you need to move styles from one publication to another, follow these steps.

1. Open the publication containing the style you want to move.

2. Select a path that's tagged with the style and press Command-C to copy the path to the Clipboard.

3. Open the publication you want to copy the style into.

4. Press Command-V to paste the path into the current publication. After you paste, the style name appears in the Styles palette. If you want, you can press Delete to get rid of the path you just pasted in. The style stays on the Styles palette.

If a style with the same name already exists in the target publication, it'll override the incoming style (the "home team" wins). The path you've pasted will be marked as if it had local formatting overriding the style.

Merging Styles

We can use FreeHand's "home team wins" rule to merge two styles into one style. Why would you want to merge two styles? If your publication needs to change from color to black and white, or from process color to spot color, you might want to change all of the paths tagged with one style into another style.

If you have two styles you'd like to combine into one style, follow these steps.

1. Select a path that's tagged with the style ("style 1") you want to end up with and copy it into another publication.

2. Change the name of the style to the name of the style you want to merge it with ("style 2").

3. Return to the original publication. Press Command-A to select everything in the publication.

4. Press Command-C to copy everything in the publication to the Clipboard.

5. Go to the second publication and press Command-V. FreeHand pastes all of the objects on the Clipboard into the current publication, changing the definition of "style 2" as it does so.

Adding Styles to Your Defaults File

You can add styles to your Aldus FreeHand defaults template by opening the template, copying in elements having the styles you want, and then saving the file as a template. This way, the styles you've added will appear in every new publication you create.

Charting and Graphing

Because FreeHand works "by the numbers," it's easy to create good-looking charts and graphs. (Good-looking or not, I've always hated the dang things.)

It might seem that the easiest way to get a chart or graph into your FreeHand publication would be to create one in Excel or Persuasion, then paste or place the chart into FreeHand. Because the chart is an object-PICT, FreeHand will convert it into FreeHand elements as it's pasted or placed.

The trouble with this method is that you often end up spending more time cleaning up the chart than you would if you were creating it from scratch. PICT-generating applications have weird ideas about how to draw things, generally using about three times as many elements as are necessary to draw any given image. For more on importing object-PICT graphics, see "Importing PICTs" in Chapter 4, "Importing and Exporting."

The best method for more complex charts is to use Aldus' Chart-Maker or Adobe Illustrator, but you can draw simple charts yourself in FreeHand.

Chart creation is best shown by example. Here are the basic steps.

◆ Choose a scale. For bar, column, and line charts, you set up the vertical and horizontal axes of the chart according to some scale—years, thousands of tons, or dollars—mapped into units of vertical and horizontal distance.

◆ Choose an equivalent unit of measure to represent the scale you've chosen. Once you know what the scale of your chart is, you can translate that scale into units of your measurement system. If the vertical axis of your chart is marked off in 10-year increments, pick some unit of measure as being equal to that scale. It doesn't matter what unit you choose as long as you're comfortable with the working size of the chart (remember, you can always scale the chart later, after you've got all of the data points plotted). For a chart with a horizontal axis spanning 100 years in one-year increments, you'd better choose something small—like a point or .001 inch—to represent each year. If the same vertical axis were marked in 10-year increments, you'd do just as well choosing a larger unit of measure—a pica, or .5 inches.

◆ Set a zero point. If you're new to charts, this is where the horizontal and vertical axes of your chart meet.

◆ Draw the horizontal and vertical axes of your chart and mark them off in the increments you want with tick marks.

◆ Plot your data onto the chart using FreeHand's numeric movement features.

Bar and Column Charts

The only difference between bar charts and column charts is that column charts plot their data vertically and bar charts plot their date horizontally. You can use the same techniques to create either type of chart.

Imagine that you want to create a column chart showing how a particular organization's budget has grown over five years. You want to mark off the vertical axis in increments representing thousands of dollars; the horizontal axis in years. We have only a single data point for each year: $12,000 for 1985; $16,000 for 1986; $23,245 for 1987; $1,011 for 1988; $24,600 for 1989.

To create the chart, follow these steps (see Figure 2-111).

1. Choose a scale. For this example, each pica represents $1,000. Two picas represent each year on the horizontal scale. You could set the publication's Snap To grid to picas to make the task of creating the chart a little easier.

2. Draw horizontal and vertical axes and set the zero point at their intersection.

3. Draw a box two picas wide by one pica tall using the Rectangle tool. Position the box to represent the budget amount for the first year.

4. Ungroup the box, select the two points along its top, and move the points down one pica. This positions the top two points of the box on the horizontal axis of the chart.

5. Press Command-M to display the Transform palette. Click the Move button at the top of the palette. Type "12" in the Y field to move the top of the box up 12 picas, a distance representing the $12,000 budget amount for 1985. Click the Apply button, and the top of the box moves to the point on the chart representing $12,000.

6. Clone the box from the first year across the other years, changing the position of the top of each box so that it matches the budget for that year. What about the data points that can't be expressed in even units of our measurement system, such as $23,245 for 1987? Simple. When you

FIGURE 2-111
Creating a
column chart

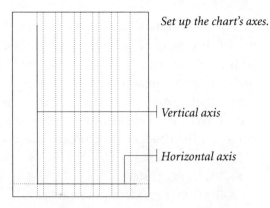

Set up the chart's axes.

Vertical axis

Horizontal axis

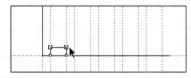

Draw a box for the first column, ungroup the box, and select the two top points. Use the Move palette to move the two points on top of the box down…

…so that they rest on the horizontal axis of the chart. Without deselecting the two points, use the Move palette again to move to the top of the bar into position.

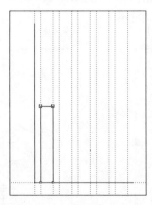

Once you've finished the first bar, use the same techniques to finish the other bars.

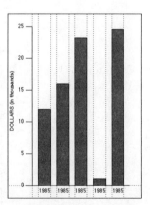

Finish the chart by adding labels and coloring the bars.

move those points vertically, we type "23.245p" in the Y field in the Move section of the Transform palette.

7. Add labels and figures to the chart.

Stacked Bar and Stacked Column Charts

Stacked bar and stacked column charts break larger bodies of data into smaller parts, plotting those parts inside the area covered by the total. If you want to break down the budget amounts shown for the nonprofit organization from the previous example to show contributions from city, state, federal, corporate, and individual sources, you'd use a stacked column chart.

For the 1985 budget, the amounts contributed were:

$2,000 from the city

$1,600 from the state

$4,400 from the federal government

$4,400 from individuals

You'd go through steps one through three as described in the previous scenario, and then create individual areas for each of the contributing sources to make up the column representing the $12,000 budget total. To do this, you'd follow these steps (see Figure 2-112).

1. Create a column representing the amount contributed by the city using the technique shown in step four in the previous scenario. In this example, create a column representing the city's contribution of $2,000 moving the top of the column up two picas.

FIGURE 2-112
Creating a stacked
column chart

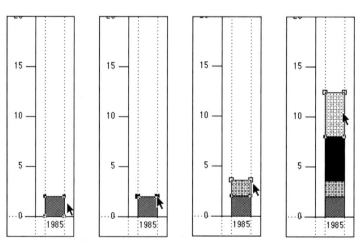

Create each part of the stacked bar chart using the moving and scaling techniques shown in Figure 2-111 (on the previous page).

2. Clone the column by pressing Command-=. Select the bottom two points on the cloned column and press Command-M to display the Transform palette, if it's not already visible. The palette should appear with the same distance as you just moved the top of the column representing the city's contribution entered in the Y field, so you can probably just click the Apply button to move the bottom of the cloned column to the same position as the top of the original column (if it doesn't, type "2" again in the Y field in the dialog box and press Return).

3. Without deselecting the points you just moved, enter the distance representing the amount contributed by the state government ("1.6p") in the Y field in the Transform palette. The bottom points you selected earlier now become the top point of a new column whose base rests precisely on the top of the column representing the amount contributed by the city.

4. Clone the column representing the state's contribution, and repeat the process of moving the bottom points on the cloned column twice to create the column representing the federal government's contribution.

5. Clone the column representing the federal contribution, and repeat the process of moving the bottom points on the cloned column twice to create the column representing contributions made by individuals in 1985.

6. Repeat this process for all of the other years in the chart.

7. Add labels, figures, and a key to the chart.

Line and Area Charts

Line charts and area charts work about the same way a bar chart works—they plot data points along a horizontal axis. A line chart plots its data along a line, rather than on a bar or column. I still think of an area chart as being a line chart with fills, rather than listening to any of the people who've tried to convince me that the two types of charts are different. All I know is that you make them the same way in FreeHand.

Imagine you want to use a line chart to plot the budget of the same nonprofit organization used as an example in the two procedures above; over the same 5-year period. Once again, you want to mark off vertical axis in increments representing thousands of dollars, and mark off the horizontal axis in years. You have a single data point for each year: $12,000 for 1985; $16,000 for 1986; $23,245 for 1987; $1,011 for 1988; $24,600 for 1989.

Set up your chart's scale by following Steps one through three in "Bar and Column Charts," and then follow these steps (see Figure 2-113).

1. Draw a path along the horizontal axis of the chart using the corner tool, placing a point along the horizontal axis every two picas (starting with a point placed at the zero point).

FIGURE 2-113
Creating a line chart

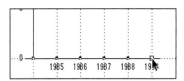

Set up the axes of your chart, select the corner tool and, draw a line with a point at each horizontal increment. Then select the first point display the Move palette.

Move the point into position using the Move palette.

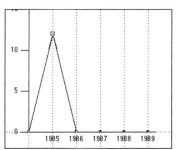

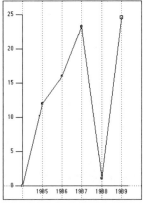

Repeat the process for each point on the line, and then finish the chart by adding labels or changing the line style or color.

2. Select the first point in the path.

3. Press Command-M to display the Transform palette. In the Move panel, type "12" in the Y field to move the point up 12 picas, a distance representing the $12,000 budget amount for 1985. The point moves to the vertical position on the chart representing $12,000.

4. Repeat the process for the four remaining points.

5. Add labels and figures to the chart.

If you wanted to make this line chart into an area chart, you'd make the line plotting the data points into the top edge of a filled path, as shown in Figure 2-114.

If you wanted to show the amounts that had been contributed by various sources, as we did using the stacked column chart, you'd use an area chart filled with different colors or tints, as shown in Figure 2-114.

FIGURE 2-114
Area charts

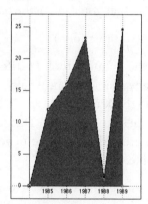

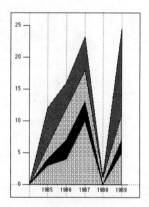

Area chart   *Area chart showing individual levels*

Pie Charts

Pie charts use degrees around a circle as their measurement system, rather than horizontal and vertical axes. Pie charts typically show parts of some total amount or percentage.

Getting there's half the fun.

If you wanted to show the contributions to our example non-profit agency's budget from 1985 as percentages in a pie chart, you'd first have to convert the raw numbers to percentages. This isn't hard: just divide the amounts by the total ($2,000 divided by

$12,000 would give us 16 percent for the city's contribution). The other contributors would be 13 percent from the state, 36 percent from the federal government, and 36 percent from individual contributors. These figures have been rounded a bit, and they do total a little over 100 percent. Don't worry about it.

Now turn these percentages into degrees by multiplying each number by 3.6 (because 360 degrees is equal, in this case, to 100 percent). This multiplication produces 57 degrees from the city, 46 degrees from the state, 129 degrees from the federal government, and 129 degrees from individuals.

To create a pie chart, follow these steps (see Figure 2-115).

1. Set a zero point on your page.

2. Draw a horizontal line using the line tool, starting at the zero point. Press Command-E and choose None from the Line popup menu. Switch to Keyline mode by pressing Command-K so that you can see the path.

3. Clone the line (Command-=).

4. Double-click the Rotation tool. The Rotate palette appears, if it's not already visible. In the Angle field, type "57". Press Tab to move to the X field and type "0". Press Tab again to move to the Y field and type "0". This tells FreeHand to rotate the line around the zero point you set. Press Return to rotate the line.

5. Select the two end points that overlap at the zero point and press Command-J to join the points. Press Command-Option-B to display the Object Inspector. Click the Closed option in the Object Inspector and press Return. FreeHand closes the path by drawing a line between the two points farthest from the zero point.

6. Clone the triangle. Select the point on the cloned triangle that's the farthest clockwise, considering the zero point as the center of a clock's face. Double-click the Rotation tool. The Rotate palette appears, with 57 still entered in the Angle field. Type "0" in both the Horizontal and Vertical fields.

FIGURE 2-115
Creating a pie chart

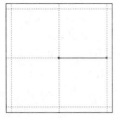 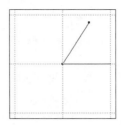 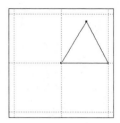

Set the zero point where you want the center of your pie chart, then draw a line out from the zero point.

Clone the line, and select the point on the cloned line that's away from the zero point. Rotate the line around the zero point by 57 degrees.

Join the two lines to make a path. Clone the triangle.

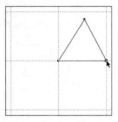 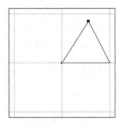 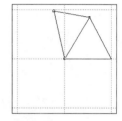

Select the point on the corner of the triangle that's in the same position as the end point of the original line.

Press Command-, to repeat the rotation you used earlier.

Without deselecting the point, use the Rotate palette to rotate the point 46 degrees.

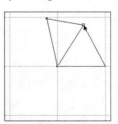 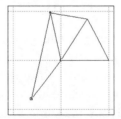

Repeat the process of cloning and rotating the triangles until you've plotted all of your data.

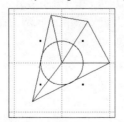 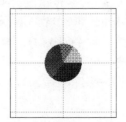 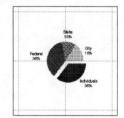

Draw a circle over the triangles. Color each triangle, and then use Intersect to create each pie wedge. Add labels, and you've got a pie chart.

This tells FreeHand to rotate the point around the zero point. Type the number of degrees for the next segment in the Angle field. In this example, this is the percentage contributed by the state government, 13 percent, or 46 degrees. Make sure that the center of rotation is still the zero point, and press Return. Repeat this process for the other two contributors.

7. Select the Ellipse tool, position the cursor over the zero point (look at the status bar to make sure you're on the zero point), hold down Option and Shift, and draw as large a circle as you can (without the edge of the circle extending past the outside edges of any of the triangles) at the center of the four triangles.

8. Use Intersect from the Path Operations submenu of the Arrange menu to create the pie wedges.

I admit that this isn't the most elegant process in the world—but it does work.

Perspective Projection

Perspective rendering (known as "central projection" in the smoke-filled back rooms of the technical illustration bars where I used to hang out) is a drawing technology dedicated to rendering an image in space much the same way as our eyes see things. Perspective rendering came into vogue during the renaissance (it wasn't invented then, it simply became fashionable) and we haven't yet found a better way of representing our three-dimensional world on two-dimensional media (such as computer screens and paper).

Perspective rendering relies on models of the physical positions of these items.

- The eye of the observer
- The object or objects being viewed
- The plane of projection
- The vanishing point or vanishing points

Scared yet? Don't be—just have a look at Figure 2-116.

The whole point is understanding where objects fall inside a frame (also called the plane of projection) which lies between you and the objects. The objects exist between the plane of projection and one or more vanishing points. When you look at a photograph, you're looking at an exercise in perspective rendering, frozen in time, where the piece of film is roughly equivalent to the plane of projection.

When did this book become a drafting class? About the time I discovered I couldn't explain how to do this stuff in FreeHand without defining some terms.

FIGURE 2-116
How perspective
rendering works

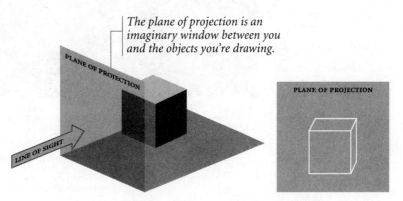

The plane of projection is an imaginary window between you and the objects you're drawing.

Purists will note that this is an isometric view.

What you see through the plane of projection.

Here's another way of looking at it.

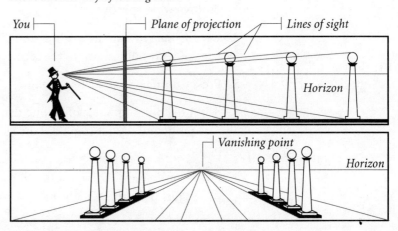

Single-View Perspective

Single-view perspective relies on a single vanishing point. You rarely see single-view perspective in the real world, because there's almost always more than one natural horizon in your field of view. The classic example of single-view perspective is that of a highway stretching into the distance on a perfectly flat plain (see Figure 2-117).

FIGURE 2-117
Single-view
perspective

Okay, so I added a few things.

To create guidelines for a single-view perspective in FreeHand, follow these steps (see Figure 2-118).

1. Designate a point as your vanishing point. Make this point your zero point. In most cases, this point should be around the vertical and horizontal center of your illustration. If it's not, you've got to ask yourself why you're not using multiview perspective.

2. Use the Line tool to draw a horizontal line from the left edge of your publication to the zero point.

3. Press Command-= to clone the line.

4. Select the point on the cloned line that's farthest from the zero point and drag it some distance up or down on the page.

5. Press Command-D to repeat the clone and drag operation you've just performed. Continue pressing Command-D

FIGURE 2-118
Creating a
perspective grid

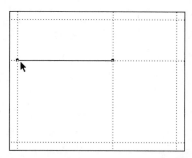 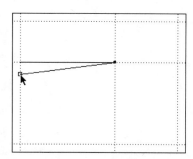

Draw a line.

Clone the line. Select the end point of the cloned line and drag it to a new position.

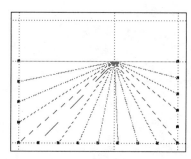

Repeat the clone-and-drag sequence until you have all of the guidelines you want.

Once you've created all of the guides you want, send them to the background to gray them out and make them inactive.

until you've created as many guidelines as you want. You'll probably have to adjust the end point from time to time to get the guidelines where you want them.

6. Select all of the lines you just drew and send them to a background layer. Now you can use them as drawing guides.

Blending and Single-View Perspective

You can use blends as an aid to perspective rendering, particularly if you've got a shape that starts near the plane of perspective and extends toward the vanishing point. You'd draw the nearest and farthest cross-sections of the object, and then blend between the two cross sections, as shown in Figure 2-119.

Multiview Perspective

Multiview perspective is much more like the way we see the world, because it uses more than one vanishing point. You can use the single-view perspective grid building techniques in multiview perspective—you just use more than one grid (see Figure 2-120).

FIGURE 2-119
Blending and
perspective drawing

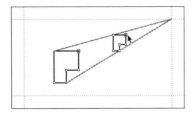

Select two reference points...   *...and blend.*

FIGURE 2-120
Multiview perspective

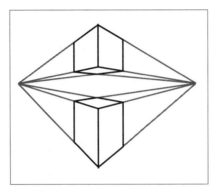

*Multiview perspective
depends on more than
one vanishing point.*

Oblique Projection

Unlike perspective projection, oblique projection is nothing like the way we see objects. It's an abstraction that's good for keeping measurements intact for manufacturing drawings, and it's also a good way to render a 3-D shape quickly.

In oblique projection, one face of an object is always against the plane of projection, and the horizontal lines in that object are always drawn 90 degrees from the vertical (what we normally think of as horizontal). The horizontal lines on the other sides of the object are always drawn at the same angle, rather than at angles that converge on a vanishing point. In oblique projection, 45 degrees, 30 degrees, and 60 degrees are commonly used angles.

The next trick of oblique projection is that the scale of the lines and objects drawn away from the plane of projection isn't foreshortened as they recede from the viewer but are drawn to a single, fixed scale.

Just to add some historical color, oblique projections in which measurements away from the plane of projection are rendered at full scale are called cavalier projections, because they were often used for drawing fortifications in renaissance and medieval times. Half-scale renderings are called cabinet projections because they were used by furniture builders (see Figure 2-121).

If you've been around the Macintosh-graphics community for long, you've seen lots of oblique projection—mainly because 45-degree lines offered the least jagged line you could get out of Mac-Paint. Early Macintosh artists created a style that's stuck with us—even now that we can draw smooth lines at any angle. I call this "Macintosh projection" (see Figure 2-122).

FIGURE 2-121
Oblique projection

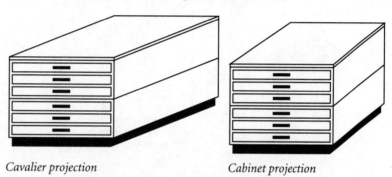

Cavalier projection   *Cabinet projection*

FIGURE 2-122
Macintosh projection

Creating a Grid for Oblique Projection

Creating grids for oblique projection drawing is easy in FreeHand. To create a grid for the most common oblique projection angle—45 degrees—use the Document Setup Inspector to set up a grid for your publication. When you draw paths, hold down Shift to constrain the angles in your drawing to 45-degree angles, and turn on Grid and Snap to Grid on the View menu. Figure 2-123 shows how it works.

If you want to create a grid for an oblique projection based on 30-degree angles, follow these steps (see Figure 2-124).

1. Create a new publication.

FIGURE 2-123
Grid for 45-degree
oblique projection

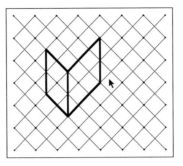

FIGURE 2-124
Grid for 30-degree
oblique projection

*Type "30" in the
Contsrain field in the
Setup Inspector.*

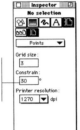

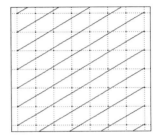

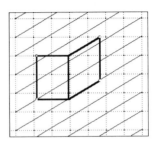

*Hold down Shift to
constrain lines as you
draw them.*

*Draw objects, using your
grid as a guide.*

2. Display the Setup Inspector.

3. Enter "30" in the Constrain field for the number of degrees,
   and then press Return.

4. Draw a series of hairlines (applying a color to them if you
   want) by placing the cursor at one of the visible grid points,
   holding down Shift, and drawing a line.

5. Select the grid of 30-degree lines you've drawn and send
   them to a specific layer. It can be either a foreground or
   background layer, depending on whether you like having a
   50-percent tint applied to your guidelines.

6. Create paths, using the grid as a reference as you draw.

If you want to create a grid for some other angle of oblique
projection, just enter that angle in the Constrain field, and draw a
series of guidelines.

Axonometric Projection

I'm sure that there are plenty of drafters that'd argue this one with me, but I think of axonometric projection as being about the same as oblique projection. In axonometric projection, the faces of the object are rotated away from the plane of perspective by some pair of different angles.

There are three types of axonometric projection: isometric, dimetric, and trimetric.

Isometric projection. In isometric projection, the object you're drawing has both of its primary axes rotated away from the plane of projection by the same angle (see Figure 2-125).

You can create grids for isometric projection using the same technique described for creating an oblique projection above, but you'll use only the grid lines—and not the horizontal guides— to draw horizontal lines perpendicular to the major axes of the object. All right, that's pretty abstruse. Figure 2-124 shows what I mean.

Circles in isometric projection are rendered as ellipses.

FIGURE 2-125
Isometric projection

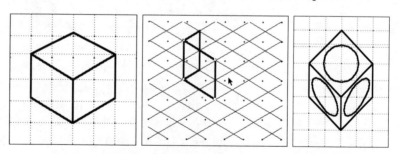

Horizontal lines in
isometric projection

Circles become
ellipses in isometric
projection

Dimetric projection. In dimetric projection, the object you're drawing has both of its primary axes rotated away from the plane of projection by different angles (see Figure 2-126). For this type of projection, the grid you create should have one angle going from left to right, and another, different angle going from right to left.

FIGURE 2-126
Dimetric projection

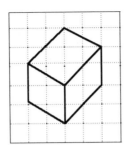

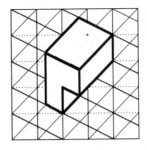

Grids in dimetric projection

Trimetric projection. You guessed it, in trimetric projection, the axes of the object you're drawing are rotated at three different angles from the plane of projection. I never really have figured out how trimetric projection differs from dimetric projection. Once again, you can create a grid that has one angle going from left to right, and another, different angle going from right to left.

Drawing Conclusions

Earlier in this chapter, I noted that I was confused by FreeHand's approach to drawing when I first encountered it. As I worked with the tools, however, I found that the parts of my brain that were used to using rapidographs (an obsolete type of pen used by the ancient Greeks), curves, and rulers quickly adapted to the new drawing environment. Eventually, I realized that this was the easier way to draw.

Then, after reading a related article in a tabloid at the supermarket, it dawned on me that the archaic methods I'd learned were nothing less than an extraterrestrial plot—forced on us in classical antiquity by evil space gods, and to some cosmic purpose which I cannot—as yet—reveal.

Just keep at it.

When you're lying awake with a dismal headache, and repose is taboo'd by anxiety, I conceive you may use any language you choose to indulge in, without any impropriety; for your brain is on fire—the bedclothes conspire of usual slumber to plunder you: first your counterpane goes, and uncovers your toes, and your sheet slips demurely from under you; then the blanketing tickles—you feel like mixed pickles—so terribly sharp is the pricking, and you're hot, and you're cross, and you tumble and toss till there's nothing 'twixt you and the ticking.

Then the bedclothes all creep to the ground in a heap, and you pick 'em all up in a tangle; next your pillow resigns and politely declines to remain at its usual angle! Well, you get some repose in the form of a doze, with hot eye-balls and head ever aching, but your slumbering teems with such horrible dreams that you'd very much better be waking; for you dream you are crossing the Channel, and tossing about in a steamer from Harwich—which is something between a large bathing machine and a very small second-class carriage—and you're giving a treat (penny ice and cold meat) to a party of friends and relations—they're a ravenous horde—and they all came on board at Sloane Square and South Kensington Stations.

And bound on that journey you find your attorney (who started that morning from Devon); he's a bit undersized, and you don't feel surprised when he tells you he's only eleven. Well, you're driving like mad with this singular lad (by the bye, the ship's now a four-wheeler), and you're playing round games, and he calls you bad names when you tell him that "ties pay the dealer;" but this you can't stand, so you throw up your hand, and you find you're as cold as an icicle, in your shirt and your socks (the black silk with gold clocks), crossing Salisbury Plain on a bicycle: and he and the crew are on bicycles too—which they've somehow or other invested in—and he's telling the tars all the particulars of a company he's interested in—it's a scheme of devices, to get at low prices all goods from cough mixtures to cables (which tickled the sailors), by treating retailers as though they were all vegetables—you get a good spadesman to plant a small tradesman (first take off his boots with a boot-tree), and his legs will take root, and his fingers will shoot, and they'll blossom and bud like a fruit-tree—from the greengrocer tree you get grapes and green pea, cauliflower, pineapple, and cranberries, while the pastrycook plant cherry brandy will grant, apple puffs, and three-corners, and Banbury's—you'll find you're as ready as ever you can be—you're a regular wreck, with a crick in your neck, and no wonder you snore, for your head's on the floor, and you've needles and pins from your soles to your shins, and your flesh is a-creep, for your left leg's asleep, and you've cramp in your toes, and a fly on your nose, and some fluff in your lung, and a feverish tongue, and a thirst that's intense, and a general sense that you haven't been sleeping in clover; but the darkness has passed, and it's daylight at last, and the night has been long—ditto ditto my song—and thank goodness they're both of them over!

Ruddigore

The Grand Duke

UTOPIA LIMITED

CHAPTER

Text and Type

3

IOLANTHE

Words.

Somehow, we can never quite get away from them. In academic circles, debate continues on whether we're born with the ability to understand language, or whether it's something we're taught. I don't know the answer, and, most of the time, I don't even know which side of the debate I'm on. What I do know is that language is the most important technology we humans have yet developed.

As I mentioned at the start of the last chapter, FreeHand serves the language of drawing very well. Does FreeHand neglect text in favor of points and paths, strokes, and fills? Not anymore—FreeHand 4 gives you almost all of the text-formatting tools you could ever ask for (though I'm still asking for paragraph and character styles). If you consider Convert to Paths a character format, FreeHand provides more character-formatting flexibility than any page-layout program.

This chapter is all about working with text and type in FreeHand. Why do I say "text and type?" What's the difference? To me, "text" means content—the stream of characters, words, sentences, and paragraphs in a publication and how they're organized. "Type," on the other hand, means how the characters of text look—their font, size, color, and paragraph formatting.

There are areas of overlap between these definitions—for example, entering a column-break character (which is really text editing) forces text to the top of the next available column—which does change the appearance of the text. It gets confusing. I've tried to cover things in order: first create some text, then arrange it on the page, and then format it. In the last part of the chapter, I'll discuss various commands and procedures that change text into something that's not quite text: text that's bound to a path, or text that's been converted into paths.

Entering and Editing Text

Before we can work with text, we've got to create some. In Free-Hand 4—unlike previous versions of FreeHand—this is easy to do: Select the Text tool from the toolbox (or press A), click the tool in the publication window, and type (see Figure 3-1). FreeHand creates a text block and enters the characters you type in the text block. For FreeHand 3 users, this should be a thrill—no more trips to the Text dialog box to enter and edit text (I admit, however, that there are times I wish it were still around).

FIGURE 3-1
Entering text

To enter text, click or drag
the Text tool in the
publication window…

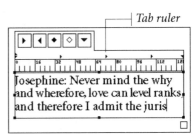

…and type. The tab ruler and tab
icons appear at the top of the text
block you've created.

Clicking to create a text block creates a text block that's a fixed size (18 picas wide by 12 picas tall). Instead of clicking to create a text block, I drag the Text tool—when I do this, FreeHand creates a text block that's the width and height I specified by dragging (see Figure 3-2).

The text in a FreeHand publication exists inside text blocks (see Figure 3-3). A text block can contain any number of different character formats, type effects, paragraph specifications, or colors.

Text blocks can also contain up to 100 columns or rows (see Figure 3-4). Columns break a text block into evenly spaced horizontal

FIGURE 3-2
Drag-creating
a text block

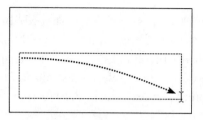

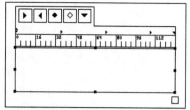

Drag the Text tool on the page...

...and FreeHand creates a text block that's the width and height you specified by dragging.

FIGURE 3-3
Text blocks

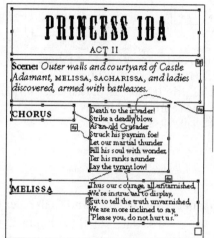

Link boxes attached to each text block show you if the text block is linked to any other text blocks. The goofy lines show you which text block it's linked to.

FIGURE 3-4
Columns, rows,
and cells

A column

A row

A cell

Trial By Jury		
A NOVEL AND ENTIRELY ORIGINAL DRAMATIC CANTATA, IN ONE ACT		
AS PERFORMED MARCH 25, 1875 AT THE ROYALTY THEATRE, LONDON		
THE LEARNED JUDGE	Baritone	Frederic Sullivan
THE COUNSEL FOR THE PLAINTIFF	Baritone	J. Hollingsworth
THE DEFENDANT	Tenor	Walter H. Fisher
THE FOREMAN OF THE JURY	Baritone	Charles Kelleher
THE USHER	Bass-Baritone	B. R. Pepper
THE ASSOCIATE	Non-singing	Unknown
THE PLAINTIFF	Soprano	Nelly Bromley

sections. Rows break the text block up vertically. I call the area of intersection between a row and a column a "cell." You can think of each cell in a text block as a miniature text block, complete with margins.

Text blocks can be resized, reshaped, and otherwise manipulated in a variety of other ways, and we'll talk more about them in "Working with Text Blocks," later in this chapter.

When you create or select a text block, FreeHand displays three things around the text block: the tab ruler, the text box selection handles, the link box (see Figure 3-5).

FIGURE 3-5
Text block controls

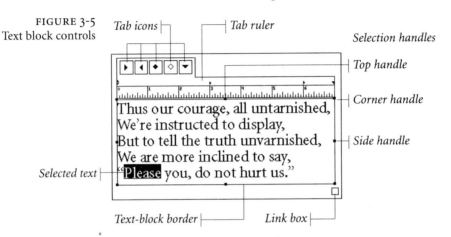

Tab icons   Tab ruler   Selection handles

Top handle

Corner handle

Side handle

Thus our courage, all untarnished,
We're instructed to display,
But to tell the truth unvarnished,
We are more inclined to say,
Selected text — "Please you, do not hurt us."

Text-block border   Link box

The tab ruler. You use FreeHand's tab ruler to set indents and tabs (see "Setting Tabs," later in this chapter). You won't see the tab ruler if your current magnification is less than 45 percent.

Selection handles. You use text block selection handles to resize the text block and to change the formatting of the text inside the text block (see "Working with Text Blocks," later in this chapter).

The link box. The link box, which appears below the lower-right corner of the text block, gives you the ability to link the text block to, or unlink the text block from, other text blocks or paths (see "Linking Text Blocks," later in this chapter).

If a text block contains more text than is currently displayed, you'll see a filled circle inside the text block's link box. When a text block is linked to any other text blocks or paths, you'll see a link symbol in the text block's link box (see Figure 3-6).

You can link text blocks to other text blocks and to open or closed paths. In this book, I'll refer to all of the text in a series of

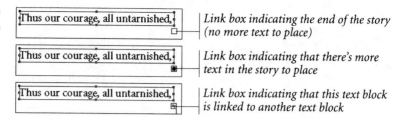

FIGURE 3-6
Link box icons

Link box indicating the end of the story
(no more text to place)

Link box indicating that there's more
text in the story to place

Link box indicating that this text block
is linked to another text block

linked text blocks (including text that isn't in any text block), as a story. Text that doesn't fit within a series of linked boxes I call "overset" or "unplaced" text.

You don't have to add text to the text blocks you create—you can leave empty text blocks on your page until you have text to add to them. This way, you can work on your publication's layout—including setting up links between text blocks—without necessarily having the publication's copy on hand.

Tip:
Applying
Formatting to
Text Blocks

When you want to apply the same formatting—character or paragraph—to all of the text inside a text block, select the text block using the Pointer tool and then apply formatting using the Type Specifications palette and the type-related sections of the Inspector palette. You don't have to select text with the Text tool to apply formatting.

Tip:
Finding Empty
Text Blocks

If you've lost track of an empty text block, switch to Keyline view. FreeHand displays the boundaries of text blocks in Keyline view.

**Moving Your
Cursor Through
Text**

When you're typing text into a text block, you shouldn't have to take your hands off the keyboard to move the cursor. While Free-Hand 4's cursor movement shortcuts aren't perfect (it'd be great to have cursor movement more like that found in PageMaker or Word), they can come in handy (see Table 3-1).

Tip:
Switch to the
Text Tool by
Clicking

Double-click a text block with the Pointer tool to position a text cursor at the end of the text block. This is the same as switching to the Text tool and clicking an insertion point at the end of the text, but it's quicker.

	Press	To move to
TABLE 3-1 Cursor movement keyboard shortcuts	Right Arrow	Next character
	Left Arrow	Previous character
	Up Arrow	Previous line
	Down Arrow	Next line
	Command-Right Arrow	Next word
	Command-Left Arrow	Previous word
	Command-Up Arrow	Previous line
	Command-Down Arrow	Next line

Selecting Text

As in most Macintosh word processing programs, pressing Shift as you press cursor movement keys selects text as you move the cursor (Command-Shift-Right Arrow, for example, selects the next word in the story). Also, as you'd expect, dragging a text cursor through text selects the text you drag over. In addition, you can use the following shortcuts.

◆ Double-click a word with the Text tool to select the word.

◆ Triple-click in a text block with the Text tool to select all of the text in the current paragraph.

◆ Triple-click a text block with the Pointer tool to select all of the text in story (same as triple-clicking with the Text tool).

◆ Press Command-A when you have a text insertion point active in a story to select all of the text in the story.

Entering Special Characters

What makes a special character special? Is it something innate, or is it upbringing? In FreeHand, it's hard to tell—some of the characters listed on the Special Characters submenu of the Type menu are active—they "tell" FreeHand to break a line or a column at a specific place. Some of the characters on the list, on the other hand, enter a character that's really no different from any other text character you can type, except that it doesn't appear printed on your keyboard. Table 3-2 shows you what FreeHand's special characters do when you enter them in text.

While you can use the Special Characters submenu of the Type menu to enter special characters in your text, I prefer typing the characters from the keyboard (after all, that's where my hands are when I'm working with text). Table 3-3 shows keyboard shortcuts for FreeHand's special characters.

TABLE 3-2
Special characters and
what they do

Character	What it does
End of column	Tells FreeHand to break the text following that character, and start the next line of text at the start of the next available column in the story. If no column is available, FreeHand stores the text as overset text and displays a solid circle in the text block's link box.
End of line	Breaks the line at the point you entered it (like a carriage return), but, unlike a carriage return, doesn't start a new paragraph. End-of-line characters are great when you're working with tables.
Nonbreaking space	Keeps the words on either side of the character together, on the same line. If you don't want FreeHand to break a line between "H.M.S." and "Pinafore," for example, enter a nonbreaking space between the two words. This space expands or contracts based on the kerning, letterspacing, and wordspacing applied to the line it appears in.
Em space	A fixed space (that is, it doesn't change size depending on the surrounding kerning, letterspacing, and wordspacing) equal in width to the point size applied to the character. An em space set to a size of 12 points is 12 points wide.

TABLE 3-2
Special characters
and what they do
(continued)

Character	What it does
En space	A fixed space equal to half an em space. A 12-point en space is 6 points wide.
Thin space	A thin space is equal to one-tenth of an em space. A 12-point thin space is 1.2 points wide.
Em dash	A dash equal to the width of an em space.
En dash	A dash equal to the width of an en space.
Discretionary hyphen	Or "dishy"—tells FreeHand that it can hyphenate the word at the point you enter the special character, if necessary. If FreeHand doesn't break the word, it doesn't display the hyphen. Whenever possible (that is, any time the character following the hyphenation point is anything other than a return or end-of-line character), use discretionary hyphens rather than entering a hyphen in your text.

TABLE 3-3
Typing special
characters

Special character	What you press
End of column	Command-Shift-Enter
End of line	Shift-Enter
Nonbreaking space	Option-spacebar
Em space	Command-Shift-M
En space	Command-Shift-N
Thin space	Command-Shift-T
Em dash	Option-Shift-hyphen
En dash	Option-hyphen
Discretionary hyphen	Command-hyphen

Working with Text Blocks

Once you've created a text block, you can work with it just as you can anything else on the FreeHand page and pasteboard. You can rotate text blocks, scale them, reflect them, skew them, group and ungroup them, and apply colors to them. You cannot, however, paste objects inside the characters of a text block without first converting the text to paths (see "Converting Characters into Paths," later in this chapter).

Copying and Pasting Text

In FreeHand 3, you couldn't select a text block with the Pointer tool, cut it, and then paste its contents inside another text block. Similarly, you couldn't copy text you selected with the Text tool and paste it as a text block. In FreeHand 4, you can do both, as shown in the next two procedures.

If you want to copy some text from an existing text block into a new text block, select the text using the Text tool, and then press Command-C to copy the text to the Clipboard. Press Command-Tab to deselect the current text block and press Command-V. Free-Hand creates a new text block and pastes the text you copied to the Clipboard into it (see Figure 3-7).

FIGURE 3-7
Creating a new
text block from
existing text

*Select the text you
want to turn into an
independent text block.*

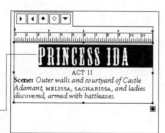

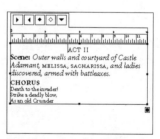

Cut the text to the Clipboard.

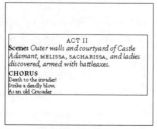

*Press Command-Tab to
deselect the text block.*

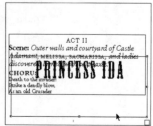

*Paste the new text block into
your publication.*

If you want to copy the contents of a text block into another text block, select the first text block with the Pointer tool and press Command-C to copy (or Command-X to cut) the text block to the Clipboard. Press A to select the Text tool, and click the Text tool in the second text block at the position you want to paste the text, then press Command-V to paste. FreeHand pastes the contents of the first text block into the second text block (see Figure 3-8).

FIGURE 3-8
Inserting text blocks

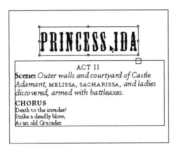

Select a text block with
the Pointer tool.

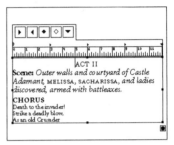

Cut or copy the text block to the
Clipboard.

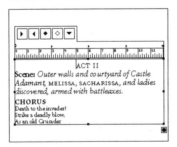

Click the Text tool where you
want to insert the text.

Paste the text into the text block.

Resizing text blocks. You can use the selection handles on a text block to resize the text block itself, resize the text inside the text block, change the kerning of the text, adjust the wordspacing used inside the text block, and change the leading of all of the lines inside the text block, as shown in Table 3-4 and Figure 3-9.

Changing the shape of a text block by dragging a corner handle recomposes the lines of text inside the text block. You don't have to enter carriage returns, end-of-line characters, or (don't even think about it!) tabs to break lines, unless you really want a line break at that specific point in your text, and want it there regardless of any changes you might make.

TABLE 3-4
Working with text-
block handles

To do this	Do this
Resize the text block	Drag a corner handle
Resize the text block proportionally	Drag a corner handle while holding down Shift
Resize the text while resizing the text block	Drag a corner handle while holding down Option
Proportionally resize the text and the text block	Drag a corner handle while holding down Shift and Option
Change the leading of text inside a text block	Drag the top or bottom handle of the text block*
Change the kerning of text inside a text block	Drag a side handle*
Adjust the wordspacing of text inside a text block	Hold down Option and drag a side handle*

* Only applies to a single-column text block

You can also use text block selection handles as a method of moving the text block. Why would you want to do this? It's some-times be difficult to drag a text block into a precise position. It always seems to snap to the wrong grid mark or ruler guide. You can get around this by simply dragging one of the corner handles to the point you want to move the text block, then adjusting the other handles (see Figure 3-10).

**Tip:
Resizing Text
Blocks to Fit Text**

To make a single-column shrink to the size of the text it contains, double-click the text block's link box with the Pointer tool. Free-Hand resizes the text block.

**Tip:
Resizing Text
Blocks Using the
Inspector**

If you want to make a text block a specific size, use the Inspector. Select the text block, then display the Object Inspector by pressing Command-Option-B (if the Inspector palette isn't currently vis-ible, you'll have to press Command-I first). In the Object Inspector for the text block, enter the width and height you want for the text block in the W (width) and H (height) fields, and press Return to apply your changes. FreeHand sizes the text block to the dimen-sions you specified.

FIGURE 3-9
Working with text
block selection handles

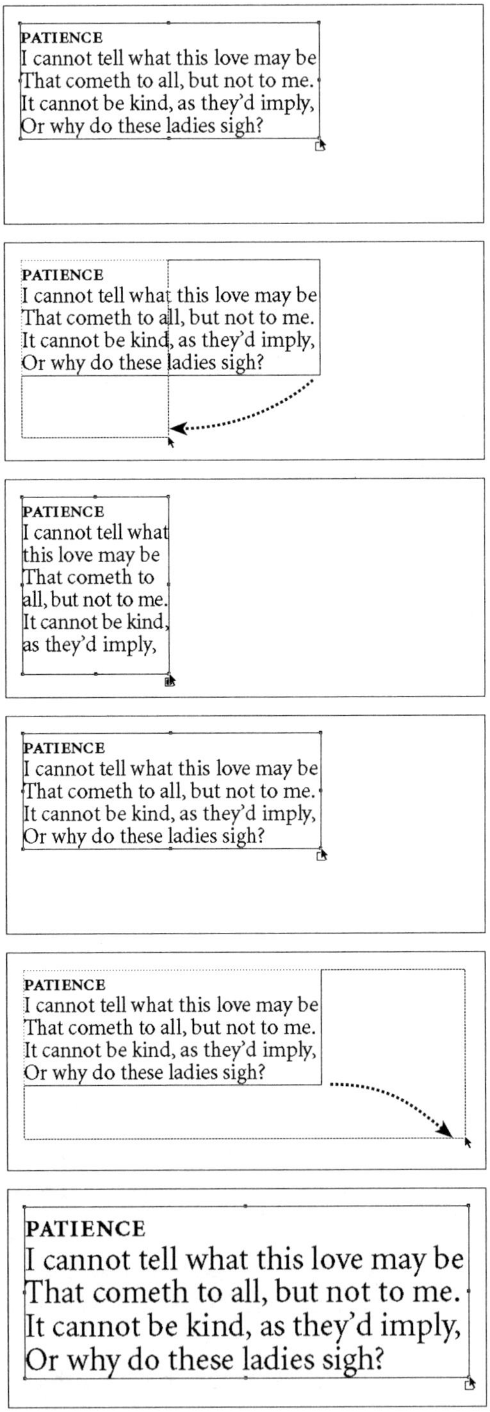

PATIENCE
I cannot tell what this love may be
That cometh to all, but not to me.
It cannot be kind, as they'd imply,
Or why do these ladies sigh?

To change the size of the text block...

PATIENCE
I cannot what this love may be
That cometh to all, but not to me.
It cannot be kind, as they'd imply,
Or why do these ladies sigh?

...drag a corner handle.

PATIENCE
I cannot tell what
this love may be
That cometh to
all, but not to me.
It cannot be kind,
as they'd imply,

FreeHand resizes the text block, reflowing the text inside the text block to fit the new shape.

PATIENCE
I cannot tell what this love may be
That cometh to all, but not to me.
It cannot be kind, as they'd imply,
Or why do these ladies sigh?

To change the size of the text inside a text block...

PATIENCE
I cannot tell what this love may be
That cometh to all, but not to me.
It cannot be kind, as they'd imply,
Or why do these ladies sigh?

...hold down Option and drag a corner handle (hold down Shift and Option as you drag to resize the text proportionally).

PATIENCE
I cannot tell what this love may be
That cometh to all, but not to me.
It cannot be kind, as they'd imply,
Or why do these ladies sigh?

FreeHand resizes the text and the block.

FIGURE 3-9
Working with text
block selection handles
(continued)

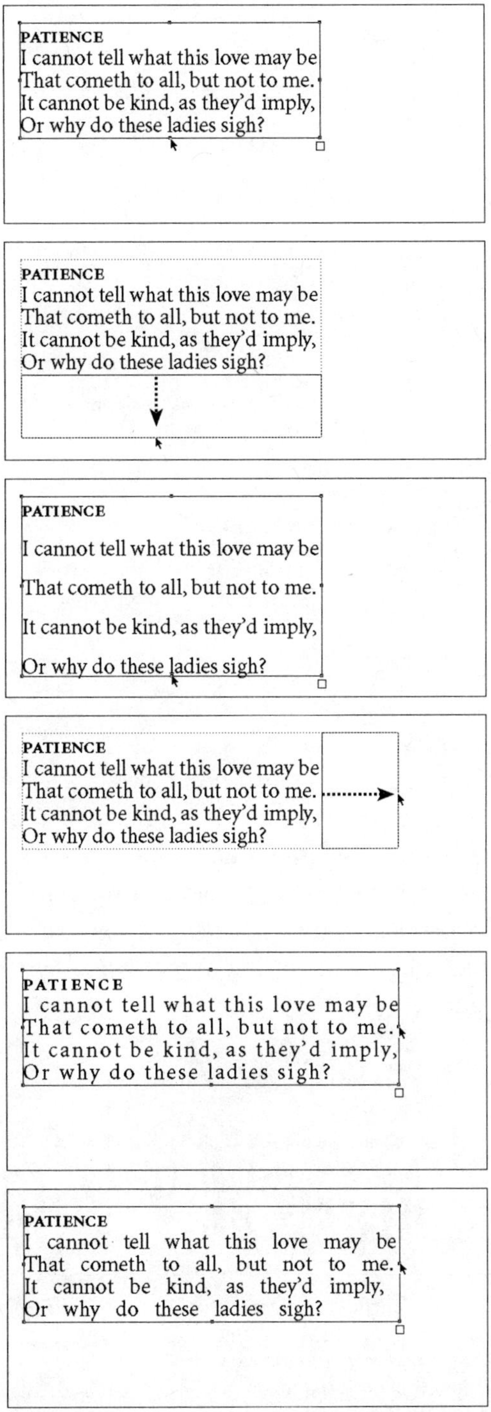

PATIENCE
I cannot tell what this love may be
That cometh to all, but not to me.
It cannot be kind, as they'd imply,
Or why do these ladies sigh?

*To change the leading of
the text in a text block…*

PATIENCE
I cannot tell what this love may be
That cometh to all, but not to me.
It cannot be kind, as they'd imply,
Or why do these ladies sigh?

*…drag a bottom or top
handle.*

PATIENCE
I cannot tell what this love may be
That cometh to all, but not to me.
It cannot be kind, as they'd imply,
Or why do these ladies sigh?

*FreeHand changes the
leading of the text in the
text block.*

PATIENCE
I cannot tell what this love may be
That cometh to all, but not to me.
It cannot be kind, as they'd imply,
Or why do these ladies sigh?

*To change the range
kerning of text in a text
block, drag a side handle.*

PATIENCE
I cannot tell what this love may be
That cometh to all, but not to me.
It cannot be kind, as they'd imply,
Or why do these ladies sigh?

*FreeHand increases or
decreases the range
kerning of the text inside
the text block.*

PATIENCE
I cannot tell what this love may be
That cometh to all, but not to me.
It cannot be kind, as they'd imply,
Or why do these ladies sigh?

*Hold down Option as you
drag a side handle, and
FreeHand changes the
wordspacing of the text in
the text block.*

FIGURE 3-10
Moving text blocks by
dragging handles

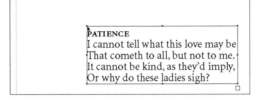

*If you're having trouble
moving a text block to a
new location...*

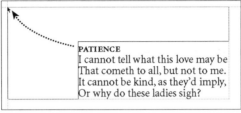

...drag a corner handle...

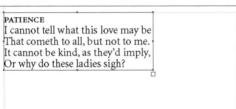

*...and adjust the shape of
the text block once you've
got one corner where you
want it.*

Tip:
Making
Text Blocks
Transparent

When you click an insertion point in a text block, FreeHand makes the background of the text block opaque white, by default. If you want to see what's behind a text block (assuming that the text block doesn't have a fill applied to it), or if you want to see the text block's background color (if the text block has a fill applied to it), check Buffered Drawing in the Display Preferences dialog box (see Figure 3-11).

FIGURE 3-11
Seeing through
text blocks

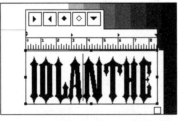

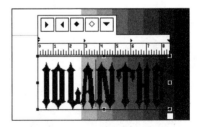

*When you turn off Buffered
Drawing in the Display Preferences
dialog box, FreeHand draws a
white box behind the text block
containing the cursor.*

*Turn Buffered Drawing on, and
you'll be able to see through the text
block as you enter or edit text.*

Tip:
Deselecting
Text Blocks

When you're editing text, you can't press Tab to deselect the text block; pressing Tab enters tab characters in the text block (which you probably don't want). Instead, hold down Command and press Tab, and FreeHand deselects the text block. Pressing Command-Tab does the same thing with any tool or object selected as Tab does, so I've gotten in the habit of pressing Command-Tab to deselect all objects. This way, I only have to remember one shortcut.

Linking Text Blocks

FreeHand's text blocks, like PageMaker's, can be linked together so that text can flow from one text block to another. By linking text blocks, you can create articles that span several magazine pages, or different panels in a brochure. Linking and unlinking text blocks, like just about everything else in FreeHand 4, is a drag-and-drop process (see Figure 3-12).

1. Select a text block.

2. Position the cursor over the link box and drag a line to the interior of another text block.

3. Release the mouse button to drop the link. You've just linked the two text blocks.

4. To see the effect of the link between the text blocks, size the first text block so that it's too small to have all of the text you entered. The text appears in the second text block you created.

FIGURE 3-12
Linking text blocks

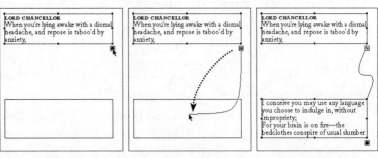

Position the Pointer tool over a text block's link box.

Drag a line out of the link box and drop it into another text block (example shown in Keyline view for clarity).

FreeHand links the two text blocks, flowing any overset text from the first text block into the second text block.

Unlinking text blocks is just as easy—select the text block before the text block you want to unlink, and then drag a line from the text block's link box to an empty area on the page or pasteboard. Linked text, if any, flows back into the other text blocks in the selected story (see Figure 3-13).

Alternatively, you can break a link between text blocks by deleting one of the text blocks. If the text block you deleted isn't the last text block in the story, FreeHand flows the text from the text block into the next text block in the story. If the text block you deleted is at the end of the story, FreeHand stores the text in the last text block in the story (as overset text).

FIGURE 3-13
Unlinking text blocks

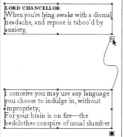  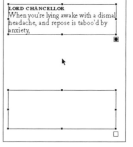

Position the Pointer tool over a text block's link box (examples shown in Keyline view).

Drag a line out of the link box and drop it on an empty area in the publication window.

FreeHand unlinks the text blocks, storing any overset text in the first text block.

Multicolumn and Multirow Text Blocks

A FreeHand text block can contain up to 100 rows and 100 columns. Any time you look at a FreeHand text block, you'll see at least one column and one row—you can't have fewer.

Multicolumn text blocks are pretty familiar from a variety of programs, but multirow text blocks may take some getting used to. In essence, they let you set up any text block as a big table. You can think of each cell inside a text block as a smaller text block, with its own margins and border. All of the cells inside a text block have the same margin and border properties, and have whatever background fill you've applied to the entire text block.

How do you add rows and columns to FreeHand's text blocks? Use the Column Inspector (see Figure 3-14).

1. Select a text block using the Pointer tool.

FIGURE 3-14
Multicolumn
text blocks

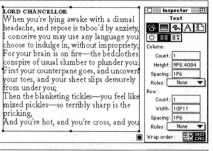

Press Command-Option-R to display the Column Inspector (if the Inspector isn't already visible, you'll have to display it by pressing Command-I).

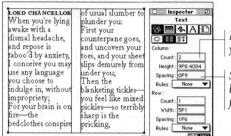

Enter the number of columns you want in the Count field.

Set the distance you want between columns in the Spacing field.

2. Press Command-Option-R to display the Column Inspector (if it's not already visible).

3. In the Column Inspector, enter the specifications you want for your rows and columns. Columns divide the text block evenly—you can't have columns of unequal width in FreeHand 4 (unless you use wrapping tabs, as shown in "Setting Tabs," later in this chapter).

The height of the rows in a text block depends on the amount of text inside each row. You can make rows taller by adding end-of-line characters in the text if you want. You can make rows taller by entering a number in the Column Height field that's larger than the height of the tallest cell in the text block (see Figure 3-15).

If you're the type of designer who prefers to work with columns of a specific width, you can specify the width of columns in Free-Hand's text blocks using the Column Inspector. It's a little confusing: the Column section of the Inspector doesn't include a setting for width—it includes a setting for the height of the columns in the text block. Instead, you enter the column width in the Width field in the Row section of the Inspector (see Figure 3-16). This makes a little more sense when you're working with a multirow text block, such as one containing a table.

FIGURE 3-15
Controlling row height

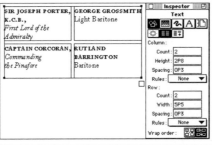

Enter a new value in the
Column Height field to make
a text block's rows taller or
shorter.

FIGURE 3-16
Specfiying column
widths

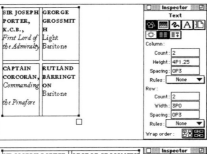

Enter a new value in the Row
Width field to make the
columns in a text block wider
or narrower.

Note that, as you'd expect, changing the column widths (or row heights) of a text block also changes the width (or height) of the text block.

You can control the order in which FreeHand flows text inside the columns and rows in a text block using the buttons at the bottom of the Column Inspector (see Figure 3-17).

FIGURE 3-17
Text flow order

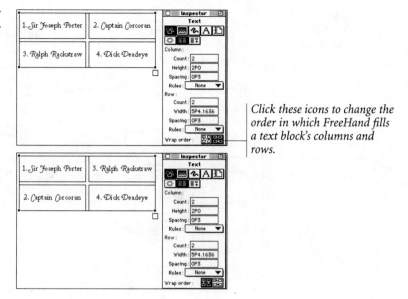

Click these icons to change the order in which FreeHand fills a text block's columns and rows.

Borders and Fills for Text Blocks

Here's how to add a border or a background fill to your text blocks (see Figure 3-18).

1. Select a text block using the Pointer tool.

2. Press Command-Option-B to display the Object Inspector.

3. Check the Display Border box.

4. Format the border and the background fill of the text block using the Fill Inspector (press Command-Option-F) and the Stroke Inspector (press Command-Option-L).

You can also set the background fill of a text block by selecting the text block with the Pointer tool and then dropping a color swatch on it. For more on applying fills using drag-and-drop, see Chapter 6, "Color."

Adding Borders to Rows, Columns, or Cells

You use the popup menus in the Column Inspector to add rules around cells (the text areas created by the intersection of rows and columns) at either the column's full height (or the row's full width) or at the inset you've specified (the inset distances are the same as you specified for the entire text block). Confused? Take a look at Figure 3-19.

FIGURE 3-18
Adding borders
to text blocks

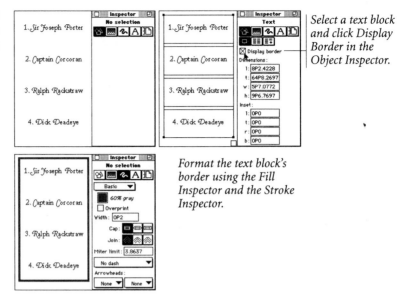

Select a text block
and click Display
Border in the
Object Inspector.

Format the text block's
border using the Fill
Inspector and the Stroke
Inspector.

A few things about column rules:

◆ Column rules don't convert to paths when you convert the text block containing them (they disappear).

◆ In the Column section, choose Full Height if you want your column rules to extend to the top and bottom edges of the text block. Choose Inset if you want the column rules to stop inside the cell (the Inset distances—from each edge of the cell—are the same as the text block's margins).

◆ In the Row section of the Column Inspector, choose Full Width from the popup menu to make the rules attached to the rows of the text block extend to the right and left edges of your text block. Choose Inset if you want the rules to stop, in each cell, at the cell's margin.

To add borders to the rows and/or columns in a text block, follow these steps.

1. Select a multicolumn text block.

2. If the Column Inspector's not already open, display it by pressing Command-Option-R.

FIGURE 3-19
Adding cell borders

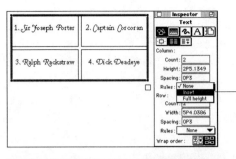

To add vertical rules around the cells in a text block, select Inset or Full Height from the popup menu in the Column section of the Column Inspector.

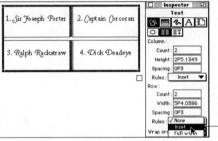

To add horizontal rules around the cells in a text block, select Inset or Full Height from the popup menu in the Columns section of the Column Inspector.

Inset positions rules inside the cell. The rules are inset from the edges of the cell the same distance as the inset distances specified in the Object Inspector.

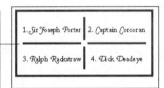

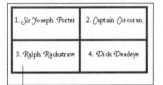

Full Height and Full Width draw rules the height or width of the cell.

3. Use the two Rules popup menus to choose the type of rules you want.

4. Press Return to apply your changes.

Tip:
If You Can't
See Your Text
Block's Border

If you've applied a stroke to a text block and still can't see the border, make sure you've checked Display Border in the Object Inspector for the text block. If Display Border is checked, and you still can't see your border when you select the text block, check Buffered Drawing in the Display Preferences dialog box. If the border you've applied to a text block is smaller than one point wide, you won't see it when you have the text box selected—it's smaller than the text block boundary FreeHand displays when you select a text block.

Tip:
Balancing
Columns

When you want to distribute your text evenly between a number of columns, so that each column contains the same number of lines of text, try this—check the Balance box in the Copyfit Inspector (press Command-Option-C to display the Copyfit Inspector if it's not visible). FreeHand tries to put an equal amount of text in each column in the current text block (or story, if the text block's linked to other text blocks), while keeping in mind the other settings for the text in the text block (see Figure 3-20). The number you enter in the Lines Together field in the Paragraph Inspector affects FreeHand's ability to balance columns.

FIGURE 3-20
Balancing columns

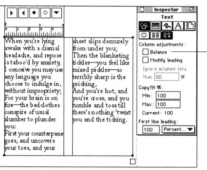

When you check Balance...

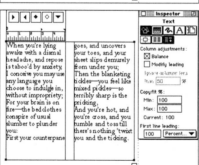

...FreeHand distributes the text in the story between the available columns.

If you set the Lines Together value for this paragraph to "2" (in the Paragraph Inspector), FreeHand takes that value into account when balancing the columns—in this case, it means the columns won't balance as well.

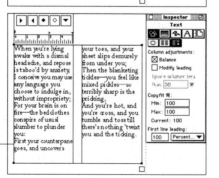

Character Formatting

Character formatting is all about controlling the way the individual letters, symbols, or punctuation of your text look. Font, type style, type size, color, and text effect are all aspects of character formatting.

I refer to all formatting that can be applied to a selected range of text as "character" formatting, and refer to formatting that Free-Hand applies at the paragraph level as "paragraph" formatting. There are definite areas of overlap in these definitions, as well. Leading, for example, is really a property that applies to an entire line of text (FreeHand uses only one leading value for a line of text), but I'll call it "character" formatting, nonetheless.

First off, let me say that while there are loads of commands on the submenus of the Type menu, I only make or change type specifications through the Type Specifications palette (see Figure 3-21). Why? Try selecting a font, type style, and size using the Font, Size, and Leading submenus a few times.

As soon as you're tired of that, display the Type Specifications palette (press Command-T if the Type Specifications palette isn't visible) and try the following steps (see Figure 3-22).

1. Press Command-~ to move to the Font field.

2. Type the first few letters of the font name you want (stop typing when FreeHand matches the font name).

3. Press Tab to move to the Type Style field.

4. Type "i" for Italic, "b" for bold, "p" for plain, or "boldi" for bold italic.

5. Press Tab to move to the Type Size field.

6. Type a number for the size of your type and press Enter to apply your changes.

FreeHand formats the text as you've specified.

FIGURE 3-21
Type Specifications
palette

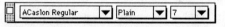

FIGURE 3-22
Changing type
specifications

Select the text you
want to format.

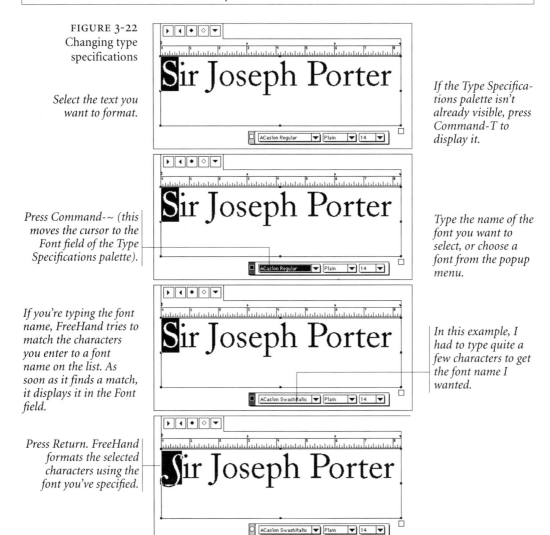

*If the Type Specifica-
tions palette isn't
already visible, press
Command-T to
display it.*

*Press Command-~ (this
moves the cursor to the
Font field of the Type
Specifications palette).*

*Type the name of the
font you want to
select, or choose a
font from the popup
menu.*

*If you're typing the font
name, FreeHand tries to
match the characters
you enter to a font
name on the list. As
soon as it finds a match,
it displays it in the Font
field.*

*In this example, I
had to type quite a
few characters to get
the font name I
wanted.*

*Press Return. FreeHand
formats the selected
characters using the
font you've specified.*

Even though the steps, when written down, sound like they'd take longer, they're much quicker—and your hands stay on the keyboard, ready to enter or select more text. Best of all, you don't have to follow those little arrows off the side of the menu and then track down the number or name you want on the submenu that pops out.

Font   To apply a particular font to text you've selected, type the name of the font you want in the Font field in the Type Specifications palette, or use the attached popup list of font names (or, if you prefer, choose the font name from the Font submenu of the Type menu). As you type, FreeHand displays the names of fonts in your system that match the characters you type. Once the font name you want appears in the field, you can stop typing. At that point, you can press Tab to move to the next field in the Type Specifications palette, or press Return to apply your font change.

Tip:
Getting the Fonts
You Ask For

This sounds pretty simple, but beware—imagesetters and different page layout programs can become confused when you specify the specialized screen font for bold, italic, or bold italic versions of a particular font.

This also makes changing fonts easier—you can change from one font to another and retain any formatting you've done using type styles. For example, you could change a text block from Minion Regular to Bodoni Book without losing italics you'd applied to individual words (their font would change, but their type style wouldn't).

How can you tell which of the screen fonts are the specialized versions? This gets very tricky. To specify Times Bold, for example, you want to choose Times, and then make it bold by choosing Bold from the Style popup menu, rather than choosing the screen font "B Times Bold." Stone Serif, on the other hand, contains two bold weights: Semibold and Bold. When you make the roman screen font for Stone Serif ("1StoneSerif") bold, you get Stone Semibold. To get the bold weight, you need to choose the screen font for Stone Serif Bold ("B1StoneSerifBold").

There's nothing for it but to experiment with the fonts you've got. If you're getting substituted fonts (usually Courier or Times) when you're trying to print a bold, italic, or bold italic version of a font, you've probably chosen the specialized screen font. Try choosing the roman version of the font, applying the type style you want, and printing again.

Why does this happen? It's history, really—the history of type on the Macintosh. See Appendix A, "System."

Tip:
Don't Be
Compulsive

When you select text that has more than one font, type style, or size applied to it, the fields in the Type Specifications palette corresponding to those attributes go blank (see Figure 3-23). Don't let this worry you—and don't fill in the fields, unless you really want to apply uniform formatting to your selection. If you leave those fields blank, FreeHand doesn't alter those attributes at all.

When you select text that's displayed using a substitute font (because you don't have the font loaded on your system; see "Font Substitution," below), FreeHand leaves the Font field of the Type Specifications palette blank. Again, don't enter anything in the field unless that's what you really want to do.

FIGURE 3-23
Mixed type
specifications

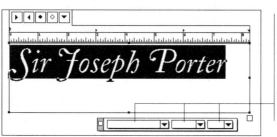

The selected text contains differing fonts, type styles, and type sizes, so FreeHand leaves the fields in the Type Specifications palette blank.

Tip:
Programming
QuicKeys to
Select Fonts

I set up QuicKeys (see Appendix A, "System") to select frequently used fonts (once again, this is to avoid submenus and popups). It's easy to remember that Control-Option-Z changes the font to Zapf Dingbats or that Control-Option-P selects Perpetua (or Palatino, or whatever you like). It's easier to program QuicKeys to choose fonts from the Font submenu of the Type menu than the Font popup menu on the Type Specifications palette. Follow the steps below to set up a font-choosing QuicKey.

1. Open QuicKeys (it's usually Command-Option-Return, since that's the default).

2. Choose Menu Selection from the Define menu.

3. Pull down the Font submenu of the Type menu and select the font you want.

4. Assign a key to your new Menu Selection QuicKey.

Font substitution. When you open a FreeHand publication containing fonts that aren't currently loaded in your System, FreeHand displays the Missing Fonts dialog box (see Figure 3-24), which tells you what fonts you're missing and also lets you substitute fonts for

FIGURE 3-24
Missing Fonts
dialog box

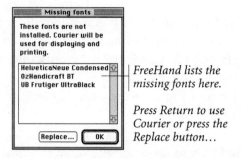

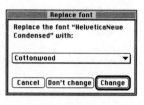

*FreeHand lists the
missing fonts here.*

*Press Return to use
Courier or press the
Replace button...*

*...FreeHand displays the
Replace Font dialog box,
where you can replace
missing fonts with specific
fonts you have installed on
your system.*

the missing fonts. If you want, you can press Return to substitute
Courier for all missing fonts.

FreeHand temporarily applies a different font to the characters
formatted with the missing font. By "temporarily," I mean that the
publication retains the information about what font was originally
applied to the text. What's the use of that? Let me use an example.

Suppose you lay out a publication on your machine at the office, save it, and take it home for the evening. At home, you open
the publication—and FreeHand warns you that you're missing Oz
Handicraft, a font you have on your office machine. You substitute
Courier for Oz Handicraft, and make a few changes to an illustration in your publication. Then—without applying any font changes
to the text—save your publication.

Note that FreeHand does not apply the spacing of the original
font to the substituted font (as PageMaker, for example, does). This
means that all of the text you formatted using the font changes
position, usually to the point that the line breaks in your publication change. When this happens, I avoid making any formatting
changes to the text. I might enter new copy, or edit the existing
copy, but it's pointless to do any kerning or text-block adjustments
when you're working with substituted fonts.

The next day, you open the publication on the Macintosh
at your office. Because you haven't applied any permanent font
changes to your text, FreeHand formats and displays the text in its
original font, Oz Handicraft.

If you don't want to work with substituted fonts, you need to
load the required fonts. If you're working with Suitcase or Master-
Juggler (see Appendix A, "System"), you can close the publication,

load the fonts, then reopen the publication. If you're loading and unloading fonts by moving them to and from the Fonts folder, you need to quit FreeHand, move the fonts, then restart FreeHand.

Obviously, loading the font is better than working with substitute fonts. If you hadn't wanted that font, you wouldn't have used it in the first place.

Tip:
Use an Ugly Font

When I have to use FreeHand's font substitution, I substitute Zapf Chancery for the missing font—I'd never use it for anything else, and it stands out from all the other text in the publication.

Tip:
SuperATM and Font Substitution

If SuperATM is running and its font substitution feature is turned on when you open a publication containing missing fonts, you won't see the Missing Fonts dialog box; instead, SuperATM will create a substitute font for the missing fonts in your publication, and FreeHand will display the text in that font. The advantage is that line breaks are more likely to stay the same. The disadvantage is that if you forget to load the real font, you can run into some serious problems when you take the file to your imagesetting service bureau.

You can keep SuperATM from substituting fonts by turning off the Substitute for Missing Fonts option in SuperATM's control panel. If you intend leaving ATM's font substitution off, you can delete the 1.4-meg ATM Font Database file from your System Folder.

Type Style

To apply a type style to text, type "p" for plain, "i" for italic, "b" for bold, or "boldi" for bold italic in the Type Style field in the Type Specifications palette, or choose a type style from the attached pop-up list (or choose a type style from the Style submenu of the Type menu). If a font doesn't have an alternate type style (bold, italic, or bold italic), FreeHand grays the name of the type style in the menus (see Figure 3-25).

When you try to type the name of a type style that's not available in the Type Style field, FreeHand beeps.

FIGURE 3-25
Grayed-out type styles

This font doesn't have these type styles, so FreeHand grays them out.

After you've chosen the type style you want, press Tab to move to the Type Size field, or press Return to apply your changes.

Type Size

Type the point size you want in the Type Size field in the Type Specifications palette, or choose a size from the attached popup menu. If you're directly entering the size, you can specify it in .0001-point increments. You can also change the size of the type in a text block by stretching the text block (see "Working with Text Blocks," earlier in this chapter).

After you've entered the size you want, press Return to apply your changes.

Tip:
Bumping Text
Up or Down
in Size

You can make selected text larger or smaller, in one-point increments, using the keyboard. To make selected text larger by one point, press Command-Shift-period. To make it smaller by one point, press Command-Shift-comma.

Tip:
Greeking

Remember that greeking—whether the type is displayed or drawn as a gray bar—is set in the Preferences dialog box. If you make the type smaller (at the current magnification) than the threshold you set in the Display Preferences dialog box, it'll appear as a gray bar (see "Preferences" in Chapter 1, "FreeHand Basics").

Leading

Text characters—usually—sit on an imaginary line, which we call the baseline. Leading is the vertical distance from the baseline of one line of text to the next text baseline. In FreeHand, leading is measured from the baseline of the current line of text to the baseline of the line of text above (see Figure 3-26). When you increase the leading in a line of text, you push that line farther from the line above it, and farther down from the top of the text block.

FreeHand's Character Inspector offers three different leading methods: Extra, Fixed, and Percentage.

Extra leading method. When you choose Extra from the Leading Type popup menu, FreeHand adds the point size of the largest character of text in the selection to the value you enter in the Leading field. If, for example, you wanted to add four points of leading between each line of type, you'd choose Extra and enter "4" in the

FIGURE 3-26
Leading

Leading is the vertical distance between baselines of type.

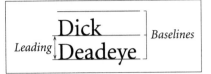

When you use FreeHand's Extra leading method, FreeHand adds the value you enter in the Leading field to the point size of the largest character in the line to calculate the leading for the line.

If want 24 points of leading, and you're working with 18-point text, enter "6" in the Leading field.

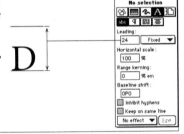

When you use the Fixed leading method, FreeHand uses the value you enter in the Leading field for the leading of the line.

If you want 24-point leading, enter "24" in the Leading field.

When you're using the Percentage leading method, FreeHand sets the leading based on the percentage of the largest size of type in a line.

If you want 24 point leading, and you're working with 18-point type, enter "133" in the Leading field.

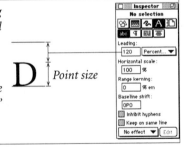

Leading field. When you change the size of the characters, the distance between the baselines changes, even though the leading value you've entered remains the same.

Fixed leading method. With Fixed leading, FreeHand sets the leading of the selected lines of text to the value you enter in the Leading field. Fixed is the most precise leading method, because you'll always get exactly the leading value you enter, regardless of the size of the selected text. You can enter a leading value in .0001-point increments.

Percentage leading method. When you choose Percentage from the Leading Type popup menu in the Character Inspector, Free-Hand calculates a leading value that's a percentage of the size of the selected text, based on the largest point size in the selection. Again, your leading will change if you change the size of the text. This may or may not be what you want.

You can set any leading amount using any one of the three leading methods. That said, however, I admit that I only use the Fixed leading method. I like knowing the distances between the baselines of the text in my text blocks, without having to do any multiplication or addition. I also believe that leading shouldn't—necessarily—have anything to do with the size of the characters in the line. Fixed is the only leading method that doesn't change as I change type sizes.

For any leading method, the largest leading value in the line predominates to the next line break. If the character containing the larger leading flows to a new line, the leading moves with it (see Figure 3-27).

FIGURE 3-27
The largest leading in a
line predominates

*This character has
more leading than the
other characters
in the line.*

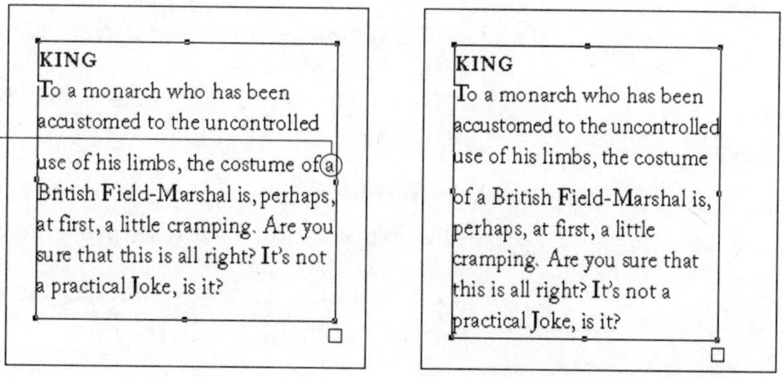

KING
To a monarch who has been accustomed to the uncontrolled use of his limbs, the costume of a British Field-Marshal is, perhaps, at first, a little cramping. Are you sure that this is all right? It's not a practical Joke, is it?

KING
To a monarch who has been accustomed to the uncontrolled use of his limbs, the costume of a British Field-Marshal is, perhaps, at first, a little cramping. Are you sure that this is all right? It's not a practical Joke, is it?

When the character with the larger leading moves to another line (if, for example, the width of the text block changes, as in this example), the larger leading is applied to that line.

Baseline Shift   Sometimes, you need to raise the baseline of a character or characters above the baseline of the surrounding text. You can't do this by changing the leading setting of the characters (remember, the largest leading in the line predominates). Instead, you use the Baseline Shift field in the Character Inspector.

Enter an amount in the Baseline Shift field to shift the baseline of the selected text by that amount. As you'd guess, positive values move the selected text up from the baseline; negative values move the selected text down from the baseline (see Figure 3-28).

FIGURE 3-28
Baseline shift

$A S C E N T$ $12^{144}/_{207}$

First Line Leading   Because I like to position and align text blocks by snapping their tops to ruler guides or the grid, it's important for me to know where the first baseline in a text block falls relative to the top of the text block.

To set the distance from the top of the text block to the first baseline, display the Inspector (press Command-I if the Inspector isn't already visible) and then press Command-Option-C. At the bottom of the Copyfit section of the Object Inspector, you'll see a section controlling first line leading.

FreeHand offers three methods: Percentage, Fixed, and Extra.

 ◆ Percentage uses a percentage of the height of the text in the first line of the text block.

 ◆ Extra adds an amount equal to the height of the first line in the text block plus some measurement you enter.

 ◆ Fixed uses the leading value that you enter, regardless of the size of the characters in the line.

I only use Fixed—I can enter a precise leading value and not worry about the leading changing because I've added a drop cap or other enlarged character. If I want the baseline of the first line of text in a text block to fall twelve points from the top of the text block, I enter "12" (see Figure 3-29).

FIGURE 3-29
Setting the first
baseline

*The trouble with the
Extra and Percentage
first line leading
methods.*

*Extra first line leading method. Where
does the baseline fall (get out your
calculator)?*

*Percentage first line leading method.
Where does the baseline fall?*

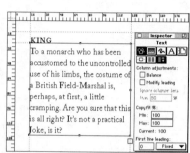

*Use the Fixed first line
leading method—and
it's easy to get the
baseline right where you
want it.*

*Fixed first line leading method. The
baseline falls precisely where you want
it (in this example, 12 points from the
top of the text block).*

*If you choose Fixed and enter zero, the
first baseline falls exactly at the top of
the text block. Don't tell any software
engineers you know how to do this.*

If you enter "0" using the Fixed first baseline method, Free-
Hand does just what it should: it hangs the characters of the first
line of text out of the top of the text block, and positions the zero
point of that line of text at the top of the text block. If you set your
text blocks up this way, you'll be able to snap the baseline of the
first line of text in a text block to a ruler guide. Since the baseline is
at the top of the text block, the characters in the first line hang out
of the top. This is sometimes just what you need, even though it's
the eventuality the other leading methods were designed to prevent (software engineers, for some reason, *hate* it when text hangs
out of text blocks).

Tip:
If Your Leading
Looks Funky

If your leading looks odd inside a text block that you think contains only one leading setting, select the text block and press Com-
mand-Option-T to display the Character Inspector (if it's not already

visible). If the Leading field is blank, you've somehow entered another leading setting inside the text block. Either reenter the leading value you want, or move your cursor through the text block until you find which character is carrying the rogue leading value (you'll see it in the Character Inspector).

Applying Colors to Text

Characters in FreeHand's text blocks can be filled or stroked with any color. While text blocks can be filled or stroked with any of FreeHand's fills (see "Borders and Fills for Text Blocks," earlier in this chapter), you can apply only basic fills and strokes to text (convert the characters to paths, of course, and you can format them as you would any FreeHand path).

FreeHand offers several ways of applying color to text and to text blocks—try them and see which methods work best for you.

Filling text. To apply a fill to the text inside a text block, follow these steps (see Figure 3-30).

1. Select the text you want to color using the Text tool.

2. Click on a color name in the Color List.

FreeHand applies a basic fill of the color you clicked to the selected text. If you select this text and display the Fill Inspector, you can specify whether the text overprints or not (for more on overprinting, see "Trapping," in Chapter 6, "Color").

You can also use the Fill Inspector to apply a color fill to text.

1. Select the text you want to fill.

2. Press Command-Option-F to display the Fill Inspector, if it's not already visible.

3. Choose Basic from the Fill Type popup menu in the Fill Inspector (the other fill types have no effect on text).

4. Click on a color in the Color List. Check Overprint in the Fill Inspector if you want the fill to overprint objects behind it.

FreeHand applies the basic fill to the text you selected.

FIGURE 3-30
Applying color to text

Select the text you want
to apply a color to.

Click a color name in the
Color List. FreeHand applies
the color to the selected text.

To apply a color to text using the drag-and-drop method, follow these steps (see Figure 3-31).

1. Select the text you want to color using the Text tool.

2. Drag a color swatch from a color well (ideally, from the Color List) and drop it on the selected text. Or drop the color swatch on the Fill icon at the top of the Color List.

FreeHand applies a basic fill of the color you dropped to the selected text.

Alternatively, you can use the drag-and-drop method to color all of the text in a text block—select all of the text, drag a color

FIGURE 3-31
Applying color to text
using the drag-and-
drop method

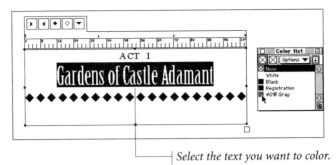

Select the text you want to color.

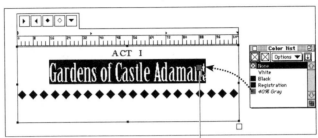

*Drag a color swatch from one of
the color wells in the Color List
and drop it on the selected text.*

*FreeHand applies the
color to the fill of the
selected text.*

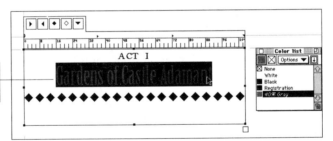

swatch from a color well, and drop it on a character in a text block. FreeHand applies the color to all of the text in the text block (see Figure 3-32).

Stroking text. To apply a stroke to text using the Stroke Inspector, follow these steps (see Figure 3-33).

1. Select the text you want to stroke.

2. Press Command-Option-L to display the Stroke Inspector, if it's not already visible.

3. Choose Basic from the Stroke Type popup menu in the Stroke Inspector (the other stroke types have no effect).

FIGURE 3-32
Another way to apply a
color using the drag-
and-drop method

Drag a color swatch from one of
the color wells in the Color List...

...and drop it onto a character.   *FreeHand applies the color to all
of the text in the text block.*

FIGURE 3-33
Applying a
stroke to text

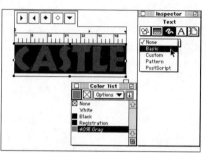

*Select the text, then apply a basic
stroke using the Stroke Inspector—
just as you would if you were
applying a stroke to a path.*

4. Click on a color in the Color List. Check Overprint in the
   Stroke Inspector if you want the stroke to overprint objects
   behind it (including the character's fill, if any).

To apply a color stroke to text using the drag-and-drop method,
follow these steps (see Figure 3-34).

1. Select the text you want to stroke using the Text tool.

2. Drag a color swatch from a color well (ideally, from the
   Color List) and drop it on the Stroke icon at the top of the
   Color List.

FIGURE 3-34
Applying a color
stroke to text using
drag and drop

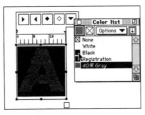

*Select the text you want to
apply a stroke to.*

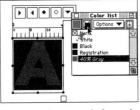

*Drag a color swatch from the
Color List...*

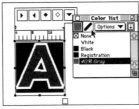

*...and drop it on the Stroke
button in the Color List.*

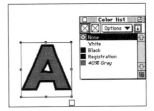

*FreeHand applies the stroke to the
selected text, using the default stroke
width.*

FreeHand applies a basic stroke of the color you dropped to the selected text. Use the Stroke Inspector to set the width of the stroke, if necessary.

Tip:
Styles and
Text Blocks

Given that you can apply strokes and fills to text, you'd think you could apply styles to text, as well. Unfortunately, FreeHand doesn't work that way. When you select text with the Text tool and apply a style, FreeHand applies the fill, stroke, and halftone properties of the style to the text block itself—not to the text contained in the text block.

Tip:
Avoid Fuzzy
Type

Even the most skilled color separators will tell you to avoid applying a process-color tint build to fine hairlines and text smaller than about 14 points (12 points for bold). It's difficult, even on the very best presses (or even the best-maintained imagesetters and film processors) to keep small type and fine lines in register, so it ends up looking fuzzy in your printed publication. So use spot colors for fine lines and type. If you're stuck, try to find a process color that gives you 80-percent cyan, magenta, or black, and try to apply it to a sans serif face; it's less likely to look fuzzy.

Stretching Characters Horizontally

Enter a value in the Horizontal Scale field in the Character Inspector to create expanded (wider) or condensed (narrower) versions of your type (see Figure 3-35). Before I became too old and tired, I used to argue that these aren't true expanded or condensed fonts, which involve custom-designed, hand-tuned character shapes and spacings, but never mind.

You can also change the horizontal scaling of type by dragging the selection handles of text blocks (see "Working with Text Blocks," earlier in this chapter).

FIGURE 3-35
Scaling characters
horizontally

A 40%   A 60%   A 80%   A 100%   A 120%   A 140%   A 160%

Text Effects

Text effects are just that—special effects for your type. They're frequently (maybe a little to frequently) used to create eye-catching display type. To apply one of FreeHand's text effects, select some text and choose an effect from the Text Effects popup menu at the bottom of the Character Inspector. Press Enter, and FreeHand applies the text effect to the text you've selected. If you can't see the text effect, make sure that Display Text Effects is checked in the Display Preferences dialog box. If Display Text Effects is checked and you still can't see the text effect, are you sure you're not in Keyline view? (Text effects don't display in Keyline.)

Inline. Remember Trace Edges from MacPaint? Inline does much the same thing—drawing outlines around solid characters. To set the number and thickness of the outlines, click the Edit button at the bottom of the Character Inspector. FreeHand displays the Inline Effect dialog box (see Figure 3-36).

FIGURE 3-36
Inline text effect

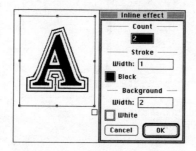

Shadow. Use Shadow to apply a drop shadow to the selected text. This drop shadow is offset to the right and below the text it's applied to (see Figure 3-37). The distance that the drop shadow is offset is based on the size of the characters. The drop shadow is set to 50 percent of the color of the selected text.

FIGURE 3-37
Shadow text effect

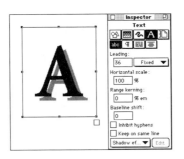

Printed example

Zoom text. Zoom text creates a string of characters that appear to recede toward a vanishing point. You see zoom text all the time in television commercials, usually for furniture and carpet dealers' goin' out of business/liquidation/oncoming recession sales.

Use this one with caution, though, and it can be a useful tool. To control the distance, offset, and color range of the Zoom effect, click the Edit button at the bottom of the Character Inspector. FreeHand displays the Zoom Effect dialog box, where you can specify the size of the most distant character in the zoom, the offset of that character, and the change in color from one end of the zoom to the other (see Figure 3-38). If you're using process colors or are zooming from one spot color to white or a tint of the same spot color, you can even zoom from one color to another.

FIGURE 3-38
Zoom text effect

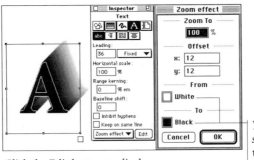

Printed example

You can drop color swatches into the color wells in the Zoom Effect dialog box.

Click the Edit button to display the Zoom Effect dialog box.

Tip:
Bounding Boxes
and Zoom Text

If you're exporting text that has the Zoom text effect applied to it, make sure that the bounding box of the EPS is large enough to accommodate the full extent of the zoomed text. The easiest way to do this is to draw a no-line, no-fill box around the text that extends to the edge of the effect.

Kerning

Kerning brings characters closer together horizontally or (these days) moves them farther apart (once, kerning meant only decreasing the space between characters) by fine increments (see Figure 3-39). FreeHand kerns in percentages of an em and can kern in increments as fine as .0001 (or .01 percent) of an em. Just as a reminder: an em is equal to the size of the type in the line. An em space in 24-point type is 24 points wide. You can use kerning to add up to 10 ems (1000 percent) or subtract two ems (-200 percent) of space.

While some "conventional" (that is, expensive, dedicated, obsolete) typesetting systems kern in absolute increments (fractional points, generally), most current typesetting systems (desktop and otherwise), kern in units relative to the size of the type. Practically, this means that you can make the type larger or smaller and retain the same relative amount of kerning.

You can kern any amount of text in FreeHand 4—from an individual character pair to all of the character pairs in all of the text blocks in a publication.

To kern a pair of characters, position the text cursor between the two characters and press the appropriate keyboard shortcuts (see Table 3-5) or enter a value in the Kerning field in the Character Inspector (see Figure 3-40). Enter positive values in the Kerning field to move the characters farther apart; enter negative numbers to move them closer together.

To kern a range of text, select some text—select text with the Text tool, or select a text block (or blocks) using the Pointer tool—and enter a value in the Kerning field (see Figure 3-41).

FIGURE 3-39
Kerning

Unkerned text   Kerned text

TABLE 3-5	To kern	Press
Kerning keyboard shortcuts	.1 em (10 percent) closer	Command-Left Arrow
	.01 em (one percent) closer	Command-Option-Left Arrow
	.1 em (10 percent) apart	Command-Right Arrow
	.01 em (one percent) apart	Command-Option-Left Arrow

FIGURE 3-40
Kerning a pair of
characters

*Position the cursor
between the characters
you want to kern.*

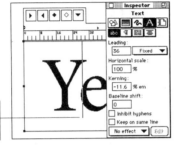 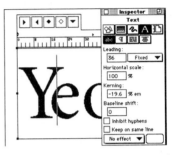

*The Kerning field shows you any
kerning that's already in effect
between the characters.*

*Press keyboard shortcuts to kern the
characters. As you kern, the Kerning
field shows you the kerning amount.*

FIGURE 3-41
Kerning a range of
characters

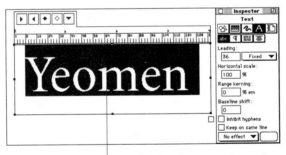

Select the range of text you want to kern.

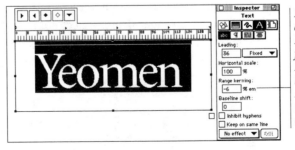

*Enter a kerning
amount in the
Range Kerning
field and press
Return, or press
keyboard shortcuts.
FreeHand kerns
the selected range
of text.*

Range kerning is often referred to as "tracking," but tracking is actually something different. Range kerning adjusts intercharacter spacing by a set amount (.5 percent of an em, for example), regardless of the size of the type. Tracking, on the other hand, adjusts intercharacter spacing by different amounts for different type sizes. For example, 12-point text in a particular font might be adjusted by one-half of a percent of an em, while 48-point type of the same face might be adjusted by -2 percent of an em. FreeHand doesn't offer a tracking feature.

Paragraph Formatting

What's a paragraph? FreeHand's definition is simple—a paragraph is any string of characters that ends with a carriage return or an end-of-column character (see "Entering Special Characters," earlier in this chapter, for an explanation of end-of-column characters).

When you apply paragraph formatting, the formatting applies to all of the characters in the paragraph. Paragraph alignment, indents, tabs, spacing, and hyphenation settings are all examples of paragraph formatting.

You don't have to select all of the text in a paragraph to apply paragraph formatting. To select a paragraph, all you have to do is click an insertion point in the paragraph. To select more than one paragraph for formatting, drag the cursor through the paragraphs you want to format—the selection doesn't have to include all of the text in the paragraphs, it only has to *touch* each paragraph.

If you want to select all of the paragraphs in a text block for formatting, click the text block with the Pointer tool. If you want to select all of the paragraphs in a story, triple-click one of the text blocks in the story with the Pointer tool, or click the Text tool on one of the text blocks in the story and press Command-A (for Select All).

Alignment Click the buttons in the Alignment Inspector (press Command-Option-A to display the Inspector if it's not already visible) to set the alignment of the selected paragraphs. You can align paragraphs in all the usual ways—Right (also known as "rag left"), Left (also known as "rag right"), Center, and Justify (see Figure 3-42). Free-Hand 4 dropped FreeHand 3's kooky Vertical Alignment feature, probably because no one was using it.

FIGURE 3-42
Aligning paragraphs

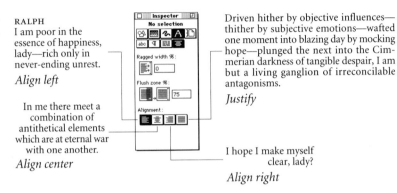

RALPH
I am poor in the essence of happiness, lady—rich only in never-ending unrest.
Align left

In me there meet a combination of antithetical elements which are at eternal war with one another.
Align center

Driven hither by objective influences—thither by subjective emotions—wafted one moment into blazing day by mocking hope—plunged the next into the Cimmerian darkness of tangible despair, I am but a living ganglion of irreconcilable antagonisms.
Justify

I hope I make myself clear, lady?
Align right

Tip:
Forced
Justification

Sometimes, you want to justify a single line of text—for example, when you want to spread a heading across the width of a column. When you select the text and click the Justify button in the Alignment Inspector, nothing happens. What gives? When you justify a paragraph, FreeHand sets the last line of the paragraph flush left, ragged right. This is good, because (most of the time) you don't want the last line of the paragraph stretching all the way across the column.

How can you get your text to stretch across the column? Use the Flush Zone setting (see Figure 3-43).

1. Select the paragraph.
2. Display the Alignment Inspector, if it's not already visible, by pressing Command-Option-A.
3. Enter "0" in the Flush Zone field (and click the Justify button if the paragraph isn't already justified).
4. Press Return to apply your changes. FreeHand spreads the line of text across the column.

Tip:
Unjustified
Justification

You may know people who call align right "right justify" or align left "left justify." Feign ignorance until they correct themselves. As you know, justification means, "to spread a line from one margin to the other," so there can't be anything called "right justify" or "left justify."

FIGURE 3-43
Forced justification

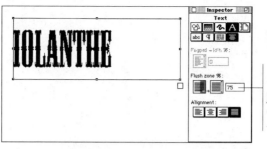

This text is justified, but doesn't spread out to fill the column...

...because the width of the line is less than the percentage of the column width set in the Flush Zone field.

To spread the text across the column, enter "0" in the Flush Zone field.

Tip:
QuicKeys for
Alignment

Because other page-layout programs use keyboard shortcuts Command-Shift-R for right alignment and Command-Shift-L for left alignment, Command-Shift-C for centered text, and Command-Shift-J for justified text, consider adding these keyboard shortcuts with QuicKeys. You'd create a Sequence QuicKey that does just what you do to align a paragraph—display the Alignment Inspector and click the alignment icon you want.

If you do this, you'll have to redefine some of FreeHand's default keyboard shortcuts—Command-Shift-J, for example, usually means Split Element.

Spacing

Now that FreeHand has paragraph formatting features, you're faced with a dilemma you didn't have to face in previous versions of the program. I call it the text composition balancing act. Word- and letterspacing, hyphenation, alignment, and the values you enter for Ragged Width and Flush Zone (in the Alignment Inspector) *all* interact, with FreeHand using each setting to compose the best-looking text it can.

What do I mean by "the best-looking text"? It's more than a little subjective. In general, I think that the right edges of your left-aligned type shouldn't be too ragged (that is, there shouldn't be extreme variation in the widths of the lines in a paragraph), and the word- and letterspacing inside lines of justified text shouldn't be noticeably tight or loose or vary too much from line to line.

I do know three, entirely objective things about spacing text in FreeHand.

◆ What constitutes "good spacing" varies from font to font and line width to line width. There is no "master" spacing setting that will work every time.

◆ FreeHand's default settings will not produce good text spacing and hyphenation for all fonts and all column widths.

◆ It's up to you to space your text the way you like it. The best thing you can do for the appearance of the type in your FreeHand publications is to experiment until you see what you like.

When FreeHand composes a line of text, it has to make decisions—decisions about where to hyphenate words and about how much type to fit on a line. FreeHand needs your help in these tasks; it can't figure out what sort of spacing is appropriate for your text. You use the Spacing Inspector and the Alignment Inspector to give FreeHand spacing guidelines.

To display the Spacing Inspector, press Command-Option-S (see Figure 3-44). The spacing percentages you enter in the Spacing Inspector apply to all selected paragraphs.

FIGURE 3-44
Spacing Inspector

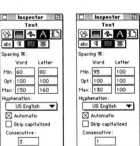

ROBIN
For a week I have fulfilled my accursed doom! I have duly committed a crime a day! Not a great crime, I trust, but still, in the eyes of one as strictly regulated as I used to be, a crime. But will my ghostly ancestors be satisfied with what I've done, or will they regard it as an unworthy subterfuge?

These spacing settings allow FreeHand to letterspace the text (sometimes too much).

ROBIN
For a week I have fulfilled my accursed doom! I have duly committed a crime a day! Not a great crime, I trust, but still, in the eyes of one as strictly regulated as I used to be, a crime. But will my ghostly ancestors be satisfied with what I've done, or will they regard it as an unworthy subterfuge?

These spacing settings tell FreeHand to increase or decrease wordspacing, and leave letterspacing alone.

What are the percentages in the Spacing Inspector based on? What does 100 percent mean? FreeHand bases word- and letterspacing percentages on values specified in the font itself, by the font designer. These values represent the designer's vision of the ideal spacing for the font, and they're different for every font. You don't need to agree with these values—both wordspacing and letterspacing for the font Utopia Regular, for example, seem extremely wide to me—you just need to know that they're where FreeHand gets its ideas about how to space the font.

All of this means that there aren't any "perfect" spacing values that work for all fonts, line widths, and alignments. What can you do? There's nothing for it—you have to work with each font (and, frequently, each publication) until you come up with spacing settings that look good to you. After awhile, you'll develop a "feeling" for certain fonts, and you'll be able to space them well without even thinking about it.

What spacing values should you start with? For nonjustified type, set everything to 100 percent to start with, and then work from there. For justified type, start with wordspacing percentages of 95, 100, 120 (that's Minimum, Optimum, and Maximum, respectively) and letterspacing percentages of 100, 100, 100. I prefer letting FreeHand set wordspacing up to 180 percent before I even think about using letterspacing.

Ragged Width. When FreeHand varies word- and letterspacing in nonjustified type, it's just trying to make your text match the value you entered in the Ragged Width field (in the Alignment Inspector). The percentage you enter in the Ragged Width field sets the minimum width for lines in nonjustified paragraphs (see Figure 3-45). Smaller values produce paragraphs with more ragged edges (the right edge, in left-aligned text; the left edge in right-aligned text); larger values produce text with more uniform edges.

If you're setting nonjustified text and want FreeHand to leave your word- and letterspacing alone (that is, to use the percentages you entered in the Optimum fields in the Spacing Inspector), enter "100" for Ragged Width.

FreeHand is alone among page-layout programs in that its minimum and maximum settings for wordspacing and letterspacing

FIGURE 3-45
Ragged width
and spacing

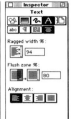

ROBIN

For a week I have fulfilled my accursed doom! I have duly committed a crime a day! Not a great crime, I trust, but still, in the eyes of one as strictly regulated as I used to be, a crime. But will my ghostly ancestors be satisfied with what I've done, or will they regard it as an unworthy subterfuge?

ROBIN

For a week I have fulfilled my accursed doom! I have duly committed a crime a day! Not a great crime, I trust, but still, in the eyes of one as strictly regulated as I used to be, a crime. But will my ghostly ancestors be satisfied with what I've done, or will they regard it as an unworthy subterfuge?

Why does spacing sometimes vary when you're working with nonjustified copy? Shouldn't FreeHand space the text according to the percentages you've entered in the Optimum fields in the Spacing Inspector?

That depends on what you've entered in the Alignment Inspector's Ragged Width field.

To keep FreeHand from using spacing values other than those you've entered in the Optimum fields, enter zero in the Ragged Width field.

apply to paragraphs of any alignment. This only happens when you've entered a value larger than zero in the Ragged Width field.

Flush Zone. The percentage you enter in the Flush Zone field controls the spacing of the last line of a justified paragraph. FreeHand's asking the following question: "If the last line in your paragraph gets within a certain distance of the right side of the column, should I justify it?" When you enter anything less than "100" in the Flush Zone field, you're specifying the line width—expressed as a percentage of the width of the column—at which you want FreeHand to start justifying text (see Figure 3-46).

FIGURE 3-46
Flush Zone

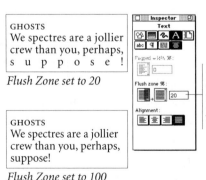

GHOSTS

We spectres are a jollier crew than you, perhaps, s u p p o s e !

Flush Zone set to 20

GHOSTS

We spectres are a jollier crew than you, perhaps, suppose!

Flush Zone set to 100

Enter a percentage in the Flush Zone field to tell FreeHand how to justify the last line of a justified paragraph. Most of the time, you can leave it set to 100.

In my opinion, you should set Flush Zone to either "100", to leave the last lines of justified paragraphs alone (that is, flush left, ragged right), or "0", to force-justify a single line of text (see "Forced Justification," earlier in this chapter). I have, however, met people whose typographic opinions I respect who set the Flush Zone to 95 percent.

Hyphenation

Another key factor in the appearance of your text is hyphenation—when and where FreeHand can break words in order to compose lines of text as you've specified using the spacing settings (see Figure 3-47). Like spacing, hyphenation settings are very subjective, and what "looks good" varies from person to person and publication to publication.

FreeHand's hyphenation controls are very simple.

◆ Use the Language popup menu to choose the dictionary you want to use. FreeHand uses the same dictionaries as PageMaker, so any additional dictionaries you've installed for PageMaker will appear on the popup menu. FreeHand doesn't use any user dictionaries you've created for use with PageMaker—only the base dictionary for a specific language.

◆ Check Automatic to use the hyphenation points defined in the hyphenation dictionary. Automatic has no bearing on any discretionary hyphens you've entered.

◆ Check Skip Capitalized to tell FreeHand not to break words typed in all capital letters, such as acronyms ("SPECTRE," for example).

◆ Enter a number in the Consecutive field to set the number of consecutive hyphens you'll allow in a paragraph. The larger the number you enter here, the less difficult it'll be for FreeHand to obey your spacing settings. I enter "1", unless I'm working in an extremely narrow column, because I hate seeing stacks of hyphens at the right edge of columns of type.

FIGURE 3-47
Hyphenation

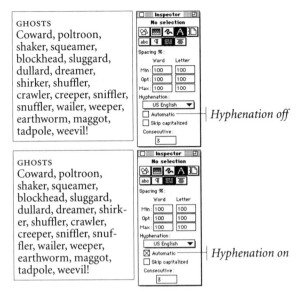

Hyphenation off

Hyphenation on

Paragraph Indents

FreeHand's paragraphs can be indented from the left and right sides of the column using the Left and Right fields in the Paragraph Inspector. You can enter positive or negative numbers in either field. Enter positive numbers to push the edges of the paragraph in from the edges of the column it occupies; enter negative numbers to push the edges of the paragraph beyond the column's edges (see Figure 3-48).

In addition, there's a special indent, First, that applies to the first line of the paragraph alone. The value you enter in First sets the distance between the first-line indent and the left indent, and can be positive or negative. You can even enter a first-line indent that causes text to hang outside the text block (see Figure 3-49).

Hanging Punctuation

Because we don't "see" punctuation when we're reading, a line beginning (or, in some cases, ending) with punctuation (especially quotation marks) doesn't look like it aligns with other lines in the surrounding text. It's a kind of typographic optical illusion. To compensate, typographers since Gutenberg have "hung" punctuation—moving the punctuation slightly beyond the edge of the text column. (Gutenberg also changed the spelling of words to fit his justification scheme—just as we do today when we're in a hurry or desperate.)

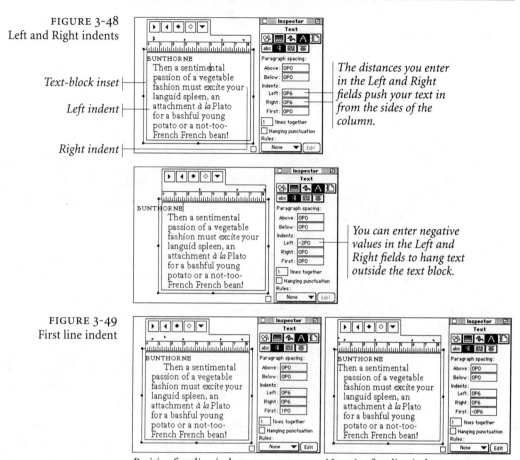

FIGURE 3-48
Left and Right indents

Text-block inset

Left indent

Right indent

The distances you enter in the Left and Right fields push your text in from the sides of the column.

You can enter negative values in the Left and Right fields to hang text outside the text block.

FIGURE 3-49
First line indent

Positive first line indent

Negative first line indent

You can think of FreeHand's hanging punctuation as something like a special, negative indent for a specific line. In fact, you can hang punctuation manually using FreeHand's right and left paragraph indents—just enter the distance you want the punctuation to extend beyond the edge of the text box. When text reflows, however, you have to start again from scratch.

FreeHand gives you an easy way to apply hanging punctuation that automatically adjusts as text reflows (see Figure 3-50). Hanging punctuation applies to ' ' " " . , ; : ` -

1. Type some text that begins with a quotation mark.

2. If the Paragraph Inspector isn't already visible, display it by pressing Command-Option-P.

FIGURE 3-50
Hanging punctuation

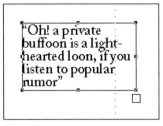
Normal punctuation

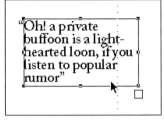
Hanging punctuation

3. Without deselecting the text block you created, check the Hanging Punctuation box. Watch as FreeHand hangs the quotation mark outside the text margins of the text block, which produces a better visual alignment. FreeHand does this any time one of the special characters appears at the left or right edge of a text block or column.

You can't set the distance the special characters hang outside the text block, and you can't add characters to the list of characters hanging punctuation affects.

Setting Tabs

Tabs (which we knew as "tab stops" when we used manual typewriters—that is, sometime before we came down from the trees) define what FreeHand does when it encounters a tab character in your text. You use tabs to control the horizontal position of text in your text blocks. FreeHand 4 features left, right, center, decimal, and wrapping tabs (see Figure 3-51).

You can also use FreeHand's tab ruler to set indents—this is handy, because indents and tabs often work together.

A few things about tabs:

◆ Use tab characters and tabs, not spaces, to add horizontal space in your lines of text.

◆ Tabs apply to entire paragraphs—you can't have different tabs inside a single paragraph.

◆ Don't force line breaks using tab characters—use returns, end-of-column characters, or end-of-line characters when you want a line to break in a specific place.

FIGURE 3-51
FreeHand's tab icons
and tab ruler

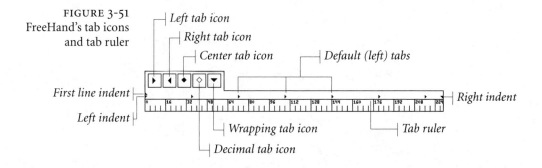

Left tab icon

Right tab icon

Center tab icon

Default (left) tabs

First line indent

Right indent

Left indent

Wrapping tab icon

Tab ruler

Decimal tab icon

◆ Use tabs and indents to create hanging indents—not carriage returns and tab characters (or, worse, spaces).

Left, right, and center tabs. FreeHand's left, right, and center tabs are the same as the basic tabs you'll find in any word processor (see Figure 3-52).

Left tabs push text following a tab character to a specific horizontal location in a column and then align the text to the right of the tab.

Right tabs push text to a location and then align the text to the left of a tab character.

Center tabs center a line of text at the point at which you've set a tab character.

FIGURE 3-52
Left, right,
and center tabs

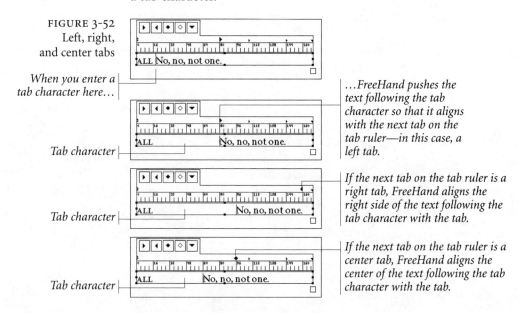

When you enter a
tab character here…

…FreeHand pushes the text following the tab character so that it aligns with the next tab on the tab ruler—in this case, a left tab.

Tab character

If the next tab on the tab ruler is a right tab, FreeHand aligns the right side of the text following the tab character with the tab.

Tab character

If the next tab on the tab ruler is a center tab, FreeHand aligns the center of the text following the tab character with the tab.

Tab character

Decimal tabs. Decimal tabs push text following a tab character so that any decimal point you've entered in the text aligns with the point you set the tab (see Figure 3-53). If there's no decimal in the text, FreeHand treats the decimal tab as a right tab.

FIGURE 3-53
Decimal tabs

This decimal tab...

...aligns the decimals in these numbers.

Wrapping tabs. Wrapping tabs create a column inside a column of your text block (see Figure 3-54). Wrapping tabs are unique to FreeHand—no other page layout or illustration program I know of has anything like them. They're great for creating columns within columns, or for creating columns of unequal widths inside a text block (columns set with the Column Inspector always divide a text block evenly).

FIGURE 3-54
Wrapping tabs

Wrapping tabs create a column inside a column of text.

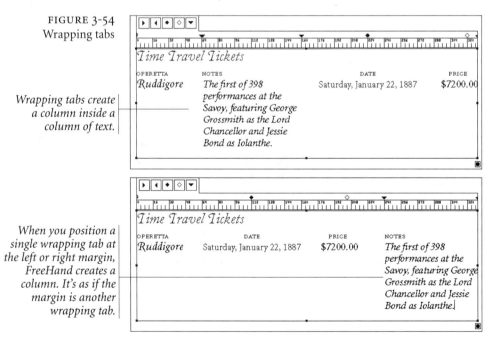

When you position a single wrapping tab at the left or right margin, FreeHand creates a column. It's as if the margin is another wrapping tab.

To set a tab, follow these steps (see Figure 3-55).

1. Select the text you want to format.

2. If you haven't already entered tab characters in the text, enter them.

3. Drag a tab icon for the type of tab you want to set onto the tab ruler. As you drag, the Info Bar shows you the position of the tab icon.

4. When the tab icon reaches the position at which you want to set the tab, drop it onto the ruler.

To change a tab's position, drag the tab on the tab ruler (see Figure 3-56).

To change a tab's alignment, drag a tab of the alignment you want onto the tab's position (see Figure 3-57). You've got to drop the new tab icon precisely on the old one, or you'll end up with two tabs on your tab ruler right next to each other.

To remove a tab, drag the tab icon off the tab ruler and drop it on your page or pasteboard (see Figure 3-58). Note that this doesn't remove tab characters you've typed in your text, though it does make them behave differently.

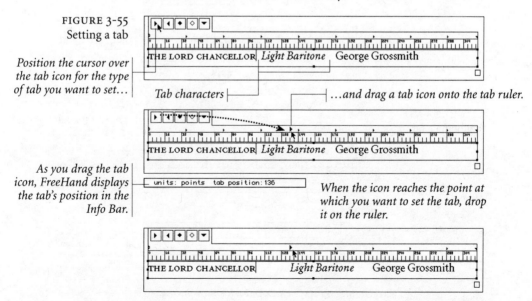

FIGURE 3-55
Setting a tab

Position the cursor over the tab icon for the type of tab you want to set...

Tab characters

...and drag a tab icon onto the tab ruler.

As you drag the tab icon, FreeHand displays the tab's position in the Info Bar.

When the icon reaches the point at which you want to set the tab, drop it on the ruler.

FIGURE 3-56
Changing a tab

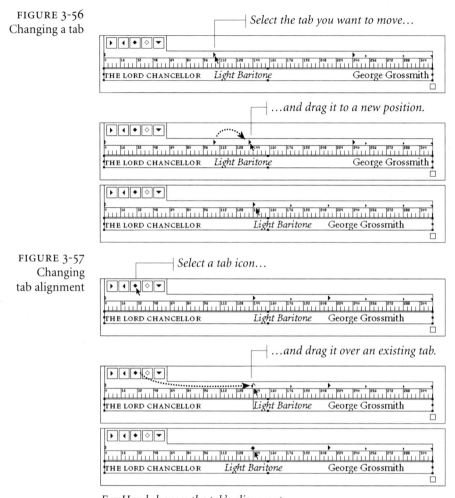

Select the tab you want to move…

…and drag it to a new position.

FIGURE 3-57
Changing
tab alignment

Select a tab icon…

…and drag it over an existing tab.

FreeHand changes the tab's alignment.

FIGURE 3-58
Removing a tab

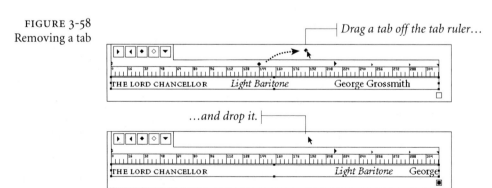

Drag a tab off the tab ruler…

…and drop it.

FreeHand removes the tab and reformats the text.

Creating a hanging indent. As in both Word and PageMaker, you create a hanging indent by dragging the left margin icon to the right of the first-line indent icon, then setting a left tab at the same position as the left margin icon (see Figure 3-59).

FIGURE 3-59
Creating a
hanging indent

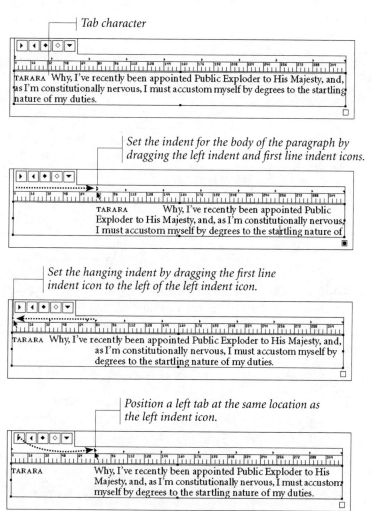

Tab character

TARARA Why, I've recently been appointed Public Exploder to His Majesty, and, as I'm constitutionally nervous, I must accustom myself by degrees to the startling nature of my duties.

Set the indent for the body of the paragraph by dragging the left indent and first line indent icons.

TARARA   Why, I've recently been appointed Public Exploder to His Majesty, and, as I'm constitutionally nervous, I must accustom myself by degrees to the startling nature of

Set the hanging indent by dragging the first line indent icon to the left of the left indent icon.

TARARA Why, I've recently been appointed Public Exploder to His Majesty, and, as I'm constitutionally nervous, I must accustom myself by degrees to the startling nature of my duties.

Position a left tab at the same location as the left indent icon.

TARARA   Why, I've recently been appointed Public Exploder to His Majesty, and, as I'm constitutionally nervous, I must accustom myself by degrees to the startling nature of my duties.

Tip:
Hanging Side
Heads

Headings that appear in a column next to text (such as the heading for this tip) are difficult to create in most publishing or word processing software (only FrameMaker and Corel Ventura Publisher feature automated methods of creating hanging side heads). Using FreeHand's wrapping tabs, it's easy, as shown in Figure 3-60.

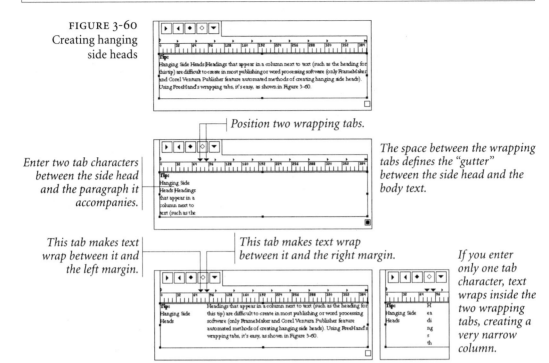

FIGURE 3-60
Creating hanging
side heads

Position two wrapping tabs.

*Enter two tab characters
between the side head
and the paragraph it
accompanies.*

*The space between the wrapping
tabs defines the "gutter"
between the side head and the
body text.*

*This tab makes text
wrap between it and
the left margin.*

*This tab makes text wrap
between it and the right margin.*

*If you enter
only one tab
character, text
wraps inside the
two wrapping
tabs, creating a
very narrow
column.*

Spacing Before and After Paragraphs

To increase or decrease the amount of space above or below a paragraph, enter a value in the Above or Below fields in the Paragraph Inspector (press Command-Option-P to display the Paragraph Inspector, if it's not already visible) and press Return. FreeHand adds the space above or below the paragraph, as you specified (see Figure 3-61).

You can enter positive or negative numbers in the Paragraph Spacing fields. Enter a negative number in the Above field, and FreeHand moves the paragraph up—even to the point where the paragraph hangs out of the top of the text block or collides with the paragraph above. Enter a negative number in the Below field, and FreeHand moves the following paragraph up in the text block. I haven't found any limit to the numbers you can enter in these fields—either positive or negative.

Controlling Widows

Everyone has a different definition for the typographic terms "widow" and "orphan." To me, a "widow" is a single line of a paragraph at the top or bottom of a page or column, and an "orphan" is when a paragraph ends with a single, short word on a line by itself. To

FIGURE 3-61
Vertical spacing
around paragraphs

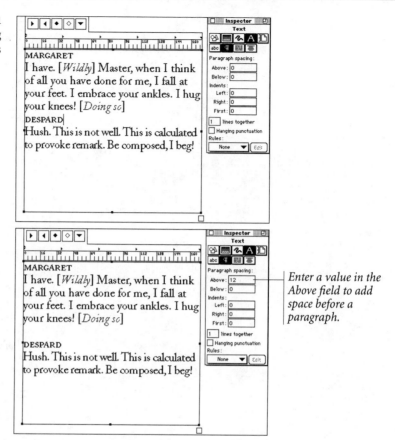

*Enter a value in the
Above field to add
space before a
paragraph.*

FreeHand, a "widow" is a single line of a paragraph at the top of a
text block or column. I don't know what it thinks an "orphan" is.

The Lines Together field in the Paragraph Inspector controls
the way FreeHand breaks a paragraph between columns or linked
text blocks. When you enter "1" here (the default), you're telling
FreeHand that it's free to break paragraphs however it sees fit. When
you enter "2", or a larger number, FreeHand always breaks paragraphs so that two (or more) lines of the paragraph appear at the
top of the next text block (see Figure 3-62).

Paragraph Rules   In the old days, we had to add rules between paragraphs manually,
dragging the rules around every time the text changed. Many of
today's page-layout applications and word-processors feature
rules you can attach to a paragraph, which then move with the

FIGURE 3-62
Keeping lines together

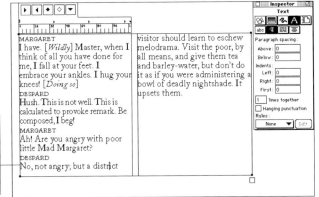

With "1" entered in the Lines Together field, FreeHand leaves the first line of this paragraph at the bottom of the column.

If you enter "2" in the Lines Together field...

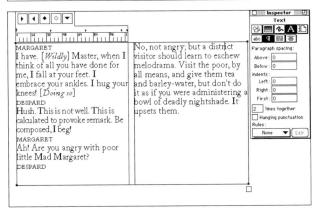

...FreeHand pulls the first line of the paragraph to the top of the next column.

paragraph as the text reflows. FreeHand has a very limited version of this feature (compared, at least, to PageMaker and QuarkXPress).

To attach a rule to a paragraph, position the text cursor inside the paragraph, press Command-Option-P to display the Paragraph Inspector, choose a rule type (Centered or Paragraph) from the popup menu at the bottom of the Inspector, and press Return. Centered rules are centered in the column or text block; paragraph rules have the same alignment as the paragraph they're attached to (see Figure 3-63).

A few notes about paragraph rules:

♦ You can't select paragraph rules by clicking on them with the Pointer tool.

♦ When you convert text to paths, any paragraph rules selected with the text are not converted—they disappear.

◆ FreeHand vertically centers paragraph rules in the space between their paragraph (the paragraph where you specified the rule) and the following paragraph, taking leading, paragraph space before, and paragraph space after into account.

◆ FreeHand strokes the paragraph rules with the stroke that's applied to the text block. You can't apply different strokes to a text block's border and to the paragraph rules within that text block (you can, however, uncheck Display Border in the Object Inspector and draw a path around the text block—it's easier than drawing paragraph rules, most of the time).

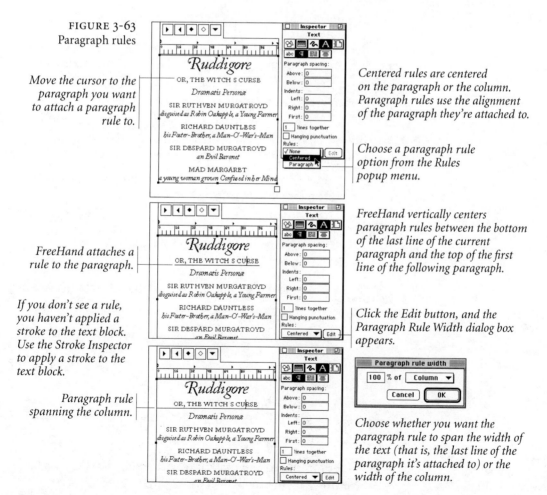

FIGURE 3-63
Paragraph rules

Move the cursor to the paragraph you want to attach a paragraph rule to.

Centered rules are centered on the paragraph or the column. Paragraph rules use the alignment of the paragraph they're attached to.

Choose a paragraph rule option from the Rules popup menu.

FreeHand attaches a rule to the paragraph.

If you don't see a rule, you haven't applied a stroke to the text block. Use the Stroke Inspector to apply a stroke to the text block.

FreeHand vertically centers paragraph rules between the bottom of the last line of the current paragraph and the top of the first line of the following paragraph.

Click the Edit button, and the Paragraph Rule Width dialog box appears.

Paragraph rule spanning the column.

Choose whether you want the paragraph rule to span the width of the text (that is, the last line of the paragraph it's attached to) or the width of the column.

Automatic Copyfitting

When you've got to make your text fit into a particular space, there are several things you can do. I've arranged your options, from best to worst, in the following list.

◆ Edit the text.

◆ Range kern the text.

◆ Reduce or increase the size, leading, and interparagraph spacing of the text.

◆ Use FreeHand's automatic copyfitting features (essentially an automated method of performing the previous step).

What if you can't edit the text, and there's too much text to range-kern into the space you have available? At that point, you're stuck, and the only thing you can do is to add or remove space and/or increase or decrease type size until your copy fits in your publication. The best way to do this is to try different combinations of type size, leading, and interparagraph spacing. The disadvantage is that this "hit and miss" method takes time—and sometimes time is the last thing you have. Sometimes, FreeHand's automatic copyfitting might be just what you need.

To use FreeHand's automatic copyfitting, follow these steps (see Figure 3-64)

1. Select a text block.

2. Press Command-Option-C to display the Copyfit Inspector.

3. Check the Modify Leading box if you want FreeHand to change the leading as it tries to fit your text.

4. In the Ignore Columns Less Than field, enter a number. Entering "0" tells FreeHand to fit all of the columns in the story equally, which is probably what you want. If not, experiment with values until you get what you want (sorry, you're on your own with this one).

5. Enter minimum and maximum percentages in the Min and Max fields. The value you enter in the Min field specifies

FIGURE 3-64
Automatic copyfitting

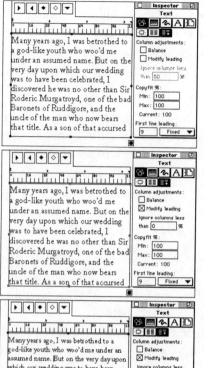

There's too much text in this story to fit in this text block. For whatever reason, the text has to fit in the text block, and we can't edit it. What can we do?

Check the Modify Leading box to tell FreeHand to try to fit the text by changing the leading. In this case, FreeHand changes the leading, but still can't make all of the text fit. In my experience, Modify Leading works best when you're trying to fill a text block.

Direct FreeHand to make the text fit by changing its size using the Min and Max fields. In this example, I told FreeHand it could make the text as small as 80 percent of its original size.

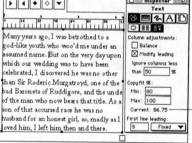

FreeHand reduces the size of the text in the story to make it fit in the text block.

This (noneditable) field displays the current text reduction (or enlargement).

how small you'll let FreeHand make the type (as a percentage of the type's current size), Max specifies how large FreeHand can make the type to fit it in the text block.

6. Press Return to apply your changes.

FreeHand changes the type size and leading of the lines in the selected story so that the text vertically fills all of the text blocks in the story.

A few things about copyfitting:

◆ When you select a text block for copyfitting, FreeHand applies copyfitting changes to any text blocks linked to that text block. That is, copyfitting applies to entire stories, not just to individual text blocks.

◆ When you check Modify Leading in the Copyfit Inspector, you're telling FreeHand that it can decrease or increase the leading in the selected story. When FreeHand changes the leading in a story, it changes all of the leading by the same percentage.

◆ The Min and Max fields in the Copyfit Inspector set the minimum and maximum percentage change in type size FreeHand can use to try to fit the story in the space you have available. Like Modify Leading, this control changes all of the type in your text block by a fixed amount. If you want FreeHand to leave the size of your text alone, enter "100" in both fields.

◆ The Current percentage (displayed below the Max field) shows you the current scaling of the text in the story, if any. What's the use of this? If FreeHand's been unable to copyfit a story, it's probably because the percentage you entered in the Min field is too large. If you see that the Current percentage is the same as the minimum or maximum percentage, and the text still doesn't fit in the space available, you know that you have to lower the percentage in the Min field or increase the percentage in the Max field.

Joining Text to a Path

One of FreeHand's signature features is the ability to place text along paths of any shape or length. To join text to a path, select some text, press Shift and select a path, and then press Command-Shift-Y (or choose Bind to Path from the Type menu). FreeHand joins your text to the path (see Figure 3-65).

Once you've joined text to a path, you select the text and the path as you'd select any other text—select the Text tool and drag it through the characters you want to select, double-click to select a word, or triple-click to select all of the text on the path. Selecting the path itself can be a little more difficult, but switching to Keyline view can make it easier to see and select the path.

FIGURE 3-65
Joining text to a path

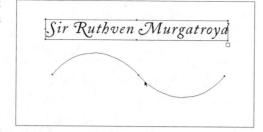

*Select some text,
select a path, and press
Command-Shift-Y...*

*...and FreeHand binds
the text to the path.*

*To edit text that's been
bound to a path, drag
the Text tool through
it, just as you'd do to
select any other text on
your page (FreeHand 3
users note—no more
trips to the Text dialog
box).*

If you want to unjoin, or split, the text from the path, select the path and choose Remove From Path from the Type menu. The text and the path become separate objects again.

Joining text to a path is a great—if somewhat overused—feature. It's often confusing, though. People have a hard time understanding why the text they've just joined to a path falls where it does on the path. There are a few simple rules to keep in mind when you're joining text to a path.

◆ Text joins the path according to the alignment of the text block; left-aligned text starts at the first point in the path, right-aligned text starts at the last point on the path, centered text is centered between the first and last points, and force-justified text is spread out over the whole length of the path.

◆ If the path is shorter than the first line of text, the excess text gets shoved off the end of the path.

◆ The first line (that is, text in a text block up to the first carriage return) of text in the text block you join to the path gets joined to the top of the path; the second line of text gets joined to the bottom of the path.

◆ Justified text will bunch up when joined to a path that's shorter than the text.

If you're confused, I understand. Take a look at Figure 3-66.

In the Object Inspector, you can set the way that the text you've joined to a path follows that path. The Top and Bottom popup menus in the Object Inspector control the way the baseline of your text aligns to a path (see Figure 3-67). The Orientation popup menu controls the way that your text follows the path (see Figure 3-68).

FIGURE 3-66
Joining text and
text alignment

First point in the path

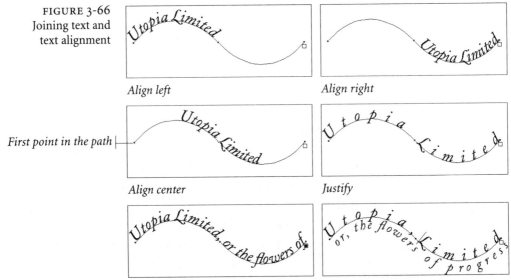

Align left

Align right

Align center

Justify

FreeHand composes as much text on a path as it can (according to the settings in the Spacing Inspector), then stores the rest as overset text.

The first paragraph of text in a text block joins to the top of the path; the second paragraph of text joins to the bottom of the path. If you join more than two paragraphs of text to a path, the other paragraphs are stored as overset text.

The new system (the Top and Bottom popup menus) takes some getting used to—particularly if you're a FreeHand 3 user. The weirdest thing is that if you choose None from both the Top and the Bottom popup menus, FreeHand doesn't display any text on the path at all. If the text you've bound to the path is linked to any other text, FreeHand flows the text into the next text block in the story. This is all perfectly logical, but it still took me months to understand it.

Beyond these options, the Show Path option makes the path a visible and printing path. You can alter the stroke and color of the path as you would any other path.

FIGURE 3-67
Baseline alignment
options for text
on a path

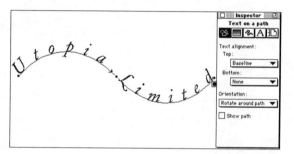

Choose Baseline to align the baseline of the text with the path.

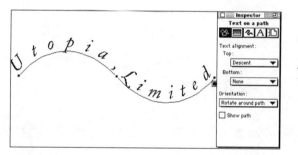

To align the bottoms of the characters to the path, choose Descent.

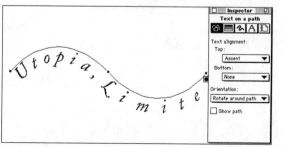

To align the tops of the characters to the path, choose Ascent.

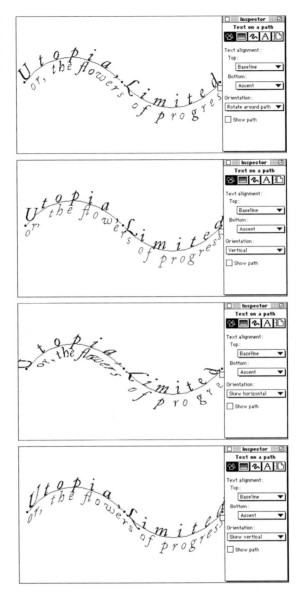

FIGURE 3-68
Controlling the
orientation of text
on a path

Tip:
Autoskewing
Text

The Skewing tool (see "Skewing" in Chapter 5, "Transforming") is lots of fun, but this trick is even more fun. When you need to make some text appear as if it's on a plane that's rotated away from the plane of the page and pasteboard, follow these steps (see Figure 3-69).

1. Draw a path using the Line tool.

FIGURE 3-69
Autoskewing text

Select the text and the line.

Press Command-J to join the text to the line.

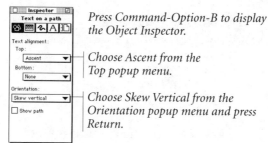

Press Command-Option-B to display the Object Inspector.

Choose Ascent from the Top popup menu.

Choose Skew Vertical from the Orientation popup menu and press Return.

Skew the text by dragging the path around.

Why you want to do stuff like this

2. Type some text.

3. Select the text and the path.

4. Press Command-Shift-Y to join the text to the path.

5. Press Command-Option-B to display the Object Inspector (if the Inspector isn't already visible, you'll have to press Command-I first).

6. Choose Ascent from the Top popup menu, and choose Skew Vertical from the Orientation popup menu. Press Return to apply your changes.

7. Now you can skew the text by dragging either end of the path anywhere you want.

Flowing Text Inside Paths

When you need a text block that's not rectangular, you can flow text inside a closed path of any shape. To flow text inside a path, follow these steps (see Figure 3-70).

1. Select the text block containing the text you want to flow inside the path.

2. Shift-select the path you want to flow the text inside (this only works with closed paths).

3. Select Flow Inside Path from the Type menu (or press Command-U). FreeHand flows the text in the text block inside the path.

If you flow a multicolumn text block inside a path, FreeHand converts it to a single column.

When you flow text inside a path, you won't be able to scale the text or change its leading, kerning, or wordspacing by dragging the corner handles of the text block. In fact, you won't see the selection handles of the text block at all—only those of the path. When you drag the corner handles of the path, FreeHand reflows the text inside the path as if you'd dragged a corner handle (that is, line breaks change, but the type formatting remains the same).

FIGURE 3-70
Flowing text
inside a path

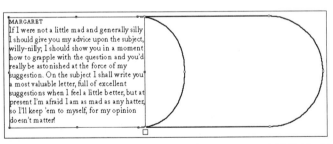

To remove text from the inside of a path, choose Remove From Path from the Type menu. FreeHand separates the path and the text block, and places them on your page as individual objects.

Tip:
The Quick Way
to Flow Text
Inside a Path

If you want to flow text inside a path, and you haven't already created the text block, here's a quick way to get text inside a path. Select the path, press Command-Shift-U (or choose Flow Inside Path from the Type menu), and start typing text (see Figure 3-71). FreeHand flows the text you type inside the path.

FIGURE 3-71
Typing text into a path

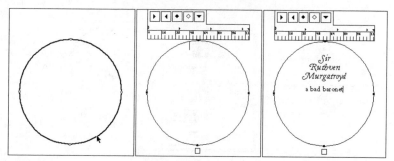

Select a path.

Press Command-Option-U. FreeHand positions a cursor inside the text block and displays the tab ruler.

Enter and format text as you would in any text block.

Wrapping Text Around Objects

Wrapping text around an object is something like the opposite of flowing text inside a path. In the former, you want to keep text out of—or away from—an object; in the latter, you want text to stay inside a path. To wrap text around an object, follow these steps (see Figure 3-72).

1. Place a basic shape or path on top of a text block that contains a few paragraphs of text. If the text block is in front of the object, the text won't wrap around the object.

2. Select both the text block and the path.

3. Press Command-Shift-W (or choose Text Wrap from the Arrange menu). FreeHand displays the Text Wrap dialog box.

FIGURE 3-72
Wrapping text around
an object

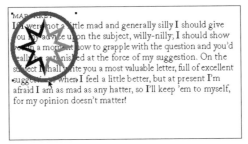

*Select the object you want to wrap text around
and bring it to the front (in this example, I've
selected the circle). Press Command-Shift-W…*

*…and FreeHand
displays the Text
Wrap dialog box.*

*Enter the standoff
distances you want for
your text wrap and
press Return.*

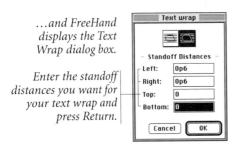

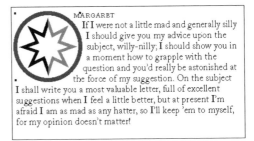

FreeHand wraps text around the object.

4. Click the Wrap icon (the one on the right) and press Return
   (or click the OK button) to close the dialog box. FreeHand
   wraps the text in the text block around the object.

You can apply a text wrap to any single object in FreeHand,
including other text blocks. If you want to apply a text wrap to all
of the objects in a group, subselect (hold down Option to subselect
grouped objects) the objects in the group and apply a text wrap to
them.

Converting Characters into Paths

When you work in graphic design, you frequently need to alter
characters of type for logos or packaging designs. For years, we
dreamed about the ability to turn type into paths we could edit.
Finally, applications such as FreeHand and Illustrator added this
feature.

You can convert characters from just about any font (TrueType, PostScript Type 1, and Fontographer PostScript Type 3 fonts) for which you have the printer (outline) font into freeform paths.

Once you've converted the characters into paths, you lose all text editing capabilities, but you gain the ability to paste things inside the character outline, to apply lines and fills that you can't apply to normal text (including Tiled, Graduated, Radial, or PostScript fills), and to change the shape of the characters themselves.

To convert characters into paths, select the text block (or text blocks) you want to convert, and then choose Convert to Paths from the Type menu. FreeHand converts the characters into paths (see Figure 3-73).

FIGURE 3-73
Converting text
to paths

 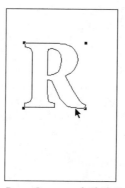 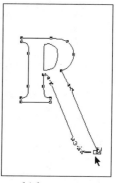

Select the text you want to convert to paths.

Press Command-Shift-P (or choose Convert to Paths from the Type menu). FreeHand converts the characters to paths...

...which you can edit as you would any other path.

When you first convert characters into paths, all of the converted characters are grouped together. To work with an individual character, choose Split Element from the Element menu. If FreeHand runs out of memory while converting characters to paths, select fewer characters and try again (or increase the amount of RAM available to FreeHand; see "Increasing FreeHand's RAM Allocation" in Chapter 1, "FreeHand Basics").

When you convert characters containing interior space (such as "P" or "O") into paths, FreeHand turns them into composite paths (see "Composite Paths" in Chapter 2, "Drawing"). This is handy.

Not only are multiple-part characters (such as "i," "é," and "ü") treated as single paths, but characters with interior paths (such as "O," "P," "A," and "D") are transparent where they should be, and fill properly (see Figure 3-74).

FIGURE 3-74
Text converted into
composite paths

When you convert characters to paths, FreeHand groups the converted characters.

To work with individual characters, choose Ungroup from the Arrange menu.

Characters with internal spaces are converted to composite paths.

To work with paths inside a composite character, hold down Option as you click on points inside the path (to subselect the points) or choose Split Element from the Arrange menu to convert the composite path to a series of normal paths.

You can always make the characters into normal (that is, not composite) paths, if you want, by selecting the character and choosing Split Element from the Element menu.

Tip:
If Your
Characters
Won't Convert

If you weren't able to convert the text into paths, make sure that you have the outline (printer) fonts and that they're somewhere FreeHand can find them (see Appendix A, "System"). If you don't have the outline fonts, FreeHand won't be able to convert your text into paths.

Tip:
Don't Worry
About Down-
loadable Fonts

If you've exported FreeHand files containing lots of downloadable fonts as EPS and then imported them into other page-layout applications, you've probably had trouble getting the EPS to print with the proper fonts. For whatever reason, EPS graphics and downloadable fonts don't mix very well.

So why bother with fonts at all? Instead, you can convert all of your text to paths (though this might not work for zoom text and other text effects) before you export your publication as an EPS (clearly, this isn't going to work if your publication contains lots of text). This way, the application that's printing your EPS doesn't have to worry about getting the downloadable fonts right. Your EPSs will print faster, too.

Tip:
Justifying
Character
Outlines

Here's something that happens to me all of the time: I convert a force-justified line of characters into paths, and then I find that I need to make them fill a different horizontal distance. Instead of creating a new text block, formatting and force-justifying it, and then converting the characters to paths again, you can follow these steps (see Figure 3-75).

1. Drag the first character of the line to the left edge of the space you want to spread the text across.

2. Drag the last character of the line to the right edge of the space you want to fill.

3. Select all of the characters in the line.

4. Press Command-Shift-A to display the Align palette, if it's not already visible.

5. Choose Distribute Widths from the Horizontal popup menu in the Align palette.

FreeHand distributes the characters you selected across the width defined by the first and last character in the line. If the text contains more than one word, you'll have to adjust the wordspacing manually, and then use the Align palette again to distribute the characters in each word—but it's still quicker than the alternative methods.

Tip:
Making
Type Glow

When you want to add a glowing outline to your type, follow these steps (see Figure 3-76).

1. Convert the text to paths.

2. Press Command-= to clone the paths.

FIGURE 3-75
Justifying character
outlines

*You've converted some
characters to paths, and,
later, realize you want
them to fill a wider (or
narrower) column.
What can you do?*

Select the converted characters.

Ungroup the paths.

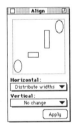

Drag one character to the width you want to fill.

*Select all the characters and press Com-
mand-Shift-A to display the Align palette
(if it's not already visible).*

*Choose Distribute Widths from the Horizon-
tal popup menu and click Apply to distribute
the characters.*

FreeHand spreads the characters to fill the line.

*If there are spaces in the text, you'll have to adjust the positions of
the characters, then redistribute the characters inside each word.*

3. Apply a stroke to the cloned paths. This stroke width should be two times the width of the glow you want to create and should be the color you want for the outside of the glow effect.

4. Press Command-B to send the cloned paths behind the original paths.

5. Apply a stroke to the original paths. This stroke should be the color you want for the inside of the glow effect.

6. Character by character, blend the original paths with their corresponding background paths. For characters with internal spaces (such as "O"), you'll have to split the paths and then blend the interior spaces separately.

FIGURE 3-76
Creating glowing type

Select the text.

Convert the text to paths.

Ungroup the converted paths, clone them, and then apply a thick, colored stroke to the cloned paths.

Printed example

Send the cloned paths to the back. Apply a thin stroke to the original characters.

Select corresponding points on the original characters and clones (sometimes, it'll be hard to see what's selected)…

…and press Command-Shift-E to blend the paths.

After Words

A picture might be worth a thousand words, but 3,000 bytes of text are worth about 1,000,000 bytes of image data. There are lots of words you'd have a hard time getting across with a thousand pictures ("mellifluous," for example).

Aldus and Altsys found that most FreeHand users wanted easier and more powerful ways to work with text and type in their publications, and, to their credit, added on-screen text editing, multi-column text blocks, the wrapping tab (a great new feature), and good paragraph formatting tools. These additions make FreeHand 4 one of the best—if not the best—tools for creating shorter documents. Now if they'd just add paragraph styles and character styles, I could do this entire book in FreeHand. As it is, around one-eighth of the pages in this book are, in fact, FreeHand pages—can you tell which?

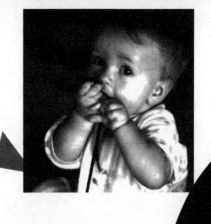

Importing and Exporting

PRINCESS IDA

Someday you'll need something FreeHand's native drawing and typesetting abilities can't give you. You'll need the to use paragraph styles, or edit color TIFFs, or to do 3-D rotation and rendering. Other applications do these things better than FreeHand does. But once you've done the work you need to do using some other application, you can bring the files you create into your FreeHand publication. And you can export your Free-Hand publications in forms that can be used in other page-layout and drawing programs.

Opening and Importing

There's a big difference between opening a file and importing, or "placing," a file. When you open a file, FreeHand converts the file's contents into objects that behave like FreeHand's own paths and text. When you import, or "place" a file, you won't be able to edit the contents of the file, though you will be able to move, scale, rotate, reflect, and skew it.

FreeHand can open EPS files saved in most Adobe Illustrator formats (FreeHand now supports Illustrator 1.1, Illustrator 88, and Illustrator 3.0—but not, at the time of this writing, Illustrator 5.0—formats), from other PostScript drawing programs, and you can import place (as opposed to import) any EPS file.

You can use word processors and page-layout programs to generate and format text using paragraph indents and tabs, and then bring the formatted text into FreeHand as RTF (Rich Text

Format—a Microsoft text-only format capable of describing anything—including text formatting and graphics—in a Microsoft Word document). You can import text-only (ASCII) files from text editors and databases. You can scan an image in either color or grayscale, edit it with an image-editing program, then place it in FreeHand, and use it as part of your FreeHand publication—including generating color separations of the images when you print. You can also create graphics in other drawing programs, and open or import them into FreeHand.

Exporting   FreeHand's no slouch at exporting graphics for use in other applications—FreeHand's exported EPS formats can be imported into every major page-layout or illustration program and combined with text and graphics created in those programs. In addition, you can now create EPS files you can open in FreeHand—no more keeping two versions of the same file on your tired hard disk. And, if exporting as an EPS doesn't work, there are several ways to export object-PICT graphics (with attached PostScript, so you won't lose any details or PostScript effects) to applications that don't support EPS import.

Last, but not least, you can export text from a FreeHand publication as either RTF or text-only files.

Importing Anything

It doesn't matter what kind of file you're importing; it always works the same way (see Figure 4-1). If all you want to know is how to get a file into your publication, read the next procedure and skip the rest of the chapter. If you really want to know all the tricks to working with the different file types, read on!

1. Press Command-Shift-D (or choose Place from the File menu). FreeHand displays the Place Document dialog box.

2. Choose a file and click the OK button (or press Return). The cursor changes into an icon, which I call a Place Gun.

FIGURE 4-1
Placing any file

Press Command-Shift-D (or choose Place from the File menu). FreeHand displays the Place Document dialog box.

Double-click on a file name in the Place Document dialog box (or select a file name and press Return)...

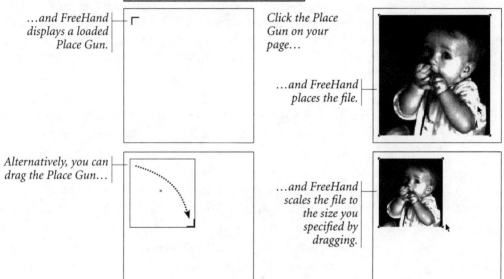

...and FreeHand displays a loaded Place Gun.

Click the Place Gun on your page...

...and FreeHand places the file.

Alternatively, you can drag the Place Gun...

...and FreeHand scales the file to the size you specified by dragging.

3. Click the Place Gun on your page (or on the pasteboard), and FreeHand imports the file you selected. Instead of clicking, you can drag the Place Gun to size the file (whether it's a graphic file or a text file) as you place it. Hold down Shift as you drag, and FreeHand sizes incoming graphics proportionally, or, if you're importing text, creates square text blocks.

About Graphic File Formats

FreeHand can import a wide range of graphic file formats, including most Adobe Illustrator EPS formats, Adobe Streamline files, grayscale and color TIFFs, EPS files, paint-type images, and PICT type graphics. From FreeHand's point of view, there are certain limitations and advantages to each of these file formats.

Just to refresh everybody's memory, here are a few quick definitions, rules, and exceptions regarding graphic file formats.

First, each Macintosh file contains information on the type of file it is (the "file type") and what application was used to create it (the "creator"). Both the file type and creator are stored as distinct, four-letter codes. You can view or edit these using programs such as Apple's free ResEdit, PrairieSoft's DiskTop, or DeBabelizer. We don't have to worry too much about the creator, but the file type code makes an enormous amount of difference in how FreeHand deals with the file.

PNTG and TIFF

File types PNTG and TIFF are bitmap, or image, formats which store their pictures as matrices (rows and columns) of pixels, each pixel having a particular gray or color value (also known as a gray depth or color depth).

PNTG-type graphics are also called paint-type graphics (because they are in the format created by the venerable MacPaint). Each pixel in a paint-type graphic has a value of either one or zero, on or off, black or white. One-bit TIFFs, often called often called bi-level TIFFs, work the same way.

Pixels in grayscale TIFF images are typically stored as values between zero and 255, which means that each pixel in these images can be one of 256 possible color (or gray) values—that's an eight-bit, grayscale TIFF. Color images can use over 16 *million* possible different values per pixel—that's a 24-bit color TIFF.

PICT and EPS

File types PICT and EPS store their pictures as sets of instructions for drawing graphic objects. Because of this, they're often called "object-oriented," which you shouldn't confuse with the "object-oriented programming" you hear so much about these days. The drawing instructions say, "Start this line at this point and draw to that point over there"; or, "This is a polygon made up of these line segments." The instructions contain values for fills and colors: "This polygon is filled with a specific gray level."

The main difference between these two formats is that the instructions in PICT graphics are expressed in QuickDraw, which is the language your Macintosh uses to draw lines, images, and characters on its screen; while the instructions in EPS graphics are written in PostScript, the language your PostScript printer uses to make marks on paper. PostScript is a far richer language for describing graphic objects.

Because the EPS graphics aren't written in the Macintosh's display language, they often carry a bitmapped PICT rendition along as a screen preview of their contents. How do they get this image? Remember that FreeHand can convert its internal database into QuickDraw (what you see on the screen) or into PostScript (what FreeHand sends to your PostScript printer). Once the file's exported as an EPS, it's not in FreeHand's native format anymore, so FreeHand can't convert it into QuickDraw commands for your screen display. When you choose to export an EPS as Macintosh EPS, FreeHand generates and attaches a QuickDraw version of the graphic to the PostScript code.

Here are the exceptions to the above descriptions.

◆ Some PICT files contain only bitmaps (I call these "bitmap-only PICT" files to differentiate them from "object PICT" files, such as those created by MacDraw). Because of problems and limitations associated with image PICT files (FreeHand can't color-separate them, and has trouble printing them), FreeHand converts them to TIFF as you import them.

◆ Object-PICT files can contain bitmapped images. FreeHand converts the images stored inside object PICTs to TIFF on import, as noted above.

◆ EPS files can also contain bitmapped images.

FreeHand can open or import both image- and object-PICT files. When you import a PICT, FreeHand converts the file to a group of FreeHand objects you can position on your page. When you want to create a new file containing only the objects in the PICT file, use Open. Once the PICT files have been converted, you can work with them as you would any other FreeHand element.

FreeHand can also directly open a number of EPS file types. You can open all files saved in the Adobe Illustrator 1.1, Adobe

Illustrator 88, and Adobe Illustrator 3.0 formats. If you can't open an Illustrator EPS file, it's probably because it's been saved in the Illustrator 5.0 format. When this happens, you can open the file with Illustrator 5.0 and save it in one of the Illustrator formats FreeHand can open. If you don't need to edit the contents of the file, you can always add it to your publication using Place.

When you open an EPS file (as opposed to placing it), the objects in the file are converted into FreeHand elements and can be edited as you'd edit any FreeHand element.

Most graphics applications can save their files in more than one file format, and almost every illustration or page-layout application can write at least one file format that FreeHand can read. If you're having trouble placing or opening a file, try opening it again in its original application (or another application that can read its original file type) and save it in a file type FreeHand can read.

FreeHand can import or open the following file types.

◆ Aldus FreeHand 2.0 through 4.0

◆ Adobe Illustrator 1.1, Adobe Illustrator 88, and Adobe Illustrator 3.0

◆ EPS (including DCS)

◆ TIFF

◆ PICT and PICT2

◆ ASCII text

◆ Rich Text Format (RTF)

Some programs are real "Swiss Army knives," and can open and save files in lots of different formats. Photoshop, for example, can open and save files in a dozen different bitmap formats. If you're working in a studio that has to deal with files from MS-DOS systems and/or dedicated computer-graphics workstations (such as the Quantel Paintbox), Photoshop is a great program to have around even if you use it for nothing more than file conversions.

There are several different file-conversion programs on the market that can make it easier to convert an unreadable image file into a file type that FreeHand can read, but the best by far is DeBabelizer. For more on DeBabelizer, see Appendix A, "System."

Tip:
There's Always
Pasting...

If the application you're trying to get something out of isn't able to save in any format FreeHand can read, try copying elements out of it and pasting them into FreeHand. This will sometimes work when all else fails.

Importing Object PICTs

FreeHand imports PICT graphics created by charting programs (such as Aldus Persuasion or Microsoft Excel), PICT tables created by Microsoft Word or Aldus Table Editor (left over from Page-Maker 4.2—PageMaker 5 didn't include it), and graphics created by PICT drawing programs (such as MacDraw II). Once you've opened or placed these files, each of the elements drawn in the original illustration is converted to a FreeHand element. Often, it'll seem like you've got two or three times as many elements as you need. This is just because PICT has weird ideas about how to draw things (see Figure 4-2).

FIGURE 4-2
"Extra" elements in
converted PICT

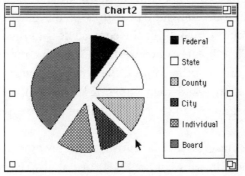

This chart looks fine in Excel...

Each filled object becomes at least two paths (one for the line; one for the fill). In this example, each line segment is a separate path.

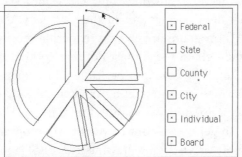

...but when you paste it into FreeHand you see that it has far more objects than you'd think it would.

Tip:
Before you
import that
PICT...

Before you place or open an object-PICT file, make sure you've checked the Convert PICT Patterns to Grays option in the Editing Preferences dialog box. This way, the nasty patterns PICT drawing applications use to represent shades of gray will get converted into what they should be—shades of gray—as you import them.

Importing Charts from Microsoft Excel and Aldus Persuasion

Both Excel and Persuasion have good charting features, and you can bring their charts into FreeHand with a minimum of fuss. To save a chart created in Persuasion, go to the slide containing the chart and choose Export from the File menu. Choose PICT from the Format popup menu, type a name for your chart, and press Return to export the chart. Now you can open and convert the chart with FreeHand (see Figure 4-3).

Excel can't export its charts as PICTs, so you'll have to copy them to the Clipboard, and then paste them into FreeHand. As you paste the chart into FreeHand, it's converted into FreeHand elements.

Tip:
For Fewer
Converted
Objects

Before you export (or copy) your chart from a PICT-type charting program, set the line widths of the filled objects in the chart to None (or whatever the equivalent is in the program you're using). When FreeHand converts PICTs, a line means one object, and a fill means another object. Because you always end up deleting all of the lines and then applying a line to the filled object, doesn't it make sense to get rid of the lines before exporting the PICT?

Importing PICTs from CAD Programs

Because most Macintosh CAD programs are capable of saving their drawings in the PICT format, it's easy to bring engineering or architectural drawings into FreeHand. Why would you want to take the drawings out of their native CAD program? Macintosh CAD programs are great at rendering precise views of an object or building, but they're just not that good at making a drawing sexy or handling type in a professional manner. Often, versions of the drawings for marketing and technical illustration need the PostScript drawing features found in FreeHand.

To get objects out of your CAD program and into FreeHand, export or save your drawing as a PICT and then open and interpret the PICT file with FreeHand. If your CAD program can't save

FIGURE 4-3
Exporting a slide
from Persuasion

In Persuasion, go to the slide you want and choose
Export from the File menu.

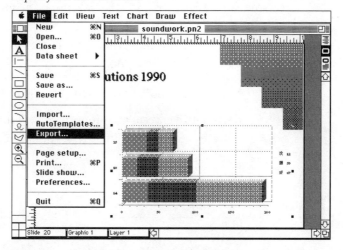

Type a name for your
chart and choose
PICT.

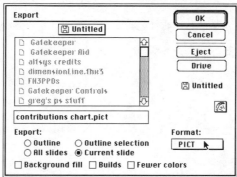

When you open the
chart, FreeHand
converts the PICT
objects into FreeHand
elements.

You can edit the
converted objects as you
would any FreeHand
elements.

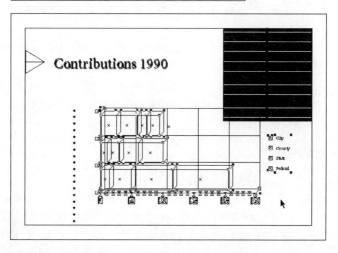

as PICT, you can still get the drawing into FreeHand by copying the objects out of the drawing program and pasting them into FreeHand.

There are a few things about converted CAD drawings you need to keep in mind (see Figure 4-4).

◆ FreeHand converts each line segment into a closed path.

◆ Arcs and ellipses are often converted into sets of closed paths made up of single straight line segments.

◆ Line joins will often miss, particularly where lines meet arcs.

FIGURE 4-4
Imported CAD
drawing

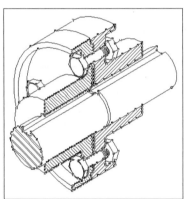

CAD drawing (from VersaCAD) pasted into FreeHand

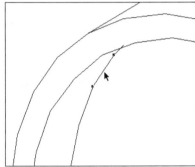

When you zoom in on the imported drawing, you'll see that all of the curves in the drawing are rendered as straight, closed paths.

The good news, however, is that you've still got the fundamental shape of the object you want. Once the objects are in a FreeHand publication, you can do as much—or as little—clean-up as you want or have time for.

Working with TIFFs

FreeHand can place and separate color TIFF images, and its TIFF printing has been improved from version 3 (which was itself much faster than FreeHand 2). I mention FreeHand 2 because I've met several FreeHand users with habits left over from that version of the program. They don't dare apply a color to a grayscale TIFF, or paste a TIFF inside a path, because they're afraid their publications will take forever to print (or won't print at all). FreeHand 3's TIFF printing improvements made it possible to use those features in your publications.

If you prefer separating your color images before final production, or if you prefer another program's separations, you can preseparate your color images, then save them as EPS graphics and place them in FreeHand. See "Importing EPS Graphics," later in this chapter.

Halftones

Commercial printing equipment can only print one color per printing plate at one time. We can get additional "tints" of that color by filling areas with small dots; at a distance (anything over a foot or so), these dots look like another color. The pattern of dots is called a halftone (for more halftoning, see Chapter 6, "Color").

To print photographic images, we use halftones for the different shades inside the photograph. The eye, silly and arbitrary thing that it is, tells our brain that the printed photograph is made up of shades of gray (or color)—not different patterns of large and small dots.

TIFFs, Screen Frequency, and Resolution

Let me introduce you to the TIFF balancing act. It goes like this: for any printer resolution (in dots per inch, or dpi) there's an ideal screen frequency (in lines per inch, or lpi)—a frequency that gives you the largest number of grays available at that printer resolution. If you go above this screen frequency, you start losing gray levels.

To find the line screen that'll give you the largest number of grays for your printer's resolution, use this equation.

$$\text{number of grays} = (\text{printer resolution in dpi/screen ruling in lpi})^2 + 1$$

If the number of grays is greater than 256, the number of grays equals 256. PostScript has a limit of 256 gray shades at any resolution.

So if you want 256 grays, and your printer resolution is 1270 dpi, the optimum screen ruling would be around 80 lpi.

What if you want to use a higher screen frequency? Something's got to give—and, usually, what gives is resolution. When you print at higher imagesetter resolutions, you can use much higher line screens before you start losing grays.

There's another part to the balancing act—the resolution of your scanned images.

It's natural to assume that by scanning at the highest resolution available from your scanner you can get the sharpest images. This bit of common knowledge, however, doesn't hold true for grayscale or color images; for these, scan at no more than twice the screen frequency you intend to use. Higher scanning resolutions do not add any greater sharpness, but the size of your image files increases dramatically. To determine the size of an image file, use this equation.

file size in kilobytes = (dpi^2*bit depth*width*height)/8192 (bits in a kilobyte)

Bit depth is eight for an eight-bit image, 24 for an RGB color image, and 32 for a CMYK image.

There's one guy I know who always complains about the size of the TIFF files he's working with. He told me the other day about a color magazine cover that took up 60Mb on his hard drive. I didn't say anything, but I think he's overscanning. Here's why—if the size of his image is 8.5 x 11 inches, and he's using a 150 lpi screen, and he's working with an RGB image, his file should be 21.4Mb (because 300^2*24*8.5*11/8192=24653.3—divide the result by 1024 to get megabytes). If he's working with a CMYK TIFF, his file size should be 300^2*32*8.5*11/8192=32871.1/1024, or 32.1Mb—still nowhere near the file size he's griping about.

Ideally, you should scan at the same size as you intend to print the image. Resolution changes when you change the size of the image, so if your scanner won't create an image at the size you want, you can compensate for the effect of resizing the image in FreeHand using this equation.

(original size/printed size)*original (scanning) resolution = resolution

If you'd scanned a three-by-three-inch image at 300 dpi and reduced it to 2.25 inches square (a reduction of 75 percent), the resolution of the image is 400 dpi.

Tip:
Scanning
Line Art

If you're scanning line art, save the files as bilevel TIFFs rather than as grayscale. You'll save lots of disk space, and your line art TIFFs will be just as sharp as they'd be if you saved them as grayscale TIFFs. Also, scan your line art at the highest resolution you can get out of your scanner. Line art, unlike grayscale and color images, does benefit from increased resolution, because you're not creating halftones.

Tip:
Increasing Line
Art Resolution

Sometimes, your scanner can't scan at a high enough resolution to give you a good scan of line art. This is especially true when you're scanning those great, copyright-free engravings from Dover's clip art books. In this case, try this trick, which I stole (with permission) from Steve Roth and David Blatner's excellent *Real World Scanning and Halftones* (also from Peachpit Press, see Appendix C, "Resources," for an address). This process produces a bilevel image at twice the resolution of your scanner.

1. Scan the image as grayscale at the highest resolution your scanner offers.

2. Resample the image to twice its original resolution using Photoshop (or other image editing program).

3. Select Threshold from the Map submenu under the Image menu. Drag the arrow back and forth to adjust the break point for black and white. Click OK.

4. Sharpen the image.

5. Convert the image to a bilevel TIFF and save it.

TIFF Controls

When you select a paint-type graphic, bilevel TIFF, or grayscale TIFF file, FreeHand adds three controls to the Object Inspector: the Edit Image button, the Transparent checkbox, and a color well (see Figure 4-5).

When you click the Edit Image button in the Object Inspector, FreeHand displays the Image dialog box (see Figure 4-6), where you can change the brightness, contrast, and (in a very rudimentary way) the gray map for the image.

FIGURE 4-5
TIFF controls

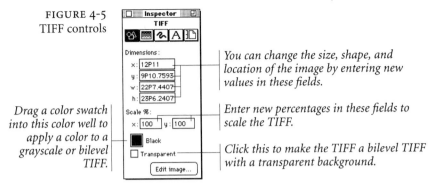

You can change the size, shape, and location of the image by entering new values in these fields.

Drag a color swatch into this color well to apply a color to a grayscale or bilevel TIFF.

Enter new percentages in these fields to scale the TIFF.

Click this to make the TIFF a bilevel TIFF with a transparent background.

FIGURE 4-6
Image dialog box

Gray level presets

Click to increase contrast

Click to increase brightness

The Image dialog box isn't modal; you can drag it out of your way if you need to see an image behind it.

Click to decrease brightness

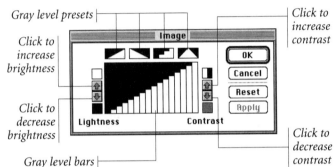

Click to decrease contrast

Gray level bars

The dialog box above is for a grayscale TIFF. If you select a bilevel TIFF or a paint-type graphic, the gray level bars show that there are only two gray levels in the image.

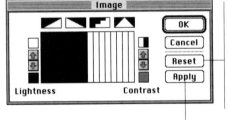

Click the Reset button to reset the image's gray levels to the default gray map (it's the same as clicking the first gray level preset).

If you make changes to the gray level bars, the Apply button becomes active. Click it to apply your changes to the image. By clicking the Apply button, you can see your changes without closing the Image dialog box.

To apply a color to a grayscale or bilevel TIFF, drag a color swatch into the color well (or you can drop a color swatch on the TIFF itself). You can't use these controls with a color TIFF, so FreeHand grays them out when you have a color TIFF selected.

Transparent. When you check the Transparent box in the Object Inspector, the white areas of a TIFF become transparent (see

Figure 4-7). If you choose this option when you've got a grayscale TIFF selected, FreeHand converts the TIFF to a bilevel TIFF. It'll seem like you've lost some image information, but don't worry—you can always uncheck Transparent again and all of your grayscale information will reappear.

Ordinarily, FreeHand treats the background of a grayscale or bilevel TIFF as an opaque white box the size of the TIFF's selection rectangle. This differs from PageMaker, where bilevel TIFFs are always transparent (unless you choose Gray or Screened in Page-Maker's Image Control dialog box) and grayscale TIFFs are always opaque (unless you choose Black and White in the Image Control dialog box).

FIGURE 4-7
Making the background of a TIFF transparent

Paint-type graphics set to Black and White have an opaque background.

Click Transparent, and you'll be able to see through the background of the image.

Tip:
Set Bilevels to
Transparent for
Faster Printing

Bilevel TIFFs (and paint files) set to Transparent print four times faster than the same images set to Black and White. Why? To make a long story short, it has to do with conformance to the OPI specifications. If you need an opaque background, why not draw a box with an opaque fill behind the transparent image?

Lightness and Contrast. The Lightness slider controls the brightness of the entire image. Increase the brightness of the image by clicking the up arrow; decrease the brightness of the image by clicking the down arrow. Note that clicking on the arrow moves the slider bars in the window to the right of Lightness (see Figure 4-8).

FIGURE 4-8
Changing lightness

*Default
lightness*

*Image
darkened by
pressing on the
down arrow in
the Lightness
control*

If you want to increase the contrast of the image, click the up arrow above Contrast. If you want to decrease the contrast of the image, click the down arrow. As you click on the arrow, the slider bars in the window to the left of Contrast move (see Figure 4-9).

FIGURE 4-9
Changing contrast

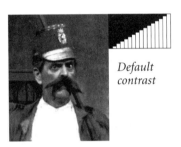

*Default
contrast*

*Increased
contrast*

Gray level sliders. Each slider inside the window in the of the Image dialog box applies to $1/16$ of the gray levels in the image, so each slider in four-bit TIFF equals one gray level (there are 16 possible gray levels in a four-bit TIFF); each slider in an eight-bit TIFF represents 16 adjacent gray levels, because there are 256 possible gray levels in an eight-bit TIFF. The gray level bars control gray levels from the darkest to the lightest in your image as they go from left to right. Slide a gray level bar up to increase the lightness of all of the pixels with that group of gray levels; slide it down to decrease their lightness (see Figure 4-10).

Gray level presets. The Image dialog box contains four default settings for the grayscale slider bars: Normal, Negative, Posterize, and Solarize. Clicking the Normal icon returns the image control settings for the TIFF to the position they were in when the TIFF was first imported. Clicking the Negative icon reverses all of the grayscale slider bar settings from their Normal setting. Posterize

FIGURE 4-10
Working with
gray level bars

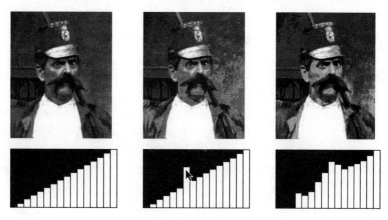

Default gray levels   *You can adjust individual gray bars until you've achieved the effect you want.*

maps all of the gray levels in the TIFF to four gray levels. Solarize maps all of the gray levels to a kind of bell curve. This produces an effect similar to the photographic effect "solarization," which is produced by exposing photographic film to light before developing the film (see Figure 4-11).

FIGURE 4-11
Gray level presets

Normal   *Negative*   *Posterize*   *Solarize*

Reset. Click the Reset button to undo any changes you've made in the Image dialog. Clicking Reset returns the gray bars to their default position—the "normal" ramp.

Apply. Click Apply button to see what the changes you've made in the Image dialog box look like without having to close the Image dialog box (remember, you can drag the dialog box around to get a better look at the TIFF).

Resizing Images to Your Printer's Resolution

Paint-type images and bilevel TIFFs often use regular patterns of pixels to represent gray areas in the image. You can see these patterns of black and white pixels in the scroll bars in most Macintosh applications. You'll also see them if you're scanning and saving images as halftones from most popular scanner software (see Figure 4-12).

When you print graphics containing these patterns, you'll often get moiré patterns in the patterned areas (see Figure 4-153).

Purists will argue that these aren't true moiré patterns, because moiré patterns are created by the mismatch of two (or more) overlapping screens. While it's true we have only one overlay, we nevertheless have two overlapping, mismatching screens—the resolution of the image and the resolution of the printer. Both are matrices of dots.

When the resolution of the image you're trying to print and the resolution of the printer don't have an integral relationship (that is, when the printer resolution divided by the image resolution equals other than a whole number), some rounding is going to have to occur, because your printer can't render fractional dots.

FIGURE 4-12
Pixel patterns
representing grays

Paint-type graphics and bilevel TIFFs often use patterns of black and white pixels to represent grays.

FIGURE 4-13
Moiré patterns

Moiré patterns

Not resized to printer resolution

Resized to match printer resolution

When this happens, parts of pixels get cut off or added to make up the difference (see Figure 4-14).

Instead of figuring out the scaling percentages for each bilevel image you're working with, take advantage of FreeHand's "magic stretch" feature, which resizes images to match the resolution of your target printer.

FIGURE 4-14
Integral and non-integral resolutions

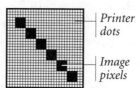

Printer dots

Image pixels

Your printer can't print fractional dots—they're either on or off. When your image pixels and printer dots have an integral relationship (4:1 in this example), the printer can match your image's pixels.

When the image pixels don't match your printer's resolution, the printer has to guess which printer dots it should turn on or off...

...which distorts your image.

Hold down Option as you resize an image and the image snaps to sizes that have an integral relationship with the selected printer resolution. Hold down Shift and Option as you size the graphic both to size the graphic proportionally and to match the printer's resolution (see Figure 4-15).

FIGURE 4-15
Magic-stretching an image

 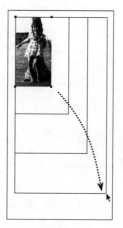 

Point at a corner of an image, hold down Option-Shift...

...and drag. The image snaps to possible sizes as you drag.

When you've reached the size you want, stop dragging.

Where do you set the printer's resolution? Enter a value in the Printer Resolution field in the Setup Inspector that matches the resolution of the printer you'll be use for the final printing of the publication (not the resolution of your proof printer).

The value you enter in the Printer Resolution field does not affect the actual resolution of your printer; it's just there to give FreeHand a value to use when calculating magic stretch sizes.

Magic stretching doesn't improve the printing of grayscale or color TIFFs—even though they'll snap to the same sizes—and it doesn't have any effect on object-PICT or EPS graphics.

Extracting Paint-Type Graphics

If you need to extract sized paint files from your FreeHand publication so that you can edit them in a paint program, you can't just copy them out of FreeHand and paste them into the paint program. If you do, the graphics will look distorted when you paste them into the paint program. You'd need this trick if the original paint-type graphics had been lost, because FreeHand has to link to an external file to be able to print images.

What you have to do is return them to their original, glorious, 72-dpi state. You can do this using the Image dialog box.

1. Select the graphic you want to extract.

2. Double-click the Scaling tool in the toolbox to display the scaling section of the Transform palette.

3. Type "100" in the Horizontal and Vertical scale fields and press Return. The graphic pops back to its original size.

4. Copy the image to the Clipboard.

5. Paste the image into a paint program.

6. Save the image.

7. Replace the unlinked image in your FreeHand file with the file you've just created. You can use the numeric position and scaling information in the Object Inspector to get the image into the same position as the original.

This trick won't work with images that have an original resolution of other than 72 dpi, because FreeHand constructs a 72-dpi screen image of each image as it's placed. For images with resolutions over 72 dpi, a file you'd create this way would lack some of the information found in the original image.

Cropping TIFF Images

If you're used to PageMaker's Cropping tool, and are looking for a similar tool in FreeHand, you're out of luck—there isn't one. Instead, however, you can use FreeHand's Paste Inside feature to crop your image. It's better than the Cropping tool anyway. When you want to use just part of a TIFF image in your FreeHand publication, try this (see Figure 4-16).

1. Size the TIFF to the size you want.

2. Draw a path around the part of the TIFF you want to use.

3. Select the TIFF and press Command-X to cut it to the Clipboard.

4. Select the path and choose Paste Inside from the Edit menu. FreeHand pastes the TIFF inside the path.

FIGURE 4-16
Cropping a TIFF

Draw a path around the area you want to crop.

Cut the TIFF image to the Clipboard, then select the path and paste the image inside the path.

While I'm telling you about cropping images, I should also mention that it's better to create your images in your scanning or image-editing software so that you don't have to crop. When you crop an image, the parts of the TIFF you can't see don't just go away; FreeHand still has to keep track of the entire TIFF, which means slower screen redraw. It also means you've got a larger TIFF than you need stored somewhere. So don't crop in FreeHand unless you have to.

Tip:
Adjusting
Cropping

If you just need to make a minor adjustment to the way you've cropped a TIFF, try this (see Figure 4-17).

1. Select the cropped TIFF.

2. Press Command-M to display the Transform palette, if it's not already visible. If the Move panel of the Transform palette isn't already visible, click the Move icon to display it.

3. Uncheck Contents, then drag the path (or move the path using the X and Y fields in the Transform palette. FreeHand moves the clipping path without changing the position of the TIFF inside the clipping path.

FIGURE 4-17
Adjusting cropping

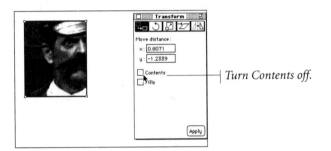

Turn Contents off.

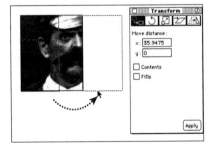

Drag the path to a new location.

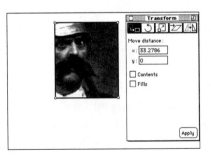

FreeHand moves the path, but leaves the path's contents in their original position. To move the path back to its original position, turn Contents on again, so that the TIFF moves with the path.

Creating an Outline Mask for a TIFF Image

Something that people often miss when they think about cropping images in FreeHand is that the path you're using to crop the image can be any size or shape. You can paste TIFFs inside ellipses, characters, or totally freeform paths. This comes in handy when you've got to pull a particular object out of a placed TIFF file. Trace the part of the TIFF you want, cut the TIFF to the Clipboard, and paste it inside the shape you've just drawn (see Figure 4-18).

Voilà! Instant outline mask. Note that you can adjust the cropping by dragging individual points on the clipping path to get it just right, and that you can stroke the path to trap the image if you need to (for more on trapping images, see Chapter 6, "Color"). Just for fun, go ask your local prepress outfit what they'd charge to do this.

FIGURE 4-18
Creating an outline mask

Draw a path around the parts of the image you want (it helps to send the image to the background before tracing).

Paste the image into the path. You can adjust the points on the path to change the cropping of the image.

Creating a Vignette Mask for a TIFF Image

Here's another photographic effect that used to cost a bundle—creating a vignette. What's a vignette? It's where a photo progressively lightens as it approaches the edge of some shape (traditionally, an ellipse) until the photographic material is entirely white at the point at which it reaches the edges of the shape. Think of the photos of your 19th-century ancestors—they're probably vignettes.

While this technique is still going to be cheaper than doing the same thing photographically, it's going to take some time to print, especially on an imagesetter. It's also much easier to do using Photoshop (or other image-editing application), and should only be done in FreeHand in desperation. Still, desperation is what this book's about. The process is illustrated in Figure 4-19.

1. Draw a path around the part of the TIFF that you want to leave unchanged. This area is the center of the vignette effect. The TIFF should extend for some distance beyond this area in all directions.

2. Cut the TIFF to the Clipboard and paste it inside the path.

3. Clone the clipped TIFF.

4. Scale the cloned clipping path so that it's larger than the original clipping path (in the example shown below, I scaled each path in the vignette so that it was 105 percent of its original size).

5. Select the cloned clipping path and choose Cut Contents from the Edit menu. FreeHand places the TIFF on top of the path.

6. Without deselecting the TIFF, apply a color the TIFF so that it's lighter than the original TIFF. In our example, I made each TIFF 10 percent lighter than the previous one.

7. Cut the TIFF to the Clipboard, select the cloned path, and choose Paste Inside from the Edit menu to paste the TIFF inside the path.

8. Send the path to the back, or to another layer that's behind the original clipping path.

9. Repeat steps 3 through 8 until all or nearly all of the color values inside the TIFF are white.

When you work through this procedure, you end up with a stack of cropped images, with the TIFFs inside each clipping path getting lighter and lighter as they get farther and farther from the center of the vignette.

It's occurred to me that you could probably produce the same effect using the Lightness control in the Image dialog box instead

FIGURE 4-19
Creating a vignette

Create several paths.

Create several clones of the image. Paste the images into the paths, pasting the lightest image into the largest path.

of coloring each TIFF a lighter shade. I used colors because it's easier to control the amount of a color—there's no numeric way to adjust lightness. Another point is that you can do this technique much faster if you work in Keyline view—you don't have to spend any time redrawing the TIFF. Finally, you can probably do a better job of this in an image-editing program.

Enhancing Images Using Aldus PrePrint

Because FreeHand's got the ability to color separate color images, you don't necessarily need Aldus' color-separation application PrePrint. But its image-enhancement controls are worth taking a look at (and, if you have a copy of PageMaker 4.2, you already have a copy of PrePrint 1.5—but it wasn't included with PageMaker 5).

To enhance an image with PrePrint, start PrePrint, open a TIFF image, and use the commands on the Image menu to alter the TIFF. Once you've applied the commands you want, save the TIFF and place it in FreeHand.

Auto Enhance, in particular, is a shocker. It actually does a great job of improving images for printing. It doesn't, and shouldn't, replace the manual controls you'll find in image-editing programs, but it's a quick and painless way to get pretty good results when you don't have time, experience, or patience enough to twiddle with more sophisticated programs, such as Photoshop.

When you're through working with the image in PrePrint, you can save the file as either a color TIFF or as a set of DCS separations (for more on DCS separation, see "Preseparating Color TIFFS" later in this chapter).

Importing EPS Graphics

If you work with other programs that can export files as EPS, or if you write your own PostScript programs, you can import those files into FreeHand and combine them with text and graphics you've created in FreeHand. You have the choice of placing EPS files as imported graphics or—with some EPS formats—converting the graphic into FreeHand objects.

If You See an "X" Instead of a Graphic

When you import an EPS graphic (and you're not in Keyline mode), if you see a box with an "X" through it, instead of a screen preview, you've imported a file that doesn't have a screen preview attached. The file contains the dimensions of the graphic, and it'll probably print correctly, but there's nothing for you to look at as you lay out your page. This happens in these scenarios.

- There's not enough memory to display the preview. Increase FreeHand's application size (see "Increasing FreeHand's RAM allocation" in Chapter 1, "FreeHand Basics"), or close some publications.

- There was too little memory available to create the screen preview when FreeHand (or other application) created the EPS file. If you're placing a FreeHand EPS, think again: wouldn't it be better to paste that graphic into the current publication instead of placing it?

- The graphic has no screen preview attached. This happens if the file is a PostScript program written by an application that doesn't support preview images, or if the file was created using word processor, or if the person creating the EPS saved it without a screen preview. This also happens if you've edited a normal EPS with a word processor and have not reattached the screen preview PICT. See "Converting FreeHand 3 EPS Files to Illustrator 1.1 EPS Format" below on editing old EPS graphics with a word processor.

If you can't get by without a screen preview, see the section "Creating a Screen Preview for EPS Graphics," later in this chapter.

Importing FreeHand EPS

Think about it—why do you want to import a FreeHand EPS instead of copying the elements out of one publication and pasting them into the current publication? When you import an EPS, there's a whole bunch of information attached to the FreeHand objects that you just don't need. And it takes longer to print—have a look at Figure 4-20.

If you're placing the EPS because you want to deal with the objects as a single graphic, why not group them?

FIGURE 4-20
Importing FreeHand
EPS versus pasting
FreeHand objects

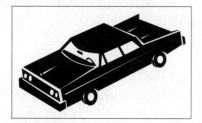 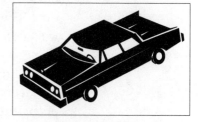

FreeHand EPS placed in FreeHand. Processing time: 34 seconds

FreeHand elements pasted from one publication to another. Processing time: two seconds

Importing Illustrator EPS

If I had to choose between FreeHand 4 and Illustrator 5.0, I'd take FreeHand. In fact, I don't use Illustrator much, these days, though it's an excellent program. But I do know lots of people who swear by Illustrator, and I know even more people who strongly prefer using both. Luckily, the path from Illustrator to FreeHand is clear. FreeHand can open or place EPS files created by Adobe Illustrator 1.1, Adobe Illustrator 88, or Adobe Illustrator 3.0. I've been able to open EPS files created in Illustrator 5.0 some of the time.

When you open an Illustrator EPS, FreeHand converts the paths and type into FreeHand elements. If you place an Illustrator EPS, FreeHand displays the screen-preview image (if there is one) and treats the file as an imported graphic—you can transform it, but you can't edit its contents.

When you open an Illustrator EPS, some of Illustrator's features are converted; some aren't.

Paths. FreeHand imports paths in Illustrator EPSs just as they were drawn in Illustrator. FreeHand converts Illustrator points into curve points whenever possible, though points defining sharp angles or sudden changes of curve direction are converted into corner points. As points are converted, FreeHand adds handles to each converted point so that the path matches the path you drew in Illustrator.

Text. FreeHand converts Illustrator text into FreeHand text blocks. Typically, the Illustrator text is converted one line at a time, though any changes in type style or font will create new text blocks, as will any kerning (including automatic kerning pairs). If the EPS was saved in the Illustrator 1.1 format, each line of text will be an individual text block.

Color. Process colors you've defined in Illustrator are imported as you defined them, but the color names don't appear in your Colors palette. To add colors from a converted Illustrator file to your Color List, follow the stesp described in "Adding Colors from Illustrator" in Chapter 6, "Color."

Blends. Illustrator blends are often made up of separate, colored objects, so you can't change the blend once you've imported it except by deleting the intermediate blend steps and blending again.

Complex Paths. Compound paths you've created using Illustrator's Make Compound command are converted to FreeHand's composite paths. ("Composite path" and "compound path" are just two ways of saying the same thing.)

Creating Your Own EPS Graphics

You can create EPS graphics using a word processor or LaserTalk (see Appendix A, "System," for more on LaserTalk), but you've got to remember two things.

◆ If it doesn't print when you download it, it won't print after you've placed it in FreeHand. Always test every change you make in your word processor by downloading the text file to the printer and seeing what you get before you place the file in FreeHand, or at least before you take the FreeHand file to a service bureau.

◆ When you edit an EPS graphic with a word processor and save it in the text-only (ASCII) format, you break the link between the PostScript text part of the EPS and the screen preview PICT resource. You can use ResEdit to rejoin the two parts of the EPS, provided you don't overwrite the original file.

Why would you want to create your own EPS graphics? There are lots of things you can do with PostScript that FreeHand doesn't do (yet). See Chapter 8, "PostScript," for some examples and more on creating your own EPS graphics.

Creating Invisible EPS Graphics

I often want to use full-page EPS backgrounds but I can't stand waiting for the background's screen preview to redraw every time I do something. In FreeHand, of course, the easiest thing to do is to set the layer the background's on to be invisible. But if you're creating a FreeHand EPS background to place in some (other) page-layout program, you need this trick (see Figure 4-21).

FIGURE 4-21
Creating an invisible
EPS graphic

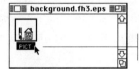

Locate and open the EPS file using ResEdit.

Once the file's open, double-click on the PICT resource class icon.

ResEdit displays the EPS file's screen-preview image. Select the image and press Delete.

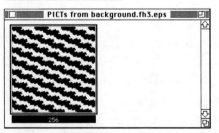

Press Command-K to create a new PICT resource.

Press Command-I to display the Info dialog box. Type "256" in the ID field.

Press Command-S to save your work, and quit ResEdit.

When you place the EPS file, you won't see the screen preview, but it'll print just as it did before.

1. Open the EPS file with ResEdit (for more on ResEdit, see Appendix A, "System").

2. Open the PICT resource.

3. Choose Clear from the Edit menu.

4. Press Command-K to create a new PICT resource.

5. Make sure that the new PICT has a resource ID of 256 by pressing Command-I and typing 256 in the ID field in the Info window that appears.

6. Press Command-S to save the file, and quit ResEdit.

Now, when you place the edited EPS file, you'll get a transparent bounding box that's the size of the graphic, but no screen preview will appear, and it won't take any time to redraw the image. The image will print out, though.

Creating Visible, Nonprinting Graphics

If you want to place a graphic on the page, but don't want it to print, the best thing to do is to move it to some nonprinting layer. Use this trick when you want to create a FreeHand EPS to import into a page-layout program, and want the contents of the graphic to display but not print.

1. Open a copy of the EPS file with a word processor.

2. Delete everything in the document from the line that begins with "%%BoundingBox:" to the line that says "%%EndDocument" and save the file as text-only.

3. Launch ResEdit.

4. Locate and open the text file you just created. When ResEdit asks if you want to add a resource fork to the file, click OK.

5. Open the original EPS file and select the PICT resource class.

6. Copy the PICT resource class out of the original EPS file and paste it into the resource listing for the text file.

7. Press Command-S to save the file, and quit ResEdit.

Why would anyone want to do this? It's handy to be able to place nonprinting notes ("type headline here") in page-layout programs. Sometimes people want to lay out and proof their publications without having to take the time to print the EPS.

Preseparating Color TIFFs

If you prefer the color separations of color TIFF images created by some other program—Adobe Photoshop and Aldus PrePrint come to mind—to the separations created by FreeHand, you can preseparate color TIFFs and place them in FreeHand as EPS or DCS files.

EPS files created this way contain all of the information the color-separation application would have sent to a printer to create color separations of an image. DCS is a variation of EPS, and stores the color separated image as five files (one for each color plus a "header" file that's the part you work with).

When you place the preseparated file (either EPS or DCS) in FreeHand and print the publication, FreeHand separates the file as the original application would have.

The following steps show how you'd preseparate an image using Adobe Photoshop.

1. In Photoshop, make sure that your separation settings are the way you want them. Switch to CMYK mode, and Photoshop separates the image.

2. Choose Save As. In the Save As dialog box, choose EPS from the File Format popup menu. Click the Save button. The EPS Options dialog box appears.

3. In the EPS Options dialog box, pick a screen preview from the list of preview options, choose either ASCII or Binary as your encoding scheme (binary files are smaller), check the Include Halftone Screens and Include Transfer Functions options (if you want to include Photoshop's screening). Check the Desktop Color Separation option if you want to use the DCS method of storing the file as five separate files. Press Return to save your image as an EPS file.

Place this file in FreeHand, and it'll be separated like any other imported EPS graphic.

Importing Text

After I'd finished producing the documentation for FreeHand 2 at Aldus, FreeHand's product manager asked me what one feature I'd like to see in FreeHand 3. "Give me a Text Place Gun," I said. In FreeHand 4, I've finally gotten my wish (though I doubt it had much to do with my request)—you can import, format, and edit both formatted (RTF) and unformatted (text-only) text files.

Importing Text-Only Files

Word-processing programs, databases, spreadsheets, and almost all other applications speak one common language—they can all save their documents as text-only, or ASCII files. Text-only files don't include any formatting information—no font, size, leading, or paragraph spacing—they're just characters.

Sometimes you want to save files as text-only to strip out any formatting that's been applied to them (usually, you do this because the person who entered the text applied formatting you don't want). Sometimes text-only is the only kind of file an application can write. Either way, you can import the text files into FreeHand and format them there.

The only real trick to working with text files has do with where they come from. Often, text files generated by applications running on other platforms (you know, DOS/Windows boxes, Sun Workstations, and NeXT machines) or from online services (such as Compuserve and the Internet) are full of weird characters, or, most often, have carriage returns at the end of every line in a paragraph. In general, you need to run these text files through a conversion utility before you place them in FreeHand. I use Apple File Exchange (part of Apple's basic system software) and McSink (a shareware text editor) to convert text files. For more on text file conversion utilities, see Appendix A, "System."

Tip:
Inserting Text into an Existing Text Block

When you're placing a text file in FreeHand, you can't choose to insert the text into an existing text block (unlike PageMaker, where you have the option of either inserting the incoming text in existing text, or of replacing the existing text with the incoming text).

So you have to place the text, then copy text out of the new text block and paste it into the original text block. The following steps show you the least-painful method I've come up with for doing this (see Figure 4-22).

1. Drag-place the text file in your FreeHand publication (drag-placing means you can keep the text block small). After you place the file, FreeHand selects the new text block.

2. Press Command-X to cut the text to the Clipboard.

3. Click the Text tool where you want to insert the text, or, if you want to replace all of the text in a story, triple-click one of the text blocks in that story with the Pointer tool.

4. Press Command-V to paste the text you copied to the Clipboard. FreeHand inserts the text in the text block (or text blocks).

Using this technique, you can set up your text blocks *before* you have any text to place in them. It gives you something to do while you're waiting for someone else to finish writing or editing the text—a handy think, especially if you're laying out a magazine or newspaper in Freehand.

FIGURE 4-22
Inserting text in an
existing text block

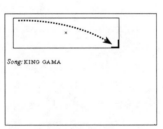

Drag-place the text.

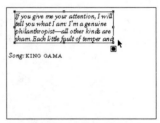

Cut the text to the Clipboard.

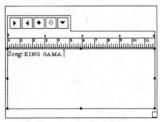

*Click the text tool where you
want to insert the text.*

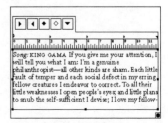

Paste the text into the story.

Importing RTF

Being able to import text-only files is wonderful, but what if you need to import formatted text from your word processor or page layout application? That's where Microsoft's Rich Text Format (RTF) comes in. Technically, RTF isn't a file format—RTF files are saved as text-only format—it's a specific way of organizing text inside a file. RTF files contain text codes and values capable of describing anything and everything that can appear in a Microsoft Word document. The best way to understand how RTF works is to look at a sample RTF file, created by FreeHand (see Figure 4-22). This example file shows almost all of the text formatting FreeHand can import or export from an RTF file.

One of the peculiarities of RTF is that it repeats local formatting for each paragraph, even if the formatting hasn't changed between paragraphs, ass you can see in the sample. This is just how RTF, as defined by Microsoft, works. If you leave out the repetition for a paragraph, FreeHand formats the text with the current default text formatting when you import the file.

If you look at a Microsoft Word RTF file, you'll see a lot more information at the start of the file than you see in Figure 4-22—most of it, from FreeHand's point of view, useless. Word, when it writes an RTF file, includes every font that's currently installed in your system in the font table (the section starting with "\fonttbl"), whether that font is used in the document or not (FreeHand includes only the fonts you've actually *used*, which makes more sense to me).

Following the font table, most RTF files will include a color table ("\colortbl"), and sometimes a table containing the styles defined in the document ("\stylesheet").

A few notes about RTF files.

◆ Most measurements in an RTF file are in *twips*, or twentieths of a point (.05 point). Type size is measured in half-point increments. If you export FreeHand text containing measurements finer than a twip (a leading value of 10.12, for example), or type sizes finer than half a point (10.7, for example), FreeHand rounds to the nearest twip, or half point, respectively.

FIGURE 4-22
FreeHand RTF file

```
{\rtf1\mac{\fonttbl{\f3\fnil Times;}{\f4\fnil Bembo;}}
{\colortbl\red0\green0\blue0;\red0\green0\blue0;\red158\green48\blue0;}
\deftab720\pard \li0 \ri0 \fi0 \sb0 \sa0 \fs48 \f4 \cf1 \ql \sl-200 RTF Test
Document\par
\pard \li0 \ri0 \fi0 \sb0 \sa0 \fs20 \f4 \cf1 \ql \sl-200 {\b bold}\par
\pard \li0 \ri0 \fi0 \sb0 \sa0 \fs20 \f4 \cf1 \ql \sl-200 {\i italic}\par
\pard \li0 \ri0 \fi0 \sb0 \sa0 \fs20 \f4 \cf1 \ql \sl-200 {\b \i bold italic}\par
\pard \li0 \ri0 \fi0 \sb0 \sa0 \fs20 \f4 \cf1 \ql \sl-200 {\up6 baseline shift
up}\par
\pard \li0 \ri0 \fi0 \sb0 \sa0 \fs20 \f4 \cf1 \ql \sl-200 {\dn6 baseline shift
do}{\dn6 wn}\par
\pard \li0 \ri0 \fi0 \sb0 \sa0 \tqr\tx2162 \fs20 \f4 \cf1 \ql \sl-200 \tab right
tab\par
\pard \li0 \ri0 \fi0 \sb0 \sa0 \tqr\tx727 \fs20 \f4 \cf1 \ql \sl-200 \tab left
tab\par
\pard \li0 \ri0 \fi0 \sb0 \sa0 \tqc\tx1322 \fs20 \f4 \cf1 \ql \sl-200 \tab center
tab\par
\pard \li0 \ri0 \fi0 \sb0 \sa0 \tqdec\tx2162 \fs20 \f4 \cf1 \ql \sl-200 \tab
decimal tab.\par
\pard \li0 \ri0 \fi0 \sb0 \sa0 \fs20 \f4 \cf1 \ql \sl-200 align left text\par
\pard \li0 \ri0 \fi0 \sb0 \sa0 \fs20 \f4 \cf1 \qr \sl-200 align right text\par
\pard \li0 \ri0 \fi0 \sb0 \sa0 \fs20 \f4 \cf1 \qc \sl-200 centered text\par
\pard \li0 \ri0 \fi0 \sb0 \sa0 \fs20 \f4 \cf1 \qj \sl-200 justified text\par
\pard \li0 \ri0 \fi0 \sb120 \sa0 \fs20 \f4 \cf1 \ql \sl-200 {\expnd20 range
k}{\expnd20 er}{\expnd20 ned text}\par
\pard \li0 \ri0 \fi0 \sb120 \sa0 \fs20 \f4 \cf1 \ql \sl-200 space above\par
\pard \li0 \ri0 \fi0 \sb0 \sa1440 \fs20 \f4 \cf1 \ql \sl-200 space below\par
\pard \li720 \ri0 \fi0 \sb0 \sa0 \fs20 \f4 \cf1 \ql \sl-200 left indent\par
\pard \li720 \ri0 \fi0 \sb0 \sa0 \fs20 \f4 \cf1 \ql \sl-200 right indent\par
\pard \li0 \ri0 \fi240 \sb0 \sa0 \fs20 \f4 \cf1 \ql \sl-200 first line indent\par
\pard \li0 \ri0 \fi0 \sb0 \sa0 \fs20 \f4 \cf1 \ql \sl-200 end of \line line
character \par
\pard \li0 \ri0 \fi0 \sb0 \sa0 \fs20 \f4 \cf1 \ql \sl-200 dis\-chy\par
\pard \li0 \ri0 \fi0 \sb0 \sa0 \fs20 \f4 \cf2 \ql \sl-200 color\par
\pard \li0 \ri5330 \fi0 \sb0 \sa0 \fs48 \f4 \cf1 \ql \sl-480 {\shad shadow}\par
\pard \li0 \ri5330 \fi0 \sb0 \sa0 \fs48 \f4 \cf1 \ql \sl-480 {\outl outline}\par
\pard \li0 \ri5330 \fi0 \sb0 \sa0 \fs48 \par }
```

◆ Type styles and baseline shift are typically enclosed in "curly" brackets (for example: "{\b \i bold italic}")—the brackets mark the beginning and end of the formatting.

◆ Wrapping tabs are not supported by RTF.

◆ Column breaks are not supported by RTF.

◆ Horizontal scaling of text is not supported by RTF.

◆ Text colors are imported as unnamed, process colors (they're represented as RGB colors in the RTF file, but they're converted to CMYK as FreeHand imports the file).

◆ FreeHand doesn't support case changes you can specify in a word processor or page layout application. When FreeHand imports an RTF file containing "\caps" (all capitals) or "\scaps" (small capitals), it ignores the codes and draws the text as it was typed (small caps will appear in lowercase).

◆ FreeHand doesn't support the type styles Strikethrough and Underline. FreeHand imports text coded with the RTF codes "\strike" (strikethrough), or "\ul" (underline) without those formatting attributes.

◆ Hidden text ("\v"), table of contents markers ("\tc'), and index entries ("\xe" and "\:") are stripped out of RTF files on import into FreeHand.

◆ FreeHand doesn't support graphics (PICT, EPS, or TIFF) embedded in RTF files.

◆ FreeHand's Zoom and Inline text effects aren't supported by RTF.

◆ RTF codes specifying page layout information, such as page headers and footers, explicitly specified paragraph positions, or page margins, are stripped out of the RTF file on import into FreeHand.

Table 4-1 shows the RTF codes you'll see and use most often.

	Code	What it means
TABLE 4-1 Frequently used RTF codes	\sn	Style number. This won't make any difference to FreeHand, but you might see it in RTF files generated by other applications. In addition, RTF files generated by applications which support paragraph styles, such as PageMaker, QuarkXPress, and Microsoft Word, will have a table (like the RTF font table or color table) at the start of the document listing the styles and style names used in the document.
	\fn	Font number. The number of the font in the font table at the start of the RTF document.

TABLE 4-1
Frequently used
RTF codes (continued)

Code	What it means
\fs*n*	Font size in half points
\b	Bold
\i	Italic
\sl-*n*	Leading. For some reason, both FreeHand and Word put a "-" in front of the leading amount.
\li*n*	Left indent
\ri*n*	Right indent
\fi*n*	First line indent
\tx*n*	Tab position
\cf*n*	Text color. The number of the color determined by the color's position in the color table at the start of the RTF document.
\par	Carriage return
\pard	Start of a new paragraph (you can think of "\par" and "\pard" as a carriage return/line feed combination—it's what they might be if you transfer this RTF file to a DOS/Windows PC—on the Macintosh, of course, all you really need is "\par," but FreeHand adds "\pard" because that's how the RTF specification says it's done).
\ql	Left alignment
\qr	Right alignment
\qj	Justified alignment
\qc	Centered alignment
\tqr	Right-aligned tab
\tql	Left-aligned tab

TABLE 4-1
Frequently used
RTF codes (continued)

Code	What it means
\tqc	Center tab
\tqdec	Decimal tab
\txn	Tab position (always follows "\tqr," "\tql," "\tqc," or "\tqdec")
\'n	Special character expressed as a hexadecimal number
\upn	Baseline shift up (from some applications, superscript)
\dnn	Baseline shift down (from some applications, subscript)
\-	Discretionary hyphen
\tab	Tab character
\deftab	Distance between default tabs
\line	End-of-line character
\~	Nonbreaking space
\shad	Shadow text effect
\outl	Stroked text
\expndn	Range-kerning amount
\sbn	Space above. Should be space below, but I think there's an error in the FreeHand RTF export filter.
\san	Space below. Should be space above, but, again, I think something's wrong with the filter.
\fnil, \froman	Alternate fonts—RTF includes its own font substitution scheme. "\froman" and "\fswiss" tell Word on DOS/Windows PCs to use Times (or even "TmsRmn") or Helvetica instead of the original font, if the original font's not found. FreeHand always uses "\fnil,"—no substitution.

Importing Text Tagged with XPress Tags

Part of the "Real World" tradition of this book is the idea that you might, someday, have to convert files from one format to another using nothing but a text editor. For example, let's say you're stranded in the middle of the Sahara, you have a file that's been exported from QuarkXPress as an XPress Tags (Quark's text-only equivalent to RTF) file you need to import into FreeHand, and you don't have a copy of QuarkXPress (if you did, you could export the text as RTF, a format FreeHand understands). Do you wait until a passing caravan offers you the use of their copy of XPress, or do you roll up your sleeves and convert the file yourself?

Now that your forearms are bare, take a look at Table 4-2, which shows the RTF equivalents for commonly-used XPress Tags.

TABLE 4-2
Converting XPress
Tags to RTF

Attribute	XPress Tag	RTF equivalent
Plain	<P>	\plain
Bold	<B>	\b
Italic	<I>	\i
Outline	<O>	\outl
Shadow	<S>	\shad
Baseline shift up/superscript	<+> (or <bn>)	\up
Baseline shift down/subscript	<-> (or <b-n>)	\dn
Font	<f"name">	\f$n$ (Where *name* is the name of the font in your system and n is the number of the font in your font table.)
Type size	<zn>	\fs$n$ (multiply the XPress Tag specified font size by 20 to convert it to twips.)
Color	<c"name">	\cf$n$ (Where *name* is the name of the color in your XPress publication and n is the number of the color in your RTF color table.)

	Attribute	XPress Tag	RTF equivalent
TABLE 4-2 Converting XPress Tags to RTF (continued)	Left align	<*L>	\ql
	Right align	<*R>	\qr
	Center	<*C>	\qc
	Justify	<*J>	\qj
	Paragraph format	<*p(*n*, *n*, *n*, *n*, *n*, G or g>	The values in the tag specify left indent, first-line indent, right indent, leading, space before, and space after, respectively (so you'd convert them to twips by multiplying them by 20, and then use \li *n*, fi *n*, ri *n*, \sl-*n*, \sb *n*, and \sa *n* to render them in RTF syntax. "G or g" specifies whether the paragraph is locked to XPress' baseline grid, and has no RTF counterpart.
	Tabs	<*t(*n*, *n*, "character")>	The first value in the tag is the tab's position, the second value is the tab's alignment (where 1=center, 2=right, 3=decimal, and 4=left), followed by the tab's leader *character*. In RTF, you'd set the tab's alignment first using \tqr, \tql, \tqc, or \tqdec, and then set the position (again, convert the value in the XPress Tag file to twips by multiplying by 20) using \tx *n*. FreeHand doesn't have tab leaders, so you can omit the leader character.

Attribute	XPress Tag	RTF equivalent
Return	<\n>	\par
End-of-line character	<\d>	\line
Dishy	<h>	\-
Kerning or range kerning	<kn> or <tn>	Convert the values in the tags to twips by multiplying them by .0005 (each increment is $1/200$ of an em), then multiplying them by the current type size, and then dividing by 20 to convert to twips. An XPress Tag value of 4000, in 24-point text, therefore, is equal to an RTF value of two, because 4000*.0005*24/20=2.4 (which we round down, because you can't have fractional twips).

You can automate most or all of this conversion process using the incredible search-and-replace utility Torquemada the Inquisitioner. For more on Torquemada, see Appendix A, *System*.

Fixing PageMaker's RTF

As I write this book, PageMaker's RTF export filter isn't working properly, which means you can't export text from PageMaker for use in FreeHand. In addition, you can't reliably copy the text from PageMaker into FreeHand and have it retain its formatting, because the RTF PageMaker copies to the Clipboard is also generated by the RTF filter.

The trouble is that PageMaker's RTF export filter doesn't work when you have more than 30 fonts on your system (that's fewer than eight typical font families, for anyone counting—and bear in mind that the required set of Geneva, Chicago, and Monaco are going to burn 12 of your available slots). When you have more than 30 fonts installed, PageMaker doesn't write a font table into the RTF files it generates.

While friends at Aldus assure me that they'll make a new RTF export filter for PageMaker available as soon as they possibly can, I'll show you how to fix PageMaker's RTF yourself.

The easiest route is to export the text from PageMaker in Word or Word Perfect format (these export filters, at least, work), then use either word processor to save the text as RTF. If you can't do that—if you've only got the RTF file to work with, here's what to do (see Figure 4-23).

1. Create a new FreeHand file. In the file, create a text block containing the font (or fonts) you want to use in the PageMaker RTF file.

2. Export the FreeHand file as RTF.

3. Using your word processor, open both RTF files (the one generated by PageMaker, and the one you just created using FreeHand).

FIGURE 4-23
Fixing
PageMaker's
RTF

Before editing

```
{\rtf1\mac\deff20{\info{\doccomm generated by an Aldus
application}}\hyphhotz720 {\colortbl\red0\blue0\green0
;}\sl260\tx720\tx1440\tx2160\tx2880\tx3600\tx4320\tx5040\tx5760\tx6480\tx7200
\tx7920\tx8640\tx9360\tx10080\tx10800\tx11520\tx12240\tx12960\tx13680\tx14400
\tx15120\tx15840\tx16560\tx17280\tx18000\tx18720\tx19440\tx20160\tx20880
\tx21600\tx22320\tx23040\tx23760\tx24480\tx25200\tx25920\tx26640\tx27360
\tx28080\tx28800\cf0 This text should be in Bembo and this text should be in
Courier.\par}
```

After editing

Font table ├──

```
{\rtf1\mac\deff20{\info{\doccomm generated by an Aldus application}}
{\fonttbl{\f3\fnil Bembo;}{\f4\fnil Courier;}
}\hyphhotz720 {\colortbl\red0\blue0\green0
;}\sl260\tx720\tx1440\tx2160\tx2880\tx3600\tx4320\tx5040\tx5760\tx6480\tx7200
\tx7920\tx8640\tx9360\tx10080\tx10800\tx11520\tx12240\tx12960\tx13680\tx14400
\tx15120\tx15840\tx16560\tx17280\tx18000\tx18720\tx19440\tx20160\tx20880
\tx21600\tx22320\tx23040\tx23760\tx24480\tx25200\tx25920\tx26640\tx27360
\tx28080\tx28800\cf0 \f3 This text should be in Bembo and \f4 this text
should be in Courier.\par}
```

4. Select the font table in the FreeHand RTF file (it starts at "{\fonttbl" and ends at the second enclosing "}"). A typical font table looks like this:

```
{\fonttbl{\f3\fnil Bembo;}{\f4\fnil Courier;}}
```

5. Paste the font table into the PageMaker RTF file immediately after the phrase "{\info{\doccomm generated by an Aldus application}}".

6. Enter the font codes in the appropriate places in your PageMaker RTF file.

7. Save the RTF file as text-only and place it in FreeHand.

Tip:
Learning more about RTF

If you want to learn more about RTF, you can get a copy of the RTF specification (the specification is updated every few months) by writing to: Microsoft Corporation, Department RTF, 16011 NE 36th Way, Box 97017, Redmond, Washington, 98073-9717.

Exporting

All of the tricks shown earlier in this chapter for importing data from other applications make it clear that FreeHand's good at importing. But what about exporting? FreeHand supports three EPS export formats (with no screen preview, Macintosh screen preview, and MS-DOS screen preview), and you can Option-Copy FreeHand elements out of FreeHand to create a PICT with attached PostScript that can be pasted into just about anything. Besides the "stock" EPS formats, you can export your files as Adobe Illustrator 1.1, Adobe Illustrator 88, and Adobe Illustrator 3.0 EPS files. You can also export as PICT (don't), PICT2 (don't, unless you have to), and you can export the text in your publication as text-only (without formatting) or as RTF (with formatting).

Something you should understand about exporting: unless you choose to include your original FreeHand file in one of the EPS formats (check Include FreeHand document in EPS when you're exporting the file), *the file is going to change.* I don't mean that objects in the EPS are going to move around, or change color, or anything like that. What I mean is that the layers, styles, and other attributes of a typical FreeHand document are going to be lost. Everything will look the same, but the structure of the file will be different.

That's not—necessarily—a bad thing. I mention it here because I don't want you to be surprised the night before a deadline.

When you export a FreeHand page as PICT or PICT2, its appearance will change significantly (objects will *move*—PICT is a less accurate format than EPS, and rounding errors do occur when you save files as PICTs). If you save the file in any of the Adobe Illustrator formats, you'll lose features specific to FreeHand, such as graphic styles and wrapping tabs.

In all of the cases mentioned, you'll be able to open and edit the file again. If you export the file as EPS and don't include the FreeHand page inside the EPS, you might not even be able to open the EPS.

The first half of this chapter covered how to get from there to here. Here's the dope on how to get from here to there. Exporting works the same way for any type of file, as shown in the following steps (see Figure 4-24).

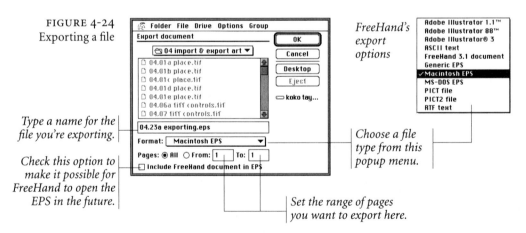

FIGURE 4-24
Exporting a file

FreeHand's export options

Type a name for the file you're exporting.

Check this option to make it possible for FreeHand to open the EPS in the future.

Choose a file type from this popup menu.

Set the range of pages you want to export here.

When you export more than one page, FreeHand creates separate files and numbers them sequentially "filename1.eps", "filename2.eps", etc.)

1. Choose Export from the File menu (or press Command-E). FreeHand displays the Export Document dialog box.

2. Choose a file format from the Format popup menu.

   If you choose and of the Adobe Illustrator formats, EPS formats, or PICT formats, FreeHand displays page export options at the bottom of the dialog box. You an export any or all of the pages in your publication as EPS, with FreeHand creating one EPS file for each page you export.

   If you choose any of the EPS formats, you can include the FreeHand page in the EPS file by checking Include FreeHand Document in EPS. The FreeHand file that's included in the EPS is exactly the same file as FreeHand creates when you save the file, so all of your layers and styles are available when you open the EPS. (Note that you can't include the FreeHand document in any of the Adobe Illustrator formats.)

   FreeHand exports all of the text in your publication when you choose ASCII text or RTF.

3. Type a name for your file and direct it to the folder and volume you want.

4. Press Return to export the file, and FreeHand creates the file on disk.

That's all there is to the mechanics of exporting a file. Now, on to the fun stuff—the details.

Creating EPS Graphics

Actually, exporting EPS graphics is what most people think of when they think of using FreeHand with other applications. It's only because of the twisted orientation of this book (that FreeHand is your main publishing program for short, complex documents) that exporting FreeHand elements appears in this chapter as a kind of afterthought.

EPS Output Options. Before you export a file as EPS, choose Output Options from the File menu. FreeHand displays the Output Options dialog box (see Figure 4-25). These options affect both printing and EPS export.

FIGURE 4-25
Output Options
dialog box

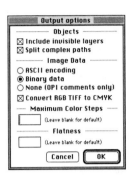

- ◆ Check Include Invisible Layers when you want to print all of the foreground layers in the publication.

- ◆ Check Split Complex Paths to make paths containing graduated, radial, and tiled fills—or paths you've pasted other objects inside—easier to print. Don't check this option if If you're exporting an EPS containing a large TIFF you've pasted inside a path—it can cause the TIFF to download over and over again, increasing your printing time dramatically.

- ◆ ASCII Encoding and Binary Data determine how FreeHand saves any imported TIFF images. ASCII Encoding is a little more forgiving of network and disk errors, but, most of the time, you should click Binary Data—images saved as Binary Data are more compact and are quicker to transmit to your printer.

- ◆ If you're taking your EPS to an OPI system, such as Kodak's Prophecy, click "None (OPI comments only)". Since you'll be linking to another version of the image, your FreeHand file need only contain the location and size of the image, and doesn't need to contain the image data.

- ◆ If you plan to print the EPS from another application, check Convert RGB TIFF to CMYK. PageMaker can't separate RGB TIFFs, but can separate CMYK TIFFs, so check this if you're exporting the file for use in PageMaker. QuarkXPress can't separate RGB TIFFs on its own, either— you need an XTension, such as the EfiColor XTension, which you may or may not have.

◆ If you're printing to a color prepress system, or a continuous-tone film recorder, enter 256 in the Maximum Color Steps field. This limits the number of shades of color FreeHand uses to render blends and graduated and radial fills. These devices can only handle a limited number of colors at once.

◆ For faster printing, enter a value above zero in the Flatness field (for more on flatness, see "Thinking Like a Line" in Chapter 2, "Drawing"). You can safely enter up to "3" with no noticeable change in your publication's printed quality on most printers and imagesetters.

Incredible as it might sound, the Output Options dialog box is one of the most important new features in FreeHand. In previous versions, you could set global flatness for a publication only when you were printing from FreeHand—you couldn't set the flatness for all of the paths in an EPS without editing the EPS in a word processor. Similarly, the Split Complex Paths feature affected only FreeHand printing, not EPS files exported from FreeHand.

Embedding FreeHand files in EPS graphics. When you check Include FreeHand Document in EPS in the Export Document dialog box, FreeHand writes the FreeHand page you're exporting into the EPS file. When I first heard of this feature, I assumed that FreeHand attached the file to the EPS as a resource (like the PICT screen preview). Not so—FreeHand exports a special version of the file as text, and embeds it in the text of the EPS file (that is, in the file's data—not resource—fork). When you place the EPS in another program, the text version of the FreeHand file gets sent along to your printer when you print.

What good is this? In previous versions of FreeHand, you had to keep two versions of a FreeHand file on your disk—the EPS, which you could import into other programs, and the original FreeHand file, which you could open and edit in FreeHand. In FreeHand 4, you can choose to store one file, which you can use in other programs, and which can be opened and edited by FreeHand.

When you use a word processor to open an EPS file that's been exported with "Include FreeHand document in EPS" checked, you'll see the line "%%BeginAGDEmbeddedDoc: version 1.0," lots of gibberish, and the line "%%EndAGDEmbeddedDoc." What is that stuff? It's your FreeHand page, saved as text. You can leave it alone or throw it away—it's up to you. If you can't stand the idea that you're sending your printer more bytes that are absolutely necessary (these extra characters do take a little time to transmit from your Macintosh over your network to your printer), by all means delete the text. Don't throw it away if you want to open the EPS file again in FreeHand, of course.

Tip:
Breaking a
Multi-Page
Publication into
Single Pages

When you want to create a new publication from a single page of a multipage publication, you could make a copy of the file and then delete all of the pages you don't want, or you can export the page as an EPS, checking Include FreeHand Document in EPS as you do so. You can then open the EPS file and save the page as a separate FreeHand document, complete with the styles, layers, and colors you defined in the original publication.

Generic EPS. When you need to create an EPS file containing the PostScript required to print the FreeHand publication you've created, but don't want the file to have a screen preview attached, choose Generic EPS from the Format popup menu.

If you place a Generic EPS file in FreeHand, you'll see a box with an "X" through it. There's a way to add a screen preview to a Generic EPS file, as described in "Creating a Screen Preview for EPS Graphics," earlier in this chapter.

Use Generic EPS when you're exporting a FreeHand graphic for use in a non-Macintosh, non-MS-DOS system (if you're preparing a graphic that'll be placed in a FrameMaker publication on a Sun workstation, for example), or if you just don't want to bother with a screen image. The Generic EPS file is a straight text file.

Macintosh EPS. A Macintosh EPS file is a PostScript text file with a PICT resource attached to it. When you place the EPS file in FreeHand or any other Macintosh program that can import EPS, the PICT is what you see on your screen.

MS-DOS EPS. Because MS-DOS files are structurally different from Macintosh files in that they're data files only (there's no concept of different forks for data and resources in the MS-DOS world) MS-DOS EPS files have a TIFF image of the graphic embedded in the file as hexadecimal data.

If you're exporting a FreeHand file as MS-DOS EPS, don't forget to use a file name your MS-DOS system can understand (eight characters or fewer), and add the extension ".eps" to the file name. Most MS-DOS applications have no way of knowing what type a file is without the extension.

Exporting Publications in Adobe Illustrator Format

FreeHand partisans might ask "Why would you want to export a FreeHand publication as an Illustrator file?" While I think there are lots of good answers to this question, the best one is "So I can import the file into Adobe Photoshop."

When you export in the Adobe Illustrator 3 file format, several things happen.

◆ You lose all layer information. The appearance of the objects on your page won't change (that is, they'll still be stacked up in the same order), they just won't be assigned to layers.

◆ You lose all style information. The objects on your page are all formatted using local formatting—their appearance doesn't change.

◆ Graduated and radial fills get rendered as Illustrator blends—versions of Illustrator prior to Illustrator 5 didn't feature graduated and radial fills.

◆ Illustrator doesn't support the import of TIFF images, so any TIFF images in your FreeHand publication are omitted from the Illustrator file.

◆ Multicolumn and multirow text blocks are converted to linked, single-column text blocks.

◆ Any Custom or PostScript line or fill effects you've used in your FreeHand publication are omitted from the exported Illustrator file. You just get the paths.

When you export to Adobe Illustrator 88 or Adobe Illustrator 1.1 format, a few other things happen (in addition to the changes described for the Adobe Illustrator 3 format).

◆ Composite paths are converted to individual paths.

◆ The text blocks in your FreeHand publication are converted to single-line text blocks in the exported Illustrator 88 file.

Tip:
Breaking Text
Blocks into
Single Lines

A friend of mine needed to break all of the text in a text block into separate text blocks, each text block containing a single line of text. He didn't want to copy and paste the text (it was a large text block, containing captions he wanted to position on a map). He asked me if I had any idea how he could do this.

I told him to export the text block in the Illustrator 88 format, then open the file he'd exported in FreeHand. Sure enough, his text block had been broken into many smaller text blocks, each one containing a single line of his text.

Copying:
Another Way
to Export

There's another way to get objects out of FreeHand, and this one doesn't involve the Export dialog box—copying. There's not much to it: select the objects you want to use in another application and press Command-C (or choose Copy from the Edit menu). Switch to the other application and paste. Use this technique when you want to use a FreeHand graphic in an application that can't import EPS files, but can handle PICTs.

Note some points about copying.

◆ The screen image that results when you copy a graphic to another application is not as good as the image FreeHand adds to an EPS file when you're exporting a file as EPS.

◆ Graphics that you copy to another application do not include any downloadable fonts, and it's often difficult to get the fonts to download from whatever application you've pasted the graphics into; so be prepared to manually download fonts if you're using these graphics. Or you can convert type to paths before copying,

◆ When you copy objects out of FreeHand, FreeHand copies the objects as PICT (with attached PostScript), RTF, AGD1 (native FreeHand format), and ASCII (or text-only). When you paste the Clipboard's contents into another application, that application pastes the data in the format it likes best. For more on which data types get sent to the Clipboard, see Appendix B, "Your FreeHand Installation."

Placing FreeHand Graphics in Page-Layout Programs

If you need to produce documents longer than a few pages, you're going to have to look to a page layout program. Luckily, you can take your FreeHand illustrations with you. There are a few tricks and twists to this process.

Bounding boxes. You'll note that FreeHand's bounding boxes are sometimes just a little bit larger than the edges of the graphic, or that the graphic is not positioned inside the bounding box the way you'd like it. The edges of your FreeHand graphic might even be getting clipped off when you print.

What's going on? According to Adobe's EPS specification, EPS bounding box measurements should be expressed in integers (such as 100, 612, or 792). FreeHand, written by engineers with a mania for accuracy, uses EPS bounding boxes accurate to $\frac{1}{10000}$ of a PostScript point (which means you'll see numbers such as 100.0125, 612.0005, or 792.9999). Some applications don't observe the fractional part of the EPS bounding box when they create a box to put the graphic in, so you can lose up to half a point (more or less) of the edge of your graphic.

If this happens to you, draw a box around the graphics you're exporting, making the box a little larger than the objects it encloses. Set the line and fill of the box to None, and export the EPS.

EPS files and downloadable fonts. You've probably heard that EPS graphics include any downloadable fonts used in the file. It's not necessarily true—sometimes EPS files contain the fonts; sometimes they only list the fonts.

When your page-layout program's printing, it creates the image of the page in your printer's memory by starting with the objects on the page that are the farthest to the back (actually, I'm only certain of this for PageMaker and QuarkXPress). When the application starts to print an EPS graphic, it reads the fonts listed in the EPS and downloads any needed fonts to your printer.

This does not guarantee that the fonts will still be in the printer's memory when they're called for inside the EPS, because a lot can happen between the start of the file (when your page layout program downloads the font) and whenever the font is needed.

Your page-layout application cannot manage the printer's memory once you're inside the EPS—only before and after your printer processes the EPS. By contrast, when you're printing objects you've created using your page-layout program's tools, your page-layout application manages font downloading and printer memory on an object-by-object level—it can always download another copy of the font if necessary.

If you've got an older printer with one megabyte of RAM, like a LaserWriter or LaserWriter Plus, it's much more likely that this will be a problem, because it's much more likely that your page-layout program will have to flush the downloadable font out of the printer's RAM to make room to print something else. It's also something you'll sometimes run into when you're printing to an imagesetter, because the higher resolution of imagesetters also means that these printers will run short of RAM.

If you have enough RAM in your printer, or if your printer has a hard disk, manually download the fonts to your printer. This guarantees they'll print, and your file will print faster, too.

Tip:
Importing
Named Process
Colors into
QuarkXPress

When you import a FreeHand EPS into a QuarkXPress picture box (in version 3.3), XPress adds the spot colors used in the EPS to its list of colors, but doesn't add any named process colors you might have used in the graphic. You can add them yourself, or follow these steps.

1. Select the named process color in the Color List and choose Duplicate from the Color List's popup menu. FreeHand adds a duplicate of the color to the Color List.

2. Select the duplicate color and choose Make Spot from the popup menu.

3. Apply the new spot color to an object on your page.

4. Export the page as an EPS.

5. Import the EPS into XPress. XPress adds the spot color to its color list.

6. Delete the EPS.

7. Convert the spot color to a process color. Now you can apply the named process color to other elements in your XPress publication.

Converting FreeHand 3 EPS Files to Illustrator 1.1 EPS Format

It's going to happen to you someday. You'll need to edit a Free-Hand 3 graphic and will have only an EPS version of the file—not the original file. Here's what to do. First, try opening the EPS with FreeHand—it can open some simple FreeHand 3 EPS files.

If that didn't work, you'll just have to give up and start re-creating the illustration—unless you know how to translate FreeHand's EPS file into an Illustrator 1.1 format EPS file. Once it's in Illustrator 1.1 format, you can open it in either Illustrator or FreeHand.

Before you go any further, please note that this section doesn't deal with FreeHand 4 EPS files—only those EPSs created by Free-Hand 3.0, 3.1, and 3.1.1. The instructions provided here won't work with FreeHand 4.0 EPSs.

The best way to learn about the differences between the two formats is to take a look at the EPS files written in them.

1. Create a file in FreeHand and export it as an Illustrator 1.1 EPS.

2. Export the same file as Generic EPS.

3. Open both files with a word processor and compare them. You'll start seeing similarities and differences almost at once.

Focus on the parts of the files between the "%%EndSetup" comment and the "%%PageTrailer" comment. These are the parts that describe points, paths, and other objects. Table 4-3 shows the significant part of two EPS files describing the same path. Note

TABLE 4-3
Illustrator and
FreeHand syntax
compared

Illustrator 1.1 version	FreeHand version
0 i 0 J 0 j 1 w 4 M []0 d[]	0 d
%%Note:	3.863708 M
192 1044 m	1 w
192 -252 L	0 j
N	0 J
-342 480 m	0 O
954 480 L	0 R
N	0 i
-342 336 m	false eomode
954 336 L	[0 0 0 1] Ka
N	[0 0 0 1] ka
336 1044 m	vms
336 -252 L	u
N	234 468 m
0 G	234 324 L
192 480 m	378 324 L
192 336 l	378 324 378 406 327 382 C
336 336 l	276 358 285 362 285 362 C
336 418 285 394 v	278 400 L
234 370 243 374 y	378 413 L
236 412 l	378 468 L
336 425 l	234 468 L
336 480 l	4 M
192 480 l	s
s	U
	vmr

that these lines show the same object, but that the line on the right does not necessarily match the line on the left.

First of all, note that the coordinate systems differ slightly. In this case the Illustrator coordinate system starts 42 points farther along the horizontal axis and 12 points earlier along the vertical axis than the FreeHand coordinate system. Differences in coordinate systems will vary between publications. In this case, "192 480 m" ("m" is for *moveto*) in the Illustrator file equals "234 468 m" in the FreeHand EPS.

In general, don't worry about differences in coordinate systems; the point is to get the objects into one program or the other. You can always adjust their positions once you've opened the file.

The first thing you need to do to convert a FreeHand EPS file into an Illustrator 1.1 format EPS file is to edit the file's header. To do that, follow these steps.

1. Open the file with your word processor. If you're using Microsoft Word, hold down Shift as you choose Open from the File menu, press Shift-F6, or select Open, and then select All Files from the List Files of Type popup menu. The first six lines of the file should look like this (the words shown in italics will vary—don't worry about them).

```
%!PS-Adobe-2.0 EPSF-1.2
%%Creator: FreeHand
%%Title: filename
%%CreationDate: date and time
%%BoundingBox: x1 y1 x2 y2
%%DocumentProcSets: FreeHand_header 3 0
```

2. Change the line beginning with "%%DocumentProcSets" to look like this:

```
%%DocumentProcSets: Adobe_Illustrator_1.1 0 0
```

3. Delete the line beginning with

```
"%%DocumentSuppliedProcSets:".
```

4. Leave the line beginning with "%%ColorUsage:" as it is.

5. Delete the line beginning with "%%FHPathName:".

6. Leave the line "%%EndComments" as it is.

7. Select from the line beginning with "%%BeginProcSet:" to the end of the line "%%EndProcSet" and delete the selection. Leave the two lines following ("%%EndProlog" and "%%BeginSetup").

8. Select from the beginning of the line "FHIODict begin" to the start of the line "%%EndSetup" and delete the selection. Type two lines between "%%BeginSetup" and "%%EndSetup" as follows.

    ```
    Adobe_Illustrator_1.1 begin
    ```

    The text you see between the line "%%EndSetup" and the line "%%Trailer" is the body of your FreeHand EPS file. Table 4-4 shows you how to convert paths, while Table 4-5 covers converting text objects.

Text is tricky. You'll usually have to guess for *alignment* and *kerning*, and you'll have to derive *horizontalScale* from the *size* specified in FreeHand, because FreeHand's already done all of the positioning and scaling before exporting the file as EPS. Still, I've had good luck moving text back and forth.

TABLE 4-4 Converting from FreeHand to Illustrator syntax		
If you see this in a FreeHand EPS	**Convert it to**	**What it does**
[]0d	[]0d	The numbers between the brackets set the dash pattern, if any, of the path. In this example, the line's not dashed, so the array inside the brackets is empty. For a dashed line, the code would look something like "[2 1]0d" for a two-unit-on, one-unit-off dashed pattern. This code is the same as PostScript's *setdash* operator.

TABLE 4-4 Converting from FreeHand to Illustrator syntax (continued)	If you see this in a FreeHand EPS	Convert it to	What it does
	x M	*x* M	The number before this code sets the miter limit of the path. This code is the same as the PostScript *setmiterlimit* operator.
	x w	*x* w	The number before this code sets the width of the path, in points. This shortcut is the same as the PostScript operator *setlinewidth*.
	x i	*x* i	The number before this code sets the flatness of the path. "i" is the same as the PostScript operator *setflat*.
	x j	*x* j	The number before this code sets the line join of points inside the path. 0 = miter joins; 1 = round joins; 2 = beveled joins. This code is the same as the PostScript operator *setlinejoin*.
	x J	*x* J	The number before this code sets the line cap style. 0 = butt caps; 1 = round caps; 2 = projecting caps. This code is equivalent to the PostScript operator *setlinecap*.
	x1 y1 m	*x1 y1* m	Moves to the specified point. This code is the same as the PostScript operator *moveto*.

TABLE 4-4
Converting from
FreeHand to
Illustrator syntax
(continued)

If you see this in a FreeHand EPS	Convert it to	What it does
x1 y1 L	*x1 y1* l	Draws a line to the specified point and places a curve point (a "smooth" point in Illustrator parlance) with no curve control handles extended at that point. If you want to place a corner point, use "L" instead of "l." This code is the same as the PostScript operator *lineto*.
x1 y1 x2 y2 x3 y3 C	*x2 y2 x3 y3* v or *x1 y1 x3 y3* y	Sets a curve point and control handles. If *x1 y1* in the FreeHand version equals the previous point (usually *x1 y1* L), then convert it to a "v"; otherwise, convert the curve point to a "y."
s	s	Close and stroke the current path with the predefined line weight, miter specifications, and color. Exactly the same as the PostScript operator *stroke*.
b	b	Close the current path, and then fill and stroke the path with the predefined line weight, miter specifications, and colors.
[*c m y k*] Ka	*c m y k* K	Sets the fill color. 80C0M10Y10K would be written as .8 0 .1 .1 K.

TABLE 4-4 Converting from FreeHand to Illustrator syntax (continued)	If you see this in a FreeHand EPS	Convert it to	What it does
	[*c m y k*] ka	*c m y k* k	Sets the stroke color. 20C5M0Y0K would be written as .2 .5 0 0 k.
	x O	Delete this line	
	x R	Delete this line	
	Vms	Delete this line	
	Vmr	Delete this line	
	Vmrs	Delete this line	
	U and u	U and u	"u" indicates the start of a group, "U" indicates the end of a group. You can delete these if you want.

TABLE 4-5 Converting text	FreeHand	Illustrator
	%%IncludeFont: *fontName*	/_*fontName size leading kerning alignment* z
	MacVec 256 array copy /*fontNumber* /|_____*fontName* dup RF findfont def { *fontNumber* [*size* 0 0 *leading* 0 0] makesetfont *x y* m 0 0 32 0 0 (*textString*) ts } [*c m y k*]	[*horizontalScale* 0 0 1 x y]e* (*textString*)t T
	sts	

* Use "e" for text that's filled but not stroked, "o" for text that's both filled and stroked, and "r" for text you want stroked but not filled. These options use the current fill and stroke settings—see Table 4-3, above, for more information on setting strokes, fills, and colors. Table 4-6 shows an example of text set in FreeHand 3 and Illustrator 1.1 formats.

TABLE 4-6
Text conversion
example

FreeHand	Illustrator
%%IncludeFont:/_Utopia-Regular	.8 0 .2 0 K
MacVec 256 array copy	/_Utopia-Regular 14 16 0 0 z
/f2 /|_____Utopia-Regular dup	
RF findfont def	[.8 0 0 1 200 200]e*
{	(Pinafore)t
f2 [11.2 0 0 16 0 0] makesetfont	T
200 200 m	
0 0 32 0 0 (Pinafore) ts	
}	
[.8 0 .2 0]	
sts	

Once you've reached the line "%%Trailer" you've finished converting the body of the file. Select through the line "%%Trailer" to the end of the file and delete the selection. Type in the Illustrator 1.1 codes for the end of the file as shown below.

```
%%PageTrailer
%%Trailer
_E end
%%EOF
```

Save the file as Text Only. Try opening it with Illustrator. If you've made a mistake, Illustrator displays a dialog box containing a hint (see Figure 4-26). FreeHand displays a dialog box, but doesn't give you the hint.

Make a note of what Illustrator thinks is wrong with the file, return to the file, and try to fix it.

FIGURE 4-26
Illustrator's hint

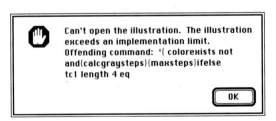

Publishing and Subscribing

One of the features that appeared in System 7 is Publish and Subscribe—a way of linking data between applications. With Publish and Subscribe, you can import a chart from Excel into a Word document in such a way that the graphic in the Word document updates when you change the chart in Excel. It's an alternative to the usual export-and-then-import process, and features the ability to open the originating application (Excel, in the above example) from the subscribing application (Word).

I don't use Publish and Subscribe, myself—I find the process of saving files and importing them using Place easier to work with. I have been told that Publish and Subscribe is most useful when you need to update FreeHand graphics placed in multiple documents, or when you want to be able to launch FreeHand from an application containing a FreeHand EPS (though you can do this from PageMaker without using Publish and Subscribe; see "Linking to PageMaker," later in this chapter).

When you make a file available to Publish and Subscribe, you're "publishing" an "edition," and the application the file came from is called the "publisher." When you import the edition file, the application you're using is called the "subscriber." Just to make things a bit confusing, the edition file, once placed in your subscribing application, is also called the "subscriber."

FreeHand can act as both a publisher and a subscriber.

To subscribe to an edition file, follow these steps.

1. Publish the file (precisely how you do this differs from application to application, but it's usually the Create Publisher menu item under the Edit menu).

2. Switch to FreeHand and choose Subscribe To from the Editions submenu of the Edit menu. FreeHand displays the Subscriber dialog box.

3. In the Subscribe To dialog box, select the edition file you want to subscribe to and click OK. FreeHand changes the cursor into a Place Gun.

FIGURE 4-27
Subscribe To
dialog box

When you select an
edition file, FreeHand
displays a preview of
the file's contents.

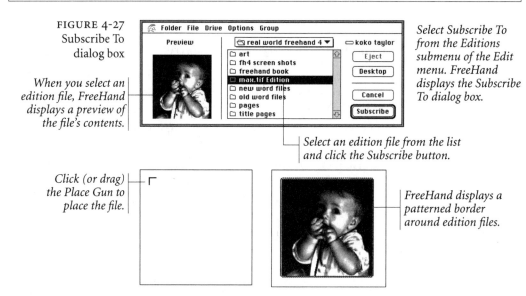

*Select Subscribe To
from the Editions
submenu of the Edit
menu. FreeHand
displays the Subscribe
To dialog box.*

*Select an edition file from the list
and click the Subscribe button.*

Click (or drag)
the Place Gun to
place the file.

*FreeHand displays a
patterned border
around edition files.*

4. Click (or drag) the Place Gun in the publication window to
   position the edition file you're subscribing to.

When you're subscribed to an edition, you can set the update
options for that edition—do you want it to update (change) when
and if the edition file changes? Do you want to update the edition
now? Do you want to stop your subscription to the edition? To
do any or all of these tasks, choose Subscriber Options from the
Editions submenu of the Edit menu. FreeHand displays the Subscriber Options dialog box (see Figure 4-28).

FIGURE 4-28
Subscriber Options
dialog box

*Click Automatically if
you want the edition file
you've placed in
FreeHand to update
whenever the original
edition file changes.*

*Select an edition file from
this popup menu.*

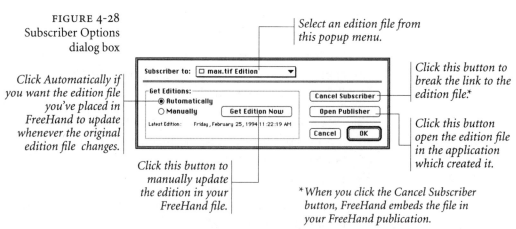

*Click this button to
break the link to the
edition file.**

*Click this button
open the edition file
in the application
which created it.*

*Click this button to
manually update
the edition in your
FreeHand file.*

**When you click the Cancel Subscriber
button, FreeHand embeds the file in
your FreeHand publication.*

To publish an edition, follow these steps.

1. In FreeHand, turn to the page you want to publish as an edition file. FreeHand publishes whole pages only—you can't publish selected items.

2. Choose Create Publisher from the Editions submenu of the Edit menu. FreeHand displays the Create Publisher dialog box.

3. In the Create Publisher dialog box, you can choose to publish your edition as either an EPS or a PICT file. Unless the application in which you're planning to place the edition file can't accept EPS graphics, use EPS, rather than PICT.

4. Enter a name for your edition file and press Return. FreeHand publishes the file, making it available to any application that supports Publish and Subscribe.

FIGURE 4-29
Publishing an edition

Create the objects you want to publish.

Choose Create Publisher from the Editions submenu of the Edit menu.

FreeHand displays the Create Publisher dialog box.

Type a name for your edition file here.

Choose an edition file format (choose EPS, unless you'll be printing to a non-PostScript printer, or know that the subscribing application can't subscribe to EPS).

Here's your edition file, as seen from PageMaker's Subscribe To dialog box.

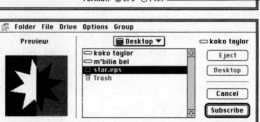

You can choose to update an edition you published with Free-Hand (and, potentially, the way that edition appears in all subscribing documents), or cancel an edition, from FreeHand. To do this, choose Publisher Options from the Editions submenu of the Edit menu. FreeHand displays the Publisher Options dialog box.

If you're in FreeHand and you want to edit an edition file in its originating application, choose Edit Original from the Editions submenu of the Edit menu. Your Macintosh switches to the application (if it's running) or locates and launches the application (if it's not), and then opens the edition file in that application.

Keep the following things in mind when you're working with Publish and Subscribe.

◆ When you subscribe to an edition that's been published as a PICT or as an EPS, FreeHand doesn't convert the file to FreeHand elements (as it would if you placed the file). It acts like an imported graphic.

◆ You can't apply text wrap to a subscriber.

◆ Instead of the usual selection handles, edition files display a dotted border when you select them in your FreeHand publication. When you cancel a subscription to a particular edition, the file displays normal selection handles.

When you want to delete an edition file published by FreeHand, thereby breaking the link between the edition and all subscribing documents, choose Subscriber Options or Publisher Options from the Editions submenu of the Edit menu. In either dialog box, click the Cancel Publisher button. FreeHand deletes the edition file. When you do this, the appearance of your subscribing publications doesn't change—they'll still contain the edition file, just as if you'd placed it.

Tip:
Linking to
PageMaker

PageMaker and FreeHand have their own link—hold down Option and double-click a selected FreeHand EPS in a PageMaker publication, PageMaker switches to FreeHand (if it's running), or launches FreeHand (if it's not running), and opens the original file (or the EPS file, if the EPS file contains the FreeHand file). When you save the file from FreeHand, FreeHand exports the file and updates the EPS in your PageMaker publication.

Managing Linked Files

When you import a TIFF or EPS file, FreeHand doesn't include the file in your publication, but establishes a link between the publication and the imported file. Linking means you don't have to store two copies of the original file—one on disk, and one in your Free-Hand publication—which saves disk space.

When you move a linked file, or change its name (including any changes you might make to the name of the folder you've stored it in—or the volume you've stored it on), you break the link between the file and any FreeHand publication you've placed it in. You can also break the link when you move the publication file to another volume.

When you do this, FreeHand displays a box where the linked graphic would appear in your publication (see Figure 4-30). Don't worry—FreeHand maintains the link information. This means you can still link the the file, once you find it.

If FreeHand can't find a linked file when you're opening a publication, it looks in the folder containing the illustration for the linked file. If FreeHand doesn't find the linked file there, it displays the Locate File dialog box (see Figure 4-31). Use the Locate File dialog box to locate and link to the file.

If you can't find the original file, you can close the Locate File dialog box without linking to a file. Locate the original file, and put it inside the same folder as the publication, and FreeHand updates the link (unless you're in keyline mode, you'll see the image replace the placeholder in the publication window).

FIGURE 4-30
Losing links

When you move, delete, or rename a linked file, FreeHand displays a box where the file appeared in your publication.

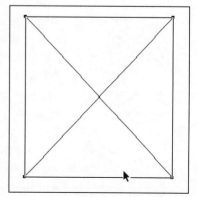

FIGURE 4-30
Locate File dialog box

Tip:
Losing Links
on Purpose

I work on my FreeHand documents at my office and at home. When I need to work on a FreeHand publication at home, I frequently leave linked TIFF images behind, and take just the FreeHand publication file. This means that I can still work on any text or paths in the file, but that I don't have to carry the TIFF files around (also, working with TIFFs on my slow home machine is pretty painful). I can even change the position and size of the TIFF placeholders. When I open the file back at my office, FreeHand re-links to the TIFFs.

The Best of All Possible Worlds

Can you get there from here? When you're working with Free-Hand, you can almost always export or save files in a form you can use in another program, and you can usually produce files in other programs you import or open using FreeHand.

There are definitly bumps in the road—PageMaker's broken RTF export filter, for example. Sometimes, you've got to go through an intermediate program—such as the amazing De-Babelizer—to convert files from one format to another (particularly if the files came from another type of computer).

Someday, we'll have a more complete, universal, and sophisticated file format for exchanging publications than the Adobe Illustrator 1.1 format. We'll be able to take page layouts from Free-Hand to PageMaker to Photoshop—using each program for what it's best at—without losing any formatting.

And the streets will be paved with gold, mounted beggars will spend the day ducking winged pigs, and the Seattle Mariners will win the World Series.

CHAPTER

Transforming

5

In the previous chapters, I've covered the process of creating FreeHand elements. This chapter talks about what you can do with those elements once you've drawn, typed, or imported them. The process of rotating, reflecting, skewing, scaling, cloning, or moving objects is called *transformation.*

Many of the topics in this chapter have been touched on in the preceding chapters—mainly because everything you can do in Free-Hand is interconnected. In the old days, software was entirely linear or modal: one had to proceed from this screen to that screen following a particular set of steps. These days, software is extremely nonlinear and nonmodal (that is, you can do things many different ways in many different orders), and, therefore much harder to write about. Your purchase of this book will make my time at Looney Farm that much more pleasant. Thank you.

Transformations are the key to using FreeHand efficiently. I don't know how many times I've seen people laboriously drawing and redrawing shapes when they could have been using the Clone, Rotate, and Reflect commands to accomplish the same ends faster and with far less trouble. Any time you can see a similarity between the shapes on one side of an object and another, you should be thinking about reflection. Any time you see an object that's made up of the same shape rotated about a center point, you should be thinking about rotation. Start looking at the paths you draw as patterns of clones and transformations, and you'll be a long way toward becoming a FreeHand wizard.

331

Like the Inspector, the Transform palette has several, different subpanels (for moving, rotating, scaling, skewing, and reflecting objects). I refer to each panel as a separate palette: the Move, Rotate, Scale, Skew, and Reflect palettes. This beats saying "the Rotate panel of the Transformation palette."

In addition to the operations corresponding to the transformation tools, I think of several other FreeHand features as "transformations." Specifically, I include clipping paths (using Paste Inside), locking objects, and alignment and distribution. You'll find these topics at the end of the chapter.

There are two ways to transform any object on a FreeHand page. After you select an object, you can drag using the specific transformation tool, or you can type numbers in the Transform palette (see Figure 5-1). There's no "right" or "best" way to do transformations—you can experiment with the different methods and see which you like best. I change methods depending on the situation (and my mood).

If that's all there is to transforming, then what's in the rest of this chapter? Homespun philosophical insights guaranteed to make this book a checkout counter bestseller? Nope. As you might expect, there's more to transforming objects than meets the eye. The rest of the chapter covers the down-and-dirty details.

Grouping and Transformation

When you transform a group, FreeHand transforms all of the lines and fills inside the group proportionally, unless you've checked Transforms As Unit (which you'll find in the Object Inspector for the group). Check this option if you want to transform the line weights and fills inside the group nonproportionally, resulting in an effect that resembles perspective drawing (see Figure 5-2).

When you ungroup objects you've transformed with Transform As Unit turned on, any lines and fills applied to those objects revert to their undistorted appearance.

Transformation Shortcuts

As you think about transforming object, keep in mind two of Free-Hand's most important keyboard shortcuts: Command-, (comma) and Command-D.

Command-, means "transform it again"; it performs the previous transformation you used (see Figure 5-3). You don't even have

FIGURE 5-1
Transforming
anything

*Transforming objects
by dragging*

Rotation tool |———

Axis of transformation |———

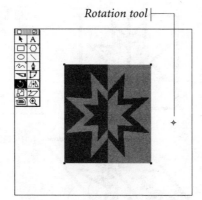

*Select the object you want to trans-
form, then select the transformation
tool you want to use. In this example,
I've selected the Rotation tool.*

Keyline preview of |———
transformation. |

*Drag the transformation tool in the
Publication window. As you drag,
FreeHand displays a preview of the
transformed object.*

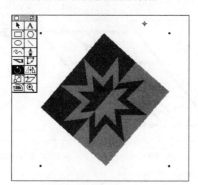

*When the object looks the way you
want it to, stop dragging. FreeHand
transforms the object.*

*Transforming objects
using the Transform
palette*

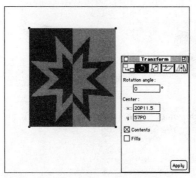

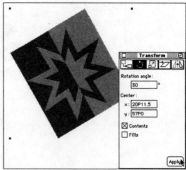

*Select the object you want to rotate
and press Command-M to display the
Transform palette. Click the buttons
at the top of the palette to display the
transformation you want. In this
example, I'm using the Rotate palette.*

*Enter the values you want in the
Transform palette (in this example,
the Rotate palette), check any
appropriate checkboxes (they vary
from palette to palette), and click the
Apply button (or press Return).*

FIGURE 5-2
Transforming groups

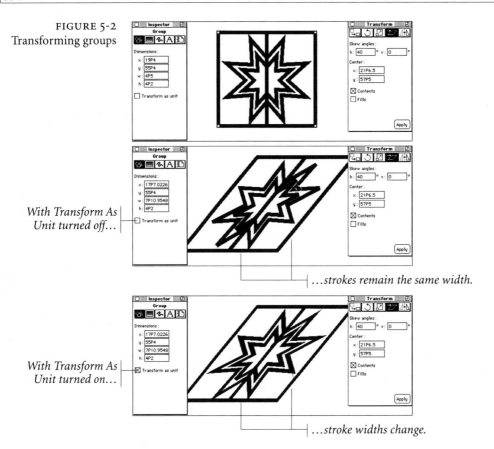

With Transform As
Unit turned off...

...strokes remain the same width.

With Transform As
Unit turned on...

...stroke widths change.

FIGURE 5-3
Transform again

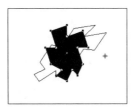  

Transform an object (in this example, I'm skewing the object using the Skewing tool).

Press Command-comma, and FreeHand applies the most recent transformation again.

to have the same object selected as the one you originally transformed—you can transform an object, select a different object, and then transform that object using the same settings.

Command-, is great for experimentation, because just by pressing the keyboard shortcut you can ask, What if I moved it a little bit more? or What if I skewed it a little bit more? If you don't like what you've done, press Command-Z to Undo it.

If you haven't done any transformations lately, Command-D actually does what the menu item (Duplicate) says—it duplicates the object, placing the duplicate at a slight distance from the original object. Most of the time, however, Command-D means, "Clone it and transform it again," and performs the most recent transformation while cloning the currently selected object. You can use Command-D to do all kinds of things (see Figure 5-4).

Note that the transformation (whatever it was) persists until the next transformation. That is, if you rotate something, drag out some ruler guides, copy something to the Scrapbook, then select an object and press Command-, FreeHand rotates the object as you specified in the earlier transformation—*even if it's not the same object you originally transformed.*

FIGURE 5-4
Clone and
transform again

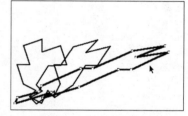

Clone an object, then transform it (in this example, I've skewed the clone of the object using the Skewing tool).

Press Command-D, and FreeHand clones the selected object and applies the last transformation to it.

Moving

Moving an object from one place to another is probably the task you do most often in FreeHand. There are four ways to move objects in FreeHand.

◆ Dragging the objects with the Pointer tool.

◆ Entering values in the Move palette.

◆ Changing coordinates in Object Inspector.

◆ Pressing the arrow, or "nudge" keys.

Moving Path Contents and Fills

Check the Contents box when you want objects that you've pasted inside a path to move with that path (see Figure 5-5). Check Fills to move the fill you've applied to the path (see Figure 5-6)—though it only makes a difference when you're moving paths filled with tiled fills. If you don't want the paths' contents or fill to move, uncheck the appropriate checkbox (or checkboxes).

Note that these checkboxes affect movement whether you're using the Move palette to move objects or not.

These checkboxes have no effect on objects other than paths.

FIGURE 5-5
Moving contents

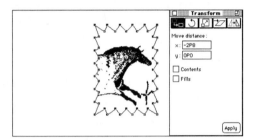

In this example, I'll use the Move palette to move the selected path to the left.

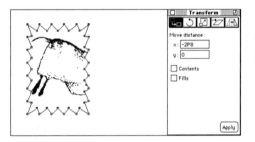

With Contents off, objects you've pasted inside a path don't move when you move the path.

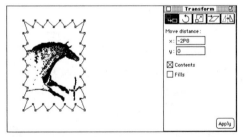

With Contents turned on, objects you've pasted inside a path move with the path.

**Tip:
Moving Selected Points**

When you drag some, but not all, of the points on a path, Free-Hand doesn't move anything you've pasted inside the path, regardless of the state of the Contents checkbox in the Move palette. This comes in handy when you need to adjust a path you've used to crop a TIFF image (see Figure 5-7).

FIGURE 5-6
Moving fills

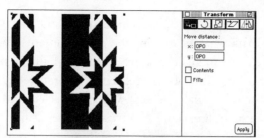

In this example, I'll use the Move palette to move the selected path to the right.

With Fills off, the path's tiled fill doesn't move with the path.

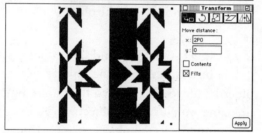

With Fills turned on, the tiled fill moves as you move the path.

FIGURE 5-7
Moving selected points

Regardless of the setting of the Contents check-box in the Move palette, moving points does not move the contents of the path (unless, that is, you select all of the points in the path).

This is a good thing, because it makes it easy to edit paths you've used to crop TIFFs.

Tip:
A Trick that No
Longer Works

In FreeHand 3, you could select and move all of the points in a path without moving the path's contents, regardless of the state of the Contents checkbox in the Move dialog box (in FreeHand 3, all of the controls in FreeHand 4's Transform palette were found in separate dialog boxes). When you select and move all the points in a path, FreeHand 4 moves—or doesn't move—the contents of the path, depending on the state of the Contents field in the Move palette.

The good news, however, is that the control is no longer buried—it's in the Move palette, where you can always check the setting before you move a path (the original tip was great, because it saved you a trip to a dialog box).

Moving by Dragging

FreeHand's just like any other Macintosh program—if you want to move something, select the object with the Pointer tool and drag.

Tip:
Dragging Things
Quickly Versus
Dragging Things
Slowly

If you select something and immediately start dragging, you'll see only a box the shape of the object's selection rectangle. If, on the other hand, you hold down the mouse button for a second before dragging, you'll see the object as you drag it (whether this works for multiple selected objects or not depends on the setting you've entered in the Preview Drag field in the Editing Preferences dialog box; see "Setting Preferences" in Chapter 1, "FreeHand Basics").

Dragging quickly is great for snapping objects into position by their outlines; waiting a second before dragging is best for seeing things inside a selection as you position them on the page (see Figure 5-8).

FIGURE 5-8
Seeing objects as
you drag them

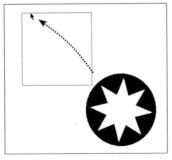

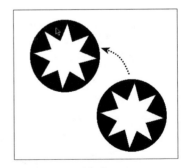

Drag quickly, and you'll see only an outline of the objects.

Pause a second before you start dragging, and you'll see the objects.

Tip: Seeing What You Drag	To make FreeHand show you a screen display of the object you're dragging—no matter how many objects you've selected and no matter what the setting of the Preview Drag preference—hold down Option before you start dragging (that is, after you've pressed the mouse button down, but before you've moved the mouse). Wait for FreeHand to draw the objects you've selected (in some cases, this can take a while), and then drag the objects. As you drag, FreeHand displays the objects you're moving.
Tip: Constraining Movement	Holding down Shift as you drag elements constrains their movement to 45-degree angles (just as in almost every other Macintosh graphics application), which makes it easy to drag objects only horizontally or vertically. FreeHand adds another wrinkle, however: the axis from which those 45-degree increments are derived can be set to present any angle (see "Constraining Tools" in Chapter 1, "FreeHand Basics").

Moving "By the Numbers"

When I need precision, I always move objects by entering numbers in the Move palette (see Figure 5-9). And it's not just because I'm a closet rocket scientist; it's because I don't trust a 72-dpi screen, even at 800 percent magnification. You shouldn't either, when it comes to fine adjustments in your FreeHand publication.

1. Select the object you want to move.

2. Display the Transform palette, if it's not already visible (you can double-click any of the transformation tools in the toolbox to display the palette, or press Command-M). Click the Move icon button at the top of the Transform palette to display the Move palette, if necessary.

3. Enter values in the fields. Type positive numbers to move objects up (toward the top of the screen) or to the right; type negative numbers to move them down or to the left).

4. Set the Contents and Fills checkboxes the way you want them (see "Moving Contents and Fills," earlier in this chapter).

5. Press Return (or click the Apply button). FreeHand moves the selected object.

FIGURE 5-9
Moving with
the Move palette

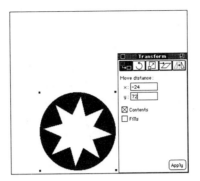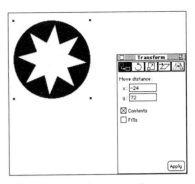

*Select the object you want to
move and type distances in the
Move palette.*

*Click the Apply button, and
FreeHand moves the object the
distance and direction you specified.*

Moving with the Object Inspector

The X and Y fields in the Object Inspector aren't only there to show you where the object is; you can use them to move the object to a specific location on your page. To move the object to a new location, type coordinates in the X and Y fields (remember, coordinates are measured from the current position of the zero point, and specify the location of the lower-left corner of the selected object), and press Return (see Figure 5-10).

If you're looking at the Object Inspector, and you don't see the X and Y fields, you're looking at an ungrouped path. Group the path, and the fields appear in the Object Inspector. You can always ungroup the path after you've moved it.

FIGURE 5-10
Moving with
the Object Inspector

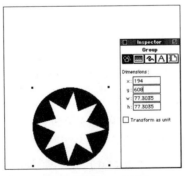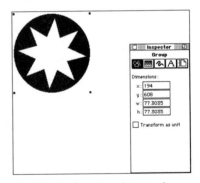

*Enter the coordinates at which
you want to position the lower-
left corner of the object in the X
and Y fields of the Object
Inspector and press Return.*

*FreeHand moves the object to the
new coordinates.*

Moving by Pressing Arrow Keys

As if dragging by eye and specifying coordinates weren't enough movement options, FreeHand also sports "nudge" keys. Select an element and press one of the arrow keys, and the element moves in that direction in the increments you set in the Cursor Key Distance field in the Editing Preferences dialog box (see "Setting Preferences" in Chapter 1, "FreeHand Basics").

Scaling

In FreeHand, you can change the size of objects using any of the following techniques.

- Dragging the Scaling tool on the page.

- Entering values in the Scale palette.

- Dragging a selection handle with the Pointer tool.

- Changing values in the Object Inspector.

In addition, you can change the size of text boxes by changing the size of the column heights and row widths in the Column Inspector (see "Multicolumn and Multirow Text Blocks" in Chapter 3, "Text and Type").

Scaling Contents, Fills, and Strokes

When you scale a path, you can choose to scale the path's contents (that is, whatever you've pasted inside the path), or the fill and stroke you've applied to the path. To scale these items, check the Contents, Fills, or Lines boxes, respectively, in the Scale palette (see Figure 5-11). To keep the paths's attributes from scaling as you scale the path, uncheck the appropriate box or boxes.

Using the Scaling Tool

When you want to scale an object until it "looks right," use the scaling tool (see Figure 5-12).

1. Use the Pointer tool to select the object you want to scale.

2. Select the Scaling tool from the toolbox.

FIGURE 5-11
Scaling path attributes

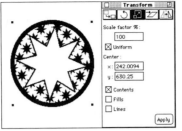

*Original object
before scaling*

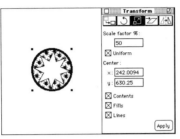

*When you check the Fills and Lines
boxes, FreeHand scales those path
attributes as it scales objects.*

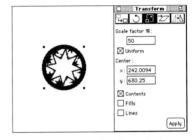

*When you uncheck Fills and Lines,
FreeHand does not scale any strokes
or fills as it scales objects.*

FIGURE 5-12
Using the Scaling tool

 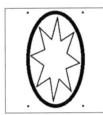

*To scale an object vertically,
select the object and drag the
Scaling tool up (to make the
object larger) or down (to make
the object smaller).*

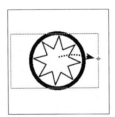 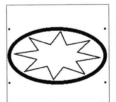

*To scale an object horizontally,
select the object and drag the
Scaling tool to the left (to make
the object smaller) or to the
right (to make the object
larger).*

*To proportionally scale an
object, select the object and hold
down Shift as you drag the
Scaling tool.*

*To scale from an object's center,
hold down Control as you drag
the Scaling tool.*

3. Position the Scaling tool at the point around which you want to scale. Most of the time, you'll want to hold down Control to scale an object around its center.

4. Drag the Scaling tool horizontally to scale the object's width, or drag vertically to scale the object's height. Dragging diagonally sizes the object's width and height. Hold down Shift as you drag to scale the object proportionally.

   If the object you're scaling is a paint-type graphic or a bilevel TIFF, you can hold down Option and Shift to scale the object both proportionally and to the printer's resolution (which you set in the Target Printer Resolution field in the Setup Inspector; see "Using the Setup Inspector" in Chapter 1, "FreeHand Basics").

5. When the object's the size you want it, stop dragging.

Using the Scale Palette

When you know you want to make an object larger or smaller by an exact percentage, use the Scale palette (see Figure 5-13).

1. Select the object you want to scale.

2. Display the Scale palette (if it's not already visible, double-click the scaling tool in the toolbox).

FIGURE 5-13
Using the Scale palette

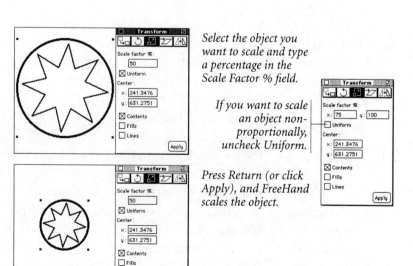

Select the object you want to scale and type a percentage in the Scale Factor % field.

If you want to scale an object non-proportionally, uncheck Uniform.

Press Return (or click Apply), and FreeHand scales the object.

3. Uncheck Uniform if you want to scale the object's width and height by different percentages (leave Uniform checked to scale both dimensions by the same percentage).

4. Set the Contents, Fills, and Lines checkboxes the way you want them (see "Scaling Contents, Fills, and Lines," earlier in this chapter).

5. Enter percentages in the Scale Factor field (or, if you're scaling width and height separately, enter percentages in the X and Y fields).

6. Press Return to scale the object.

Tip:
Resetting the
Center of Scaling

If you want to use the Scale palette to resize an object around its center point, and see that the coordinates in the X and Y fields in the Scale palette aren't at the center of the object (it's easy to accidentally set them to other coordinates—all it takes is clicking the scaling tool on the page), you can reset them to the object's center.

Click on the object with the Pointer tool (hold down Command to turn the current tool into the Pointer tool, if necessary), and FreeHand enters the coordinates of the object's geometric center in the X and Y fields.

Tip:
Picking a Point
To Scale Around

Suppose you want to enlarge or reduce an object, but you want the lower-left corner of the object to stay in its original location (that is, you want the object to grow up, and to the right). If you know the location of the point you want to scale around, you can enter that point in the Scale palette—but I rarely go to all that trouble—I simply click the Scaling tool on that point (being careful, as I do so, that I don't drag the tool). FreeHand enters the coordinates of the point I click on in the X and Y fields in the Scale palette.

Tip:
Positioning
Objects by
Setting the
Zero Point

One of the easiest ways to set the center of transformation is to position the zero point where you want the center of the object to fall, and then enter "0" in the Horizontal and Vertical fields in the Center options section of the Scale dialog box. It's easier than entering "23.0476" and "47.135" (for example).

Scaling with the Pointer Tool

As in any other Macintosh drawing or page-layout application, you can change the size of objects by dragging their corner handles with the Pointer tool (see Figure 5-14). As you drag, the object you're dragging gets larger or smaller. Hold down Shift as you drag to resize the object proportionally.

I confess: I use this method far more often that I use the Scaling tool (mainly because I can switch to the Pointer tool from any tool by holding down Command, while there's no keyboard shortcut for the Scaling tool).

When you resize a rectangle, ellipse, or grouped path by dragging a selection handle, FreeHand doesn't resize anything you've pasted inside the object, regardless of whether Contents is checked in the Scale palette.

Tip:
Resizing from an Object's Center

Hold down Option as you drag a selection handle to resize an imported graphic, group, rectangle, or ellipse from its center point. This trick doesn't work for ungrouped paths.

FIGURE 5-14
Scaling objects by dragging selection handles

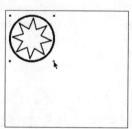 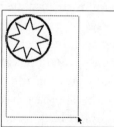 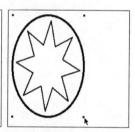

With the Pointer tool, position the cursor over a corner handle...

...and drag to scale the object.

When the object is the size and shape you want, stop dragging.

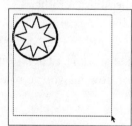 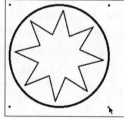

To scale an object proportionally, hold down Shift as you drag a corner handle.

To scale a group, imported graphic, or basic shape from its center point, hold down Option as you drag.

Scaling with the Object Inspector

When you select an object other than an ungrouped path, that object's width and height appear in the W and H fields in the Object Inspector (to see the width and height of a path, first select the path and press Command-G to group it). To change the object's width or height, enter new values in these fields, and press Return. FreeHand changes the size of the object.

I find this feature particularly useful when I'm working with rectangles I've drawn with the Rectangle tool. I use rectangles a lot when I'm laying out a page, and I usually know what size they need to be, so I use the Object Inspector to set their width and height. Doing that is often easier than drawing them to precisely the right size.

Rotating

Some applications (such as PageMaker) store the original orientation and angle of objects on their pages. To these applications, rotation is an absolute measurement—the current angle of an object always refers to that object's original rotation angle (usually zero degrees). In FreeHand, rotation is a relative—the object's current angle of rotation is always considered to be zero degrees, regardless of any previous rotation.

This approach has advantages and disadvantages. You can't rotate an object back to its original state by giving it a rotation angle of zero, as you can in PageMaker (in FreeHand, a rotation angle of zero means the object doesn't rotate at all). In FreeHand, however, you can always rotate the object another 12.5 degrees, without adding that value to the object's existing rotation angle to derive the angle you enter (as you would in PageMaker).

You can always rotate an object back to its original angle, provided you keep track of how far you've rotated it away from that angle.

Using the Rotation Tool

To rotate an object "by eye," follow these steps (see Figure 5-15).

1. Select the object you want to rotate.

2. Select the Rotation tool from the toolbox.

FIGURE 5-15
Rotating an object
using the Rotation tool

FIGURE 5-15
Rotating an object
using the Rotation tool

*Select the object you
want to rotate.*

Position the
Rotation tool at
the point you
want to rotate
around.

*Drag the Rotation tool in the
publication window. As you
drag, FreeHand displays a
keyline preview of the rotated
object.*

units: points cx:112.0688 cy:477.9829 angle:46

*As you drag the Rotation tool,
FreeHand displays the angle
of rotation in the Info Bar.*

*When the object looks the
way you want it to, stop
dragging. FreeHand rotates
the object.*

3. Position the Rotation tool at the point where you want to position the center of rotation. Hold down Control to set the center of rotation at the center of the object.

4. Drag the Rotation tool. As you drag, FreeHand displays the angle of rotation in the Info Bar.

5. When the object looks the way you want, stop dragging.

Using the Rotate Palette

To rotate an object using FreeHand's Rotate palette, follow these steps (see Figure 5-16).

1. Select the object you want to rotate.

2. Display the Rotate palette (if it's not already visible, double-click the Rotation tool in the toolbox).

3. If you're rotating a path, make sure that the Contents and Fills checkboxes are set the way you want them (see "Rotating Contents and Fills," later in this chapter).

FIGURE 5-16
Rotating an object
"by the numbers"

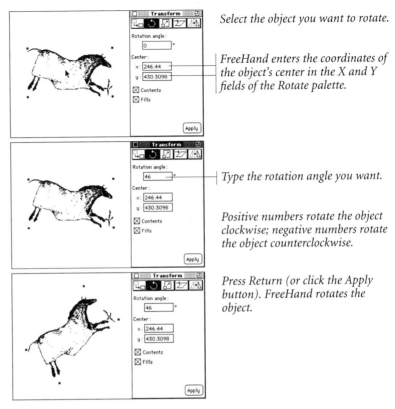

Select the object you want to rotate.

FreeHand enters the coordinates of the object's center in the X and Y fields of the Rotate palette.

Type the rotation angle you want.

Positive numbers rotate the object clockwise; negative numbers rotate the object counterclockwise.

Press Return (or click the Apply button). FreeHand rotates the object.

4. Enter values in the Rotation angle field.

    FreeHand's Rotate palette isn't picky. You can enter positive numbers (such as "45"), negative numbers (such as "-270"), and absurd numbers (such as "478") in the Rotation Angle field. Positive rotation angles rotate the selected object clockwise; negative values rotate the object counterclockwise. You can enter rotation angles in .1 degree increments.

5. Press Enter (or click the Apply button in the Rotate palette) to rotate the object.

Tip:
Rotating Around
a Specific Point

When you're rotating an object using the Rotate palette, it's easy to get it to rotate around its center. What if, instead, you want to rotate the object around some other point?

You can always enter the coordinates of the location you want to rotate around in the X and Y fields in the Rotate palette, but wouldn't it be nice to click on a spot on the page, as you can when you're rotating using the Rotation tool?

You can: just click the Rotation tool on the page before you enter anything in the Rotate palette. Don't drag the Rotation tool, and don't click too quickly—I find it takes a second for the palette to update. When the X and Y fields in the palette change to match the current location of the cursor, release the mouse button and press Command-` to move your cursor to the Rotation Angle field. Enter an angle and press Return to rotate the object. FreeHand rotates the object around the point you specified by clicking.

Rotating Multiple Selected Objects

When you rotate more than one object (in this sense, I'm counting groups as a single object), the objects rotate around a single point (see Figure 5.17). This point can be their joint geometric center, the point where you started dragging the Rotation tool, or a point you specified in the Rotate palette. They don't all rotate around their individual center points.

FIGURE 5.17
Rotating multiple objects

When you rotate multiple objects in FreeHand…

…they rotate around a single center of rotation.

Like this: Objects rotated around a single point.

Not like this: Objects rotated around their individual centers.

Rotating Contents and Fills

You can choose to have a path's contents (objects you've pasted inside the path) or fills rotate with the path as you rotate the path (see Figure 5-18). To rotate the path's contents, check the Contents checkbox in the Rotate palette before you rotate the path. To rotate the path's fill, check Fills.

Rotating a fill doesn't change the screen angle of any halftone screen you've applied to the fill (you control screen angles using the Halftone palette).

FIGURE 5-18
Rotating contents
and fills

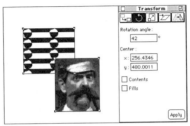

In this example, I'll use the Rotate palette to rotate two paths. One path is filled with a tiled fill; the other has a scanned image pasted inside it.

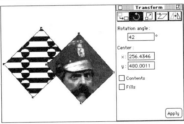

With Contents unchecked, objects you've pasted inside a path don't rotate when you rotate the path. Turn Fills off, and tiled fills won't rotate when you rotate the path.

Turn on Contents, and objects inside paths rotate with the paths. When you want tiled fills to rotate with the path, turn on Fills.

Rotating Selected Points

You don't have to select all of the points in a path to apply rotation to that path; you can rotate some or all of the points. What possible use is this? Look at Figure 5-19.

Rotation and Path Direction

While you're rotating things, remember that the direction, or winding, of rotated paths does not change (for more on PostScript path direction, see "Thinking Like a Line" in Chapter 2, *Drawing*)—it still starts from the same point as it did before you rotated it (see Figure 5-20).

FIGURE 5-19
Rotating selected
points

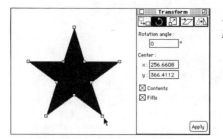

*Select some, but not all, of the
points on a path.*

*The selected
points rotate...*

*...the unselected
points stay in their
original positions.*

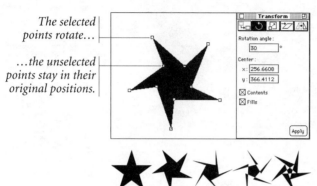

Rotate the selected points.

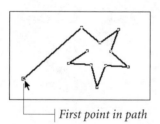

FIGURE 5-20
Rotation doesn't
change the direction
of a path

First point in path

First point in path

*Even though you've rotated
this path 180 degrees...*

*...the first point in the
path remains the same.*

Rotation and Perspective Drawing

You can use rotation and scaling to create isometric projections of 3-D objects in FreeHand (for more on perspective drawing, see "Perspective Projection" in Chapter 2, "Drawing"). The following steps show you how (see Figure 5-21).

1. Create an orthographic view of the object (also called a plan view: front, top, and side views of the object).

2. Select the top view of the object. Display the Rotate palette. Type "90" in the Rotation Angle field and press Return. FreeHand rotates the top view of the object 90 degrees.

FIGURE 5-21
Rotating and scaling
create an isometric
projection

*Draw the front, side,
and top of an object.*

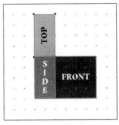

*Rotate the top of the
object 90 degrees.*

*Rotate all three objects
-45 degrees.*

*Scale the top and front
vertically by 57.735
percent.*

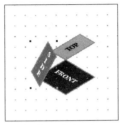

*Scale the side horizon-
tally by 57.735 percent.*

*Rotate the front
60 degrees.*

*Rotate the side
30 degrees.*

*Snap all the pieces
together.*

3. Select all three views of the object. Display the Rotate palette. Type "-45" in the Rotation Angle field and press Return. FreeHand rotates the top view of the object 45 degrees counterclockwise.

4. Deselect the side view (keep the top and front views selected). Display the Scale palette (double-click the scale tool in the toolbox). With the Uniform box checked, enter "57.735" in the Scale Factor field and press Return. FreeHand scales the top and front views.

5. Select the side view and deselect the front and top views. Uncheck Uniform in the Scale palette. Type "57.735" in the X field and press Return. FreeHand scales the side view horizontally.

6. Select the front view of the object. Display the Rotate palette. Type "60" in the Rotation Angle field and press Return. FreeHand rotates the front view 60 degrees clockwise.

7. Select the side view. Type "30" in the Rotation Angle field and press Return. FreeHand rotates the side view 30 degrees clockwise.

8. Snap the three pieces of the object together, and you've got an isometric projection of the object. You can enhance the 3-D effect of the projection by shading the sides of the object, if you want.

Reflecting

Reflection flips a selected object or objects across a specified axis. When we're drawing, we very often work with paths which are mirror images of each other around some axis. FreeHand's reflection tool makes it possible for us to work the way we think.

You can reflect selected objects by dragging the Reflection tool, or by entering values in the Reflect palette

Using the Reflection Tool

To reflect an object "by eye," follow these steps (see Figure 5-22).

1. Select the object you want to reflect.

2. Select the Reflection tool from the toolbox.

3. Move the cursor to the point where you want to place the axis of reflection.

4. Drag the object across the axis of reflection (as you drag, FreeHand displays a dotted line showing the axis of reflection). Hold down Control as you drag to locate the center of

reflection at the center of the object. Hold down Shift as you drag to constrain the reflection angle to 45-degree angles. As you drag, FreeHand displays angle of reflection in the status bar.

5. When you're through reflecting the object, stop dragging. FreeHand reflects the object as you've specified.

FIGURE 5-22
Reflecting
objects using the
Reflection tool

Select the object you want to reflect.

Drag the Reflection tool in the publication window. The point where you start dragging determines the axis around which FreeHand reflects the object.

    units: points   cx:230.3909   cy:442.5912   angle:90

As you drag, FreeHand displays the angle of reflection in the Info Bar...

...and displays a preview of the reflected object.

Hold down Shift and drag toward the top or bottom of the publication window to reflect the object across its vertical axis. Hold down Shift and drag left or right to reflect the object horizontally.

**Using the
Reflect Palette**

Most of the time, I know precisely how I want to reflect an object, so I use the Reflect palette (see Figure 5-23). Come to think of it, I don't think I ever use reflection to do anything other than flip objects across their vertical or horizontal axes. More candidates for keyboard shortcuts...

To reflect an object using the Reflect palette, follow these steps.

1. Select the object you want to reflect.

2. If the Reflect palette isn't already visible, display it by double-clicking the reflection tool in the toolbox.

3. Set the Fills and Contents checkboxes the way you want them (see "Reflecting Contents and Fills," later in this chapter).

4. Type the values you want in the Reflect Axis field (enter "90" to reflect the object across its vertical axis, "180" to reflect the object across its horizontal axis). Positive values entered in the Reflect Axis field reflect the selected object counterclockwise; enter negative values to reflect the object clockwise.

5. Press Return. FreeHand reflects the object as you specified.

FIGURE 5-23
Reflecting contents
and fills

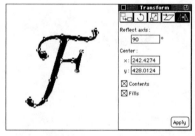 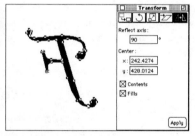

Select the object you want to reflect,   *…and press Return (or click the Apply*
type an angle in the Reflect Axis field   *button). FreeHand reflects the selected*
of the Reflect palette…   *object across the axis you entered.*

**Reflecting
Contents and Fills**

When you're reflecting a path, you can choose to reflect the path's contents (what's pasted inside the path) or fills as you reflect the path (see Figure 5-24). To reflect path contents, check Contents. To reflect the path's fill, check the Fills box.

**Reflection and
Path Direction**

Reflection changes the winding, or direction, of reflected paths (for more on PostScript path direction, see "Thinking Like a Line" in Chapter 2, "Drawing"). The path still starts from the same point as it did before you reflected it, but the path's direction now goes the opposite direction (see Figure 5-25).

FIGURE 5-24
Reflecting contents and
fills

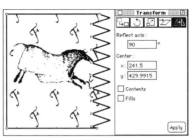

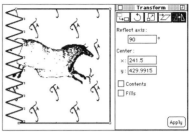

In this example, I'll use the Reflect palette to reflect a path containing both a tiled fill and an image.

With the Contents and Fills checkboxes off, FreeHand reflects the path, but doesn't reflect the object pasted inside the path or the path's tiled fill.

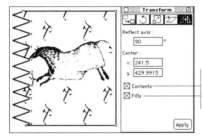

With the Contents and Fills checkboxes turned on, FreeHand reflects the image and the tiled fill.

FIGURE 5-25
Reflection and
path direction

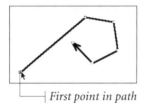

First point in path

Before reflection, this path winds clockwise.

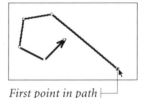

First point in path

After reflection, the path winds counterclockwise.

Skewing

Skewing an object makes it appear that the plane the object's resting on has been rotated. It's good for creating perspective effects.

Skewing is hard to get used to at first, because vertical skewing seems to affect the horizontal lines in an object, while horizontal skewing affects the vertical lines in an object. It's just something you'll have to get used to (see Figure 5-26).

Using the Skewing Tool

Follow these steps to skew an object by eye (see Figure 5-27).

1. Select the object you want to skew.

FIGURE 5-26
Horizontal and
vertical skewing

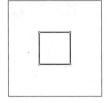

Original object

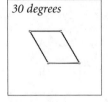

30 degrees

Horizontal skewing

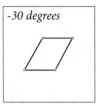

-30 degrees

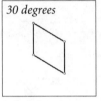

30 degrees

-30 degrees

Vertical skewing

FIGURE 5-27
Skewing an
object by eye

*Select the object you
want to skew.*

*Position the cursor to
define the center point
you're skewing around
and drag the cursor in
the publication window.*

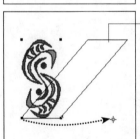

*FreeHand displays a rectangular preview of the
skewed object as you drag.*

*As you're dragging, the Info Bar
shows you what's going on.*

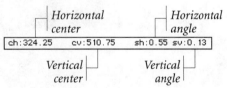

*Horizontal
center*

*Horizontal
angle*

ch:324.25   cv:510.75   sh:0.55 sv:0.13

*Vertical
center*

*Vertical
angle*

*Hold down Shift as you
drag to constrain the
skewing to either
vertical or horizontal.*

*When you stop
dragging, FreeHand
skews the object.*

2. Choose the Skewing tool from the toolbox.

3. Position the cursor where you want the skew to start.

4. Drag the Skewing tool to skew the object. As you drag the cursor, the skewing angles display on the status bar.

5. When the object looks the way you want it, stop dragging.

Using the Skew Palette

To skew an object using the Skew palette, follow these steps (see Figure 5-28).

1. Select the object you want to skew.

2. Display the Skew palette by double-clicking the Skewing tool in the toolbox, if necessary.

3. Set the Contents and Fills checkboxes (see "Skewing Contents and Fills," later in this chapter).

4. Enter skewing angles the H (horizontal) and V (vertical) fields in the Skew palette.

5. Press Return (or click the Apply button in the Skew palette) to skew the selected object.

FIGURE 5-28
Skewing with
the Skew palette

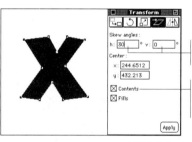

Select the object you want to skew.

Enter skewing angles in the H (for horizontal) and V (for vertical) fields.

Check the Contents box if you want FreeHand to skew any objects pasted inside the path when it skews the path.

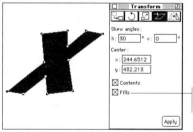

Press Return (or click the Apply button), and FreeHand skews the selected object.

Check the Fills box if you want FreeHand to skew the path's fill.

Skewing Contents and Fills

If you want to skew a path's contents (objects you've pasted inside the path) as you skew the path, check the Contents box. To skew the path's fill, check Fills.

Skewing and Perspective Drawing

If you survived the parts of Chapter 2, "Drawing," covering perspective, oblique, and axonometric projections, here's your reward: skewing is a fantastic way to automate drawing oblique and axonometric projections. In many cases, these simple projections can substitute for (much more complicated) perspective rendering. The following steps show you how to create an oblique projection of an object (see Figure 5-29).

1. Draw the orthographic views (top, side, and front) of an object.

2. Select the side view of the object.

FIGURE 5-29
Skewing to create an oblique projection

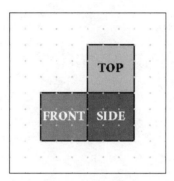

Draw the top, front, and side of the object.

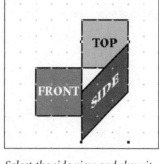

Select the side view and skew it 45 degrees vertically.

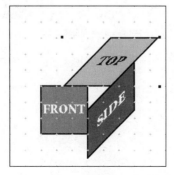

Select the top view and skew it -45 degrees horizontally.

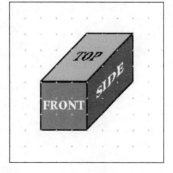

Snap the three views together.

3. Display the Skew palette (if the palette's not visible, double-click the skewing tool in the toolbox). Type "45" in the V field and press Return. FreeHand skews the front view of the object.

4. Select the top view of the object.

5. Type "-45" in the Horizontal field and press Return. FreeHand skews the top view.

6. Snap all of the objects together, and, voilà, you've got an oblique projection.

Skewing is also a great help in creating axonometric views of an object. Axonometric views differ from oblique views in that they're both skewed and scaled, and that the front view is skewed away from the plane of perspective.

Creating Clipping Paths

Another of FreeHand's basic transformations is Paste Inside—the ability to use any path as a clipping path for any object or objects. Paste Inside has already gotten some coverage in Chapter 2, "Drawing," but here's more. Clipping paths are the key to three other FreeHand techniques.

◆ Cropping imported graphics (this technique is covered in Chapter 4, "Importing and Exporting").

◆ Trapping objects which cross color boundaries (this technique is covered in depth in Chapter 6, "Color").

◆ Creating transparency and translucency effects.

Clipping paths are also just plain fun. Be aware, however, that clipping paths increase the complexity of your publication by an order of magnitude as far as the PostScript interpreters in printers and imagesetters are concerned. This doesn't mean they should be avoided! Just remember that publications containing clipping paths will take longer to print, and may produce overtime charges at your imagesetting service bureau. In other words, make sure that the effect you hope to achieve by using clipping paths is worth the added expense and time.

Use the following steps to create a clipping path (see Figure 5-30).

1. Draw, type, or import an object.

2. Draw a path on top of the initial object.

3. Select the original object and press Command-X to cut it to the Clipboard.

4. Select the first object and press Command-Shift-V (or choose Paste Inside from the Edit menu). The parts of the second object which fell within the first object's area appear inside the first object.

What happens when you use Paste Inside more than once for the same clipping path? Each successive Paste Inside places the

FIGURE 5-30
Creating a
clipping path

Draw, type, or import something...

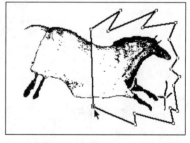

...and draw a path on top of it. Select the original object and cut it to the Clipboard.

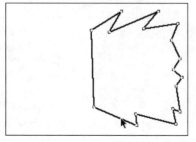

Select the path...

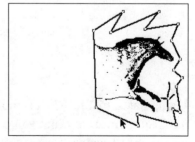

...and choose Paste Inside from the Edit menu. FreeHand pastes the object inside the path.

contents of the Clipboard on top of any objects already inside the clipping path. You'll still be able to see any objects not obscured by opaque lines or fills (see Figure 5-31).

If you need to edit the objects you've pasted inside a path, or if you want to remove them, select the object that contains them and choose Cut Contents from the Edit menu (or press Command-Shift-X). The objects which had been pasted inside the path you selected are pasted on top of the path you cut them from (see Figure 5-32). The objects retain the stacking order they had inside the path (the last object pasted inside it on top).

FIGURE 5-31
Multiple Paste Insides

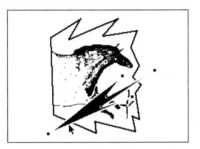
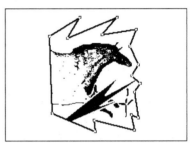

When you paste a new object inside a clipping path that contains other objects...

...FreeHand pastes the new object on top of the other objects already inside the path.

FIGURE 5-32
Removing objects from
inside a clipping path

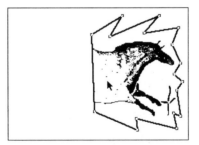
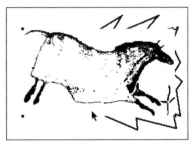

Select the clipping path...

...and choose Cut Contents from the Edit menu. FreeHand pastes the path's contents on top of the path.

Using Paste Inside to Crop Imported Images

FreeHand lacks a tool analogous to PageMaker's Cropping tool, but you can simulate the behavior of the Cropping tool using Free-Hand's Paste Inside feature. Actually, the ability to create clipping paths of any shape in FreeHand is more powerful and flexible than the PageMaker's Cropping tool (which crops only in rectangles).

For more on cropping images, see "Cropping TIFF Images" in Chapter 4, "Importing and Exporting."

Creating a Color Change Where an Object Crosses a Color Boundary

Here's an effect that we used to sweat over in the dark days when everything was done with a copy camera, hot wax, cold beer, and a knife. Suppose you have some black text that crosses from a white background onto a black background. If the edge of the black background is a straight line, the effect is pretty easy to create. But if the edge of the black background is a curved or jagged line, it's nearly impossible to create this effect using a copy camera. With FreeHand, it's so easy that a number of power users I know have missed it (see Figure 5-33).

1. Create your type.

2. Create the black background object.

FIGURE 5-33
Changing colors as you cross a color boundary

Create two paths. Fill one with black; fill the other with white. Create a text block that crosses both paths. Color the text block black.

Clone the text block and cut the clone to the Clipboard. Select the white shape and choose Paste Inside from the Edit menu.

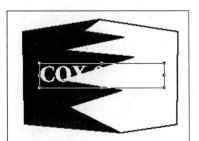

Select the text block and color it white.

Cut the white text block. Select the black shape and choose Paste Inside from the Edit menu.

3. Position the type and the black background object in the alignment you want.

4. Clone the text block.

5. Color the clone of the text block white and press Command-X to cut it to the Clipboard.

6. Select the black object and press Command-Shift-V (or choose Paste Inside from the Edit menu). FreeHand pastes the white text block inside the black object. Can't see it? Select the black text block and send it to the back.

Note that this same trick works just as well for colored text and a colored background, and that, by extension, it works for multiple adjacent color fields which have multiple overlapping objects which change color as they pass through the different color fields. For an example of this trick, refer to the color section of this book. And don't forget to trap!

Creating the Illusion of Transparency Using Clipping Paths

Have you ever wondered why you can't just select a FreeHand element and click an option that makes the object transparent? (You can, of course, for placed images, but that's not what I'm talking about.) When PostScript fills an object, it assumes that the fill is opaque. FreeHand, being a child of PostScript, adheres to this assumption, but also gives you a number of ways to fool PostScript into rendering objects that look transparent.

When an object passes behind some transparent or translucent plane, it changes color—sometimes very subtly. To simulate this effect in FreeHand, clone the partially obscured object and change the colors of the cloned objects from their original colors. Then paste those objects inside the transparent or translucent object (see Figure 5-34).

You can use this optical illusion to simulate the effect of viewing an object through a number of simple transparent/translucent planar surfaces. The main difficulty of rendering transparency and translucency in two-dimensional work is that you walk a fine line. If the color shift is too great, it'll look like you've created another object; if the color shift is too slight, it won't look like an object's transparent. Transparency is harder to simulate than translucency.

FIGURE 5-34
Creating transparent
objects

*This object is colored
20-percent gray, and
has lightened copies of
the background objects
pasted inside it.*

Creating three-dimensional transparency is both easier and more difficult. It's easier because color shifts and perspective shifts around three-dimensional objects provide more cues to the eye and so are more easily simulated; it's more difficult because you've got to figure out what those shifts are to be able to simulate them.

Once again, you'll have to look at my example and figure out how the techniques I use work with the publication and effect you're creating (see Figure 5-35).

FIGURE 5-35
Creating three-
dimensional
transparent and
translucent effects

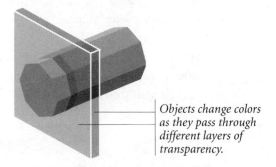

*Objects change colors
as they pass through
different layers of
transparency.*

Creating Transparent Text

An effect you see very often, especially in television video advertising, is that of a character or word superimposed on an image where the characters are wholly or partially transparent. Here's how you can you achieve this effect in FreeHand (see Figure 5-36).

1. Place an image.

2. Create some type and position it over the image. Without deselecting the text block, choose Convert to Paths from the Type menu. FreeHand converts the characters to paths.

FIGURE 5-38
Transparent text
above an image

*Create some type above an image
you've placed.*

*Convert the text to paths, then paste
a lightened clone of the image inside
the text.*

3. Select the image and press Command-= to clone the image. Without deselecting the cloned image, display the Object Inspector (press Command-Option-B) and click the Edit button at the bottom of the Inspector. FreeHand displays the Image dialog box. Change the image's gray levels so that it's about half as dark as the original image. When you're through changing the gray levels, press Return to close the Image dialog box.

4. Press Command-X to cut the altered image.

5. Select the text (which is now a composite path) and press Command-Shift-V (or choose Paste Inside from the Edit menu).

FreeHand pastes the altered image inside the characters. This produces the illusion that you're looking through transparent text. You can enhance this illusion by cloning the type and offsetting the clone slightly from the original text to create a drop shadow, and then pasting another clone of the original image inside the drop shadow.

Locking Objects

In the previous edition of this book, I mentioned locking objects only once, in the section on alignment and distribution. It's the way I was brought up—out in the mountains in Idaho we never locked anything (our car keys spent the night, undisturbed, in the ignition switches of our cars). I view the difficulties of urban living as the result of a large-scale conspiracy of keys and locks.

In FreeHand, locking an object means that you can't transform it or change its appearance. You can still select the object, and you can copy it or clone it, but you can't do anything to it.

`🔒 units: points   x:78       y:576`

To lock an object, select the object and press Command-L (or choose Lock from the Arrange menu). When you select a locked object, you'll see a lock icon in the info bar.

To unlock an object, press Command-Shift-L (or choose Unlock from the Arrange menu).

Aligning and Distributing

For most people, MacDraw ushered in the era of object alignment. You could align the left, right, top, bottom, or center of selected objects. It was the greatest. I spent whole afternoons just aligning things. You couldn't do that in MacPaint.

FreeHand, which counts MacDraw as one of its forebears, also features object alignment. FreeHand aligns objects based on the rectangular area each object takes up, which I'll call the object's bounding box. The selection handles of the object show you the object's bounding box (to see the bounding box of a path, group the path). Note that imported EPS graphics and TIFF files can have bounding boxes that have nothing to do with the actual content of the graphic (see Figure 5-39).

FreeHand's object alignment capabilities include both Align, which does exactly what you'd expect; and Distribute, which means, "Evenly arrange the selected objects inside the selection rectangle formed by the objects." Align and Distribute can be used at the same time; you can, for example, vertically align objects while horizontally distributing them.

FIGURE 5-39
Object bounding boxes

FIGURE 5-39
Object bounding boxes

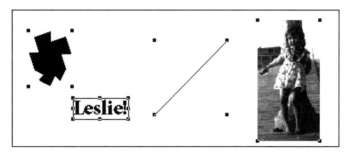

Aligning Objects

When you've selected the objects you want to align, press Command-Shift-A to display the Align palette, pick an alignment using the popup menus, and then click the Apply button in the palette (pressing Return doesn't work, for some reason). FreeHand aligns the selected objects as you've specified (see Figure 5-40).

Tip:
Locking as an
Adjunct to
Alignment

If any of the selected objects is locked, FreeHand aligns objects based on that object's position (see Figure 5-41). If more than one of the selected objects is locked, FreeHand bases alignment on the object nearest the alignment specified (that is, the topmost locked object for Top alignments, the leftmost locked object in Left alignments, etc.).

I use this technique all the time—and it's virtually the only reason I lock individual objects. When I want to protect part of my publication from accidental editing, I usually put that part of the publication on a layer and lock that layer. Unlocking a layer is easier than tracking down individual, locked objects.

Tip:
Centering Text
Vertically

When you want to center text vertically inside an object, simply choosing to align by object centers doesn't usually work. Why? Because the alignment is based on the size of the text block—not on the size of the text.

Convert the characters to paths, however, and the bottom of the path will truly be the bottom of the character and the characters align properly to the center of the object (see Figure 5-42).

Distributing Objects

Have you ever wanted to align a bunch of objects at even distances from each other (from each other's centers, at any rate) across a particular horizontal measurement? If you have, FreeHand's Distribute feature should make your day.

FIGURE 5-40
Aligning objects

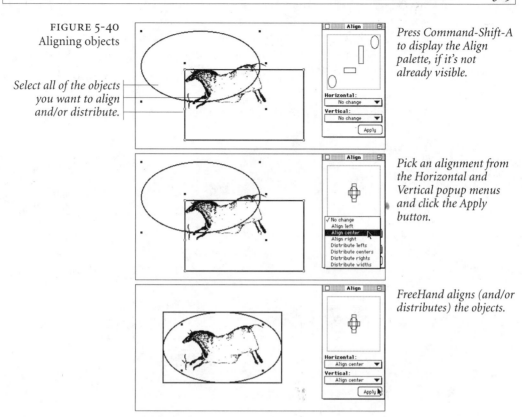

Select all of the objects you want to align and/or distribute.

Press Command-Shift-A to display the Align palette, if it's not already visible.

Pick an alignment from the Horizontal and Vertical popup menus and click the Apply button.

FreeHand aligns (and/or distributes) the objects.

FIGURE 5-41
Locking and alignment

This object is locked

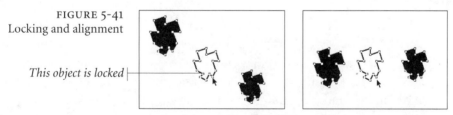

Align the tops of these objects, and they'll align to the top of the locked object—even if it's not the topmost object selected.

FIGURE 5-43
Converting text to paths aids object alignment

Alignment is based on the top and bottom of the text block, so you can end up with extra space below the text.

If you convert the text to paths, it'll be aligned based on the actual height of the characters.

To distribute objects, select the objects, press Command-Shift-A to display the Align palette, select the alignment and distribution options you want from the popup menus, and then click the Apply button in the palette. FreeHand aligns and distributes the objects as you've specified (see Figure 5-44).

FIGURE 5-44
Distributing objects

Select the objects you want to distribute, set up the distribution and alignment you want in the Align palette, and click the Apply button.

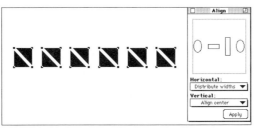

FreeHand distributes the selected objects.

My Life Was Transformed

All around you, every day, things are changing from one thing to another. Fuzzy caterpillars turn into moths. Clark Kent jumps into a phone booth and emerges as Superman. Werewolves stalk the moors under the full moon. The bat shown on page 122 is, by day, a harmless graphic designer with prominent canines. These transformations are all everyday, natural, phenomena.

I didn't understand this when I first approached FreeHand's transformation tools. The tools seemed alien, awkward, and I didn't use them very much. Then, one day, I saw them as extensions of the way I already thought about drawing. Now, I use them more than I use the drawing tools.

Make FreeHand's transformation tools an integral part of how you work with the program, and you'll have their powerful, almost magical forces on your side. And that means you'll have more time for other things. Like howling at the moon.

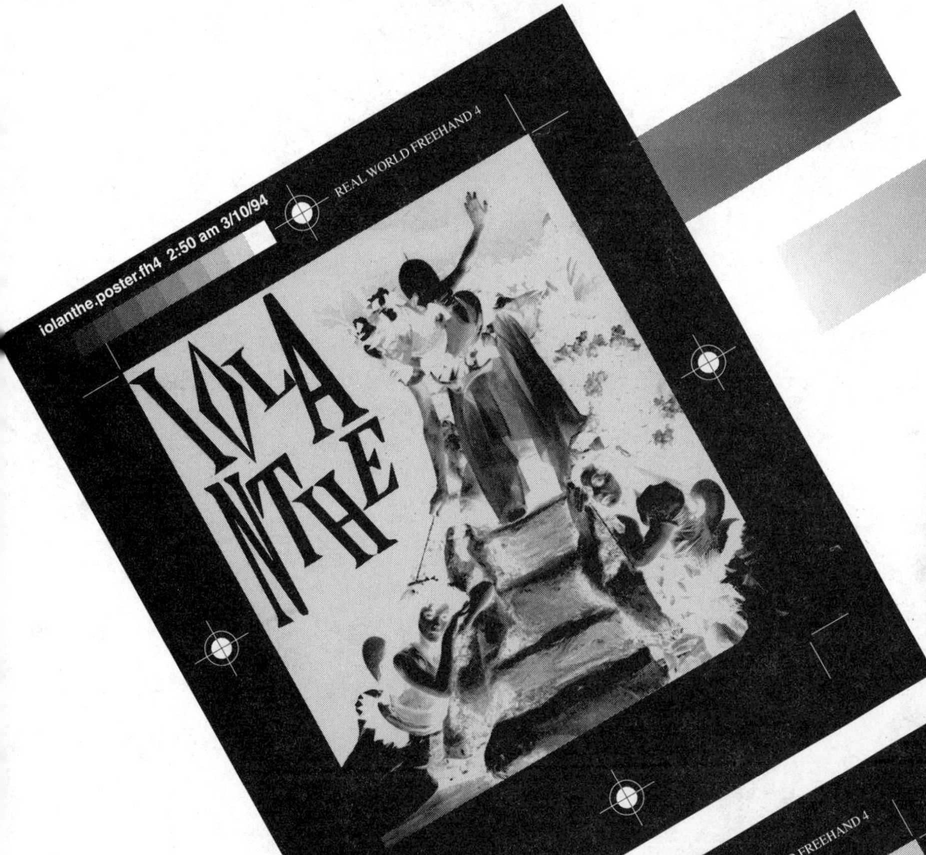

CHAPTER

Color

6

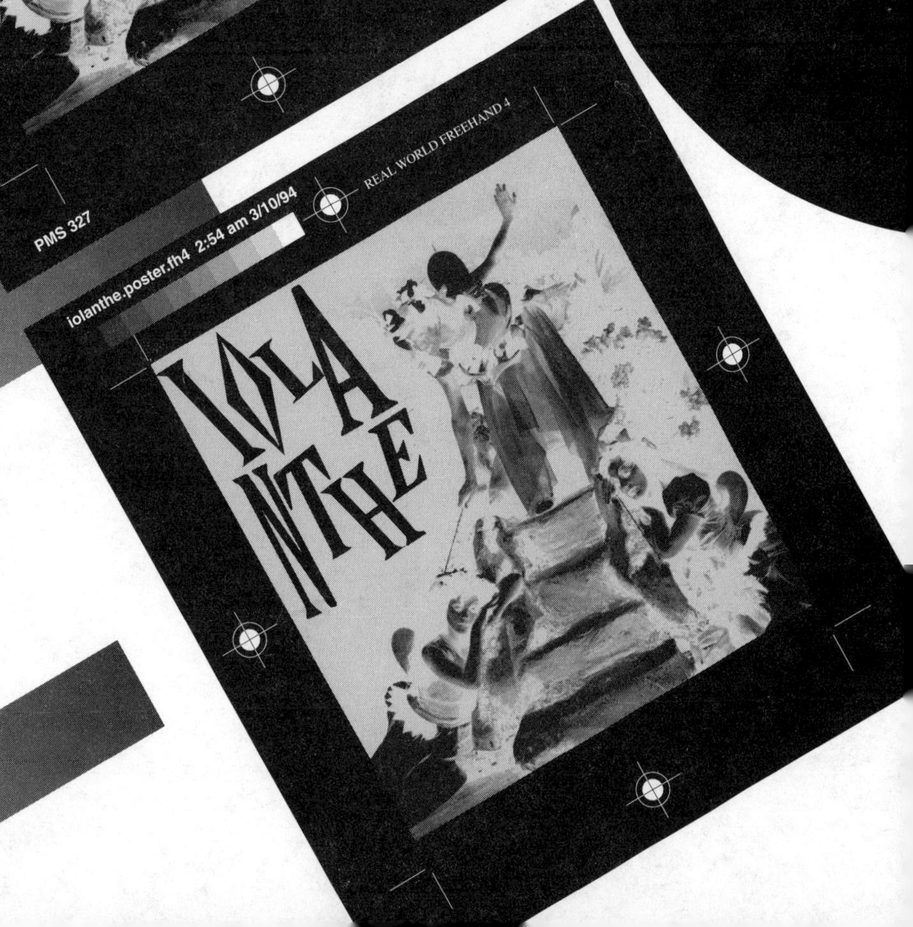

I remember drawing things when I was a kid. I enjoyed drawing with a pen or pencil, but I didn't really get excited until someone got out the crayons. Or the finger-paints. Or the watercolors and brushes. Drawing black lines on paper was fun, but that color stuff was *what it was all about.*

Color communicates, telling us things about the object bearing the color. Without color cues, we'd have a hard time guessing the ripeness of a fruit or distinguishing a poisonous mushroom from an edible one. And many animals would have a hard time figuring out when to mate, or with whom.

We associate colors with human emotions: we are green with envy; we've got the blues; we see red. Colors affect our emotions, as well. Various studies suggest that we think best in a room of one color, or relax best in a room of another color.

What does all of this mean? Color's important. A rule of thumb in advertising is that a color advertisement gets something like 10 times the response of a black-and-white ad.

FreeHand's always been one of the best desktop-publishing tools for creating color publications. FreeHand 3 added color TIFF separation, support for the optimized screen angles in PPDs, automatic trapping, and OPI support. In some ways, FreeHand 4's color enhancements are more modest. So what's new?

For starters, everything's different. The Colors dialog box you knew in FreeHand 3—the place where you created colors, edited colors, and picked colors from libraries—is gone. In its place are three floating palettes—the Color List, the Color Mixer, and the Tints palette.

Does putting the controls in palettes mean you'll spend more time mousing around? Maybe. Some tasks—such as adding a color from a color library—are much quicker. Other tasks, such as editing a color, take a few more mouse actions than they did in Free-Hand 3. In the procedures in this chapter, I'll show you the quickest ways I've found to navigate through the color palettes.

You won't miss it. FreeHand 3's "automatic trapping" (the Spread Size field in the Print Options dialog box) is gone. My hat's off to Aldus and Altsys for recognizing that the pain this caused Free-Hand users wasn't worth the favorable press they got for it (and they did; believe me).

Spread Size was one of those features that seemed like a good idea at the time—a way to get something, in some cases, for almost nothing. If you understood what it could do, and used it sparingly, you could get it to do very simple trapping. Unfortunately, people expected it to do more (automatically trap everything in a Free-Hand publication) than it did (it increased the stroke width of all paths), or was intended to do.

Aldus could throw away the Spread Size field because they'd created TrapWise—an automatic trapping program so good that you don't even have to think about trapping anymore unless you want to (or don't have access to TrapWise).

At more than $5,000, TrapWise sounds like a very expensive FreeHand utility—but you don't have to buy it. Look for an image-setting service bureau near you that can trap your FreeHand files with TrapWise. It'll cost something to have them trap your file, but it'll cost far less than it would if you did it yourself.

Drag-and-drop color. Most color-related procedures in FreeHand 4 involve dragging a color swatch from one color well to another (Figure 6-1). Want to change a color? Drag a color swatch out of the large color well at the bottom of the Color Mixer and drop it into a color well in the Color List.

In addition, you can apply color directly to objects using drag and drop—drag a color swatch over the object you want to color

FIGURE 6-1
Color wells and
color swatches

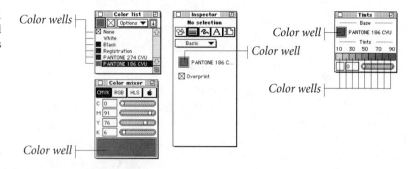

*To see a color swatch, position the cursor over
any color well, and drag.*

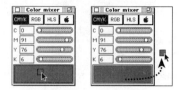

(from any color well), and drop it. FreeHand applies the color to
the object. If you're dropping the color swatch in the middle of a
shape, FreeHand applies the color to the shape's fill. If you drop
the color swatch on the outline of the path, FreeHand applies that
color to the path's stroke.

For more on drag-and-drop color, see the procedures in the
rest of this chapter.

New color libraries. FreeHand 4 supports the most-frequently used
color-matching systems in the graphic arts industry.

◆ **DIC.** A spot-color specifying system corresponding to inks
manufactured by Dainippon Ink and Chemicals, Inc. It's
something like Japanese version of Pantone—and not seen
frequently in North America or Europe, except in printing
subsidiaries of Japanese printers. Still, it's a nice set of
colors, which you might want to use if you can get a printer
to match them.

◆ **Focoltone.** A process-color specification system (mostly
used in Europe). Colors in the Focoltone library are organized in sets of colors with common percentages of at least

one process color. The idea is to create a library of colors that, when applied to objects, are easy to trap, or don't need trapping at all.

- **Pantone.** The basic set of spot-color inks manufactured by Pantone, Inc. These inks are the industry-standard for spot color in the North American printing business (as always, ask your commercial printer).

- **Pantone Process.** A set of process-color simulations of Pantone's spot colors, corresponding to their *Pantone Process System Guide*—*not* their *Process Color Imaging Guide* (where the process colors have great names like "MOGO," "POOH," and "TFOB"). These colors have no relation to the Pantone spot colors.

- **Toyo.** A spot-color library for matching inks from the Toyo Ink Manufacturing Company, Ltd, and corresponding to their Toyo 88 Color Guide ink sample book. Like DIC, Toyo is primarily used in Asian countries, and isn't seen much in Europe or North America.

- **TruMatch.** A process-color specifying system featuring small percentage changes from one process color to another. Their swatch book is often preferred over any of the others by designers for specifying process color.

In addition, FreeHand's color libraries are in the same format as PageMaker's. If you get a new color library for PageMaker, that library's name appears on the Color List's popup menu in Free-Hand. Watch the Aldus Forum on Compuserve (see Appendix C, "Resources") for more, or updated, color libraries.

If you have PageMaker 5 installed, you might also see other color libraries—notably Pantone Coated and Pantone Uncoated (these libraries contain the same colors as the Pantone library, but they've been edited so that their onscreen appearance more closely matches the swatches shown in the *Pantone Color Selector 1000/Coated* and the *Pantone Color Selector 1000/Uncoated* color sample books)

You can create your own color libraries by exporting colors from FreeHand, or you can create them youself using a word processing program (or a spreadsheet, or a database—anything that can write text-only—or ASCII—files)—see "Creating Color Libraries," later in this chapter.

Color Printing

It's impossible to discuss creating and using colors in FreeHand without talking a little about printing. If you already know about color printing, feel free to skip ahead, though you'll miss all the jokes if you do. Everyone else should note that this is a very simple explanation of a very bizarre and complex process.

The Printing Process

After you've printed your FreeHand publication to film and delivered it to your commercial printer (I like to walk in through the loading dock), your printer takes your film and uses it to expose (or "burn") a photosensitive printing plate. The surface of the plate has been chemically treated to repel ink (it's "hydrophilic"). When the printing plate is exposed, the image areas from your film become able to accept ink (or "hydrophobic"). Once the plate's been exposed, your printer attaches the printing plate to the cylinder of a printing press.

As the cylinder holding the plate turns, the parts of it bearing your image become coated with ink, which is transferred (via another, rubber covered cylinder—the offset cylinder) to the paper. This transfer is where we get the term "offset," as in "offset printing," because the plate itself does not touch your paper.

Printing presses put ink on paper one ink color at a time. Some presses have more than one printing cylinder (also called a printing "head" or "tower") and can print several colors of ink on a sheet of paper in one pass through the press, but each printing cylinder carries only one color of ink. We can make it look like we've gotten more than one color of ink on a printing plate by using screens—patterns of dots that, from a distance, fool the eye into thinking it sees a separate color (see Figure 6-2).

Spot and Process Inks

Spot-color printing is simple: the printer just mixes solid-color inks to get exactly the color we want, then we load our press with that

FIGURE 6-2
Black and…gray?

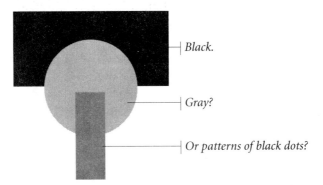

Black.

Gray?

Or patterns of black dots?

ink. In process-color printing, we use different screens of four inks (cyan, magenta, yellow, and black) to simulate a large part of the visible color spectrum by printing screens of the different colors so that they overlap. If everything's gone well, the dots of the different colored inks are placed near each other in a pattern called a rosette (see Color Figure 6 on the color pages for an example of a rosette).

Process-color printing can't simulate all of the colors our eyes can see (notably metallic and fluorescent colors), but it can print color photographic images. Spot colors can print any color you can make with pigments, but can't be used to print color photographic images. Technically, you *can* print color photographs using spot colors, but—unless you were very careful—you'd end up either compromising color-matching in the photographs, or printing more than four inks.

Avoiding Rosettes

Recently, some companies have been experimenting with color separation methods that do not produce rosettes.

Flamenco screening. One method (sometimes called "Flamenco" screening) prints all process inks at the same screen angle and line screen, producing a grid of color dots. Once again, the eye reads these juxtaposed dots of the four process inks as any number of colors. While this method can produce good-looking images that lack moiré patterns at fairly low line screens, higher line screens often show severe color shifting from one part of the image to another. In effect, it's a huge moiré pattern.

Flamenco screening is mostly used in the newspaper industry.

Stochastic screening. Another method, called "stochastic" screening, avoids halftoning altogether. Stochastic screening converts grayscale information into high-resolution dithered bitmaps (shades of MacPaint!). When you print bitmaps you've applied colors to (that is, cyan, magenta, yellow, and black) on top of each other, the eye sees more colors—just as it does when you print rosettes. It's like a Seurat painting.

As I'm writing this (in March 1994), imagesetter manufacturers have begun to offer stochastic screening hardware and software for their RIPs under various tradenames (Agfa's, for example, is called Cristal Raster). Third-parties have also released software that works with software RIPs running on desktop computers.

You don't have to print your publication on a specially-equipped imagesetter to experiment with stochastic screening—you can do it yourself, using Photoshop and FreeHand (see "Do-It-Yourself Stochastic Screening," later in this chapter, for more information on separating color images using stochastic screening).

Hi-Fi color. You'll often hear stochastic screening mentioned in the same breath as a new process-color printing method, high-fidelity color (usually called "hi-fi" color). The most popular current hi-fi color scheme uses seven inks—cyan, magenta, yellow, orange, green, violet, and black—to simulate more of the visible spectrum than can be simulated using four-color process printing. (Other schemes use six or eight colors, or a different set of seven inks.). The idea's still the same—put dots close together, and people see more colors than you've printed. In any case, you don't have to use hi-fi color to use stochastic screening.

The samples of hi-fi color I've seen have been very impressive—the technique makes it possible to print fluorescent and more intense colors than would be possible to print with four-color process printing.

As I write this book, very few commercial printers are set up to do hi-fi color (in fact, you can probably count the number of printers in North America equipped to print seven colors in a single pass through the press on your fingers and toes). The printing giant R.R. Donnelly, however, is writing software and building printing and hardware systems that will allow them and their clients to take advantage of hi-fi printing and stochastic screening sooner than anyone else. The technology is on the horizon, however, and it's getting closer. Is it the next "revolution" in printing? Will all printers be using hi-fi color in five years?

I have no idea.

Color in FreeHand

Now that you know all about color printing, it's time to get down to specifying colors in your FreeHand publication.

The colors you work with in your publication correspond to the inks you'll use to print your publication. When you create, edit, or import a color in FreeHand, you're working with a single ink, or a tint of that ink, or a set of inks (a "tint build") which, when printed, optically blend together to produce the color.

How you specify colors affects what you can do with objects you apply the colors to. You can blend between objects with different process colors applied, or create graduated or radial fills from one process color to another. You can't do that with spot colors (well, actually, you *can*, but FreeHand turns all of the intermediate blend steps into process colors)—though you can go from one spot color to white, black, or another tint of that same spot color.

When it comes time to print, your ink list (in the Print Options dialog box) displays the four process inks and any spot colors you've defined in your publication. If you need to convert any of your spot colors to process colors, or vice versa, you need to redefine the colors; you can't, as in Adobe Separator or Aldus PrePrint, select an ink and convert it to a process color from the Print options dialog box.

Spot Color or Process Color or Both? Whether you use spot colors, process colors, or both depends on the needs of your specific publication—which has to do with your printing budget, your communications goals, and, most importantly, your mood. If you plan to use color photographs in your publication, you're going to have to use at least the four process inks. If you're printing on a tight budget, you'll probably want to use one or two inks.

When you're creating a color, you're offered a variety of choices: is the color a spot color or a process color or a tint? If you don't yet know how your publication will be printed, don't worry too much about whether a color is defined as a spot or process color—you can always change it later. It's much easier to go from spot to process than the other way around.

Is What You See Anything Like What You'll Get?

Any time you're working with colors, refer to printed samples of the colors, rather than looking at the colors on your screen. Remember that, unlike the paper you'll be printing on, your screen is backlit, so it displays colors very differently from what they'll look like when printed.

If you're using uncoated paper, look at samples of the ink (spot color) or ink mix (process color) printed on uncoated stock. If you're using coated paper, look at examples printed on coated paper. If you're using a colored paper, try to find an example of the ink printed on a colored paper—though these examples are much harder to find.

If you're working with Pantone (or PMS) colors, Pantone makes a line of swatch books showing their colors printed as spot colors and books of process color conversions of their colors; they're printed on both coated and uncoated stocks, and although they're kind of expensive, they're not as expensive as pulling a job off of a press because you didn't like the press check. They're downright cheap if you consider what it must cost to print them.

Though I know everybody does it, I never use Pantone spot colors (the ones you find in the Pantone library) to specify a process color. The Pantone Matching System is a spot-color specifying system, and the colors don't convert to process colors particularly well because you can't make any given hue just using process colors (see the discussion earlier in this chapter). Still, Pantone has included the process color conversions for these colors (as seen in their *Process Color Imaging Guide*) in the definition of these spot colors.

Next, don't rely on a color PostScript printer to give you an accurate version of what your colors are going to look like. They can't do it, because they simply lack the resolution and color range to produce good process colors. (and bear in mind that, because color PostScript printers print using something akin to the process-color method, your spot colors will be converted to process colors during printing).

When you need to create a color proof of your publication, but aren't yet ready to have your commercial printer set up their press to print a sample for you, use one of the color proofing processes (such as Chromalin or Press Match) to create your proofs from the film you've gotten out of your imagesetter. Imagesetting service bureaus frequently offer color proofing as part of their business. Some of these proofing processes can give you a proof on the paper you're intending to use, or can give you transparent overlays that you can place on top of your selected paper to get an idea of what your publication will look like when printed.

Controlling Your Color-Viewing Environment

If it's important to you that what you see on your screen looks as much like what the printed version of your publication as possible, there are a few rules you need to follow.

◆ Use a monitor and video card capable of displaying 24-bit color. Eight-bit color, as built into the Macintosh IIci, IIsi, and Centris series, is simply not going to do the trick. Neither is the 16-bit color you'll find on most Quadras.

◆ Calibrate your monitor. Radius, SuperMac, and Tektronix all make color monitor calibrators that work with FreeHand's onscreen display of colors. Find the one that works with your monitor and use it.

◆ Control the lighting around your monitor and keep it consistent when you're working. Just about everyone agrees that the fluorescent lighting used in most of our office buildings is the worst possible lighting for viewing colors. Turn it off, if you can, and rely on incandescent lighting (desk lamps with one sort of bulb or another) to light your work area. If you can't turn it off, try getting some "full spectrum" (or "amber") fluorescent tubes to install above your monitor. These also reduce eye strain.

◆ Control the lighting of the area where you'll be viewing your color proofs. Ideally, you'd have a room or small booth equipped with "daylight" (or 5000-degree Kelvin) lamps—but few of us can afford the money or space required.

Why is lighting important? Basically, the temperature of the light affects what a color "objectively" looks like. You can't assume ideal-viewing conditions, but you have to work in them to be able to do consistent work.

These rules have been passed on to me by people who are serious about color, and whose opinions I respect. But, this being a "Real World" book, I have to point out that these conditions are difficult to achieve. My Macintoshes run in eight-bit color 98 percent of the time, and their monitors have never been anywhere near a calibration system. The lights above my desk are fluorescent tubes—and white ones, at that. And as for having a special booth or room for viewing color proofs—hah!

To compensate, I base my design decisions on printed examples of spot and process colors and pay little attention to what's on the screen except to remind me of what colors I've put where. When I get a color proof, I look at it in several different lighting environments: outdoors, indoors under typical fluorescent lighting, and indoors under typical incandescent lighting. These are, after all, the conditions under which people will be viewing it.

Color Models

FreeHand lets you define colors using any of four color models—CMYK, RGB, HSB, and HLS. Which one should you use? It's pretty simple:

Spot colors. If you're working with spot colors, it doesn't matter what color model you choose, and it really doesn't matter what the color looks like on the screen, as long as you let your commercial printer know what color of ink they need to use to print your publication. How do you know what ink to use? If you use Pantone colors the most likely scenario), you can tell them the PMS color number. If you don't, it's trickier, but your printer can help you match the color you want to an ink they can mix.

Process colors. If you're working with process colors, *specify your color using the CMYK color model or a CMYK color-matching* *system*, or be ready for some nasty surprises when your publication gets printed. Once again, look at a printed sample of the process color, and enter the values given in the sample book for the color. It might seem too obvious to state, but don't enter other CMYK values unless you want a different color!

Tints. In addition, if you're trying to create a tint of an existing color (process or spot), use the Tints palette—don't try to approximate the right shade using the Color Mixer. You can base your tint on a spot color, a process color, or another tint. Don't base your tints on other tints unless you want to lose your mind. What's a 20-percent tint of a 67-percent tint of a 45-percent tint of PMS 327?

FreeHand's Color Controls

You create and add colors using three palettes—the Color List, the Color Mixer, and the Tints palette.

Color List   The most important of the three color palettes is the Color List (see Figure 6-3). You use the Color List to import colors from color libraries, export colors to color libraries, name colors, apply colors, duplicate colors, and convert colors from spot to process (or from process to spot).

Fill and Stroke buttons. At the top of the Color List, just below the palette's title bar, you'll see the Fill and Stroke buttons (see Figure 6-3). These aren't labelled in any way, but the Fill button is the one on the right (here's proof that FreeHand's new user interface, while easier to use, is harder to write about). When you want to work with an object's fill, click the Fill button; to work with an object's stroke, press the Stroke button. FreeHand shows you which button is active by displaying a black border around the outside of the button.

The Color List popup menu. The Color List's popup menu, to the right of the Fill and Stroke buttons, is what you use to duplicate colors, delete colors, choose color libraries, and and convert colors from one color type (spot or process) to another.

FIGURE 6-3
Color List

Stroke button ⊢   ⊣ Zoom box

Close box ⊢

Fill button ⊢   ⊣ Add arrow

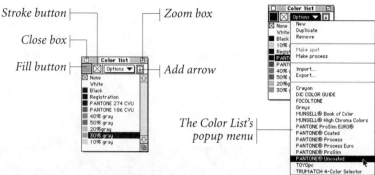

The Color List's
popup menu

To change the position of a color in the Color List...

Select the color...   *...and drag it up or*   *When the color's where you*
                             down in the Color List.   *want it, stop dragging.*

The Add arrow. The Add arrow is another unnamed feature of the Color List. It's to the right of the popup menu—a little box with an arrow in it. You add colors to the Color List by dropping color swatches into the open area at the bottom of the list. If you can't see the bottom of the list, drop the swatch on the Add arrow. Free-Hand adds the color to the end of the list.

For more on adding new colors to the Color List, see "Creating New Colors," later in this chapter.

Changing the order of the colors in the Colors List. To change the order in which colors appear in the Color List, point at a color name and then drag the color name up or down in the Color List. Once you've got the color where you want, drop it. This can be handy when you've got a long list of colors and want to position the most-used colors near the top of the palette.

Tip:
The Quick Way
to Display the
Color List

To display the Color List, double-click any color well (in the Inspector, in the Tints palette, or in the Color Mixer, for example). FreeHand displays the Color List.

The Color Mixer

The Color Mixer is FreeHand's palette—you use it to specify the colors you use in your publications. The Color Mixer gives you four different color models to choose from: CMYK, RGB, HLS, or HSB (also known as the Apple color model or Color Picker). To display the controls for a color model, click the corresponding button in the Color Mixer (see Figure 6-4).

Tip:
The Quick Way
to Display the
Color Mixer

To display the Color Mixer, double-click one of the color wells in the Color List. FreeHand displays the Color Mixer, and loads the Color Mixer with the color definition of the color you clicked.

FIGURE 6-4
Color Mixer

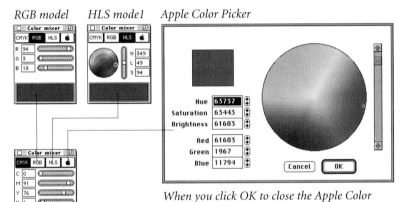

RGB model   *HLS model*   *Apple Color Picker*

Click the buttons in the Color Mixer to change the color model you're using.

CMYK model

When you click OK to close the Apple Color Picker, FreeHand displays the HLS color model in the Color Mixer.

Double-click a color swatch ...   *...and FreeHand displays the Color Mixer, loaded with that color.*

The Tints Palette

You use the Tints palette to quickly generate a set of tints of a color (see "Creating Tints," later in this chapter). The Tints palette generates 10-percent tints (from 10 to 90 percent) of any color you drop into the palette's color well. You can also create a custom tint by entering a value in the Tint Percentage field, or by dragging the slider at the bottom of the Tints palette (see Figure 6-5).

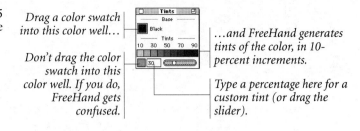

FIGURE 6-5
Tints palette

Drag a color swatch into this color well...

Don't drag the color swatch into this color well. If you do, FreeHand gets confused.

...and FreeHand generates tints of the color, in 10-percent increments.

Type a percentage here for a custom tint (or drag the slider).

Creating and Adding Colors

Now that you know what the new tools are, you're probably wondering how they work. FreeHand 3 users sometimes find the process of creating colors in FreeHand 4 more difficult than the process they're used to. I think that creating and editing colors is somewhat quicker, overall, in FreeHand 4 than in previous versions of FreeHand—but you have to get used to the tools and learn the "tricks." Read on.

Adding Colors from a Color Library

Most of the time, you'll be adding colors from FreeHand's color libraries. Why should you do this? Because your commercial printer wants you to (when they talk in their sleep, they call out Pantone numbers), and because it's the quickest way to add a named color to your publication. To choose a color from a color library, follow these steps (see Figure 6-6).

1. Display the Color List (if it's not already visible, press Command-9).

2. Choose a color library from the popup menu at the top of the Color List. FreeHand displays the Library dialog box.

3. Pick a color by clicking on one of the color swatches in the Library dialog box. To select more than one color, hold down Shift as you click on the color swatches. You can also hold down Shift and drag the cursor to select a series of adjacent colors (in fact, you can Shift-drag through the entire library to select all of the colors in the library).

4. Press Return (or click the OK button). FreeHand closes the Library dialog box and adds the selected color or colors to the Color List.

FIGURE 6-6
Adding a color from
a color library

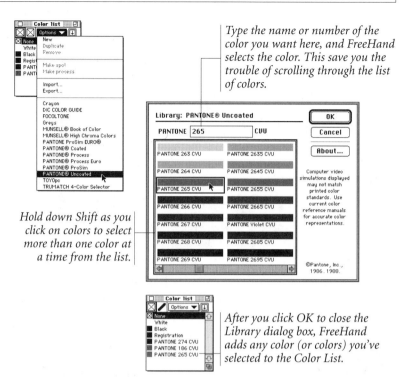

Type the name or number of the color you want here, and FreeHand selects the color. This save you the trouble of scrolling through the list of colors.

Hold down Shift as you click on colors to select more than one color at a time from the list.

After you click OK to close the Library dialog box, FreeHand adds any color (or colors) you've selected to the Color List.

Tip:
Leave the
Name Alone

If you're working with Pantone spot colors, don't rename the color unless you're working with one of the applications that names PMS colors differently from FreeHand (see "Keep Your Color Names Straight," below). Just stick with the color name that's entered in the Name field when you select the PMS color. This way, when you print, you can turn on the Separation names option in the Print options dialog box and the color name will print on the correct color overlay. Your commercial printer has a pretty good idea what "PMS 327 CV" means, but might go mad trying to guess what you meant by naming a color "angry spam."

Then again, if you know you're going to be using a PMS ink but don't know which one, you can always name the color "Spot Color" or some such, and tell the printer which ink to use when you hand over the job.

Tip:
Why Import
Colors?

What's the difference between importing colors using the Import command and choosing a listed library? The libraries shown on the menu are the ones FreeHand found in the Color folder in your

Aldus folder (in your System Folder). If you've stored a library somewhere else, you can retrieve colors from it using Import. You might want to store your color libraries somewhere else to keep the popup list shorter.

Tip:
Keep Your Color
Names Straight

If you're using FreeHand to create EPS graphics containing spot colors that will be placed in a publication created by another application, and you want to color-separate from that publication, make sure that your spot color names match between FreeHand and the other application. Color separation programs are as literal-minded as every other piece of software, so when you're separating a file containing the spot colors "OceanBlue" and "Ocean_Blue" you can expect to get two overlays. Since you only want all the spot-color items to come out on one overlay, keep your color names consistent between documents. Make sure they're identical—right down to capitalization and punctuation.

This is especially true when you're working with Pantone colors, because different applications use different names for the same Pantone colors.

Note that all of this makes no difference whatever if you're converting these colors to process colors as you separate the file.

Creating a Color

To create a new color, follow these steps (see Figure 6-7).

1. Display the Color List (if you can't see the Color List, press Command-9).

2. Double-click a color swatch in the Color List to display the Color Mixer, if it's not already visible.

3. Pick a color model by clicking the buttons at the top of the Color Mixer. If you're working on a publication that you'll be printing using process colors, use the CMYK color model. If you're creating a custom spot color (have you talked with your commerical printer about this?), it really doesn't matter which color model you use.

4. If you're using the CMYK or RGB color model, specify your color by entering numbers in the fields or sliding the sliders. If you're using the HSB or Apple Color Picker, click on a point in the color picker those models display.

FIGURE 6-8
Creating a new color

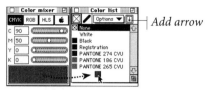

Add arrow

Display both the Color List and
the Color Mixer. Specify a new
color using the Color Mixer.

Drag a color swatch from the Color Mixer
and drop it into an empty area in the
Color List (or on the Add arrow).

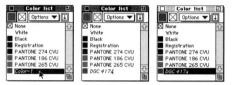

FreeHand adds the new color
to the Color List, and assigns
the color a default name.

To change the color name, double-click on
the name in the Color List, type the new
name you want, and press Return.

5. Drag a swatch of the color from the color well at the bottom
    of the color mixer onto the Add arrow at the top of the
    Color List (or drag the swatch into an empty area at the
    bottom of the Color List). FreeHand adds the color to the
    Color List, assigning it a default color name as it does so.
    You might have to scroll the list of colors to see the new
    color (it'll appear at the bottom of the list).

6. If you want to change the color's name, double-click on
    the color name in the Color List, type the new name for
    your color, and press Return. If you want, you can hide
    the Color Mixer by double-clicking a color swatch in the
    Color List.

Tip:
Keep Your Color
Definitions
Straight

If you're using FreeHand to create EPS graphics containing process
colors that'll be placed in a publication created by another application, and you want to color separate that publication, make
sure that your process-color specifications match between Free-
Hand and the other application for colors that are supposed
to print as the same color (actually, PageMaker 5.0 imports the
named process colors, so you're safe there—but QuarkXPress 3.3
doesn't import named process colors from an EPS, only named
spot colors).

Once again, you can't rely on your screen display, because different applications display colors differently. Make the CMYK settings for your process colors identical, though, and you can count on their printing identically when you separate the publication.

Creating Color Libraries

FreeHand can read two different types of color libraries—binary files, which are stored in a proprietary format, and text files, which are saved as text-only. Binary files generally have the file extension ".BCF," and text-only files have the extension ".ACF." If you create your own color libraries, you can use any file name you want, but I'd advise you to stick with FreeHand's file extensions.

Exporting color libraries. You create binary color libraries when you export colors from FreeHand. To do that, follow these steps (see Figure 6-8).

FIGURE 6-8
Exporting a binary
color library

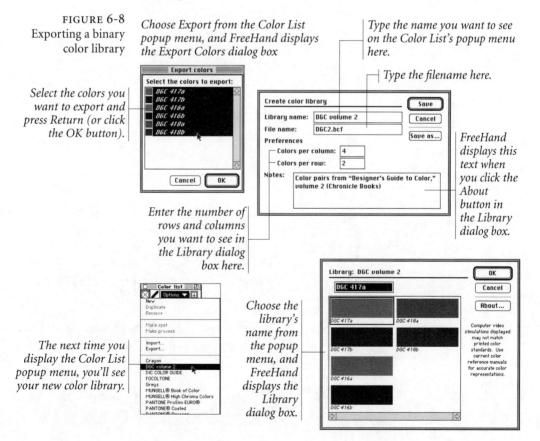

Choose Export from the Color List popup menu, and FreeHand displays the Export Colors dialog box

Type the name you want to see on the Color List's popup menu here.

Type the filename here.

Select the colors you want to export and press Return (or click the OK button).

FreeHand displays this text when you click the About button in the Library dialog box.

Enter the number of rows and columns you want to see in the Library dialog box here.

The next time you display the Color List popup menu, you'll see your new color library.

Choose the library's name from the popup menu, and FreeHand displays the Library dialog box.

1. Choose Export from the Color List's popup menu. FreeHand displays the Export Colors dialog box.

2. Select the colors you want to export from the list in the Export Colors dialog box and press Return. FreeHand exports the colors you've selected.

Creating color libraries using a word processor. You can create a color library or edit an existing color library (such as "Crayon-Library.acf") using any word processor that can save files as text-only (ASCII). If you're working from a process-color swatch book, here's your chance to enter lots of colors at once.

Color library files begin with the following text (items you enter are shown in italic). Table 6-1 shows what the different lines mean.

```
ACF 1.0
library name
LibraryVersion: number
Copyright: © your name here
AboutMessage: your message here
Names: Partial or Full
Rows: number of rows
Columns: number of columns
Entries: number of entries
Prefix: prefix you want for the colors in the library
Suffix: suffix you want for the colors in the library
Type: Process, Spot, or Mixed
Models: color models
PreferredModel: preferred color model
Data:
```

TABLE 6-1 Color Library Keywords	

Keyword	What it means
Library name	The name of the library as you want it to appear on the Color List's popup menu. Your library's name can be up to 31 characters long.
LibraryVersion	Enter a number here to represent the version number of your library. You can leave this line blank, if you want.
AboutMessage	The message you want to see when you click the About button in the Library dialog box.

Keyword	What it means
Names	Enter "Full" to display names with their suffixes and prefixes attached (see "Suffix" and "Prefix," later in this table), or "Partial" to display only the names of the colors. If you're insane, you can even enter "None", which means you won't see any color names in the Color List.
Rows	The number of vertical color swatches FreeHand displays in the Library palette. Larger numbers mean smaller swatches; smaller numbers mean bigger swatches. Enter a "1" to produce the tallest possible color swatch.
Columns	The number of horizontal swatches FreeHand displays in the Library palette. Enter a "1" to produce a the widest possible color swatch.
Entries	The total number of colors in the library
Prefix	Any text you want to appear before your color names in the Color List.
Suffix	Any text you want to appear after your color names in the Color List.
Type	The type of colors contained in the library. You can enter "Process", "Spot", or "Mixed".
Models	A list of the color models used in the library. You can enter "CMYK" and "RGB".
PreferredModel	Enter "CMYK" or "RGB" here—it doesn't seem to make any difference to Freehand. If you're creating a color library to use with PageMaker, on the other hand, the value you enter here determines which color model PageMaker's Edit Color dialog box displays when you edit the color.

After you create the library header, enter your color definitions as shown below, where *colorname* is the name you give the color and *cyan, magenta,* etc. are the color percentages for the color model being used (where 1.0 = 100 percent).

```
percentageC percentageM percentageY or percentageK
process or spot
colorname
```

For example

```
0 0 0 .1
Process
10% Gray
```

If you want define a color using the RGB color model, enter the RGB values as shown below. Enter each of the component colors ("Red", "Green", and "Blue") using a scale where "65535" equals 100 percent of that color and "0" equals zero percent.

```
Red Green Blue
spot
colorname
```

For example

```
65535 65535 0
Spot
10% Gray
```

When you're through adding colors to your color library, save the file as text-only, giving the file the file extension ".acf." An example of a very short color library is shown in Figure 6-9.

Importing Colors from PageMaker

Because it's so important to have your spot-color names—or your process-color specifications—match, it's great to be able to import objects from PageMaker into FreeHand and add the color names and specifications used in PageMaker to your Color List.

Most of the time, it's easiest to pick the colors you want from a color library—FreeHand and PageMaker can use the same color libraries. If you're working with lots of custom spot colors (i.e., colors that didn't come from a color library), follow these steps to bring those spot colors into FreeHand.

1. Create spot colors in PageMaker.

FIGURE 6-9
A very short
color library

```
ACF 1.0
ShortColorLibrary
LibraryVersion: 1.0
Copyright: ©Olav Martin Kvern
AboutMessage: Why did you click that button?
Names: Partial
Rows: 2
Columns: 2
Entries: 4
Prefix:
Suffix:
Type: Process
Models: CMYK
PreferredModel: CMYK
Data:
.4 0 .2 .5
ColorPair 1a
.6 .4 .5 .5
ColorPair 1b
0 .1 0 .7
ColorPair 2a
.7 .6 .3 .5
ColorPair 2b
```

2. Save one page containing objects with the colors you want to bring into FreeHand to disk as an EPS file. (In PageMaker, press Command-P to display the Print dialog box, enter the page number you want to print in the Range field, click the Options button, then use the controls in the Print Options dialog box to print the page to disk as an EPS file.)

3. In FreeHand, press Command-Shift-D (or choose Place from the File menu).

4. Locate and select the EPS file you just printed to disk and press Return. FreeHand displays a loaded Place Gun. Click the gun to place the PageMaker EPS. As FreeHand places the EPS file, it adds the colors defined in the PageMaker EPS to the Color List.

You can take color names and definitions created in FreeHand back to PageMaker—when you import a FreeHand EPS file, Page-Maker updates the Colors palette with any named colors in the placed EPS.

When you import an EPS from PageMaker or QuarkXPress, FreeHand doesn't import named process colors defined in the EPS. Process-colored objects in the the EPS separate correctly when you print, but the name of the color doesn't get added to the Color List. If you want to use these colors in your FreeHand publication, you'll have to either recreate them in FreeHand, or follow these steps.

1. Convert the named process colors you want to import into FreeHand to spot colors in PageMaker or XPress.

2. Export an EPS containing examples of the colors.

3. Place the EPS in FreeHand. The spot color names appear in the Color List. You can delete the placed EPS, if you want.

4. Convert the imported spot colors to process colors (select each color and choose Convert to Process from the Color List popup menu.

Adding Colors from Illustrator

You can't name process colors in Illustrator, so when you open or place EPS files created in Illustrator, FreeHand's Color List doesn't update with any custom process colors you've used in the Illustrator file.

If you've placed the EPS file, there's not much you can do to get the color specifications from the Illustrator file into FreeHand; you'll have to recreate the colors from scratch. Remember that you've got to make the color definitions identical to have the colors match when you separate the publication.

If you've opened and converted the EPS file, on the other hand, you can add the colors to your Colors palette.

1. Ungroup the converted Illustrator EPS.

2. Select an object in the converted graphic that's filled with the color you want to add to your Color List.

3. Press Command-Option-F to display the Fill Inspector.

4. Drag a color swatch from the Fill Inspector's color well to an empty area in the Color List (or drop it on the Add arrow at the top of the Color List).

5. Double-click on the name of the color in the Color List, type a new name for the color, and press Return to change the color's name.

Importing Colors from Other Applications

In general, you can import spot-color definitions from any other application that supports named colors by creating an EPS file containing the spot colors you want, and then placing the EPS in Free-Hand. The named colors in the EPS file appear in the Colors palette. At that point, you can delete the EPS graphic, if you want.

If you edit the properties of a color you've imported with an EPS graphic, don't expect the changes you've made to affect the color definitions inside the EPS—they won't. The colors inside the EPS are, in effect, locked.

If you imported the EPS only to get the color definitions and have deleted the EPS, there's no problem. If you've imported an EPS, edited the colors that are imported with the EPS, and applied the edited colors to FreeHand objects, you can expect the colors inside the EPS and the colors of the FreeHand objects to separate differently. If they're spot colors, you'll end up with (at least) an extra overlay. If they're process colors, colors that should look the same will look different.

Tip:
What's That Color?

If you want to match a color that occurs in a scanned color photograph you're using in your publication (the perfect shade of green in the leaves of a tree, or the bright red of a classic sports car, for example) so that you can color type or other graphic elements to match part of the image, and you have PrePrint, Fractal Design's Painter, or Photoshop (or some other program that can open a color TIFF and derive a CMYK value from a pixel), try this (I'll use Photoshop in my example, as shown in Figure 6-10).

1. Open Photoshop.

2. Locate and open the TIFF file.
   If the you haven't adjusted the color of the TIFF, and you want to adjust it, do it now. Once you're through, you can convert the file to a CMYK TIFF, which you'll also need to

FIGURE 6-10
Deriving colors from
photographic images

*Click the Eyedropper
tool on an area of
the color you want
to match.*

*If the Gamut Alarm
icon appears next to
the color swatch, the
color you chose
cannot be simulated
by a process color.*

*Click on the foreground
color in Photoshop's
toolbox, and Photoshop
displays the Color
Picker dialog box.*

*Read the color values
out of the fields at the
right of the Color Picker
dialog box.*

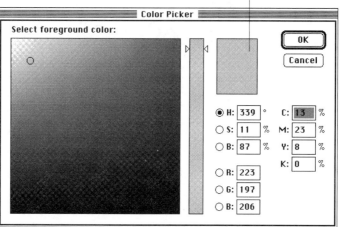

do. It won't do you any good to derive a color from part
of an image if you're going to change the colors in the
TIFF later.

Different programs have different ways of converting
RGB (all color TIFFs are RGB, at present) to CMYK.
PrePrint's values, for example, differ from those of Photoshop. Get your CMYK values from the application you're
going to use to separate your TIFF image, if possible. If
you're separating using FreeHand's built-in separations,
the values displayed by PrePrint will be very close, if not
exactly the same.

3. Select the Eyedropper tool.

4. Click the Eyedropper tool on the area in the image that contains the color you want to match.

5. Read the CMYK values for the color. In Photoshop, you double-click the foreground color swatch in the toolbox, and the Color Picker dialog box would appear.

   Photoshop tip: If the color you've chosen cannot be simulated with CMYK process color, Photoshop displays a Gamut Alarm icon next to the color swatch in the Color Picker dialog box. If you click the icon, Photoshop adjusts the color swatch and the color's CMYK values to be as close to the color as process color can get.

   Sometimes these "close" colors are farther away than you'd like—you may want to experiment and choose other colors if it's not as close as you want, and then click the alert market again.

6. Return to FreeHand and define the color using the CMYK values you captured from the photographic image.

Now you can apply the color to any graphic element you want.

Editing Colors

To edit a color, follow these steps (see Figure 6-11).

1. If the Color Mixer isn't already visible, double-click the color well for the color you want to edit in the Color List. Once the Color Mixer is visible, drag a color swatch from the color well in the Color List into the large color well at the bottom of the Color Mixer. The Color Mixer fills in with the specifications of the color you selected.

2. Drag the color sliders or type numbers in the fields (if you're using the CMYK or RGB color models). If you're using the Apple or HSB color models, pick a color in the color wheel.

FIGURE 6-11
Editing a color

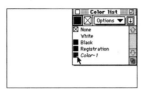

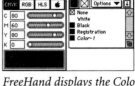

Double-click on the color you want to edit in the Color List.

FreeHand displays the Color Mixer.

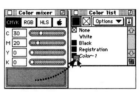

Use the fields or sliders in the Color Mixer to adjust the color.

Drag a color swatch from the Color Mixer and drop it on the color well of the color you're editing in the Color List.

FreeHand updates the color.

3. When the color has the specifications (or appearance) you want, drag a color swatch from the color well in the Color Mixer to the color well next to the color's name in the Color List.

Converting Spot Colors to Process Colors

Sometimes you need to change a color you've specified as a spot color into a process color. Your budget's expanded, you've got a sweetheart deal from your commercial printer, your client/boss/ whatever just *has* to have a color photograph—something happens so that you find you have to change your publication's color printing method from spot color to process color. Here's what you do (see Figure 6-12).

1. Select the color in the Color List.

2. Choose Make Process from the Color List's popup menu.

FreeHand converts your spot color to a process color. The process colors will rarely match the spot color—this is partly because

FIGURE 6-12
Converting spot colors
to process colors
(and vice versa)

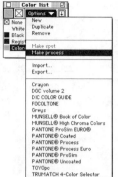

*Select the spot
color you want
to change.*

*FreeHand
converts the
spot color to a
process color
(and italicizes
the color name
in the Color
List).*

*Choose Make Process
from the popup menu.*

*To turn a process color
into a spot color, select
the color and choose
Make Spot from the
popup menu.*

the conversion process isn't perfect, but it's mostly because process color can't simulate the range of colors you can print with spot color inks (especially, as I've noted elsewhere, Pantone inks). Tweak the new process color until it looks the way you want, or until it matches the specs in your process color swatch book.

When you convert a Pantone spot color into a process color, FreeHand uses the CMYK percentages listed in Pantone's *Process Color Imaging Guide*.

Tip:
Changing from
one library color
to another

You've just changed your mind—you want all of the "PANTONE 192 CVU" in your publication to change to "PANTONE 274 CVU" You can, of course, change the name and color specifications of "PANTONE 192 CVU" to match those of "PANTONE 274 CVU"— though it's easy to make an error typing the name. Or you could tell your commercial printer that the film overlay labelled "PANTONE 192 CVU" should be printed as "PANTONE 274". But what if you're compulsive (I know you're out there), and really want to change the one color to another, precisely as it's listed in the color library? First deselect everything (press Command-Tab), and then follow these steps (see Figure 6-13).

1. Add (or import) the new color from a color library.

2. Double-click the name of the color you just added.

3. Press the Left Arrow or Right Arrow key, then drag the

FIGURE 6-12
Changing from
one library color
to another

Select the new color's name and press Command-C to copy it to the Clipboard.

Drag a color swatch from the new color into the original color's color well.

Remove the new color from the Color List.

Double-click on the original color's name and press Command-V to paste the color name from the Clipboard.

Press Return. FreeHand updates the color name.

cursor to select the color name (for some reason, double-clicking on the name doesn't work). Press Command-C to copy the color name to the Clipboard.

4. Drag a color swatch from the new color's color well into the color well of the color you want to change. FreeHand changes the color specifications of the color.

5. Delete the new color.

6. Double-click on the name of the original color.

7. Press Command-V to paste the color name you copied earlier, then press Return. FreeHand changes the name of the color in the Color List.

Applying Colors

Once you've selected an object, you use any of the following techniques to apply a color to the object (see Figure 6-14).

◆ Click the Fill or Stroke button and then click on a color in the Color List. FreeHand applies the color to the object's fill and/or (if it's a path or a text block) stroke.

◆ Drag a color swatch from the Color List to the Fill or Stroke button at the top of the Color List.

◆ Drag a color swatch from any color well and drop it on
an object. If you drop the swatch inside a closed path,
FreeHand applies the color to an path's fill. If you drop
the swatch on the path, FreeHand applies the color to
the object's stroke.

◆ Drag a color swatch from any color well and drop it into
the color well in the Fill or Stroke Inspector and press
Return, and FreeHand applies the color to the fill or stroke
of the object.

FIGURE 6-14
Applying colors

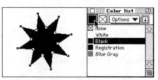

*Select an object. Click the
Stroke or Fill button...*

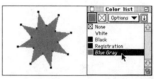

*...and click a color name. FreeHand
applies the color to the selected object.*

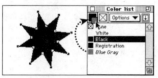

*Select an object. Drag a color
swatch from a color well...*

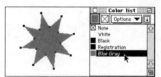

*...and drop it on the Fill or Stroke
button. FreeHand applies the color.*

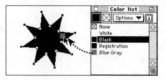

*Drag a color swatch
from a color well...*

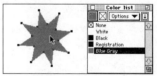

*...and drop it on top of an object
(the object need not be selected).*

*Select an object. Drag a color
swatch from the Color List (or
the Tints palette, or the Color
Mixer) and drop it in the color
well in the Fill (or Stroke)
Inspector.*

*Press Return, and FreeHand
applies the color.*

Applying Colors to Text

You can apply a fill or stroke to the characters of text in your publication. To apply a color to text, select the text with the Text tool and apply a color using any of the techniques described in the previous section. If you select the text block with the Pointer tool and apply a color, FreeHand applies the color to the text block's background—not to the text.

Applying Colors to Groups

You can apply a color to a group, changing the stroke and fill of all of the objects inside the group. There are some odd wrinkles to this.

◆ Objects inside the group with any basic fill or a fill of None will be filled with a basic fill of the color you apply.

◆ Patterned fills are colored with the color you apply, but remain patterned fills (you shouldn't be using these anyway, as explained in "Fills" in Chapter 2, "Drawing").

◆ Graduated and radial fills change so that the color you've applied to the group is their starting color.

◆ Tiled and PostScript fills are unaffected.

You can still subselect objects inside the group and change their color and fill specifications, regardless of any color you've applied to the group.

Applying Colors to Imported Graphics

FreeHand separates imported EPS graphics according to the color definitions inside the EPS, so applying a color to an EPS image has no effect.

You can apply colors to paint-type graphics, bilevel TIFFs, and grayscale TIFFs. When you print, FreeHand separates the image (or prints it as tints of a spot color, if you've applied a spot color to it). Applying a color to a color TIFF has no effect on the way that TIFF is separated by FreeHand.

Creating Duotones

Contrary to what you may have heard elsewhere, a single grayscale TIFF with two process colors applied to it does not a duotone make. It doesn't even make a "fake" duotone—which you create by printing a grayscale image on top of a tint of some color.

The trouble is, I haven't found two people who agree on how to create a duotone. Some people change the screen frequency of the image for one color. Some people enhance the highlights in the image that prints on the overlay for the more dominant color and enhance the shadows in the image that prints on the overlay for the subordinate color. Some people do both. And so on.

Inside this book, I'm the absolute dictator, and I say that a duotone is created by printing two slightly different TIFFs on top of each other. The TIFF for the more dominant color in the color scheme has had its shadows enhanced; the TIFF for the subordinate color has had its highlights enhanced. By "enhanced," I mean that the darkest five percent (or so) of the pixels in the image become black and that the lightest five percent become white. The darkest—or lightest—areas in the image seem to spread out slightly. The screen frequencies and screen angles are the same for the two TIFFs.

If you have Photoshop, of course, you can use it to create your duotones. But if you don't, read on.

To create duotones using FreeHand and Photoshop or PrePrint, follow these steps (see Figure 6-15 and Color Figure 8).

1. Open your original grayscale TIFF with PrePrint (or Photoshop—I mention PrePrint because so many people got "free" copies with PageMaker 4.2).

2. Enhance the shadows in the image. In PrePrint, you'd choose Shadows from the Enhance submenu on the Image menu (in other programs, you'd change the map of the lowest gray levels so that more of them became black). Save this version of the TIFF under a different name.

3. Open the original grayscale TIFF again. Enhance the highlights in the image. In PrePrint, you'd choose Highlights from the Enhance submenu on the Image menu (in other programs, you'd change the map of the highest gray levels so that more of them became white).

4. Place the two TIFFs into your FreeHand publication, making sure that one is exactly on top of the other. Color the one with its shadows enhanced with the dominant color

FIGURE 6-15
Creating duotones

Create two copies of the image using Aldus PrePrint or Adobe Photoshop. Enhance the shadows in one image, and enhance the highlights in the other.

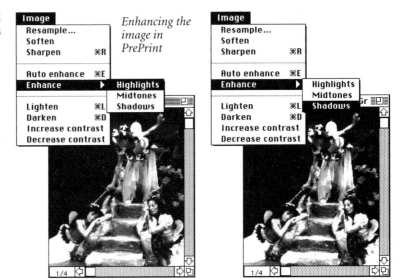

Place the two images on top of each other in FreeHand, color them different colors, and print them so that they overprint each other.

you intend to use to create the duotone. Color the TIFF with enhanced highlights with the subordinate color you intend to use to create the duotone.

5. When you print the publication, print the ink colors you've applied to the TIFFs one color at a time, starting with the color of whichever TIFF is on top. Once that overlay's printed, bring the other TIFF to the top of the stack (remember that you can Control-click through the stacked objects to select it) and print the other color used to create the duotone. When plates are made from the two overlays, the TIFFs overprint each other, producing a real duotone.

Why couldn't you just stack up the TIFFs and use ink-level overprinting commands to make them overprint? You can, if you modify your copy of FreeHand as instructed in "Overprinting TIFFs" in Chapter 8, "PostScript." To see what this effect looks like, see Color Figure 5 in the color pages in this chapter.

Removing Colors

To remove a color, select the color name in the Color List and choose Remove from the popup menu attached to the Color List. If there are other colors in the publication based on the selected color (tints, mostly), or if there are objects with that color applied to them, or if the color is used in a style's defintion, FreeHand complains that that color is in use somewhere in the publication and cannot be removed. Locate the objects or colors containing the color you want to remove and (for objects) change their colors or (for tints) remove them.

This is something of a bother. FreeHand should make it easier to merge or change all of one color to another color. Until that feature's added, it's something you've got to be aware of, and plan for.

Copying Colors

If you need to copy a color or set of colors from another FreeHand publication into the current publication, just open the source publication, select some objects with those colors applied, copy them out of the source publication and into the target publication. Remember FreeHand's "home team wins" rule—any colors in the target publication with names the same as those of the incoming colors override the incoming color definitions.

Creating Spot-Color Tint Builds

When you're working with spot-color publications, you often want to create tint builds (also known as stacked screens) of the colors you're working with to broaden the range of colors in your publication. Since you can't create a color containing percentages of two or more spot colors (20-percent black and 60-percent PMS 327, for example), it'd seem, at first glance, that you're stuck. You're not, though, as the following exercise demonstrates.

1. Open a new publication and add a spot color (create your own, or use one from the Pantone spot-color library). If one doesn't already exist, create a 20-percent tint of black.

2. Draw a rectangle.

3. Without deselecting the rectangle, fill it with the spot color you created in step 1. Set the rectangle's stroke to None.

4. Clone the rectangle by pressing Command-=.

5. Fill the clone with the 20-percent tint of black.

6. Press Command-Option-F to display the Fill Inspector. Check Overprint to make the rectangle overprint.

That's all there is to it. When you print, the gray rectangle overprints the spot-color rectangle, creating a combination of the two spot colors. Unfortunately, you can't see the tint build onscreen or on color printouts; you just see the color of the frontmost object. The next section shows another, more flexible, means to this same end.

Using Blending to Create Process - Color Tint Builds

Here's a trick I use to create a palette of tint builds for my publications (see Figure 6-16).

1. Draw a rectangle, fill it with 100-percent cyan, magenta, or yellow, and set the rectangle's stroke to None.

2. Clone the rectangle, move it away from the original rectangle, and fill it with 100-percent black.

3. Select both rectangles, press Command-U to ungroup them, and select a blend reference point on each rectangle. Press Command-E (or choose Blend from the Path Operations submenu). FreeHand blends the rectangles.
   Display the Object Inspector by pressing Command-Option-B (if the Inspector's not visible, press Command-I first to display it). Type the number of tint builds you'd like to create in the Number of Steps field and press Return to change the blend. The intermediate objects in the blend are colored with tints. These new colors do not appear in your Colors palette.

4. Ungroup the blended objects.

5. Select an object filled with one of the colors you want and press Command-Option-F to display the Fill Inspector. The color well in the Fill Inspector displays the color of the path you selected.

6. Drag a color swatch from the color well to the Add Arrow at the top of the Color List. FreeHand adds the color to your list of colors (change the name of the color, if you want).

FIGURE 6-16
Creating a palette
of tint builds

FIGURE 6-16
Creating a palette
of tint builds

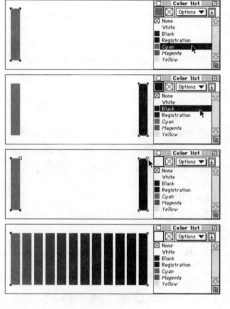

*Draw a rectangle and fill it
with 100-percent cyan,
magenta, or yellow.*

*Clone the rectangle and drag the
clone away from the original
rectangle. Color the clone 100-
percent black.*

*Press Command-U to convert
the rectangles to paths. Select a
point on each path and blend
the rectangles.*

*Adjust the number of blend
steps using the Object Inspector.
Ungroup the blend (press
Command-U twice) and select
a rectangle that's filled with a
color you like.*

Display the Fill Inspector.

*Drag a color swatch
from the color well in
the Fill Inspector to an
empty area in the
Color List (or to the
Add arrow).*

*FreeHand adds the color to the
Color List. You can change the
name of the color, if you want,
by double-clicking on the color
name, typing a new name, and
pressing Return.*

7. Repeat steps 5 and 6 until you've defined all of the colors
you want.

Substituting Process Colors for Spot Colors

Blending's a great way to create a set of tint builds, but blending
one spot color into another produces blended objects that are filled
with process color simulations of the original spot colors. This
makes it tough to quickly create a set of spot-color tint builds in
FreeHand. What to do? Substitute process colors for your spot colors. But what if you want to see something like the spot color you're
working with on screen, instead of looking at cyan, magenta, or
yellow?

The following procedure shows you how to change the on-screen
display of a process color to match that of a spot color.

1. Choose a Pantone color in the Color List.

2. Drag a color swatch from the color well for the Pantone color into the large color well at the bottom of the Color Mixer.

3. Click the RGB button in the Color Mixer.

4. Write down the Red, Green, and Blue percentages for your spot color. Multiply each percentage by 65535 and write the numbers down. Close the dialog box.

   Example:
   PMS 299 CV = R15 G56 B75
   or
   R9830.25 G36699.6 B49151.25

5. Choose Preferences from the File menu. The Display Preferences dialog box appears.

6. Click the Calibrate button. The Display Color Setup dialog box appears.

7. Click the swatch of process color you're using to substitute for your spot color. The Apple Color Picker dialog box appears.

8. Type the numbers you derived in the Red, Green, and Blue fields and press Return three times to close all of the dialog boxes.

Your process color now matches (or comes close to matching) your spot color.

When you change the color display options via the Preferences dialog box, the changes remain in effect until you change them again. They're not stored in the individual publications. This means you'll have to change the color display options again when you want to display a normal process-color publication. You can make a QuicKey to reset your color display options. Create a QuicKey sequence containing the QuicKeys shown in Table 6-2.

Now that you've got onscreen correspondence, you can create stacked screens to your heart's content using individual process colors as substitutes for individual spot colors.

COLOR FIGURE 1
Overprinting
and knockouts

Objects colored with spot color 1 set to knock out (Overprint box unchecked).

Spot color 1 plate

Spot color 2 plate

*Color 1 knocks
out color 2*

Objects colored with spot color 1 set to overprint (Overprint box checked).

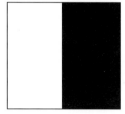

Spot color 1 plate

Spot color 2 plate

*Color 1 prints
over color 2*

COLOR FIGURE 2
Trapping an
open path

*This cyan path needs
to be trapped.*

*To create a spread, clone the
path, and then increase
the width of the cloned
path. Set the cloned
path to overprint.*

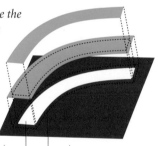

*The thinner stroke
knocks out objects
behind it.*

*The thicker stroke
overprints objects
behind it.*

*To create a choke,
clone the path and then
decrease the stroke width
of the cloned path. Set
the original path
to overprint.*

*The cloned path
overprints the
background
objects.*

*The original path knocks
out objects behind it.*

Trapped path

COLOR FIGURE 3
Trapping closed
paths and text

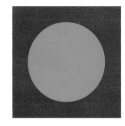

Select the object you want to trap and press Command-Option-L to display the Stroke Inspector. There, add a stroke to the object by choosing Basic from the Stroke Type popup menu.

Unless I've been very lucky, you'll see the paper showing through around the cyan circle in this example. To prevent the paper from showing, you need to trap the object.

Enter a value in the Width field that's twice the width of the spread you want, and check Overprint.

Fill ⊢

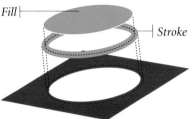

Stroke ⊣

When you print, the the stroke of the ellipse overprints the background rectangle, while the fill knocks out. This creates a spread.

To create a choke, apply an overprinting stroke the color of the background rectangle to the ellipse.

Here's the trapped version of the example.

Fill ⊢

Stroke ⊣

When you print, the stroke decreases the size of the knockout created by the fill of the ellipse.

Not trapped

Again, unless I've been lucky, you'll see the paper showing through around these characters. That means that this text needs to be trapped.

Trapped using a spread

This stroke overprints the background objects, creating a spread. Unless I've been very unlucky, you won't see the paper showing around the edges of these characters.

Trapped using a choke

The stroke decreases the size of the knockout behind the text, creating a choke.

COLOR FIGURE 4
Trapping graduated fills

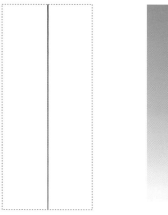

When two graduated fills abut, you run the risk of having the paper show through between the fills.

Create a new shape that's twice the width of the trap you want. Position it where the two fills abut, and fill it with a graduated fill based on both of the graduated fills of the original objects. When you print, the new fill traps the graduated fills.

COLOR FIGURE 5
TrapWise trapping

You shouldn't even think of trapping this manually.

TrapWise displays a preview of the spreads and chokes it uses to trap the file. (This screen shot is from the Windows version of TrapWise— a Macintosh version of the program should be available by the time you read this.)

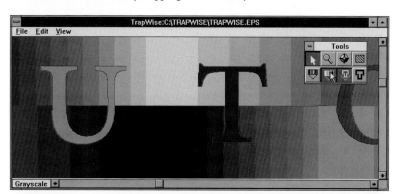

Example EPS trapped by TrapWise.

COLOR FIGURE 6
Rosettes

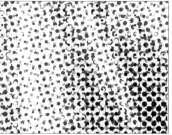

Rosettes for an area of flat color: 10C 10M 10Y 10K (ugly, but good for demonstration purposes).

COLOR FIGURE 7
Creating tint builds

You can quickly create palettes of tints using FreeHand's Blend command.

To see the color definition for a tint, drag a color swatch from the Fill Inspector's color well into the Color Mixer's color well.

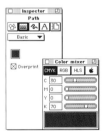

100K	50C 50K	100C
100K	50M 50K	100M
100K	50C 50K	100Y
60K	50C 30K	100C
60K	50C 30K	100M
60K	50C 30Y	100Y
20K	50C 10K	100C
20K	50C 10K	100M
20K	50C 10K	100Y

COLOR FIGURE 8
Duotones

*FreeHand duotone.
Two overlapping TIFFs
colored with different
colors (cyan and black)
and with different
settings in FreeHand's
Image dialog box.*

Photoshop duotone.

Photographs of Amy Denio by Roger Schreiber

*Two "fake"
duotones*

100 percent cyan background *50 percent cyan background*

COLOR FIGURE 9
Color Examples

FreeHand's Neon custom stroke effect is great—but you can't see it on your screen. Here's a way to create glowing lines you can see on your screen.

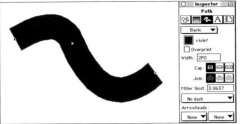

Draw a path.

Assign a thick stroke weight to the path that's the color of the outside of the "glow" you want to create.

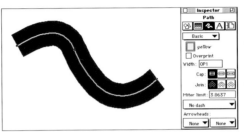

Clone the path.

Assign a thin stroke weight to the cloned path. This stroke should be the color you want for the inside of the "glow" effect.

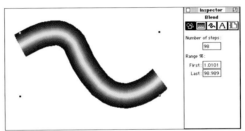

Blend the two selected paths.

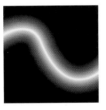 

For an effect that looks more like a neon lighting tube, blend from white to the glow color, then blend from the glow color to the background color.

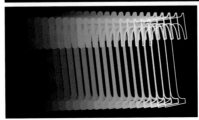

Each "neon" character above is composed of two blends. One blend goes from white to a color; the other goes from that color to black.

COLOR FIGURE 10
Separating color images

Example RGB TIFF separated by FreeHand.

Example color TIFF separated by Photoshop, saved as an EPS, and printed from FreeHand (you could also save the file as DCS from Photoshop).

Printing color
images using random
dither patterns

*If you look closely at these
images, you won't see
rosettes—you'll see
overlapping, random
dither patterns (in this
example, I've used a
600 dpi diffusion dither
from Photoshop.*

*This technique is also called "stochastic" screening, and my version of it is
still at an extremely experimental stage (I have no idea what these images
will look like when printed). See page 429 for more information on this
color separation-technique.*

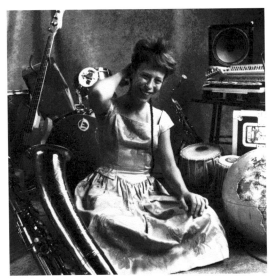

Duotone created by superimposing two dithered bilevel TIFFs.

	QuicKey	QuicKey contents	What it does
TABLE 6-2 Reset color display QuicKey	Menu/DA	Preferences	Selects Preferences from the File menu.
	Button	Calibrate	Clicks the Calibrate button in the Preferences dialog box.
	Click	120, 54*	Clicks the Cyan color swatch in the Display color setup dialog box.
	Text	ΔΔΔ0Δ65535Δ65535**	Enters the correct (in my opinion; you might want to enter something else) values for screen display of cyan.
	Literal	Enter	Closes the Apple Color Picker dialog box.
	Click	37, 202*	Clicks the Magenta color swatch in the Display color setup dialog box.
	Text	ΔΔΔ65535Δ0Δ65535**	Enters the values for screen display of magenta.
	Literal	Enter	Closes the Apple Color Picker dialog box.
	Click	204, 201*	Clicks the Yellow color swatch in the Display color setup dialog box.
	Text	ΔΔΔ65535Δ0Δ65535**	Enters the values for screen display of yellow.
	Literal	Enter	Closes the Apple Color Picker dialog box.
	Literal	Enter	Closes the Display color setup dialog box.
	Literal	Enter	Closes the Preferences dialog box.

* These coordinates might be slightly different on your system.

** Δ indicates a tab character in the QuicKeys Text dialog box. Where you see a Δ, just press Tab.

Trapping

A trap is a method of overlapping abutting colored objects to compensate for the imperfect registration of printing presses. Because registration, even on good presses with good operators, can be off by a quarter point or more, abutting elements in your publication may not end up abutting perfectly when the publication is printed by your commercial printer. What happens then? The paper stock shows through where you don't want it to show through (see Figure 6-17).

FIGURE 6-17
Why you need to trap

When you don't trap, you can end up with
paper showing through where it shouldn't.

When you trap, you enlarge (or shrink) the objects so that
they'll overlap a little bit when they print—regardless of the
paper stretching or shifting on the press.

Do I need to tell you what happens if you take your work to a less skilled printer? Or to a press that's badly out of register or run by turkeys? Disaster. Also, some printing processes, notably silk-screening, require larger traps than others. In any case, talk with your commercial printer regarding the tolerances of their presses and/or operators.

Before I start describing trapping techniques in FreeHand, you ought to know that the best technique is one you find outside Free-Hand—use Aldus TrapWise. TrapWise can trap your publications better than you can, and, if you use TrapWise, you don't even have to think about trapping. I'll provide descriptions of what you can do to trap your files, but I'll say at the outset—find a service bureau that'll trap your files with TrapWise, and save yourself time and trouble. For more on TrapWise, see Appendix A, "System."

Object-Level Overprinting

The key to trapping, in FreeHand and elsewhere, is in controlling which objects—or which parts of objects—print on top of other objects as the printing press prints your publication. While choosing to overprint entire inks can be handy (especially overprinting black), you really need to control the overprinting characteristics of individual objects to make trapping work (see Color Figure 1).

Luckily, you can. Any path you create in FreeHand can be specified as an overprinting object (that is, it won't knock a hole in any objects behind it when you print), regardless of the object's color. The controls for object-level overprinting are found in the Fill Inspector and the Stroke Inspector (see Figure 6-18).

FIGURE 6-18
Overprinting controls

Check Overprint to overprint the fill of the selected object.

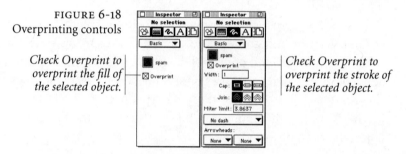

Check Overprint to overprint the stroke of the selected object.

Ink-Level Overprinting

In FreeHand's Print Options dialog box, you can choose to knock out or overprint an entire ink (see Figure 6-19). I find I usually overprint all inks, and knock out selected paths using the Overprint checkboxes in the Fill and Stroke Inspectors.

Object-level overprinting settings override ink-level overprinting settings for individual objects.

FIGURE 6-19
Ink-level overprinting

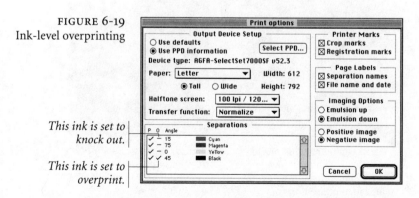

This ink is set to knock out.

This ink is set to overprint.

Manual Trapping   The keys to trapping in FreeHand are the Overprint checkboxes in the Fill Inspector and the Stroke Inspector. These controls, in combination with FreeHand's Paste Inside command, provide incredible manual trapping flexibility.

When you're working with FreeHand's trapping features, you'll be creating *spreads* (outlines of objects, in the same color as the object, that are slightly larger than the object itself) and *chokes* (outlines of the object that are the same color as the underlying object's color). Spreads make the object larger so that the edges of the object print over the underlying object; chokes make the area knocked out of the underlying object smaller than the outline of the foreground object.

In general, you use chokes when the foreground object is a darker color than the background object, and you use spreads when the color of the foreground object is lighter. In other words, trap from light colors into darker colors. Sound subjective? It is. I tend to use chokes, especially when I'm trapping type, because I feel they're less likely to give the impression that the shape of the foreground object has been distorted.

Spot-Color Trapping   In most cases, it's more important to trap abutting color fields in spot color publications than it is in process color publications. Why? Because when you're working with process colors, you've almost always got some kind of dot between objects (cyan, magenta, yellow, or black), so you're less likely to see the tell-tale paper-colored lines showing a poor trap (see Figure 6-20).

FIGURE 6-20
Spot-color trapping
and process-color
trapping

When you're trapping process colors, there's almost always some color value—dots—on one of the other plates...

...while in spot-color trapping, there's usually not.

The easiest way to demonstrate how spot-color trapping works is to show you some examples. As you work through these examples, you'll trap an ellipse into a rectangle by manipulating the color, width, and overprinting specifications of the path that surrounds the ellipse. First, draw the colored objects.

1. Create a rectangle. Fill the rectangle with a spot color (in these instructions, I'll call this color "Color 1"). Set the rectangle's stroke to None.

2. Draw an ellipse on top of the rectangle. Make sure that the ellipse is entirely inside the rectangle. Fill the ellipse with a different color from that of the rectangle (I'll call this color "Color 2"). Set the stroke of the ellipse to None.

3. Save the file.

Creating a spread. The ellipse needs to be trapped, or you'll run the risk of having paper-colored lines appear up around the ellipse when you print the publication. You can either spread or choke the ellipse, or both.

To spread the ellipse, follow these steps (see Color Figure 3).

1. Select the ellipse.

2. Press Command-Option-L to display the Stroke Inspector.

3. In the Stroke Inspector, choose Basic from the Stroke Type popup menu, set the line color to "Color 2" (the color of the ellipse), type a line width for your trap in the Width field. Finally, check the Overprint box and press Return.

The line width you enter in the Width field should be equal to twice the trap amount—if you enter "2", you'll get a stroke of one point on either side of the path defining the ellipse, because PostScript lines grow out from the line's center. If your commercial printer has asked you for a trap of .5 points, enter "1" in the Width field.

When you print, the ellipse is larger than the hole that's knocked out of the background rectangle, which means that the outside of the ellipse slightly overprints the background rectangle. You've just created a spread.

After you're through looking at the objects, or printing, choose Revert from the File menu and revert to the version of the file you saved earlier. This way, you're ready for the next procedure.

Creating a choke. To choke the ellipse, follow these steps (see Color Figure 3).

1. Select the ellipse.

2. Press Command-Option-L to display the Stroke Inspector.

3. In the Stroke Inspector, choose Basic from the Stroke Type popup menu, set the line color to "Color 2" (the color of the ellipse), type a line width for your trap in the Width field. Finally, check the Overprint box and press Return.

When you print, the hole that's knocked out of the background rectangle is slightly smaller than the ellipse. This way, the outside of the ellipse slightly overprints the background rectangle. You've just created a choke.

Choose Revert from the File menu to get the file ready for the next procedure.

Trapping across color boundaries. The techniques described above work well as long as you're working with objects that don't cross color boundaries. If the objects cross color boundaries (especially going from a color background to a white background), it's too obvious that you've changed the shapes of the objects. What do you do?

1. Drag the ellipse so that it's partially outside of the rectangle.

2. Clone the ellipse by pressing Command-=.

3. Without deselecting the cloned ellipse, press Command-Option-L to display the Stroke Inspector.

4. In the Stroke Inspector, choose Basic from the Stroke Type popup menu, set the stroke color to "Color 1" (the color of the background rectangle), enter a stroke width for your trap in the Width field. Finally, check the Overprint box and press Return to apply your changes.

5. Press Command-X to cut the ellipse to the Clipboard.

6. Select the background rectangle and choose Paste Inside from the Edit menu.

7. Select the original ellipse and press Command-B to send it to the back.

At this point, the ellipse you pasted inside the rectangle spreads slightly, while the part of the ellipse outside of the rectangle remains the same size and shape (see Color Figure 3).

Choose Revert from the File menu to get ready for the next trapping example.

What happens when the object you need to trap overlaps more than one other, differently colored object? In this case, you can run into trouble. The trap you use for one background color might not be the trap you want to use for the other. You might want to spread one and choke the other, depending on the colors you're using.

In these cases, you use the same basic techniques described above for all of the overlapping objects. Try it (see Color Figure 3).

1. Draw another new rectangle (I'll call it Rectangle 2) so that it partially overlaps the original rectangle (which I'll call Rectangle 1). Create a third spot color ("Color 3") and apply it to the rectangle's fill. Set the rectangle's stroke to None. Drag the ellipse so that it partially overlaps both rectangles.

2. Select Rectangle 2 and press Command-= to clone it. Without deselecting the clone, press Command-Option-L to display the Stroke Inspector.

3. In the Stroke Inspector, choose Basic from the Stroke Type popup menu, set the line color to "Color 1" (the color of the background rectangle), enter a line weight for your stroke in the Width field, and check the Overprint box. Press Return to apply the stroke.

4. Select the ellipse and repeat step 3. Make sure that the clone of the ellipse is in front of the clone of the rectangle, then

select both of the clones you've created and press Command-X to cut them to the Clipboard.

5. Select Rectangle 1 and choose Paste Inside from the Edit menu. You've just created chokes for the ellipse and Rectangle 2 at the points they overlap Rectangle 1.

6. Select the Ellipse and press Command-= to clone it. Change the stroke of the cloned ellipse as directed in step 3. Press Command-X to cut the new clone to the Clipboard. Select Rectangle 2 and choose Paste Inside from the Edit menu. The ellipse is now choked at the points it overlaps Rectangle 2.

Trapping Lines

The trapping techniques above work well for filled paths, but what about lines? After all, you can't apply two different line properties to a single line. Instead, you clone the line and make the width of the cloned line larger or smaller to achieve the spread or choke you want. One of the lines overprints; the other line knocks out.

Follow these steps to spread a line (see Color Figure 2).

1. Draw a rectangle. Create a spot color and fill the rectangle with it.

2. Draw a line inside the rectangle. Create another spot color and apply it to the line. Do not set this line to overprint.

3. Select the line and press Command-= to clone the line.

4. Press Command-Option-L to display the Stroke Inspector. Increase the width of the line by twice the amount of spread you need (remember, PostScript lines grow out from their centers) and check the Overprint box to make the stroke overprint.

That's all there is to it. The original line knocks a hole in the background rectangle, and the clone of the line spreads to just a little bit beyond the edges of the knockout.

To choke the line, follow these steps (see Color Figure XXX).

1. Draw a rectangle. Create a spot color and fill the rectangle with it.

2. Draw a line inside the rectangle. Create another spot color and apply it to the line. Set this line to overprint.

3. Select the line and press Command-= to clone the line.

4. Display the Stroke Inspector. Decrease the width of the line by twice the amount of choke you need, and leave the Overprint box unchecked.

5. Hold down Control and select the original line. Press Command-F to bring it to the front.

This time, the cloned line is narrower than the original line, and knocks out an area that's slightly smaller than the original line, creating a choke.

If the line you need to trap crosses a color boundary, follow the same steps described above for trapping paths: clone the line, edit the line, cut the line, select the background object, choose Paste Inside, and send the original line to the back.

Trapping Text

Text is usually the element in a publication that needs trapping the most. For whatever reason, it's easier to notice poor trapping around text than around other elements. At the same time, traps that are too large distort the shapes of the characters you're trapping. It's especially a problem with small type, especially serif type.

Here's how to create a spread for text (see Color Figure 3).

1. Draw a rectangle, create a spot color ("Color 1"), and apply it to the rectangle.

2. Type a text block. Position the text block on top of the rectangle so that it's entirely within the area occupied by the rectangle.

3. Create a second spot color ("Color 2") and apply it to the text in the text block.

4. While the text is still selected, press Command-Option-L to display the Stroke Inspector. Enter the width you want (remember, it's two times the amount of trap you want) in the Width field. Check the Overprint box and press Return.

The next example shows how you can choke text by making the shape the characters knock out of the background a little bit smaller than the characters themselves.

1. Draw a rectangle, create a spot color ("Color 1"), and apply it to the rectangle.

2. Create a text block. Position the text block on top of the rectangle so that it's entirely within the area occupied by the rectangle.

3. Create a second spot color ("Color 2"). Select all the text in the text block and click on "Color 2" in the Color List. FreeHand applies a fill of "Color 2" to the text.

4. Without deselecting the text, press Command-Option-L to display the Stroke Inspector. Enter the width you want for the trap in the Width field. Check the Overprint box and press Return.

If text crosses color boundaries, use the techniques described earlier for trapping overlapping paths.

Tip:
Type and
Black Ink

Type that's specified as 100-percent black always overprints, regardless of the settings you've made in the Fill and Stroke dialog boxes or in the ink list in the Print Options dialog box. You probably want 100-percent black text to overprint most of the time, but what if you don't? Create a color that's specified as 99-percent black and apply it to the text you want to knock out of whatever is behind it. 99-percent black works just like every other color. It can be set to knock out or overprint as you want, and it'll look just like 100-percent black.

Advanced Spot-Color Trapping

All of the trapping techniques demonstrated above assume that you're working with solid (that is, 100 percent) spot colors. What happens when you're working with tints of spot colors, and what happens when you're working with graduated or radial fills?

When you're working with tints, you simply use the above procedures, substituting the tints for the colors specified for the overprinting strokes you're using to create traps. When you're trapping graduated and radial fills, on the other hand, things get complex.

Trapping Spot-Color Graduated Fills

When graduated fills abut in your spot color publications, you need to provide for some sort of trapping between the two fills, or you'll end up with your paper color showing through between the fills. Apart from using TrapWise (see "Trapping with TrapWise," later in this chapter), the simplest thing to do is to set one or both spot colors to overprint, and then overlap the graduated fills by some small amount (something less than one point).

If you can't, or don't want to, overprint the spot colors you've used in your graduated fills, life gets harder. You'll have to create a pair of blends—one in each spot color—that mimic your graduated fills and position them where the graduated fills abut. Why create blends? Remember that each intermediate object in a blend is a solid color, or tint, and can be set to overprint.

Once again, I'll show you how to do this by leading you through a series of steps. You'll probably run into more complex examples of abutting graduated fills than the one shown in this example, but you can use these techniques for all situations in which spot color graduated fills abut (see Color Figure 4).

1. Draw two abutting rectangles.

2. Create two spot colors ("Color 1" and "Color 2").

3. Fill one of the rectangles with a graduated fill going from "Color 1" to white. Fill the other rectangle with a graduated fill going from white to "Color 2".

Next, you'll set up the objects for the blend.

1. Create two squares that are the width of the trap you want to use. Position one rectangle at either end of the point where the two graduated fills abut.

2. Fill one of the squares with "Color 1", and fill the other one with a zero-percent tint of "Color 1".

3. Set both squares to overprint using the Fill Inspector.

4. Select the same point on each of the small squares you've just created. It's probably easier to do this in Keyline view. If you can't select a point, ungroup the squares and try again.

5. Choose Blend from the Path Operations submenu of the Arrange menu. FreeHand blends the selected squares. Does the blend fill the distance from one of the objects to the other without any gaps? If not, display the Object Inspector for the blend, increase the number of blend steps, and press Return to close the dialog box and apply the new blend. Keep increasing the number of steps until there are no gaps in the blend.

6. Clone the original squares. Repeat the process substituting "Color 2" for "Color 1" in the blend.

When you print, the blended objects print over the area where the graduated fills abut, spreading the two graduations into each other. This technique brings up a point—if you can trap blends, and can't trap graduated fills, why not just use blends for all of the graduated fills you need to trap? Why not, indeed. See "The Golden Rules" in Chapter 7, "Printing," for more on why you should use blends instead of graduated fills.

Trapping Spot-Color Radial Fills

After all of the trouble we had to go through to create a trap for adjacent spot-color graduated fills, you'd think radial fills using spot colors would be more difficult. Luckily, that's not the case all of the time. When you create a radial fill inside an object, you can simply add an overprinting stroke to the object containing the radial fill that's the color of the background object, thereby creating a choke.

Where things get ugly is in those cases where two radial fills abut each other. When that happens, try this trick.

1. Clone of the objects containing the radial fill.

2. Set the fill of the clone to None, and stroke it with a one-point line that's the color of the outermost value of the radial fill (if you went from white to "Color 1", as we did in our example, you'd set the line's color to "Color 1"). Set the line to overprint.

3. Select the other object containing a radial fill and clone it.

4. Set the fill of the clone to None, and stroke it with a one-point line that's the color of the outermost value of the radial fill (if you went from white to "Color 2", as we did in our example, you'd set the line's color to "Color 2"). Set the line to overprint.

5. Cut the clone of the second object.

6. Select the first object you created and choose Paste Inside from the Edit menu.

7. Select the object you created in step 2 and cut it to the Clipboard.

8. Select the second object and choose Paste Inside from the Edit menu.

Process-Color Trapping

Process-color trapping is a bit simpler than spot-color trapping, because it's usually less critical that process-colored elements have traps (as simulated in Figure 6-20, earlier in this chapter), but it can be far harder to figure out exactly what color to make the stroke for a process-colored object. And when you're talking about trapping two process-colored graduated fills, watch out!

Simple Process-Color Trapping

In process-color trapping, you've got to make your overprinting strokes different colors from either the background or foreground objects. Why? Because process colors have a way of creating new colors when you print them over each other. It's what they do best.

As in the spot-color trapping section above, I'll demonstrate process-color trapping techniques by example. First, create a couple of objects.

1. Create a rectangle that's filled with "Color 1", which is specified as 20C 100M 0Y 10K.

2. On top of this rectangle, draw an ellipse and fill it with "Color 2", which is specified as 0C 100M 50Y 0K.

3. Select both objects and set their stroke to None.

4. Save the file.

The ellipse needs to be trapped, or you run the risk of having cyan-colored lines showing up around the ellipse when the publication is printed—which could happen if the cyan and yellow plates slipped. Whether you spread or choke the ellipse depends on its color. If the ellipse is darker than the background rectangle, choke the ellipse. If the ellipse is a lighter color than the background rectangle, spread the ellipse. In this case, the ellipse is a lighter color, so you'll use a spread. To spread the ellipse, follow these steps.

1. Create a new process color containing only those colors in "Color 2" having higher values than "Color 1". Quick quiz: what component colors in "Color 2" have higher values than their counterparts in "Color 1"? If you said 50Y, you're the lucky winner. Specify a new color: 0C 0M 50Y 0K.

2. Select the ellipse.

3. Press Command-Option-L to display the Stroke Inspector.

4. In the Stroke Inspector, choose Basic from the Stroke Type popup menu.

5. Drag a swatch of "Color 3" into the color well in the Stroke Inspector.

6. Type the width you want for your stroke in the Width field. It should be twice the width of your desired trap. Finally, check the Overprint box and press Return.

When you print, all of the areas around the ellipse have some dot value inside them, and the new colors created where the objects abut won't be too obvious.

Choose Revert from the File menu to get ready for the next example.

What if the ellipse were the darker color? If it were, we'd have to choke it. To choke the ellipse, follow these steps.

1. Select the ellipse and fill it with "Color 1". Select the rectangle and fill it with "Color 2".

2. Create a new color ("Color 3") that contains only the largest color component in "Color 1". That's 100M, so "Color 3" should be specified as 0C 100M 0Y 0K.

3. In the Stroke Inspector, choose Basic from the Stroke Type popup menu, set the line color to "Color 3", type the width of the trap you want in the Width field. Finally, check Overprint in the line section of the dialog box and press Return.

When you print, the stroke you applied to the ellipse guarantees that there's no gap around the ellipse, even if you run into registration problems when you print the publication.

Complex Process-Color Trapping

What if the ellipse in the examples given above was not completely contained by the underlying rectangle? What if, in fact, only half of the ellipse passed into the rectangle?

You don't want to make the entire ellipse larger, so limit the spread and choke of the ellipse to the area inside the underlying rectangle by using the Paste Inside techniques shown in the section on spot color trapping earlier in this chapter.

Trapping Process-Color Graduated and Radial Fills

If you've gotten this far, call me the next time you're in Seattle and I'll buy you a beer at The Trolleyman. You've mastered the basic trapping techniques for spot and process colors, and you're ready to trap abutting process-color graduated and radial fills.

Create an object which covers the area where two process-color graduated fills abut and fill this object with a graduated fill. The colors in this graduated fill are derived from the colors used in the abutting graduated fills underneath it. Once again, I'll demonstrate the technique by having you work through an example, and once again we'll start by creating some objects.

1. Create two side-by-side, abutting rectangles.

2. Fill one rectangle with a graduated fill that goes from "Color 1" (25C 30M 0Y 20K) to "Color 2" (70C 20M 0Y 0K) at 90 degrees. Fill the other rectangle with a graduated fill that goes from "Color 3" (0C 80M 45Y 0K) to "Color 4" (0C 20M 60Y 0K) at 270 degrees.

3. Select both rectangles set their strokes to None.

4. Draw a new rectangle over the abutting edges of the rectangles. Make the new rectangle the height of the existing rectangles, and make it twice as wide as the trapping amount you want. Center it horizontally over the line where the two rectangles abut.

5. Create two new process colors ("Color 5" and "Color 6"). "Color 5" should contain the highest color components from Color 1 and Color 3 (the two colors at the tops of the original rectangles): 25C 80M 45Y 20K. "Color 6" contains the largest color components from "Color 2" and "Color 4": 70C 20M 60Y 0K.

6. Fill the new rectangle with a new graduated fill going from "Color 5" to "Color 6" at 270 degrees.

It's harder to come up with a precise way to trap radial fills containing process colors, because unless the object with the radial fill is a perfect circle and the center of the fill is in the center of the circle, it's hard to know what color is at the edge of the radial fill. And it's almost never the same color all the way around the outside of the path.

So here's the sleazy way. Stroke the radial fill with an overprinting line containing about 20 percent of the background color. This way, there are at least some dots in any out-of-register areas. If you come up with a better way to trap process-color radial fills, please let me know.

Trapping Imported Images   Because you can place color TIFF images in FreeHand, you can run into some truly hairy trapping situations. What happens when you need to cut out part of a color TIFF and place it on a process-color background? This isn't actually as scary as it sounds. Just follow the instructions in the section "Cropping TIFF Images" in Chapter 4, "Importing and Exporting," to construct a clipping path for the TIFF, and then stroke the path with an overprinting line that's the same color as the background colors.

In this case, if the object passes over several color boundaries, avoid pasting both the TIFF and the path containing it into the underlying objects—it'll never print. Instead, clone the path, choose Cut Contents from the Edit menu and delete the extra TIFF. Then fill the new object with white, stroke it with your over-printing line (choke), and paste it inside the underlying object. Then place the original clipped TIFF above the area you've just choked.

Separating Color Images

FreeHand can separate color TIFFs you've placed, and can also separate DCS and EPS preseparated images. In my opinion, the fastest and best method is to use a color-separation program such as Photoshop or PrePrint to create a CMYK TIFF, an EPS file, a DCS 2.0 file, or a set of DCS 1.0 files and place the separated image in FreeHand.

Why not just place an RGB TIFF in FreeHand? The color-separation programs have controls for correcting and improving color images. FreeHand really has very few tools for working with the content of color images. Like none, now that I think of it.

Still, FreeHand's separations of RGB images aren't bad (as long as you've done a decent job of correcting them and sharpening them in advance)—take a look at Figure 10 in the color pages to see an example.

Preseparating Color Images

If you want to separate your color images using Photoshop (or Fractal Desgn's Painter, or PrePrint, or any other program capable of saving color separations in the EPS/DCS format) and then place the preseparated image in FreeHand, you can save the file as either a single EPS file, a single DCS 2.0 file (if you're using PlateMaker in Photoshop), or as DCS (five linked files).

If you save the image as a single EPS or DCS 2.0 file, place the entire file in FreeHand. If you save the image as DCS 1.0, place the DCS header file (it's the one without a C, M, Y, or K extension on its file name). In either case, when you separate the image with FreeHand, the separations will be the same as if you'd printed the separations directly from Photoshop. You might like FreeHand's separations better, though. Take a look at the side-by-side Free-Hand, Photoshop, and PrePrint separations in the color section of this book (see Color Figure 10).

Which EPS preseparation method should you use? Saving the file as a single EPS or DCS 2.0 makes a large file, but saving as DCS 1.0 creates five files you've got to look after. The four DCS 1.0 separation files (the ones with C, M, Y, or K in their file names) have to be in the same folder as the DCS 1.0 header file, or Free-Hand won't be able to find them to print.

FreeHand and OPI

Open Prepress Interface (OPI) is a standard for links between desktop systems and dedicated color prepress systems, such as those manufactured by Kodak, Scitex, Hell, and Crosfield. OPI concerns imported images (TIFFs and paint-type graphics) only.

When you export an EPS from FreeHand, the EPS contains OPI information (a set of PostScript comments) that these systems need to be able to work with the file. OPI comments are most important if you're going to do something like drop a Scitex-separated color image into a FreeHand publication.

To be entirely frank, I'm not sure it's worth it. For my purposes, separations created using FreeHand, Photoshop, and/or PrePrint and an imagesetter can produce give me excellent quality in the 150-lpi-and-under range, which is where I do most of my work. If you want better than 150 lpi, OPI might be better for you.

Additionally, if you're working with very large images, or if you're working with a large number of images, you might want to have your prepress or imagesetting service bureau store and manage the files for you (while you take lower-resolution "For Position Only" images to work with on your Macintosh). Then, when you take your files to the service bureau to produce film, use OPI to link to the stored images.

Do-It-Yourself Stochastic Screening

Warning! This section is still under construction! Use the techniques described here with extreme caution (and, I might add, at your own risk). I've only just started figuring this out myself, but had to share it with you.

You can separate your own color images using the "stochastic" screening I described at the start of the chapter, using Photoshop (or any other image-editing program capable of creating a CMYK TIFF). You don't need to print on an imagesetter equipped with a special (and expensive) RIP, and you don't need to find a press capable of printing incredibly small dots. You can print on garden-variety imagesetters, at low resolutions, and then print on whatever presses you normally use.

Here's the deal—you can split the channels of a CMYK TIFF, save each channel as a separate diffusion dither (that is, as a bilevel bitmap), stack the dithered images up in FreeHand, applying colors to them as you do.

What are the advantages? There aren't any regular patterns in the dithered images, so you don't have to worry about moiré patterns. Images look sharper, because halftone cells actually blur the focus of an image slightly. You can print at lower resolutions (to get a fine linescreen for a halftoned image, you've got to print at resoultions of 2,400 dpi or higher—but you can print dithered images at 1,200 dpi). The dithered images print faster (they're just bilevel bitmaps), and they don't take any time for FreeHand to separate (as an RGB TIFF would).

What are the disadvantages? Dither patterns are more obvious in areas of flat color than halftone screens. It's still a somewhat experimental technique, and your commercial printers might look askance at it.

To separate a CMYK TIFF using "stochastic" screening, follow these steps (see Figure 6-21).

1. Open the TIFF with Photoshop. Set up your separation options as you normally would using the various setup dialog boxes in the Preferences submenu.

2. Select CMYK from the Mode menu.

3. Choose Split Channels from the Mode menu. Photoshop creates a separate grayscale TIFF for each channel (that is,

each channel now shows what would be printed on each separation).

4. Choose Bitmap from the Mode menu. Photoshop displays the Grayscale to Bitmap dialog box. Click the Diffusion Dither button, and enter a resolution for the dithered bitmap you want to create.

Most presses (and papers) have no problem printing the dots in bitmaps in the range of 400 dpi to 600 dpi (I like 600 dpi best, but you've got to experiment). Why not make a bitmap at imagesetter resolution—say, 2,400 dpi? Because your press won't be able to print the dots making up the image (ask your printer if their press can hold a one-percent spot in a 300-lpi screen, and you'll get the idea—the dots are just too small).

5. Save each of the bitmaps.

6. Place the four bitmaps on top of each other in FreeHand, coloring each one the appropriate process color. As you import and color each bitmap, check the Transparent box in the Object Inspector. Make sure that the bitmaps are all the same size and in the same position.

When you print separations of your publication, FreeHand prints the dithered bitmaps on separate pages (or pieces of film). When you make a color proof, or print your your publication on a press, you'll see the image.

I've only started using this technique—there are about a million details that I still need to work out (for example, separation settings that work well for conventional halftoning don't really work for this technique).

Most people working with stochastic screening see it as a high-end printing method—they're working with presses that can hold 300 lpi halftone screens. I don't see it that way at all. I think this technique would be best for people working at 150 lpi and under, on cheaper papers (like newsprint).

For an example of a color image separated using this technique, see Color Figure 11 in the color pages.

FIGURE 6-21
Do-it-yourself
stochastic screening

Open the TIFF you want to separate. If you haven't already converted it to CMYK, or done any color correction or sharpening, do it now.

Display the Channels palette (choose Channels from the Windows menu). Choose Split Channels from the Channels palette's popup menu.

Photoshop displays the four, separate channels.

For each channel, choose Bitmap from the Mode menu. Photoshop displays the Bitmap dialog box.

Enter a resolution for the dithered image (the range from 400–600 dpi seems most promising). Press Return (or click OK)…

…and Photoshop converts the grayscale image (this channel) to a bilevel bitmap. Save the bitmap. Repeat this process for the other three channels.

Stack the four bitmaps on top of each other in FreeHand. Set the bitmaps to Transparent using the Object Inspector. Apply the appropriate process color to each image, and print.

Color Me Gone

When you're working with color, take it easy. Always remember that you're at the mercy of a series of photochemical and mechanical processes—from your imagesetter through your commercial printer's press—that, in many ways, haven't changed since the turn of the century (if that recently).

Temperature, humidity, and ambient static electricity play a large role, and the people who operate these systems are at least skilled craftspeople; at best, artists. Ask them as many questions as they'll answer, set your job up the way they want it, and then sit back and watch your job come off the press.

CHAPTER

Printing

7

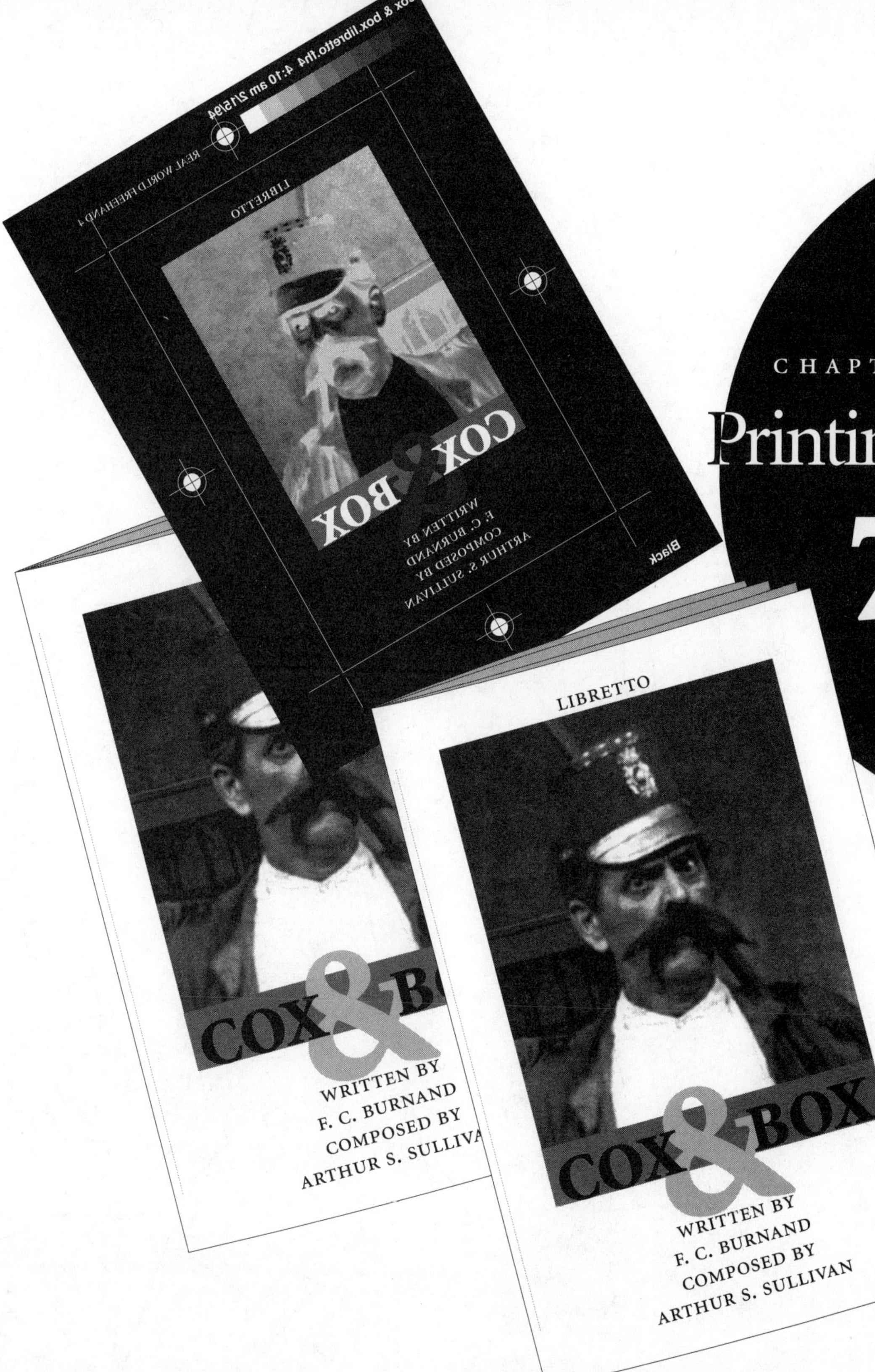

Clay.

Roll a carved cylinder over a flat sheet of wet clay, and the carvings on the cylinder are transferred—in reverse—to the surface of the clay. Once the clay hardens, the marks are there to stay.

The ancient Mesopotamians noticed this. They figured that by carving characters on the cylinders in reverse they could transfer them to the clay tablets. Roll the cylinders over several tablets, and you've made several copies of the symbols on the cylinders. They were a bureaucratic bunch, and covered their tablets with bills of lading, legal contracts, nondisclosure agreements, and other rules and regulations.

They invented printing.

We've improved on this process a little bit since then.

We found that, by smearing ink over the surface of the cylinder (or over the tablets, for that matter), we could transfer the images on the cylinder to that new invention—the white sheets of beaten, bleached papyrus reeds the Egyptians made. It was easier to carry than the tablets.

Later, somebody came up with moveable type, and scribes the world over lamented the decline in the quality of written materials. The romance novel followed closely on the heels of this technological advance. Printing—the ability to make dozens, hundreds, thousands, millions of copies of the an image—flourished.

Printing, ultimately, is what FreeHand is all about. Everything you do in FreeHand is directed toward production of a mechanical (whether an illustration or a publication) for printing. If you're using FreeHand to create on-screen (rather than printed) artwork, you might want to invest in some other (pixel-based) illustration program.

The FreeHand Print Dialog Box

When you press Command-P, FreeHand displays the Print dialog box (see Figure 7-1). Never mind that it says "Printer '*printername*'" instead of "Print." It's the Print dialog box and everybody knows it. Similarly, you'll see two Print Options dialog boxes in FreeHand—one from FreeHand itself (which appears when you click the Print button in the Print dialog box); one from the printer driver (which appears when you click the Options button in the Page Setup dialog box). I'll refer to FreeHand's as the "Print Options dialog box," and call the other one the "LaserWriter Print Options dialog box." In addition, there's FreeHand's Ouput Options dialog box, which you'll see if you choose Ouput Options from the File menu or press the Options button in the Print dialog box.

The options you see in some of these dialog boxes might differ somewhat. In this chapter, I'm assuming you're using LaserWriter 8 for your printer driver, and all the descriptions in this chapter are based on that driver. Most things, however, are the same or similar in the LaserWriter 7 printer driver.

If you're still using an earlier version of the driver because you were scared by the bugs in LaserWriter 8.0, you might reconsider—most of the problems seem to be fixed in LaserWriter version 8.1.1.

Here's a rundown of the options in the Print dialog box, and how to use them.

Copies   Enter the number of copies of the page you want to print here. You can print up to 999 copies of your publication.

Tip:
Printing More
Than 999 Copies

Honest, I get asked about this, so here it is. If you need to print more than 999 copies of your publication, print your publication to disk as PostScript (see "Printing PostScript to Disk," later in this chapter), open the file with a text editor, and search for "#copies."

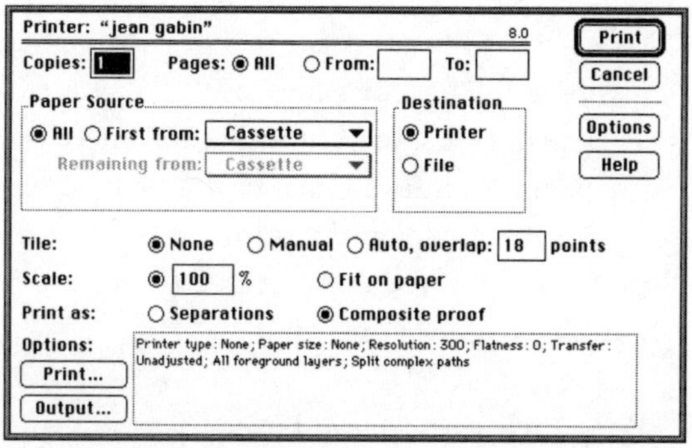

FIGURE 7-1
Print dialog box

Once you've found this string, just type the number of copies you want after it and save the file as text-only. Then download the Post-Script file to your (long-suffering) printer.

Pages

Enter the range of pages you want to print from your publication. Remember, pages in FreeHand are numbered relative to their position on the pasteboard—if you've moved pages around, your pages might be numbered differently from the last time you printed.

Paper Source

Where's the paper coming from? Some printers have multiple paper bins. You choose the one you want here.

Destination

Most of the time, you'll click Printer to send the pages to your printer. If you want to print your publication (or pages from your publication) to disk as PostScript, click File. When you do this, the Print button in the upper-right corner of the Print dialog box changes to Save. When you've set all the printing options you want (including the ones in the Output Options dialog box), click the Save button. The Create File dialog box appears.

Type a name for your PostScript file in the field, select the options you want at the bottom of the dialog box, and press Return (or click the OK button) to save your file to disk as PostScript.

Format. Choose PostScript Job from the Format popup menu. Don't use the EPS options on this popup menu to create EPS files; use Export from the File menu instead (for more on exporting EPS files, see Chapter 4, "Importing and Exporting"). Files created using the EPS options on this popup menu are larger and print less reliably than EPS files created using Export.

The options ASCII and Binary, are overridden by the settings in FreeHand's Output Options dialog box.

If you know that the printer you'll be sending the file to is equipped with a Level 2 PostScript RIP, choose Level 2 Only. Otherwise, choose Level 1 Compatible.

Font Inclusion. If you know that the printer you'll be sending the file to has the fonts you've used in your publication, or if you plan to send the fonts as separate files (if, for example, you're taking your file to an imagesetting service bureau and plan to give them copies of the fonts you've used in the publication), choose None from the Font Inclusion popup menu.

Choose All to include all of the fonts you've used in the publication in the PostScript file you create. If you do this, you won't have to worry about font substitution—but your PostScript file will take up more disk space (each font adds around 40K to the file's size).

To save all of the fonts except the Courier, Helvetica, Symbol, and Times, choose All But Standard 13 from the Font Inclusion popup menu.

Tile Use Tile when your pages are larger than the maximum page size of your printer. Auto Tile splits the pages in your publication into as many parts as FreeHand thinks are necessary; Manual Tile lets you tell FreeHand what size the individual tiles should be.

Auto Tile. When you choose automatic tiling, FreeHand bases the tile on the current printer's page size, and starts tiling from the lower-left corner of the page. Note that this is different from Page-Maker, which measures down and to the right from the zero point when tiling.

The measurement you enter in the Overlap *N* Points field is the amount of the image that's duplicated between adjacent tiles. This feature comes in handy when you're printing using a printer that won't run the image out to the edge of the paper (like most laser printers).

Manual Tile. When you choose Manual Tile, FreeHand prints a tile—a page the size of the current paper size—based on the location of the zero point on the current page.

Manual Tile is generally better than Auto Tile, because Free-Hand's automatic tiling has no idea what's in your illustration, and can't, therefore, make decisions about where the seams between the tiles should fall. When you tile manually, you can make sure that the edges of the tiles don't fall across any fills (especially graduated and radial fills). When the edge of a tile falls across anything with a halftone screen, it's difficult—if not impossible—to piece the two tiles together. It's much easier to join lines and solid fills, and you should do your manual tiling with that in mind. Even if you have to make more tiles, it's better to tile across simple lines and solid fills.

Tip:
Printing
Spreads with
Manual Tiling

When you want to print more than one FreeHand page on a single sheet of paper (or piece of imagesetter film), follow these steps (see Figure 7-2).

1. Position the pages next to each other on the pasteboard. The pages don't have to touch, but the dimensions of the area of the pages, including any bleed areas or gaps between pages, can't exceed that of the paper size you'll be printing on. The pages can be side-by-side, or on top of each other, or arranged in whatever anarchic fashion you see fit.

2. Choose Fit All from the Magnification submenu of the View menu. FreeHand fits all of the pages in your publication in the publication window.

3. Make the page that's closest to the upper-right corner of the pasteboard the active page by clicking on the thumbnail of the page in the Document Inspector.

4. Reset the zero point so that it's at the lower-left corner of the lower-left page in the group of pages you want to print (or the lower-left corner of its bleed area, if any).

5. Press Command-P to display the Print dialog box. Use the Print Options and Output Options dialog boxes to specify

FIGURE 7-2
Printing spreads
using Manual Tile

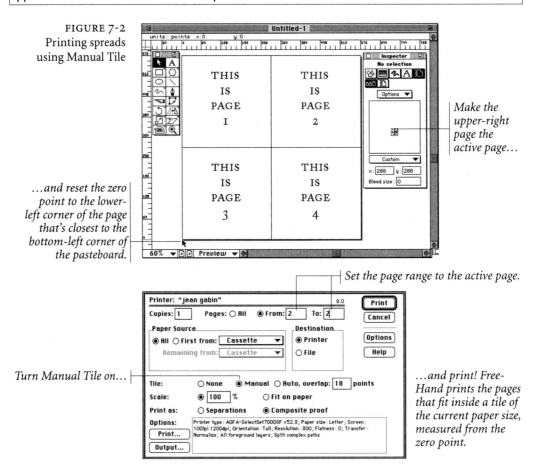

*Make the
upper-right
page the
active page…*

*…and reset the zero
point to the lower-
left corner of the page
that's closest to the
bottom-left corner of
the pasteboard.*

Set the page range to the active page.

Turn Manual Tile on…

*…and print! Free-
Hand prints the pages
that fit inside a tile of
the current paper size,
measured from the
zero point.*

the way you want the publication printed (it's especially
important to set the page size you want in the Print Options
dialog box). Finally, in the Print dialog box, enter the page
number of the active page (see step 3) in the From and To
fields, and select click Manual to turn on manual tiling.

6. Print your publication. FreeHand prints one tile, starting
   at the point you set in step 4. If your paper size is large
   enough, FreeHand prints the spread.

Scale   Enter a scaling value from 10 percent to 1000 percent of the publication's original size (in one-percent increments). The Fit on Paper
option scales your page automatically to the largest size that'll fit
on your currently selected paper size.

Print Options   Click the Separations option when you want to print color separations of your publication (which inks print depends on the specifications you've entered in the Print Options dialog box), and click the Composite Proof button when you want to print all of your colors as black and shades of gray, or when you want to print a color proof of your work on a color PostScript printer.

Printing and Page Setup

Because you're creating a publication that'll be printed on an existing PostScript printer, you've got to pay attention to the page sizes that are available. It might be too obvious to state, but if you can't print it, it's of no use to you.

You could tile your publication, but tiling only works in a few cases. Can you imagine grafting a bunch of halftoned images together? Or graduated fills? On negative film? You get the idea: it's impossible. Don't even try tiling unless you can set it up so that the edges of the tiles don't bisect anything containing a halftone screen.

That brings us back to paper sizes.

Page Size and   When I talk about page size, I'm talking about the page size you've
Paper Size   defined for your publication using the Document Inspector. This page size should be the same as the page size of the printed piece you intend to produce. "Paper size" means the size of the paper as it comes out of your printer or imagesetter. There can be a big difference between these two sizes. Try to print your publication on a paper size that is no larger than the publication's page size, unless you need printer marks (crop marks and registration marks). For more on page size and paper size, see "Paper Size," later in this chapter.

Tip: If you need printer marks (crop marks or registration marks), print
Paper Size and   your publication on a paper size that is larger than your publi-
Printer Marks   cation's page by about 60 points in either dimension.

Page Orientation and Paper Orientation

You set the orientation of your *page* in the Document Inspector by clicking either the Tall or Wide button (or, if you're working with a custom page size, by entering values in the X and Y fields). You set the orientation of the *paper* you're printing to by clicking either the Tall or Wide button in the Print Options dialog box. What do these two orientation settings have to do with each other? Lots.

If you create a tall page and print it to a normal orientation, wide paper size, expect the top and bottom of your publication to get clipped off. Ditto for a wide page size printed to a normal orientation, tall paper size.

Always print tall pages to tall paper sizes, and wide pages to wide paper sizes—even when you're printing to a transverse page size (see Figure 7-3).

◆ If you need to print a wide publication down the length of an imagesetter's paper roll (because it's too wide for the width of the roll), use a wide, transverse orientation paper size.

FIGURE 7-3
Page orientation and paper orientation

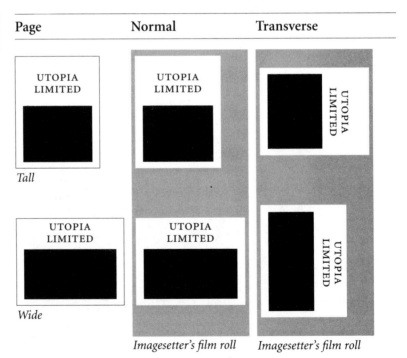

◆ If you want to save paper on the imagesetter's roll and speed up printing time, print tall page sizes to transverse paper sizes (provided that the page size isn't taller than the width of the imagesetter's paper roll). As always, ask your imagesetting service bureau what they want you to do.

Printing Signatures

FreeHand's 54-by-54-inch maximum page size is large enough that you can arrange whole press sheets for many common presses; laying out and printing multiple pages in a single FreeHand publication (see Figure 7-4). To see how to print multiple pages on a single sheet of paper, see the tip "Printing Spreads with Manual Tiling," earlier in this chapter.

Signatures can be a real brain-twister. The object of creating a signature is to get pages onto a press sheet in such a way that your commercial printer can fold and cut the sheet so that it starts on the first page of the signature and ends on the last page. This means you have to position the correct pages in the right places and in the right orientations on both the front and back of the signature. Figure 7-5 shows how it works for a very simple signature.

You should try to leave ¼ inch for trim on each end of the signature and ½ inch on each side of the signature for color bars and for the press' grippers. Also, if your pages have bleeds, make sure you add ⅛ inch to all four sides of the page to accommodate the bleeds.

You'll still have to find some way of printing your signatures—very few imagesetters can handle paper sizes as large as you'll want

FIGURE 7-4
Press sheet

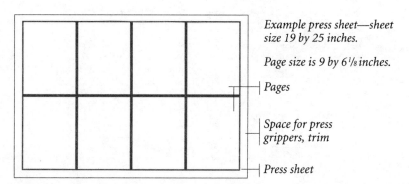

Example press sheet—sheet size 19 by 25 inches.

Page size is 9 by 6⅛ inches.

Pages

Space for press grippers, trim

Press sheet

FIGURE 7-5
Setting up a
simple signature

*After you print, fold,
and cut this press sheet,
you've got an eight-page
signature, with the
pages in the correct
order.*

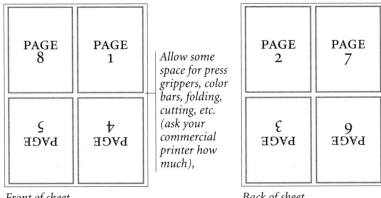

*Allow some
space for press
grippers, color
bars, folding,
cutting, etc.
(ask your
commercial
printer how
much),*

Front of sheet   Back of sheet

for signatures (the largest image area I know of right now is the a 30-by-40-inch single sheet). Table 7-1 shows some typical press sheet sizes and typical page sizes you can get out of them. Talk to your commercial printer about the sheet sizes their presses are capable of handling.

Don't despair if no imagesetters in your area can handle these sheet sizes. The most important thing about understanding how many of what size pages make up a press sheet is that you set up

TABLE 7-1
Common press sheet
sizes and signatures

Sheet size		19 x 25	23 x 29	23 x 35	25 x 38	26 x 40
Image area		18 x 24½	22 x 28½	22 x 34½	24 x 37½	25 x 39½
Pages per sheet	3	18 x 8⅛	22 x 9½	22 x 11½	24 x 12½	25 x 13⅛
	4	18 x 6½	22 x 7⅛	22 x 8⅝	24 x 9⅜	25 x 9⅞
	4	9 x 12¼	11 x 14¼	11 x 17¼	12 x 18¾	12 ½ x 19¾
	6	9 x 8⅛	11 x 9½	11 x 11½	12 x 12½	12½ x 13⅛
	8	9 x 4⅞	11 x 7⅛	11 x 8⅝	12 x 9⅜	12½ x 9⅞
	10	9 x 6⅛	11 x 51¹⁄₁₆	11 x 6⅞	12 x 7 ½	12½ x 7⅞
	15	3⁹⁄₁₆ x 8⅛	4⅜ x 11	4 ⅜ x 11	4¾ x 12½	5 x 13⅛
	16	4½ x 6⅛	5½ x 7⅛	5½ x 8⅝	6 x 9⅜	6¼ x 9⅞

All dimensions in inches

your publication to match sizes that don't waste too much paper. This isn't a comment about saving the environment—I've found it's cheaper by far to design for certain press sheet sizes.

In addition, commercial printers do lots of their printing on smaller sheet sizes. Table 7-2 shows some typical paper sizes you can use on smaller presses. You can fit signatures on these paper sizes, as well.

You need to be absolutely certain you want to do this and that you know what you're doing before you try it. Make folded dummies of the signatures you want to use, and make sure that all of the pages, front and back, fall where you want them to. When in doubt, leave it to the pros at your printer.

TABLE 7-2
Typical sheet sizes
for smaller presses

Text weights	Cover weights	Bond
19 x 25	20 x 26	8½ x 11
23 x 29	23 x 35	17 x 22
23 x 35	26 x 40	22 x 34
25 x 38		24 x 38

All dimensions in inches

FreeHand Printing Options

FreeHand's Print Options dialog box is where you control what paper size you're printing to, which (if any) printer marks you want, and which inks you want to print, among other things. You get to the Print Options dialog box when you click the Print button in the Print dialog box (see Figure 7-6).

I find that I almost always have to change settings in the Print Options dialog box before I print, I've set up a QuicKey that takes me to the Print Options dialog box when I press Command-P.

Printer Type   Click the Select PPD button to select a PostScript Printer Description file (PPD) for your printer. If no PPD matches your printer's make and model, choose General or Color General (if you're printing to a color PostScript printer).

FIGURE 7-5
Print Options
dialog box

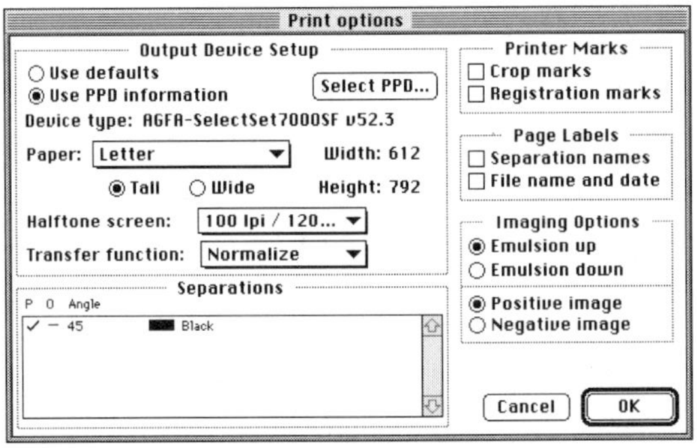

Print options

Output Device Setup
○ Use defaults
◉ Use PPD information   [Select PPD...]
Device type: AGFA-SelectSet7000SF v52.3

Paper: [Letter   ▼]   Width: 612
        ◉ Tall   ○ Wide   Height: 792
Halftone screen: [100 lpi / 120... ▼]
Transfer function: [Normalize   ▼]

Separations
P O Angle
✓ — 45   ■ Black

Printer Marks
☐ Crop marks
☐ Registration marks

Page Labels
☐ Separation names
☐ File name and date

Imaging Options
◉ Emulsion up
○ Emulsion down

◉ Positive image
○ Negative image

[Cancel] [OK]

Paper Size

When you choose a PPD, the available paper sizes for your printer appear in the Paper popup menu, including any custom paper sizes you've added to this PPD (see "Adding Custom Page Sizes to PPDs" later in this chapter).

Always choose a paper size that's at least the size of your publication's pages. If you're printing a publication that needs crop and registration marks (collectively known as printer's marks; see "Crop Marks" and "Registration Marks," later in this chapter) printed off the page, or if parts of your publication bleed (extend beyond the edge of the publication page), you'll need to choose a paper size that's larger than your publication's page size to accommodate the printer's marks and/or the bleed.

If you've chosen an imagesetter PPD, the Other option appears on the popup menu. When you choose Other, FreeHand displays the Paper Size dialog box, in which you can type whatever paper size you want. Remember, however, that the values you enter here need to take the width of the imagesetter's paper roll into account. Enter a width value greater than the width of the imagesetter's paper roll and you'll get a "limitcheck" error when you try to print.

Tip:
Line Screens and
Transverse Page
Orientation

When you choose one of the transverse page sizes/orientations from the Paper popup menu, FreeHand rotates the publication 90 degrees when printing. Halftone screens you've applied to specific objects in your publication are not rotated, which can mess things up if you're using a coarse screen like a line screen for special effects. If the direction of the halftone screen you've applied is important to your design, you can either add 90 degrees to the screen angles applied in your publication, or you can print to one of the normal-orientation page sizes.

Halftone Screen

Choosing a screen frequency for your publication can be difficult. Higher frequency screens produce smoother-looking tints, but increasing screen ruling can also result in a loss of grays—depending on the resolution of the printer. And there's a limit to how fine a screen frequency you can print with various printing methods and paper stocks. If you don't have enough gray levels available on your printer, your publications print with noticeable banding and posterization. Lower screen frequencies provide more gray levels, but also look coarser. What to do? Try using this equation to determine the number of grays you'll get from the screen ruling and printer resolution you've chosen.

number of grays = (printer resolution in dpi/screen frequency in lpi)^2+1

The key to this equation is that "number of grays" can't be greater than 256—that's the maximum number of grays a PostScript printer can render.

You can work the equation another way, and maybe this one's more useful.

screen frequency = square root(16*printer resolution)

Other people like to use this equation.

required resolution = screen frequency * 16

If you come up with a line screen that's too coarse for your taste, think about it—is your publication one where you can sacrifice a few grays for a finer screen?

Transfer Function

This option specifies how the printer's tint densities correspond to the tint densities you specify. Why do we need this? Because gray levels printed on 300-dpi printers look very different from the same gray levels printed on 2,540-dpi printers (in general, lower percentages of gray, especially 10 percent, look darker at lower resolutions). If you choose Default, FreeHand prints exactly the density you've specified, without reading any of the gray-level adjustment information from the PPD.

Ordinarily, Default is the best choice for most tasks. If you want to compensate for the differences between printers with different resolutions (to get a more accurate proof), use Normalize, which reads gray-level compensation information from the PPD.

Posterize creates special effects by converting the available gray levels into just four gray levels. Posterize works about the same way as the Posterize image preset. See "Bilevel and Grayscale TIFFs and Image control" in Chapter 4, "Importing and Exporting," for more on posterization. I can't think of any reason to use this, but that doesn't mean you're similarly impaired.

Printer Marks

Check Crop Marks to print lines, printed outside the area of your page, that define the area of your page. If your paper size is not larger than your page size, FreeHand won't print your crop marks.

When you check the Registration Marks box, FreeHand prints little targets around the edge of your page for your commercial printer to use when they're lining up, or registering, your color separations for printing. If your paper size is smaller than your page size, FreeHand won't print registration marks.

Page Labels

When you check the Separation Names checkbox, FreeHand prints the name of each ink color for each separation or overlay on each printed sheet. This way, you'll have an easier time telling the magenta overlay from the cyan overlay. If you're printing a compsite, FreeHand prints the word Composite.

Check File Name and Date to print the filename and date on your publications on each page—this makes it easy to tell which of several printed versions is the most current. It can also make it easier for your commercial printer to tell which pieces of film in a stack of separations go together (this might seem easy for you to tell, but put yourself in their shoes for a minute). If your paper size is smaller than your page size, FreeHand won't print the filename and date.

Imaging Options Use the Image Options to print a negative of your publication or to choose whether your publication prints emulsion up or emulsion down.

In the United States, most printers prefer getting their film negative, emulsion down, unless they've got stripping to do, in which case they prefer it emulsion up. Many non-North American printers—those in Japan, Hong Kong, Singapore, Italy, Switzerland, and elsewhere—like their film positive, emulsion down. Everything looks the same in the end; it's just a different standard. Printers vary a lot, though, so the best way to find out which way you should print your publication is to ask your commercial printer how they'd like to receive the film.

Separations I call the list that appears in the Separations section of the Print Options dialog box the "Ink List." The Ink List is where you determine how the inks in your publication are printed; of the choices you can make, only color definitions and object-level overprinting instructions are more important (see Figure 7-6). All of the inks used in your publication are included in the Ink List. If you've used any spot colors, they appear; and cyan, magenta, yellow, and black appear if you've specified any process colors in the document.

Using the Ink List, you can control whether or not an ink prints, and whether or not that ink overprints (though object-level overprinting instructions will override the settings in this dialog box for the objects they're applied to).

Suppress printing of an ink. To keep an ink from printing, click the checkmark to the left of the ink's name (in the column headed with a "P").

What happens when you have objects filled or stroked with percentages of process inks and turn off one of the process inks? Simple enough—you don't get any of that ink. Turning an ink off doesn't affect any of the other inks in the object.

Turning an ink off doesn't affect that ink's knockout/overprinting settings. If the ink was set to knock out other inks, it'll still knock them out—whether you print it or not.

FIGURE 7-6
Ink List

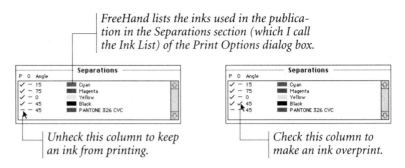

FreeHand lists the inks used in the publication in the Separations section (which I call the Ink List) of the Print Options dialog box.

Unheck this column to keep an ink from printing.

Check this column to make an ink overprint.

Overprinting inks. To make an ink overprint, click in the column headed with an "O." A check appears in the column, indicating that the ink is set to overprint. To make the ink knock out, click the checkmark—it'll turn back into a dash, indicating that the ink knocks out.

The Overprint Ink option makes all of the objects with the selected ink applied to them overprint anything that's behind them. Any object-level overprinting instructions override this setting for the objects they're attached to.

Process colors bring up some interesting questions. If you've got an object that's colored 60C 30M 0Y 10K on top of an object that's colored 10C 40M 10Y 0K, what ink percentages do you get in the areas where the objects overlap? It's simple—the process colors on top win. Even if you set cyan to overprint, you'll still get 10-percent cyan in the areas where the top object overprints the bottom object.

To see what overprinting looks like, refer to the Color Figure 1 in the color pages in Chapter 6, "Color."

Screen angles. The screen angle that's shown in the Ink List comes from the PPD file you've selected. These are the imagesetter manufacturers' optimized screen angles, which help prevent moirés from occurring, so you shouldn't alter these unless you have a really good reason to do so. Still, if you want to change the angle, double-click the angle in the Ink List, then type a new angle in the Screen Angle field FreeHand displays.

Screens you've applied to objects using the Halftone palette override the halftone screen you chose from the Halftone Settings pop-up menu in the Print Options dialog box for those objects.

Output Options

It was frustrating—in FreeHand 3, you could set the flatness of all of the paths in your document when you printed, but you couldn't do the same when you created an EPS of the same paths. Other printing controls, such as the ability to print of suppress printing of invisible layers, didn't apply to EPS files you created.

FreeHand 4 puts many of the controls that used to be in Free-Hand 3's Print Options dialog box in the new Output Options dialog box (see Figure 7-7). The settings in the Output Options dialog box apply to both files you print and files you save as EPS.

To display the Output Options dialog box, click the Output button in FreeHand's Print dialog box.

FIGURE 7-7
Output Options
dialog box

Printing Invisible Layers

If you've turned off the display of layers to speed up your publication's display on screen, you can print them by checking Include Invisible Layers. If you don't want to print invisible layers, leave this option unchecked.

Split Complex Paths

Uncheck the Split Complex Paths box when your publication contains TIFFs you've pasted into complex paths (anything with more curves than a rectangle). Why? Each time FreeHand fails to print a path, it simplifies the path (that is, cuts the path up into smaller, more manageable segments) and sends it to the printer again. If the path contains a TIFF, this means you'll spend extra time waiting for FreeHand to download the TIFF each time it sends the path (or portions of the path). Otherwise, leave this checkbox on.

Tip:
Print Only What
You Need

If you've already printed proofs of a publication, and only need to alter one part of the illustration and proof that change, consider putting the change on another layer, then printing only that layer. If you do this, you won't have to wait for the entire publication to print.

Image Data

The options in this section determine how—and if—TIFF images you've placed in your publication get sent to your printer—or to an EPS or PostScript file you save to disk.

ASCII Encoding. Choose ASCII Encoding when you're creating a file you intend to transfer to a computer other than a Macintosh, or when you're having trouble printing images over a slow network, or when you're connected to your printer through a serial cable.

Binary Data. Choose Binary Data to send images in a more compact form than ASCII Encoding.

OPI Comments Only. Choose "None (OPI Comments Only)" when you'll be linking to a high-resolution version of the image using an OPI system, such as Kodak's Prophecy or Aldus PrePrint. When you choose this option, FreeHand includes cropping and scaling information for any TIFFs you've placed in your publication, but doesn't include the TIFFs themselves.

Convert RGB TIFF to CMYK. Check Convert RGB TIFF to CMYK to include a color-separated version of any RGB TIFFs you've placed in your publication. Do this when you're saving an EPS you want to place in an application that can't separate RGB TIFFs, such as PageMaker or QuarkXPress. (if you don't have the EFIColor Xtension). You'll get better separations, however, if you separate the RGB TIFF to CMYK in Photoshop or PrePrint before you place it in FreeHand.

Maximum Color Steps. When you're printing to a slide recorder, or when you're creating an EPS you plan to convert using a color prepress system (such as those made by Crosfield or Scitex), enter

256 in this field. If you still have trouble printing or converting the file, enter a lower number. You need to do this because some of these devices can only handle a limited number of colors at a time.

Otherwise, leave this field blank.

Flatness As discussed in Chapter 2, "Drawing," flatness is a property of Post-Script paths that specifies how many tiny straight line segments a PostScript RIP has to draw to render a curve. The higher the value you enter for flatness, the fewer line segments your printer's RIP will have to draw—which means faster printing times. Even on a 300-dpi printer, the resolution of most laser printers, you won't see a difference between flatness setting of three and a flatness setting of zero, but the former will print much faster. In fact, some paths won't print at all, on any printer, unless you set their flatness to something greater than zero.

Enter a value in this field to set a flatness value for all of the paths in your publication. Any flatness settings you've applied to individual paths using the Object Inspector override any value you enter here.

Printing PostScript to Disk

The best way to send your FreeHand publication to an imageset-ting service bureau is to print it to disk as PostScript. Printing to disk creates a text file containing all of the PostScript definitions and commands needed to print the publication. If you want to print your publication at a service bureau, printing PostScript to disk can make life easier for both you and your service bureau (see "Preparing a FreeHand File for Imagesetting," in this chapter).

Printing a FreeHand publication to disk as PostScript can take a while, and can produce huge files if you've got any images (paint or TIFF) in your publication, because FreeHand has to include all of the information in the form it would normally send to the printer.

In the case of a TIFF, FreeHand sends image data as hexadeci-mal numbers written out in ASCII (or as binary numbers written out as ASCII). A one-inch square, 300-dpi grayscale TIFF saved as

ASCII takes up more than 700K in a PostScript file. A one-inch square, 300-dpi grayscale TIFF (again, saved as ASCII—the binary sizes are smaller) takes up 180K in a PostScript file. By pointing out these file sizes, I'm not trying to scare you away from including TIFFs in your FreeHand files, or even to scare you away from printing publications containing TIFFs to disk; I think both are reasonable and desirable things to do. Just be prepared.

Once you've printed your publication to disk as PostScript, you can open, view, and edit it with a word processor, because it's a text file.

Tip:
Include TIFF
Images

You should always link to TIFF and paint-type images when you're printing PostScript files to disk. If you don't link to them, they won't print. In many cases, the whole page won't print.

Learning About FreeHand's PostScript

The best way to learn about how FreeHand makes images using PostScript is to create simple files, print them to disk as PostScript, and then look at the PostScript file with a word processor. How does FreeHand draw a line? A box? Text? It's all easy to see in the PostScript FreeHand prints to disk. Having good PostScript books around is good, but FreeHand has its own dialect, and the best way to learn that dialect is to look at lots of examples of FreeHand's own PostScript.

How is a printed-to-disk PostScript file different from an EPS file? The former contains all of the instructions needed by a PostScript printer to render the page, including all of FreeHand's crop marks, page size information, and, specifically, the PostScript page-printing operator *showpage*.

The EPS file, on the other hand, counts on the application it's placed into for things like crop marks and page-positioning information. Basically, an EPS file is a FreeHand file without any options you've chosen in FreeHand's Print and Print options dialog boxes, while the printed-to-disk PostScript file includes all of those options. Further, the EPS file can include an attached PICT resource (Macintosh EPS) or TIFF (MS-DOS) for screen preview, while the printed-to-disk PostScript file doesn't.

FreeHand and PPDs

PostScript Printer Description files (PPDs) describe your printer to FreeHand and to your printer driver. PPDs are not, and should not be confused with, printer drivers. Printer drivers are pieces of software that direct information from your system and applications to a hardware port—usually, your Macintosh's printer port. For some applications, the printer driver does the work of translating the application's documents into PostScript; this isn't the case for FreeHand, which generates its own PostScript.

PPDs work in conjunction with printer drivers to give your applications information about the printer (what paper sizes are available?; what's the resolution of the printer?; what do the printer error messages mean?) and to customize the printer's operation for the application (what PostScript routine does the application use to render halftones?).

FreeHand uses the printer driver on your system, and uses PPDs to optimize printing for a specific printer.

PPDs—Who's on First?

Because of a territorial dispute—between your applications (FreeHand in particular) and your printer driver—you can get caught in a loop. You create a file, choose a PPD, and save the file. When you open the file, a different PPD is selected in the Print Options dialog box. In fact, every time you open the file, the same—incorrect—PPD appears, no matter what PPD you chose before you saved the file.

This isn't a feature.

What's going on? Both FreeHand and your printer driver want to be the entity responsible for your PPD choices. If you've chosen a PPD using the driver options available in the Chooser, this choice appears in all your FreeHand documents. Follow these steps to make the PPD choices you make in FreeHand's Print Options dialog box stick.

Note: This only works with Apple's LaserWriter 8 driver or Adobe's PSPrinter 8 driver. The Apple LaserWriter 7.1.2 driver (the previous version) doesn't let you set a PPD for the printer.

1. Select Chooser from the Apple Menu.

2. Click the LaserWriter 8 driver icon. Make sure that the correct printer shows up in the printer list to the right. If not, select it by clicking on the name.

3. Click the Setup button that appears below the list of available printers. The Chooser displays the Current Printer Description File dialog box.

4. Click the Select PPD button. The Select PostScript Printer Description File dialog box appears.

5. Click the Use Generic button.

6. Press Return (or click the OK button) to close the dialog box and apply your change.

If, on the other hand, you prefer letting the printer driver choose your PPD, select the PPD you want, or click Auto Configure in the Select PostScript Printer Description File dialog box and leave it at that.

Rewriting PPDs

You can edit your PPDs to add custom page sizes, to add new sets of screen angles, to download PostScript routines automatically, and to do a variety of other things.

What's in a PPD?

Table 7-4 shows a listing of some of the keywords you'll see when you open a PPD file. I haven't tried to cover every keyword and entry you'll find in a PPD, mainly because FreeHand doesn't use all of them. I've included keywords you might want to change, as well as keywords you shouldn't change.

Adding Custom Paper Sizes to PPDs

The main reason to edit PPDs is to add custom paper sizes. If you find yourself entering the same numbers in the Page Size dialog box over and over again, it's a job for custom page sizes. Once you've added a custom page size to a PPD file, the size appears on the Paper popup menu when the PPD file is selected.

TABLE 7-3   Keywords in PPDs (continued)

Keyword	Example	What is it?
*PSVersion	*PSVersion: "(52.3) 320"	Version of PostScript in the printer's ROMs. Change this value if your printer has a different PostScript version than that listed in the PPD.
*Include:	*Include "MyPageSizes.txt"	Includes a file at this point in the PPD. You can have any number of "*Include" keywords in a PPD.
*DefaultResolution	*DefaultResolution: 2400x2400dpi	Default resolution of the printer. If you usually run your printer in a different resolution than the one you see here, change the resolution here.
*Resolution	*Resolution 1200x1200dpi: " 1200 statusdict /setresolution get exec "	Sets the resolution of the printer, for those printers capable of switching resolutions via software commands (imagesetters, mostly). If you don't know the routine to change the setting on an imagesetter (they're all different), leave this value alone and change the resolution from the image-setter's control panel.
*ColorDevice	*ColorDevice: False	Tells FreeHand whether the selected printer is a PostScript color printer or not.
*FreeVM	*FreeVM: "992346"	Amount of the printer's virtual memory (VM) FreeHand can work with before having to flush fonts, etc. If you know your printer has more—or less—memory available, increase or decrease this value.
		Usually, a printer's startup page shows you how much VM the printer has available. If yours doesn't—or if you've turned off the *continued on next page*

TABLE 7-3   Keywords in PPDs (continued)

Keyword	Example	What is it?
*FreeVM (continued)		printer's startup page and don't feel like turning it on again—download the following code (your printer will print a page with the memory amount on it): ``` %%show FreeVM /Helvetica findfont 12 scalefont setfont 72 72 moveto /memString 256 string def vmstatus exch sub memString cvs show showpage ```
*Password	*Password: "0"	Provides a password for the printer. Do not change this, or if you do, make sure you remember the password. If you don't know the password, you might have to replace chips on your motherboard to be able to use your printer again. I can't think why Adobe put this keyword into their interpreter. In fact, I'm vaguely upset by the notion you'd want to prohibit someone on your network from printing on your printer (why not simply *ask* them?). Note: The editor and copy editor for this book have both supplied arguments for keeping people off some printers. Luckily, it's my book, and I see no reason to repeat their fascist ravings here.
*FileSystem	*FileSystem True	Lets FreeHand know if the selected printer has a hard disk attached to it. If this value is "True", FreeHand checks the printer's hard disk for downloadable fonts before looking

TABLE 7-3   Keywords in PPDs (continued)

Keyword	Example	What is it?
*FileSystem (continued)		for them on the current system. If you have a hard disk attached to your printer, set this keyword to "True"; otherwise, leave it at "False". If you have a printer that can be attached to a hard disk, FreeHand queries the printer to see if it has a hard disk attached. If you change this setting to "True", FreeHand doesn't have to ask.
*DeviceAdjustMatrix	*DeviceAdjustMatrix: "[1 0 0 1 0 0]"	Don't change this unless your printer chronically distorts the pages you're printing. If your printer does distort images, you'll have to calculate the percentage of distortion vertically and horizontally and enter it in the matrix. If you found that your printer was always stretching an image by five percent vertically, you'd change the matrix to [.95 0 0 1 0 0]. If your imagesetter is doing this, you probably ought to call a service technician. Don't even think about changing for 300-dpi printers—they're not accurate enough for it to make a difference. See the PostScript Language Reference Manual for more (lots more) information on adjusting matrices. El Greco was just Rembrandt with a matrix adjustment.
*ScreenAngle	*ScreenAngle: "45"	Sets the screen angle the printer uses to print halftones. Change this value if you want a different default screen angle for your printer. Any setting you make in the Halftone screen dialog box overrides this value.

TABLE 7-3   Keywords in PPDs (continued)

Keyword	Example	What is it?
*DefaultScreenProc	*DefaultScreenProc: Dot	Sets the default halftone screen drawing procedure for the printer. This procedure is defined in the "*ScreenProc" keyword listing.
*ScreenProc	*ScreenProc Dot: "{abs exch abs 2 copy add 1 gt {1 sub dup mul exch 1 sub dup mul add 1 sub }{dup mul exch dup mul add 1 exch sub }ifelse }" *End	Halftone screen drawing procedures for the printer. You could enter "*ScreenProc Line: "{ pop }"" or "*ScreenProc Ellipse: "{ dup 5 mul 8 div mul exch dup mul exch add sqrt 1 exch sub }"" instead, but you've got to remember to call them from the "*DefaultScreenProc" keyword to get them to work.
*ScreenFreq	*ScreenFreq: "120"	Sets the screen frequency the printer uses to print halftones. If you don't like it, change it. Any setting you make in the Halftone Screen dialog box overrides this value.
*DefaultTransfer	*DefaultTransfer Normalized	Sets the default transfer function for the printer.
*DefaultPageSize	*DefaultPageSize: Letter	Sets the default paper size for your printer. The keyword for the paper size corresponds to the name of a defined paper size existing either in the printer's ROMs or in the PPD file. For more on creating custom paper sizes, see the section "Adding Custom Page Sizes to PPDs," earlier in this chapter.
*PageSize	*PageSize Letter: "letter"	Sets up a paper size. If your printer has variable page sizes (image-setters usually do; laser printers usually don't), this entry could be: "*PageSize Letter.Extra: "statusdict begin 684 864 0 1 setpageparams end""

TABLE 7-3   Keywords in PPDs (continued)

Keyword	Example	What is it?
*DefaultPaperTray	*DefaultPaperTray: None	If you have a printer with more than one paper tray, change this to the tray you want as your default. The tray selection for your printer is defined in the "*PaperTray" section of the PPD.
*PaperTray	*PaperTray Letter: "statusdict begin lettertray end"	Defines available paper trays for your printer.
*DefaultImageableArea	*DefaultImageableArea: Letter	Sets the default imageable area (the area inside a paper size that the printer can actually make marks on) for the printer. The available imageable areas for your printer are set up using the "ImageableArea" keyword.
*ImageableArea	*ImageableArea Letter.Extra: "0 1 684 864"	Sets up the imageable area for a defined page size (in the example, a page size named "Letter.Extra").
*DefaultPaper-Dimension	*DefaultPaperDimension: Letter	Sets the default paper dimension for the printer. You set up paper dimensions using the "*PaperDimension" keyword.
*PaperDimension	*PaperDimension Letter.Extra: "684 864"	Sets up the paper dimension for a specific page size (in the example, a page size named "Letter.Extra"). Enter the width and height of the paper, in points.For a wide orientation page, the entry would read "*PaperDimension Letter.Extra.Wide: "864 684"".
*VariablePaperSize	*VariablePaperSize: True	Tells FreeHand whether your printer can accept variable paper sizes. Most imagesetters can; most laser printers can't. If your printer can accept variable paper sizes, the Paper popup menu in

continued on next page

TABLE 7-3   Keywords in PPDs (continued)

Keyword	Example	What is it?
*VariablePaperSize (continued)		FreeHand's Print Options dialog box will include Other. If you choose Other, you'll be able to enter a custom paper size in the Page Size dialog box and print to whatever size of paper you want (within the imagesetter's capabilities). You can also add your own custom page sizes to PPDs of printers capable of accepting variable page sizes. Changing this value from "False" to "True" does not give your printer the ability to accept variable page sizes.
*DefaultInputSlot	*DefaultInputSlot: Lower	Sets the default paper feed for your printer, if your printer has more than one input slot (a NEC LC 890 Silentwriter is an example of a printer with two input slots). The available input slots are set up by the entries in the "*InputSlot" keyword.
*InputSlot	*InputSlot Lower: "statusdict begin 1 setpapertray end"	Defines the available input slots for your printer.
*DefaultManualFeed	*DefaultManualFeed: False	Makes manual feed the printer's default paper feed. Don't change this unless you habitually use your printer's manual feed.
*ManualFeed	*ManualFeed True: "statusdict begin /manualfeed true store end"	Sets up the printer's manual feed mechanism, if it has one.
*Font	*Font Times-Bold: Standard "(001.002)"	Lets FreeHand know that a font is resident in the printer. Add fonts to this list if you're sure they're going to be on your printer's hard disk or memory. FreeHand will ask your printer if it has a certain downloadable font installed, unless it finds the font in this list. If you enter the

TABLE 7-3   Keywords in PPDs (continued)

Keyword	Example	What is it?

*Font (continued)		font in this list, FreeHand doesn't have to ask and prints faster. You add a font to the list by typing:
		
		`*Font: PostScriptFontName:`
		`Standard "(001.001)"`
		
		The PostScript name of the font can be a bit tricky to figure out. The best way to do it is to create a text block containing the font in FreeHand and print the file to disk as PostScript or create an EPS. Then open the file with a text editor and look at the way FreeHand names the fonts near the start of the file.
		
		The numbers following the font name are the font type and the font version. Most fonts, these days, are Type 1 (or "001"). Unless you know the font version, just enter "001" for the version.

*DefaultFont	*DefaultFont: Courier	Defines the default font for your printer. This is the default font that gets used if FreeHand can't find the font used for text in your publication. If you're tired of Courier, you can change it to any other printer-resident font you want.

If you're creating your publications on page sizes other than the paper size of the printed piece, stop (unless you're creating signatures, or have some other good excuse). Remember that paper size equals printer RAM. Your jobs will print faster if you use a paper size that's no larger than your publication's page size plus crop marks (which adds about 60 points in each dimension).

You can add custom paper sizes to PPDs for any printer that can accept variable page sizes. Usually, imagesetters can accept variable page sizes and laser printers can't.

To add a custom paper size to a PPD file, follow these steps.

1. Back up the PPD file you intend to edit. Remember that if you make a backup copy of the file you'll be able to return to where you started if you make a mistake. Without the backup, you'll have to go beg a copy of the PPD from your friends, who'll laugh at you.

2. Open the copy of the PPD with your word processor.

3. Anywhere after the "*Include" line, enter three lines defining your new page size. The lines are shown below. Variables you enter are shown in italics.

```
*PageSize PageSizeName: "Name"
"statusdict begin x y offset orientation end"
*ImageableArea PageSizeName: "0 0 x y"
*PaperDimension PageSizeName: "x y"
```

PageSizeName is the name you want to use for your custom page size. This name should not have spaces in it.

x is the width of the custom page size, in points (if you're an inch monger, just multiply the inch measurement by 72 to get the distance in points) and

y is the height of the custom page size, in points.

Offset is a value used to offset the paper size from the edge of the imagesetter's paper (or film) roll. This value should almost always be "0".

Orientation is either "1" or "0". "0" means normal orientation (with the height of the paper being measured along the length of the imagesetter's paper roll, and type in normal orientation printing across the roll); "1" means transverse (where the width of the paper is measured along the length of the imagesetter's paper roll). Here's a custom page size for a 576-by-1152-point (eight-by-16-inch) paper size with a normal orientation.

```
*PageSize myPageSize: "myPageSize"
"statusdict begin 576 1152 0 0 end"
*ImageableArea PageSizeName: "0 0 576 1152"
*PaperDimension PageSizeName: "576 1152"
```

4. Save your edited PPD file to the Printer Descriptions folder in the Extensions folder (in your system folder) as text-only. Give it a different name than the original PPD.

5. Open FreeHand.

6. Press Command-P to display the Print dialog box. Press the Change button to display the Print Options dialog box. If you edited the PPD file you currently have selected, you'll have to select another PPD, and then select the edited PPD to read the new page size information into FreeHand. Once you've selected the edited PPD file, your new page sizes should appear in the Page popup menu.

If the new page sizes didn't appear in the Page popup menu, or if the PPD can't be opened, you probably forgot to save the file as text-only. Return to your word processor and try that.

Preparing a FreeHand File for Imagesetting

I've listened long and carefully to the grievances of imagesetting service bureau customers and operators. I've heard about how this designer is suing that service bureau for messing up a job, and I've heard imagesetter operators talking about how stupid their clients are and how they have to make changes to the files of most of the jobs that come in. I've listened long enough, and I have one thing to say.

Cut it out! All of you! There's no reason that this relationship has to be adversarial. Don't throw the book across the room—I don't mean to sound harsh. I just think that we can all cooperate, to everyone's benefit.

Designers and illustrators, you have to learn the technical chops if you want to play. That's just the way it is. The technical challenges are no greater than those you mastered when you learned how to use an airbrush, X-Acto, or a rapidograph. Your responsibility to your imagesetting service bureau is to set your file up so that it has a reasonable chance of printing (the guidelines in this book should help) and to communicate to your service bureau exactly how it is you want your publication printed (or, if you're creating a PostScript file, to make sure that the settings in the publication are correct).

Service bureau folks, you've got to spell out the limits of your responsibility. If you don't think you should be fixing people's files, don't do it. If you do think it's your responsibility, tell them up front you'll do so, fix the files, and charge the customer for the time. And if you get a customer who knows what they're doing, give them a discount. This will encourage everyone else.

Okay, back to the book.

If you know what you're doing, the best way to prepare your publication for printing at an imagesetting service bureau is to print a PostScript file to disk. If you've set up your printing options correctly, the file will include everything that is needed to print the publication. This way, all your service bureau has to do is download the file, instead of having to open the file, set the printing options, link to any images included in the file, and print. The only things that can go wrong are related to film handling and processing—the wrong film's used, the film's scratched, or the film's processed incorrectly.

This means, however, that you have to be dead certain of the printing options you want before you print to disk, because it's difficult or impossible to change things after that.

What are the most critical things you have to look out for?

Links to images. Make sure any images you want to print (any that aren't on the background layer) are linked.

Tiling. If you're not tiling, make sure Tiling (Manual or Auto) is off. If you are, make sure you're tiling the way you want to. If you're tiling manually, you'll have to print a separate PostScript file to disk for each tile you want to print.

Scaling. It's easy to forget that you've scaled things for printing on your proof printer. Make sure that this is set to the scaling you want (generally 100 percent).

Separations/Composite. If you want to get separations from your service bureau, make sure you choose Separations in the Print dialog box. An obvious point, but I've forgotten it at least once.

Printer Type. If you don't choose the right printer type, your publication may not print, and may even crash the service bureau's imagesetter. They hate this, so pick the type of imagesetter they use from the popup menu. You might check with the service bureau to see if they have a custom PPD they'd like you to use.

Page Size. Pick a page size at least large enough to contain your page (this seems obvious, but I've forgotten it a time or two). If you're printing separations, pick a page size that's at least 60 points wider and taller than your page size so that printer marks can be printed. Also make sure that you understand the page orientation you're working with—wide or tall; normal or transverse.

Screen Ruling. If you haven't set a screen frequency for each item in your publication using the Halftone palette, enter the screen ruling you want here. Any screen frequency you entered in the Halftone palette overrides any entry you make here.

Printer Marks. If you're printing separations, you can live without separation names and the file's name and date, but you've got to have the crop marks and registration marks if you want your printer to speak to you again. I turn them all on most of the time.

Negative/Emulsion Up. Are you printing negatives or positives? Emulsion up or down? Set it here.

Inks. What inks do you want to print? If you don't set them to print here, don't look askance at your service bureau when you don't get an overlay/separation for the ink. If you don't want an ink to print, make sure you turn it off or expect to pay for an additional piece of film.

Tip:
Don't Forget
Your Custom
PostScript Files

If you're using a custom UserPrep file, or if you're using FreeHand extension (AGX1) files (for more on creating and using both types of files, see Chapter 8, "PostScript"), and you're giving your service bureau your FreeHand file (rather than a PostScript file), make sure you include these files with your file. Without the files, any special effects you've used won't print. If you do send these files to your service bureau, let them know that they need to put them in the same folder as their copy of FreeHand before they print.

If you print to disk, FreeHand includes the relevant information from these files in your PostScript file, so you won't need to provide them to your service bureau.

The Golden Rules

These rules are mentioned elsewhere in this book, but all of the service bureau operators I know think I should repeat them again here. The times I mention here are averages, based on a series of benchmarks.

Use blends, not graduated fills. Blends that are created to match your printer's resolution and the line screen you intend to use print more than two times faster than graduated fills covering the same area. This assumes that you're not pasting the blend inside another object, which takes longer. For more on creating blends instead of graduated and radial fills, see Chapter 2, "Drawing."

Use filled objects, not clipping paths. Illustrator users are used to creating fountains (what FreeHand calls "graduated fills") by creating a blend and then placing the blend objects inside a clipping path. In FreeHand, you should avoid doing this whenever possible, because it takes over five times as long to print as a simple graduated fill of the same path.

Use duplicated objects, not tiled fills. Tiled fills are a wonderful thing—as long as you're basing them on objects with basic lines and fills. As soon as you create a tiled fill containing a graduated or radial fill, watch out! Our benchmarks show that tiled fills containing complex objects take more than twice as long to print as an identical series of duplicated objects.

Remember that page size equals printer RAM. The size of your page corresponds directly to the amount of printer RAM consumed when you try to print the publication. A four-by-four-inch card centered on a letter-size page takes almost twice as much time to print as the same card laid out on a four-by-four-inch page. For more on page setup and page size, see "Printing and Page Setup," earlier in this chapter.

Increase flatness whenever possible. When you're printing to high-resolution imagesetters, the difference between a flatness setting of three and a flatness setting of zero isn't noticeable, but the path with a flatness of three prints almost four times as quickly. For more on flatness, see "Flatness" in Chapter 2, "Drawing."

Don't draw what you can't see. Your printer or imagesetter has to process everything on your publication's page, so why make it work rendering objects that'll never be seen on the printed publication?

Simplify your paths. If you're working with complex paths created by autotracing images, try reducing the number of points in each path by choosing Simplify from the Path Operations submenu of the Arrange menu (see Simplify," in Chapter 2, "Drawing").

Scan grayscale and color images at no more than twice your line screen frequency (and usually less). When you're scanning, it's natural to assume that you should scan them at the highest resolution available from your scanner to create the sharpest possible scans. In fact, image data scanned at a resolution greater than two times the screen frequency you intend using to print your publication does not add to the sharpness of the images, and may even harm the image's quality. For more on scanned image resolution, see "TIFFs, Line Screens, and Resolution" in Chapter 4, "Importing and Exporting.".

Don't import things when you don't have to. Whenever possible, always copy and paste from one FreeHand publication to another, rather than exporting and importing EPS graphics. If you have a FreeHand EPS, go to the original file and copy the elements you want out of it. If you're working with an Illustrator EPS, open the file (if possible), rather than placing it. In my tests, placed EPS files took up to 16 times as long to print as the same images pasted from another FreeHand file or converted from an Illustrator EPS.

Printing Troubleshooting

It's going to happen to you. Files are going to take hours to print, and some aren't going to print at all. Or they're going to print in some way you hadn't expected. While this book can be viewed as an extended treatise on printing troubleshooting, this section deals with a few of the most common printing problems and how to fix them.

First of all, what makes a file hard to print? TIFFs, PostScript fills and lines, custom fills and lines, graduated fills, radial fills, and paths with lots of points and curves all do their part to increase the amount of time your publication spends churning around in a printer's RIP. When I say paths with lots of points, I mean paths with more than 100 points—the kind you get when you autotrace the scanned picture of Aunt Martha. Don't forget composite paths, either. At some point, one of these is going to trip you up. When that happens, you'll see a PostScript error message.

PostScript error messages can be cryptic in the extreme, and, best of all, seldom say what they really mean. Almost all of the PostScript errors that have the word "VMError" in them mean that your printer's run out of memory while processing the document. If you see error messages with the word "limitcheck" in them, something in your document is pushing your printer (or PostScript) past an internal limit. If you see these errors, you're going to have to apply some or all of the golden rules to your publication. In particular, try splitting some of the more complex paths in your publication and increasing the flatness of some or all of the paths in your publication.

There are two errors that have to do with downloadable fonts that are easily fixed.

- ◆ PostScript error: "limitcheck" Offending command: "framedevice"
- ◆ PostScript error: "VMError" Offending command: "array"

If you get these error messages, go to the Page Setup dialog box and check the Unlimited Downloadable Fonts box. This should fix the problem.

If you see an error containing the word "syntaxerror," you've probably made a mistake in one of the custom PostScript fills or lines you're using. Generally, these are misplaced brackets or parentheses. Look through your code and see what you've missed.

Tip:
When TIFF
Images Look
Terrible

If your job prints, but your bilevel TIFF and paint-type images look terrible, you probably need to magic-stretch them to match them to your printer's resolution. See "Resizing Images to Your Printer's Resolution" in Chapter 4, "Importing and Exporting," for more on magic-stretching.

Tip:
When
TIFF Images
Don't Print

If your job prints, but lacks a TIFF image or paint-type graphic, you probably lost your link to the image. This often happens when you take the FreeHand file to an imagesetting service bureau for printing (rather than giving them a PostScript file). Remember to take any linked TIFF or paint-type files along when you go to your service bureau, or print your file to disk as PostScript while the files are still linked; they'll be included in the PostScript file.

Tip:
Image Polarity
and Calibration

Lots of people (including me) have said that the polarity of your image (whether it's positive or negative) should be controlled at the imagesetter. We said this because we'd had problems with old versions of PostScript ROMs not inverting images. At this point, PostScript ROMs and software developers' image polarity controls are in sync, and calibration routines for several color separation programs require that you use the application's image polarity controls. Use the image controls in your printing application, instead of setting the polarity at your imagesetter, unless you're working with PostScript ROMs 47.1 or earlier.

Printing to Non-PostScript Printers

FreeHand 4's printing to QuickDraw printers has been improved from that of version 2, which would print only the screen representation of your publication. Lines now print as smoothly as is possible at the QuickDraw printer's resolution, and, if you're using ATM, you can even use type. You can print text that's been altered by most of FreeHand's transformation tools, but you won't be able to print FreeHand's PostScript text effects.

In spite of these improvements, FreeHand is a PostScript printing program, and you shouldn't expect to get more than the roughest proofs from a non-PostScript printer.

Fortune Cookie

I love fortune cookies. "Look afar, and see the end from the beginning," one fortune told me. It could've been talking about printing with FreeHand. From the time you press Command-N to create a new file, you really should be thinking, "How am I going to print this thing?"

Whenever possible, examine the processes you use to create publications in the light of the "golden rules" presented earlier in this chapter. You can almost always make something simpler from your printer's point of view without compromising the appearance of your publication.

Finally, as I always say, if something doesn't work, poke at it.

RUDDI
GORE

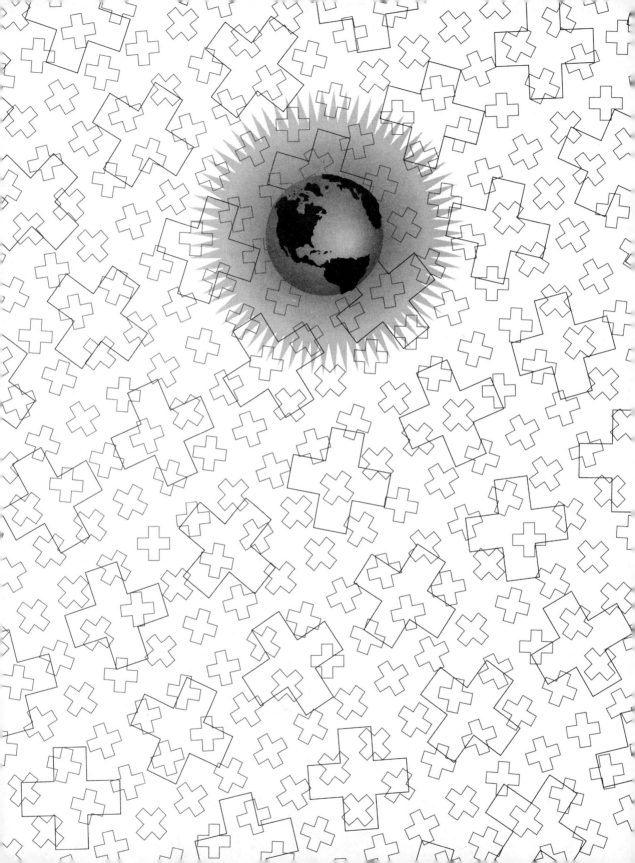

PostScript is the engine that makes desktop publishing go. If you already know all about PostScript and how your printer uses it and/or just want to know how to use it in your FreeHand publications, skip the next section. I'm about to explain PostScript, laser printing, imagesetting, and the meaning of life as I understand them, in as few words as possible. Everyone else, take a deep breath.

What Is PostScript?

PostScript is a page-description language—a programming language for describing graphic objects. It's been said that page-description languages tell your printer how to make marks on paper. This isn't quite true—your printer already knows how to make marks. Page-description languages tell your printer *what marks to make.*

PostScript has emerged as the best of the commercially available page-description languages (other page-description languages being Hewlett-Packard's PCL, Imagen's Impress, and Xerox's Interpress—these last two being "ancient history" by the standards of the computer world). This doesn't mean it's perfect, just that it's the highest standard we've got.

Inside your PostScript printer, there's a computer dedicated to controlling the printer. This computer interprets the PostScript sent to it by your Macintosh and turns it into a bitmap the size of the printer's page. The combination of printer hardware (processor and memory) and software (the version of the PostScript language in the printer's ROMs) is often called a raster image processor (RIP) because it turns a set of drawing commands into a raster image (or bitmap). You'll often hear someone talk about "ripping" a page; they mean they're running it through the RIP.

After the printer receives and processes the information for a page, the RIP transfers the bitmap from its memory to a photosensitive drum using a laser beam. The laser doesn't actually move—its beam bounces off a rotating mirror on its way to the drum. The areas where the drum is charged attract the powdered toner in the printer. When it's time to print the page, paper is pulled into the printer so that the sticky bits of toner are transferred from the drum to the paper. In an imagesetter, the laser beam directly exposes lithographic (black and white) film or paper.

What's PostScript Got to Do with FreeHand?

You can almost think of FreeHand as PostScript wearing a user interface. This isn't to say that FreeHand's internal database is PostScript (it's not), but that FreeHand approaches drawing objects the same way that PostScript does. And then there's printing. Try printing a FreeHand publication on something other than a PostScript printer, and you're in for a disappointment.

How can you use PostScript to extend FreeHand? There are three basic approaches.*

◆ You can write your own EPS files.

◆ You can examine and modify FreeHand's PostScript.

◆ You can create your own PostScript and add it to FreeHand.

---

* All of the PostScript code, PostScript special effects, and ResEdit tools discussed in this disk are included on the companion disk for this book—along with lots of other FreeHand extensions and tools. For ordering information, see the coupon inside the back cover.

Writing Your Own EPS Files

If you want to write your own PostScript files and place them in FreeHand, you'll have to convert them from "raw" PostScript to EPS. Mostly, this means you need to add the following few lines to the beginning of your file.

```
%!PS-Adobe-2.0 EPSF-1.2
%%BoundingBox: lowerLeftX lowerLeftY upperRightX upperRightY
%%EndComments
```

The variables following "%%BoundingBox" are the measurements of the image your PostScript code creates, in points. Usually, "lowerLeftX" and "lowerLeftY" are both zero. If you're not sure what the size of your image is, print the file and measure it.

The PostScript code you use inside an EPS should not include the following PostScript operators.

banddevice	exitserver	initclip
letter	nulldevice	setsccbatch
legal	renderbands	setmatrix
stop	erasepage	grestoreall
initmatrix	copypage	note
framedevice	setpageparams	initgraphics
quit		

Figure 8-1 shows an example EPS file—and what it looks like when you print it.

When you place an EPS you've created this way in FreeHand, you'll see a box, just as if you were looking at the graphic in Keyline mode. This is because the PostScript file doesn't look like anything until it's been run through a PostScript interpreter, and your Macintosh, unfortunately, doesn't have one.

Software PostScript (and PostScript clone) interpreters do exist, however. The one I'm the most familiar with is Transverter Pro, from TechPool, which does a good job of adding preview images to EPS graphics (see Appendix C, "Resources," for an address, and Appendix A, "System," for a description). In theory, you should be able to view raw PostScript files using Adobe Systems's Acrobat (it is, after all, a PostScript interpreter), but I've never been able to get it to work for that purpose.

```
%!PS-Adobe-2.0 EPSF-1.2
%%BoundingBox: 0 0 612 792
%%Creator:(Greg Stumph)
%%Title:(Fractal Tree)
%%CreationDate:(9-25-90)
%%EndComments
%% set up variables
/bdf
   {bind def} bind def
/depth 0 def
%% maxdepth controls how many branchings occur
%% exceeding 15 will be VERY time consuming
/maxdepth 10 def
%% after branching "cutoff" times, the branch angles increase
%% set cutoff higher than maxdepth to supress this
/cutoff 4 def
/length
   {rand 72 mod 108 add} bdf
/ang
   {rand 10 mod 10 add} bdf
/sway
   {rand 60 mod 30 sub} bdf
/NewLine
   {sway length 3 div sway length 3 div
   0 length rcurveto currentpoint
   depth 1 sub maxdepth div setgray
   stroke translate 0 0 moveto} bdf
/down
   {/depth depth 1 add def
   depth cutoff gt
     {/ang
        {rand 30 mod 20 add} bdf
     } if
   } bdf
/up
   {/depth depth 1 sub def
   depth cutoff le
     {/ang
        {rand 10 mod 10 add} bdf
     } if
   } bdf
%% FractBranch is the loop that does all the work,
%% by calling itself recursively
/FractBranch
   {gsave .8 .8 scale
   down NewLine
   depth maxdepth lt
     {ang rotate FractBranch
     ang 2 mul neg rotate FractBranch} if
   up grestore
   } def
gsave
```

FIGURE 8-1
EPS file
(continued)

```
306 72 translate 0 0 moveto
10 setlinewidth
1 setlinecap
currentscreen 3 -1 roll
pop 65 3 1 roll setscreen
FractBranch
grestore
%%End of file
```

*What this EPS file looks
like when you print it.*

Looking at FreeHand's PostScript

If you're curious, or if you're creating your own UserPrep file or external resource file, you should also take a look at FreeHand's PostScript to see if there's something there you can use. Knowing FreeHand's PostScript can keep you from "reinventing the wheel" when you write your own code.

One of the most beautiful things about PostScript is that it's just text—which means you can open it in any word processor.

While you can create PostScript files by turning on File in the LaserWriter driver, I use FreeHand's Export command, and choose Generic EPS. Files created this way are a little bit smaller and are guaranteed to contain only FreeHand code.

The first time you open a FreeHand PostScript or EPS file, what you see can be rather intimidating. What is all this stuff?

The most important code can be found between the lines

```
%%BeginResource: procset Altsys_header 4 0
```

and

```
%%EndProlog
```

Everything between these two lines is one or another of Free-Hand's PostScript dictionaries (see Figure 8-2). Specifically, you should look at the PostScript definitions following "/supdict 65 dict def" and "/ropedict 85 dict def." These are the support routines for FreeHand's custom PostScript fills and strokes. If you can't see these dictionaries, make sure the file you've printed to disk contains at least one custom stroke or fill.

FIGURE 8-2
Finding FreeHand's
PostScript dictionaries

*Everything from
this line...*

*...to this line is one of
FreeHand's PostScript
dictionaries.*

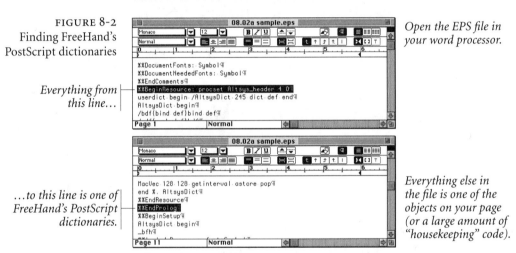

*Open the EPS file in
your word processor.*

*Everything else in
the file is one of the
objects on your page
(or a large amount of
"housekeeping" code).*

If you're looking for the objects you've drawn, scroll to the end of the file, then scroll up a couple of screens. When you see the line "%%BeginPageSetup," you've reached the start of a FreeHand page (while your publication might contain more than one page, I advise examining FreeHand's PostScript one page at a time—it's less confusing). Scroll down until you see a line ending with "m"—it's the start of the first path you've drawn (see Figure 8-3).

Don't be scared—you don't have to know this stuff to enter most of the new PostScript strokes and fills in this chapter. The code is pretty well annotated with comments (by software engineering standards) and you should be able to understand some of it just by looking at it. PostScript comments are preceded by a "%" and are ignored by PostScript interpreters.

FIGURE 8-3
Finding what
you've drawn

*Here's the start of
a path drawn in
FreeHand.*

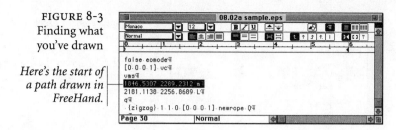

*What't the rest of the
code you can see in the
example screen mean?*

`false eomode`	*Turns off overprinting.*
`[0 0 0 1] vc`	*Sets the color to black.*
`vms`	*Manages printer memory.*
`1846.5307 2289.2312 m`	*Moves to the coordinates shown.*
`2181.1138 2256.8689 L`	*Draws a path to these coordinates, from the coordinates in the previous line.*
`q`	*Manages printer memory ("gsave")*
`{zigzag} 1 1 0 [0 0 0 1] newrope Q`	*Applies the custom line style Zigzag.*

If you're having trouble making sense of the PostScript file, remember that procedures begin with a "/" and end with a "}def" or "}bdef". Here's an example of a procedure.

```
%%procedure for picking a random integer
/randint {rand exch mod } def
```

Looking at FreeHand's PostScript Resources

The Post resources inside FreeHand contain all of FreeHand's Post-Script code. If you're creating your own PostScript code, or if you're creating external resource files, you'll probably find it helpful to take a look at these resources.

To open FreeHand's Post resources using ResEdit (a free programmer's tool from Apple available from user groups and Apple's Internet site, ftp.apple.com), follow the steps below (see Figure 8-4). If you haven't created a template for the Post resource class, you might want to skip ahead to "Creating External Resource Files" to find out how. It's much easier to look at and edit these resources if you use a template (ResEdit's existing POST template won't work).

1. Launch ResEdit.

FIGURE 8-4
Viewing FreeHand's
PostScript resources

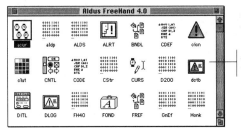

*Open a copy of FreeHand
with ResEdit.*

*ResEdit displays the resources
inside FreeHand.*

*Double-click the
Post resource class.*

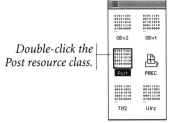

*ResEdit displays
a listing of the
Post resources
in FreeHand.*

*Double-click
one of the Post
resources...*

*...and ResEdit displays
the contents of the
resource.*

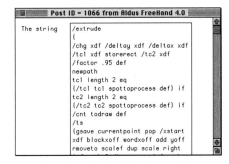

*If you haven't created a
template for Post resources,
you'll see something like this.*

*If you've skipped ahead and created a
resource template for the Post resource
class, you'll see something like this.*

2. Locate and open your FreeHand application. Always work on a copy of FreeHand so that you don't inadvertently damage the application.

3. Type "post" to scroll down to the Post resource class and press Return to open the class (or double-click the icon).

4. ResEdit displays a list of the Post resources in FreeHand.

5. Double-click any one of the resources to see its contents.

6. When you're finished looking at the resources, close the file or quit ResEdit.

The resources are labelled by number, and it can take a while to locate the code you want. Since I've already gone through the resources, I can tell you where things are (see Table 8-1). When you see "\n" inside these resources, read it as a carriage return.

Resource ID	What's in it
1066	Zoom text effect (known internally as "extrude")
1067	Inline text effect
1085	AltsysDict, FreeHand's main PostScript dictionary
1086	PostScript error handler, the code that prints PostScript error messages on your pages when something goes wrong
1125	Code for drawing crop marks
1126	Code for drawing registration marks
1145	supdict, which contains procedures used by the custom fill and custom stroke effects
1146	ropedict, the PostScript dictionary containing support routines for custom PostScript strokes
1147	texturedict, the PostScript dictionary containing code for rendering FreeHand's textured fills (Coquille, Sand, Denim, etc.)
1148	Bricks fill effect
1149	Tiger Teeth fill effect
1150	Circles fill effect
1151	Squares fill effect
1152	Hatch fill effect
1153	Random Leaves fill effect
1154	Random Grass fill effect
1155	Noise fill effect
1156	Black-and-White Noise fill effect
1158	Neon stroke effect
1160	Burlap textured fill

TABLE 8-1
Selected FreeHand
Post resources
(continued)

Resource ID	What's in it
1161	Sand textured fill
1162	Coarse Gravel textured fill
1163	Fine Gravel textured fill
1164	Light Mezzo and Heavy Mezzo textured fills
1165	Medium Mezzo textured fill
1166	Coquille textured fill
1167	Arrow stroke effect
1168	Braid stroke effect
1169	Crepe stroke effect
1170	Snowflake stroke effect
1171	Teeth stroke effect
1172	Two Waves stroke effect
1173	Three Waves stroke effect
1174	Wedge stroke effect
1175	Star stroke effect
1176	Cartographer stroke effect
1177	Checker stroke effect
1178	Dot stroke effect
1179	Diamond stroke effect
1180	Right Diagonal stroke effect
1181	Left Diagonal stroke effect
1182	Rectangle stroke effect
1183	Ball stroke effect
1184	Squiggle stroke effect
1185	Swirl stroke effect
1186	Zigzag stroke effect
1187	Roman stroke effect
1188	Heart stroke effect

What's the point of all of this? If you know where something is, you can change it, which is what most of the rest of this chapter is about. If you're happy with everything about the way FreeHand prints, or don't feel the urge to create your own PostScript effects, or aren't curious, you can skip the rest of the chapter. If you want to change the way FreeHand prints crop marks, or add new Post-Script line and fill effects, or really know what's going on under the hood, read on.

Variables in FreeHand's PostScript

Did you ever wonder how FreeHand tells your printer to change to a new font, scale the font, and draw a string of text? If you used ResEdit to open Post resource ID 1226 and 1054 inside FreeHand, you'd see the resources shown in Figure 8-5.

FIGURE 8-5
Filling out the form

When you print (or export a file as an EPS), FreeHand takes the information (in this example, some text set in Sabon) in your publication and merges it with PostScript from its Post resources.

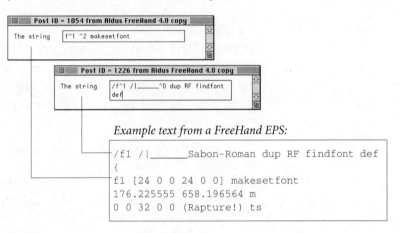

Example text from a FreeHand EPS:

```
/f1 /|_____Sabon-Roman dup RF findfont def
{
f1 [24 0 0 24 0 0] makesetfont
176.225555 658.196564 m
0 0 32 0 0 (Rapture!) ts
```

Compare the example with the Post resources. Do they look similar? You bet—the Post resource is a blank form for the code FreeHand sends (to your printer or to disk) when it specifies a font. The characters preceded by a caret (^) are FreeHand's internal representations of the data it'll use to fill out the form. Some of the tags are pretty easy to figure out—in this example, "^1" in Post ID 1226 equals "1" and "^0" equals "Sabon-Roman."

"^2" in Post ID 1226 is a little more complicated—it's an array containing the font's scaling. The example text is 24 points and hasn't been scaled horizontally (if it had been, you'd see a different number in the first position in the array).

Changing FreeHand's PostScript

There's more to opening FreeHand's PostScript resources with Res-Edit than merely snooping around, of course. Once you have an idea where things are, you can change them.

If you do change FreeHand's resources, however, bear in mind that you do so entirely at your own risk. These techniques are not supported by Aldus, Altsys, or Peachpit Press—though I'll take a shot at helping you if you get stuck (see Appendix C, "Resources," for contact information).

Making Textured Fills Transparent

If you want FreeHand's textured fills (Burlap, Denim, Coquille, etc.) to print with a transparent background, you can edit the Post resource that controls the way that they print. This is one of the simplest, easiest, and most useful changes you can make to Free-Hand's Post resources.

First, if you haven't already skipped ahead to build yourself a Post resource template, do so now. The example screens I'll show use the template, not the hexadecimal display.

To make FreeHand's textured fills transparent, follow these steps (see Figure 8-6).

1. Start ResEdit. Locate and open a copy of FreeHand.

2. Locate and select the Post resource class, and open it by pressing Return (or by double-clicking on the icon). ResEdit opens FreeHand's Post resource class and displays a list of all the Post resources inside FreeHand.

3. Select and open Post resource ID 1147.

4. Scroll through the resource until you see the following lines.

    ```
    gsave
    [0 0 0 0] vc
    filler
    grestore
    ```

5. Type "%%" in front of each of these lines.

    ```
    %%gsave
    %%[0 0 0 0] vc
    %%filler
    %%grestore
    ```

FIGURE 8-6
Making textured
fills transparent

*Default (textured fill prints
with an opaque background).*

*Edited version (textured fill prints
with a transparent background).*

Color 1 overlay　　*Black overlay*　　　*Color 1 overlay*　　*Black overlay*

*Use ResEdit to open a
copy of FreeHand.
Locate and open Post
resource ID 1147.*

*Scroll through the resource until
you locate these four lines of text.*

*Type "%%" before
each of the four lines
and save this copy
of FreeHand.*

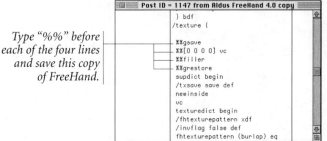

*When you use this copy of
FreeHand, textured fills will print
with transparent backgrounds.*

6. Press Command-S to save the edited copy of FreeHand.
   Quit ResEdit.

When you print textured fills from this copy of FreeHand, they'll
print with transparent backgrounds (though they'll still be opaque
on screen). If you want an opaque background behind one of your
textured fills, draw an opaque shape behind the object containing
the textured fill.

**Overprinting
TIFFs**

If you read Chapter 4, "Importing and Exporting," you'll remember that I complained about FreeHand's lack of a separate control
for overprinting grayscale TIFFs. This is no problem when you're

overprinting the ink you've used to color the TIFF, but what if you can't do that?

To find out what was going on, I printed a file to disk (with Separations turned on in the Print dialog box), then opened the file with Microsoft Word and looked through the file for anything that seemed suspicious. Immediately after the TIFF image in the PostScript file, I saw the following line.

```
[0 0 0 0] vc 0 0 21.6001 22.3201 rectfill
```

There it was: the grail. And all you have to do is comment out that line (which sets the color of the box), and the TIFF will overprint. Make the change in the resource, and all grayscale TIFFs will overprint (see Figure 8-7).

The following steps show you how. We won't alter FreeHand itself—instead, we'll create an external resource file. This way, you can turn your new "feature" on and off without editing FreeHand.

1. Launch ResEdit.

2. Locate and open a copy of FreeHand.

3. Open the Post resource class. ResEdit displays all of the Post resources in FreeHand.

4. Select Post resource ID 1209 and press Command-C. Close the copy of FreeHand (if you're asked if you want to save changes, click No).

5. Press Command-N to create a new resource. Name it "no knockout.agx1" (or something like that) and save it in the same folder as your copy of FreeHand. ResEdit creates your new, empty resource file.

6. Press Command-V to paste the Post resource you copied out of FreeHand into your new resource file.

7. Open the Post resource class and open the single Post resource inside. Scroll to the end of the resource and type "%%" at the start of the last line in the resource.

```
%%[0 0 0 0] vc 0 0 21.6001 22.3201 rectfill
```

FIGURE 8-7
Overprinting
grayscale TIFFs

*Select Post resource ID 1209,
and copy it to the Clipboard.*

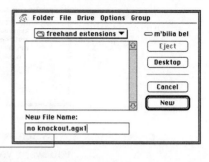

*Press Command-N to create
a new resource file. Give the
file a name and save it.*

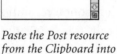

*Paste the Post resource
from the Clipboard into
the new file.*

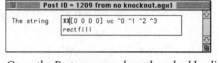

*Open the Post resource class, then double-click the
Post resource (there should be only one) to open it.
Type "%%" before the first line of the resource and
close the resource.*

*Type "AGX1" in
the Type field.*

*Type "FH40" in
the Creator field.*

*Choose Get Info
for* filename *from the
File menu.*

Save and close the file.

8. Choose Get Info for *filename* from the File menu. In the
Type field, type "AGX1". Type "FH40" in the Creator field.
Save your file and quit ResEdit.

The next time you start FreeHand, you'll see a dialog box asking if you want to load the resource or not (see Figure 8-8). You
do, so press Return (or click the OK button). To get rid of this
annoying message, you'll have to add an Xvrs resource to your
external resource file (see "Creating External Resource Files," later
in this chapter).

FIGURE 8-8
An overly grim
dialog box

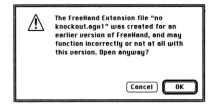

The FreeHand Extension file "no knockout.agx1" was created for an earlier version of FreeHand, and may function incorrectly or not at all with this version. Open anyway?

Cancel   OK

When you print, your grayscale TIFFs won't knock out. When you want your grayscale TIFFs to knock out again, just move the file out of the FreeHand folder and restart FreeHand, or, better, draw a box behind them.

Printing Error Messages on High-Resolution Printers

I frequently print proof pages on a printer with a vertical resolution of 1,000 dpi and a horizontal resolution of 400 dpi (the manufacturer optimistically calls this "1,000 dpi"). When there's something wrong with the PostScript I've entered in FreeHand, no error messages print on my printer. Why?

When FreeHand's PostScript detects an error during printing, it checks the resolution of the printer. If the printer's resolution is 1,000 dpi or above, FreeHand doesn't print an error message. This is great—it keeps you from printing PostScript error messages on expensive imagesetter film. But what about those of us printing to high-resolution, plain-paper laser printers?

All we have to do is raise the threshold at which FreeHand stops printing error messages. This is another great use for an external resource file.

1. Open a copy of FreeHand using ResEdit.

2. Open FreeHand's Post resources.

3. Select Post resource ID 1086 and press Command-C. Close the open copy of FreeHand.

4. Create a new resource file named "hi-res errors.agx1" (or whatever—the file extension's not important, but it does help you see what the file is in the Finder) and save it in the same folder as your copy of FreeHand.

5. Paste the Post resource you copied out of FreeHand into your new resource file.

6. Open the Post resource class and open the Post resource inside. Scroll through the resource until you see the following line.

```
printerRes 1000 lt
```

7. Change the value so that it's at least one greater than your printer's resolution.

```
printerRes 1001 lt
```

8. Choose Get Info for *filename* from the File menu. In the Type field, type "AGX1". Type "FH40" in the Creator field. Save your file and quit ResEdit.

If you do make this change, make sure that you remove the external resource file from the FreeHand folder and restart FreeHand before you print to an imagesetter (or print PostScript to the disk you intend to take to an imagesetter). If you don't, you could end up printing error messages on imagesetter film—a very expensive way to learn about a typo.

Again, without an Xvrs resource, this external resource file will make FreeHand complain as you start it (see "Adding an Xvrs Resource," later in this chapter).

Creating Your Own PostScript Effects

There are several different ways to enter your own PostScript code.

◆ You can attach your own PostScript code to FreeHand objects by choosing PostScript in the Fill Inspector or the Stroke Inspector and entering up to 255 characters of code.

◆ You can create your own PostScript effects, defining them as procedures, and save them in a special file named "UserPrep". Then you can activate those procedures by typing the procedure names (and appropriate parameters) in the PostScript sections of FreeHand's Stroke and Fill Inspectors. This gets you around the 255-character limit.

◆ You can create your own PostScript effects and turn them into FreeHand external resource files. Once you do this, they'll appear when you choose Custom from the Fill Type or Stroke Type popup menus in the Fill or Stroke Inspector.

Typing PostScript in the Fill and Stroke Inspectors

When you choose PostScript from either the Fill Type or Stroke Type popup menus in the Fill Inspector or Stroke Inspector, a large field appears at the bottom of the Inspector. You can type up to 255 characters of PostScript code in this field (or you can paste in text you've entered elsewhere). Press Return, and FreeHand applies the code you enter here to the selected object as a PostScript fill or stroke effect.

In some ways, this is the easiest way to get PostScript you've into FreeHand, provided the code fits in the field. The trouble is, 255 characters isn't a lot of code. You can cut down the number of characters used by making your variable and procedure names shorter ("ls" instead of "lineStart," for example), but this only works to a certain point.

In fact, it sometimes looks like FreeHand accepts more than 255 characters in this text edit field—the field accepts the characters without complaint. But when you press Return, FreeHand will truncate the contents of the field, leaving only 255 characters.

There are three ways around this limitation. You can rely on procedures that you know are already defined in FreeHand and use them in your PostScript code, you can rely on procedures you've created in your own UserPrep file, or you can create your own external resource files. These three techniques are covered later in this chapter.

The following steps show you how to apply a simple PostScript stroke effect (see "PostScript Strokes" in Chapter 2, "Drawing").

1. Draw a line.

2. Press Command-Option-L to display the Stroke Inspector.

3. Choose PostScript from the Stroke Type popup menu. The PostScript Code field appears at the bottom of the Inspector.

4. Type PostScript code in the field (you can delete the default code "stroke").

5. Press Return to apply your PostScript stroke.

The selected path won't look any different on screen, but when you print to a PostScript printer, the effect you've typed is applied to the path.

Figure 8-9 shows a few stroke effects you can enter. As you enter this code, you'll see procedures that don't look like "normal" Post-Script. That is, instead of typing "exch def" you'll type "xdf". I can do this because I know FreeHand's already defined "xdf" as "exch def"—it's a kind of shorthand. For a list of PostScript shortcuts defined by FreeHand, see Table 8-2.

FIGURE 8-9
PostScript strokes

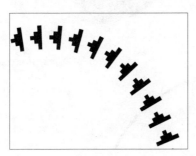

Example PostScript stroke code
```
currentlinewidth /lw exch cvi
def gsave [lw lw 4 mul] 0
setdash lw 6 mul setlinewidth
stroke grestore gsave [lw lw 4
mul] lw setdash lw 3 mul
setlinewidth stroke grestore
gsave [lw lw 4 mul] lw 2 mul
setdash lw setlinewidth stroke
grestore
```

Shorthand version of above
```
currentlinewidth /lw exch cvi
def q [lw lw 4 mul] 0 d lw 6
mul w S Q q [lw lw 4 mul] lw d
lw 3 mul w S Q q [lw lw 4 mul]
lw 2 mul d lw w S Q
```

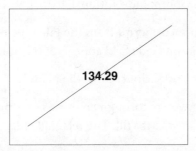

Dimension line code
```
pathbbox /t xdf /r xdf /b xdf
/l xdf /dx r l sub def /dy t b
sub def S /ts 20 string def /
Helvetica-Bold findfont 9
scalefont setfont l b trans-
late dx 2 div dy 2 div 3 sub m
dx 2 exp dy 2 exp add sqrt ts
cvs stringwidth pop 2 div neg
0 rmoveto ts show S
```

FIGURE 8-9
PostScript strokes
(continued)

Graduated line code

```
cvc /CC xdf /ks 25 def /kp 1 1
ks div sub def 0 1 ks { /c xdf
[1 ks 1 sub] c 2 add d cvc
length 4 eq {cvc {kp mul}
forall 4 array astore /cvc
xdf}{cvc 0 get kp mul /nt xdf
cvc 0 nt put} ifelse cvc vc q
S Q } for CC vc
```

Ribbon line code

```
cvc /CC xdf /ks 25 def /kp .5
ks div def 0 1 ks 2 mul {/c
xdf [1 ks 2 mul 1 sub] c 2 add
d /kz c ks le {{kp sub}}{{kp
add}} ifelse def cvc length 4
eq {cvc {kz} forall 4 array
astore}{cvc 0 get kz /nt xdf
cvc 0 nt put cvc} ifelse vc q
S Q} for CC vc
```

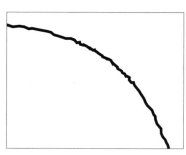

Shaky line code

```
23 srand 0 setflat /ri {cvi
rand exch mod} def flattenpath
{newpath m} {2 {1 dup 2 mul ri
sub add exch} repeat L} {} {}
pathforall S
```

PostScript fill effects work just like PostScript stroke effects. You can type up to 255 characters in the PostScript Code field (see "PostScript Strokes" in Chapter 2, "Drawing").

1. Draw a rectangle.

2. Press Command-Option-F to display the Fill Inspector.

3. Choose PostScript from the Fill Type popup menu. The PostScript Code field appears at the bottom of the Inspector.

4. Enter PostScript code in the field.

5. When you're through entering code, press Return to apply your PostScript fill. The rectangle fills with "PS".

Figure 8-10 shows a few more PostScript fill effects.

	Name	What it does
TABLE 8-2 FreeHand's shorthand for commonly used procedures	F	Fills the current path with the current color
	f	Closes the current path, then fills it with the current color
	S	Strokes the current path with the current line weight, color, and dash pattern
	s	Closes the current path, then strokes it
	q	Saves the current graphic state (more or less the same as PostScript's "gsave" operator)
	Q	Restores the previously saved graphic state (like PostScript's "grestore" operator)
	w	Sets the stroke width. Same as the PostScript operator "setlinewidth"
	n	Same as the PostScript operator "newpath"
	d	Sets the dash pattern of a path. Same as the PostScript operator "setdash"
	xdf	Defines the current variable name with whatever's on top of the operand stack. Same as "exch def"
	vc	Sets the current color
	cvc	Current color array (every time you use "vc", "cvc" updates)

Creating and Using a UserPrep File

If you've created some PostScript line or fill effects or have borrowed them from some other source (such as this book, other PostScript books, or the text files you found on someone's CorelDraw disks) and want to use them in FreeHand, the simplest thing to do is to create a PostScript dictionary of your own (see Figure 8-11).

1. Using a word processor or a PostScript programming tool such as LaserTalk from Adobe Systems, create a series of procedures you want to use.

FIGURE 8-10
PostScript fills

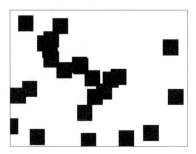

Random Squares code
```
23 srand pathbbox clipper /kt
xdf /kr xdf /kb xdf /kl xdf n
/dx kr kl sub def /dy kt kb
sub def /ri {cvi rand exch
mod} def /sz 12 def kl sz sub
kb sz sub translate 0 0 m /rl
{rlineto} def 24 {dx ri dy ri
m sz 0 rl 0 sz rl sz neg 0 rl
f} repeat
```

Random Triangles code
```
23 srand pathbbox clipper /kt
xdf /kr xdf /kb xdf /kl xdf n
/dx kr kl sub def /dy kt kb
sub def /ri {cvi rand exch
mod} def /sz 12 def kl sz sub
kb sz sub translate 0 0 m /rl
{rlineto} def 24 {dx ri dy ri
m sz 0 rl sz 2 div neg sz rl
f} repeat
```

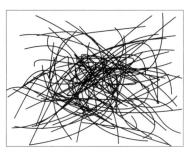

Scribble code
```
23 srand pathbbox clipper /kt
xdf /kr xdf /kb xdf /kl xdf n
/dx kr kl sub def /dy kt kb
sub def /ri {cvi rand exch
mod} def /xy {dx ri dy ri} def
kl kb translate 0 0 m 60 {q xy
m xy xy xy C .5 w S Q} repeat
```

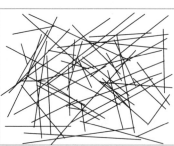

Straight Scribble code
```
23 srand pathbbox clipper /kt
xdf /kr xdf /kb xdf /kl xdf n
/dx kr kl sub def /dy kt kb
sub def /ri {cvi rand exch
mod} def /xy {dx ri dy ri} def
kl kb translate 0 0 m 60 {q xy
m xy L .5 w S Q} repeat
```

2. Save the procedures as a text-only file named UserPrep, and place the file inside the folder containing your copy of FreeHand.

3. In FreeHand, select a path to which you want to apply one of your new PostScript effects.

4. Display the Fill or Stroke Inspector.

5. Choose PostScript from the Fill Type or Stroke Type popup menu.

6. Type the name of your procedure in the PostScript code field, preceding it with any variables it requires.

7. Press Return to apply your effect to the selected path.

```
%%UserPrep
/scribble
%%on stack: random number seed, line weight, number of lines
{/ns xdf
/lineWeight xdf
/seed xdf
seed srand lineWeight w
flattenpath pathbbox clip
/top xdf
/right xdf
/bottom xdf
/left xdf
cvc /CVC xdf
cvc length 4 eq
  {/colorChange{cvc {newTint} forall 4 array astore vc} def}
  {/colorChange{cvc 0 get {newTint} mul /tint xdf cvc 0 tint put vc} def
} ifelse
/randint {rand exch mod} def
/newTint {/random {100 randint .01 mul} def random mul} def
/xy
  {rand right left sub cvi mod left add rand
  top bottom sub cvi mod bottom add
} bdf
ns {n xy m xy xy xy C colorChange S CVC vc} repeat
} def
%%End UserPrep
```

Type the parameters your new fill effect expects in the Fill Inspector, followed by the name of the procedure. In this example, you'd type a seed for the random number generator, the line width, and the number of lines you want, followed by "scribble" (the name of the fill).

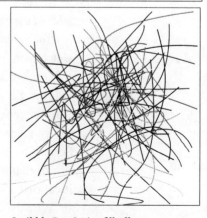

Scribble PostScript fill effect

8. Print your publication. If you get a PostScript error or if nothing prints, you've made a mistake in either your UserPrep or the way you entered the procedure. Find it and fix it. Errors containing the words "nostringval", "nocurrentpoint", and "stack underflow" are usually caused by entering a variable improperly before the procedure name in the PostScript Code field (in either the Fill or Stroke Inspector).

Creating External Resource Files

One of FreeHand 4's most significant features is that you can extend the program using external resource files. How does this work? FreeHand, on startup, loads files of type AGX1 it finds in its folder. FreeHand loads the resources found in these files as if they were resources found inside your copy of FreeHand. If the resource IDs in your AGX1 files match the IDs of resources that FreeHand's already loaded, the external resources override the internal resources.

Almost any preexisting resource in FreeHand can be replaced by an external resource file, and whole new resources can be added. Before you go off half-cocked and start trying to add charting modules to FreeHand, though, let me point out a few practical limitations. We can't easily get at how FreeHand works, because most of the active part of FreeHand is compiled code. We can, however, get at *what* this active part of FreeHand works with.

We can, for example, easily add menu items to the popup menus in the Fill and Stroke Inspectors, but it's quite another matter to add a new popup menu. FreeHand wouldn't know what to do with it (unless you added new MDEF and CODE resources—which is way beyond the scope of this book).

Don't take these limitations too hard. The number of things you can do with external resource files is mind-boggling. The Free-Hand extensions that I find most exciting are the ones that change the way FreeHand prints objects and the ones that add new Post-Script strokes and fills. I've placed most of this book's discussion of external resource files in this chapter because these exciting modifications and additions have to do with PostScript.

Why use external resource files to add PostScript effects instead of creating a UserPrep file? Because it's too easy to make mistakes entering variables for an external UserPrep. External resources make it easy to remember what variables a procedure needs, because you can add your own buttons, fields, and popup menus in the Fill and Stroke Inspectors. Creating external resource files is much more difficult than creating a UserPrep file, but it's worth it.

Creating resource templates. Before you can create any external resources for FreeHand, you've got to create four resource templates in ResEdit. Don't let that deter you, though. This part is easy. You don't have to know the theory of how this stuff works—I don't. I just know what to do to get the results I want, and I'm happy to share the results of my trial-and-error experimentation with you.

We'll be creating templates named GnEf, Post (PostScript; this resource type differs from the built-in Post resource, so don't think you can skip creating this one), UIrz, and Xvrs. We'll add the templates to a copy of ResEdit, which we'll then use to create external resource files. If you developed any FreeHand 3 external resource files, you should note that the LnEf, FlEf, and Scrn resources are not used by FreeHand 4, and that the Post resource has a new format. "Great," I said when I first opened FreeHand 4 with Res-Edit. "Everything I know is wrong."

I used ResEdit 2.1.1 to create my templates, and I strongly suggest you use this version or later. Version 2.1 is light-years ahead of earlier versions in stability, capability, and ease of use. If it gets much better, they'll have to start charging money for it.

I cannot thank Apple Computer enough for this tool, which makes it (relatively) easy for Macintosh users to augment and customize their system software and applications. Nothing like ResEdit exists on any other platform. The one problem is distribution: although it's "free," Apple charges a small fee for distribution. Consequently, you won't find it online or with shareware collections. They do keep it on their Internet site (ftp.apple.com), and many user groups have paid the small fee to distribute it.

We'll create the Post resource template first, following the steps below (see Figure 8-12).

1. Make a copy of ResEdit and open the copy with ResEdit.

2. Locate and select the TMPL resource (you can just type "T" to move to the resource). Double-click to open it. A listing of available templates appears.

3. Press Command-K to create a new template. We're going to use Command-K again several different times in this procedure, to do several different things. What Command-K does varies depending on the context you're in (usually changing based on what you've got selected). Command-K generally means "create another one," with the object being created determined by what window you're in or what you've got selected. In this case, a new, empty template appears.

4. Select the field tag "1)*****" in the template window and press Command-K to create a new field. Two new fields, Label and Type appear, along with another field tag "2)*****".

5. Type "PostScript:" in the Label field, then type "CSTR" in the Type field.

6. Press Command-I to display the Info window for the template. Type a fairly high number (I use 2000) in the ID field. You do this to keep the new resource ID from conflicting with the preexisting templates. Press Tab to move to the Name field. Type "Post" in the Name field and press Command-W twice to close both the Info window and the TMPL window.

Your new resource template appears in the listing of templates. Follow the same procedure to create three more resource templates, entering the values shown in Table 8-3 in each field as you create it. The labels aren't technically necessary—they just make the resources a little easier to decipher. Some data types (such as AWRDs and ALNGs) don't need labels—they're just byte padding in the resource and aren't displayed when you open the resource with the template.

We've just built four new ResEdit tools for creating and editing FreeHand 4 external resource files. Save your changes and quit this

FIGURE 8-12
Creating ResEdit
templates

Open a copy of ResEdit.

Double-click the TMPL resource class.

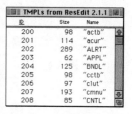

ResEdit displays a list of resource templates.

Press Command-K to create a new template. ResEdit displays a window where you can edit the definition of the template.

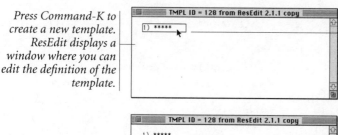

Select the first field tag in the template and press Command-K.

ResEdit creates two new fields.

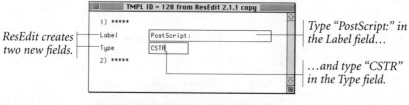

Type "PostScript:" in the Label field...

...and type "CSTR" in the Type field.

Press Command-I. ResEdit displays the Info window for your new resource.

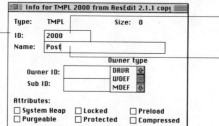

Type an ID number for the resource here.

Enter a name (in this case, "Post") for the template here.

Press Command-W twice to close the Info window and the TMPL window, and save the copy of ResEdit.

copy of ResEdit. We'll be using the copy of ResEdit we've modified, so you can throw away the original copy of ResEdit (just kidding—back it up so that you'll always be able to retrace your steps if something doesn't work).

To make sure that you've correctly created the templates, follow these steps (see Figure 8-13).

1. Open the modified copy of ResEdit.

2. Press Command-N to create a new file. Type a name for the file and press Return. A new file window opens.

TABLE 8-3
Template parameters

Name	Field	Label	Type
Xvrs	1	Just enter 0	CSTR
GnEf	1	Version:	DWRD
	2	Type:	DWRD
	3	Number of parameters:	DWRD
	4	Name:	CSTR
	5		AWRD
	6	User name:	CSTR
	7		AWRD
	8	PostScript resources needed:	0CNT
	9	*****	LSTC
	10	ID# (-1000)	DWRD
	11	*****	LSTE
	12	PostScript to invoke effect:	CSTR
	13		ALNG
	14	UIrz ID:	DLNG
	15	*****	LSTB
	16	Type:	DLNG
	17	Minimum:	DLNG
	18	Maximum:	DLNG
	19	Default:	DLNG
	20	*****	LSTE
UIrz	1	Number of items:	DWRD
	2	*****	LSTB
	3	Type:	CSTR
	4		AWRD
	5	Frame:	RECT
	6	Resource ID:	DWRD
	7	Flags:	H004
	8	Title:	CSTR
	9		AWRD
	10	Tag:	DLNG
	11	*****	LSTE

FIGURE 8-13
Testing the
resource
templates

*Create a new
resource file.*

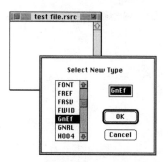

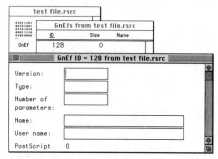

*Press Command-K to
add a new resource.*

*ResEdit creates the resource and
displays the resource template.*

3. Press Command-K to create a new resource. ResEdit
   displays the Select New Type dialog box. Scroll through the
   list of templates until you find one of the templates you
   added to this copy of ResEdit. Select one and press Return
   to close the dialog box.

If you've built the new templates correctly, ResEdit creates a
new resource and opens a view of the resource that's formatted
according to the template's instructions. If this doesn't happen, go
back to the steps above and try to figure out what went wrong. Are
you sure you're using the copy of ResEdit you modified?

Test all four of the templates. When you're through, you can
throw this dummy resource file away.

What do these resources do? When you choose a custom fill or
stroke from the Inspector's popup menu, FreeHand looks for a
GnEf matching the menu item. The GnEf then tells FreeHand where
to look for the UIrz resource, which contains the text edit fields,
buttons, and color wells that appear in the Inspector. Values in the
GnEf then set the defaults for the Inspector items. The GnEf also
tells FreeHand the IDs of the Post resources the effect needs to
print and how to invoke the effect when it's applied to a path.

GnEfs are the key to FreeHand's custom stroke and fill resources
(see Figure 8-14).

Creating new PostScript lines and fills. Even if you don't know
PostScript, this section shows you how to add a variety of new
PostScript strokes and fills to FreeHand. If you do know PostScript,

FIGURE 8-14
The GnEf resource
keeps track of other
resource locations

*These fields point to
the Post resources
required to print the
effect (the number you
enter here is 1000
less than the actual
Post resource ID).*

*This field points to the
location of the effect's
UIrz resource.*

*These fields (from
here to the end of the
resource) tell FreeHand
how to work with the
buttons and fields
for the effect (which
are found in the
UIrz resource).*

*The resource name of the
Post resource containing
the effect must match the
name you entered in the
Name field.*

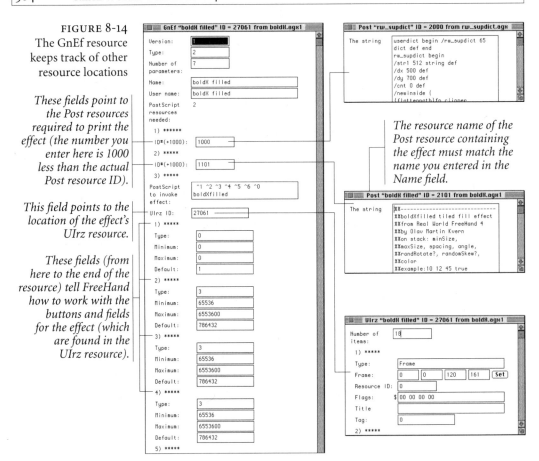

the examples in this section will show you how to fit your code into FreeHand's scheme of things. There are really three ways to add PostScript strokes and fills to FreeHand.

◆ Add new lines and fills based on support routines already inside FreeHand.

◆ Add new lines and fills based on support routines outside of FreeHand (in an external resource file).

◆ Mixing and matching the two above methods.

What's the big deal about support routines? While you can create a simple PostScript line by typing PostScript code in the PostScript dialog box, remember that you're limited to 255 characters. If you want an effect that repeats some shape along a path or changes shape randomly, you'll probably need more room. Most PostScript is based on pieces of code that are used over and over again to do some particular function (picking a random integer, for example). These pieces of code are called support routines. They can't create the effect you want by themselves, but they keep you from having to reinvent the wheel (that is, retype the same routines) every time you want to create a new PostScript effect.

Why would you want to use FreeHand's existing routines? Free-Hand's PostScript user dictionary contains routines for repeating an object along a path (stroke effects), for filling a path with a repeated shape (fill effects), and for filling a path with a randomly rotated and scaled shape (more fill effects). I don't know about you, but it would take me literally years to write PostScript code that'd do these things. And there's more good stuff inside Free-Hand for you to take advantage of. The drawback to using the internal support routines? You have to know what they are and how to use them.

Why would you want to use your own routines? Because you know them better. If you're a PostScript hack like David Blatner of PSpatterns fame, you've already written totally different routines for doing the same things (and different things, too) and have a certain number of PostScript effects you created for FreeHand 3 you want to convert to FreeHand 4 external resources.

Clearly, mixing and matching has the potential to give you the best of both worlds. Whenever possible, you can use the code that Altsys and Aldus spent blood, sweat, and person-years creating. And then, when necessary, you can create your own support dictionary to do things beyond the scope of the built-in code.

Creating Custom PostScript Strokes

You can use FreeHand's built-in custom stroke drawing routines to create virtually any line pattern you can imagine. Here's how it works. FreeHand's custom PostScript stroke routines (found in the "newrope" procedure) take instructions for one object and repeat that object along a path. The procedures scale, space, and color the objects on the path according to the values you enter in the Stroke Inspector (see Figure 8-15).

FIGURE 8-15
How FreeHand draws
custom PostScript lines

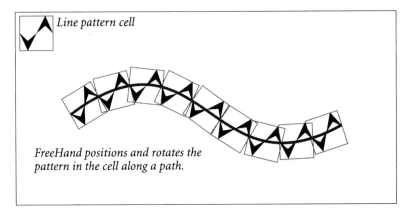

Line pattern cell

*FreeHand positions and rotates the
pattern in the cell along a path.*

Creating a GnEf resource. First, we need to fill in a GnEf resource
for our custom stroke (see Table 8-4).

1. Start ResEdit and create a new resource file.

2. Press Command-K and create a new GnEf resource. Fill in
   the fields in the GnEf resource as shown in Table 8-4.

3. Press Command-I and give the GnEf resource an ID that's
   higher than that of any GnEf ID in FreeHand (above 23000
   is safe, but keep the ID number under 28000—I've gotten
   weird "out of memory" errors for higher IDs). Enter the
   same name for the effect as you entered in the User name
   field of the GnEf.

4. Save your work.

TABLE 8-4
Creating a GnEf
resource for a custom
stroke effect

Field	Example	What it means
Version	1	Version number
Type	3	Type (2 = custom fill, 3 = custom line)
Number of parameters	4	Number of PostScript parameters—all custom fill effects have four: color, width, length, and spacing

TABLE 8-4
Creating a GnEf
resource for a custom
stroke effect
(continued)

Field	Example	What it means
Name	~Hexagon	The internal name for your custom stroke effect. This name must match the name of the last Post resource you refer to. Use a tilde (~) or other character to put your new effect at the end of the popup menu (see "On Beyond Z," later in this chapter, for the reason we need to do this).
User name	~Hexagon	Name of the custom stroke effect as you want it to appear on the popup menu in the Stroke Inspector. Again, see "On Beyond Z," later in this chapter, for the reason for the tilde (~).
Post resource #1	145	Location of supdict (this resource ID is 1000 less than the actual Post ID—the actual Post containing the support dictionary is 1145).
Post resource #2	146	Location of ropedict (again, this ID is 1000 less—the actual Post ID is 1146).

Field	Example	What it means
Post resource #3	1200	This is the location of the PostScript you need to draw the object you're repeating along the path (again, this number is 1000 less than the actual ID of the Post resource you're referring to).
PostScript to invoke effect	{~Hexagon} ^1 ^2 ^3 ^0 newrope	PostScript needed to draw the effect. The variables ^1, ^2, ^3, and ^0 refer to the Width field, the Length field, the Spacing field, and the color in the color well, respectively.
UIrz ID	0	All custom PostScript stroke effects use the same UIrz.

Control	Field	Value
Control 1	Type	0 0 = color well, 2, 3 = text edit field, in points, 4 = text edit field, in degrees, 6 = text edit field, integer, 7 = boolean (a checkbox), 8 = text edit field, percentage
	Minimum	0
	Maximum	0
	Default	0

	Control	Field	Value
TABLE 8-4 Creating a GnEf resource for a custom stroke effect (continued)	Control 2	Type	3
		Minimum	0*
		Maximum	19660500*
		Default	1572840*
	Control 3	Type	3
		Minimum	0*
		Maximum	19660500*
		Default	1572840*
	Control 4	Type	3
		Minimum	0
		Maximum	19660500*
		Default	1572840*

* Multiply the measurement you want by 65,535 to come up with the value you enter here.

Tip:
On Beyond Z

When you're creating new custom PostScript stroke effects, you've got to make sure that they appear on the Stroke Inspector's popup menu following the built-in effects. To do this, type characters in front of the names of your effect so they'll get sorted to the end of the list. I use "~" ("~Hexagon", for example).

Getting the PostScript code you need. Next, we'll create the PostScript for your new custom stroke effect. The heart of a FreeHand custom stroke effect is a kind of cell—like a tiny FreeHand page that's one unit square. The size of the unit itself doesn't matter because the scale of the cell gets determined later by the values you enter in the Width and Length text edit fields in the Stroke Inspector. The zero point of this line-drawing cell is at its center, and all of FreeHand's drawing commands (which you use to construct the line pattern) get their coordinates relative to this zero point.

You can create an enlarged version of this cell to use in plotting the placement of line segments and paths inside the cell, as shown in Figure 8-16.

FIGURE 8-16
Coordinate matrix for
creating custom lines

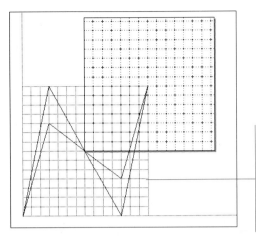

Draw whatever you want in this area, then export the graphic in one of the Adobe Illustrator formats and extract the pattern for your custom line using your word processor.

1. Open FreeHand and press Command-N to create a new file.

2. In the Document Inspector, select Custom from the popup menu. Enter "0p100" for both the width and height of the page, and enter a bleed amount of "0p50".

3. In the Setup Inspector, enter "0p10" in the Grid Size field and press Return.

4. Create a grid that's 100 points square, drawing grid lines every ten points.

5. Select the grid, press Command-G to group it, and press Command-Option-B to display the Object Inspector (if the Inspector's not visible, display it first by pressing Command-I).

6. Type "-50" in both the X and Y fields and press Return. FreeHand moves your grid so that its center point is precisely above the bottom-left corner of your publication's page.

7. Send the grid to the background layer.

Now that you can use the grid as a guide for creating your new line style, draw anything you want inside the grid. When you've got something you think would make a good line pattern (start with a simple shape), export the file as an Adobe Illustrator file (any format), and then use a word processor to extract the line pattern from the EPS graphic.

Why not export the graphic as a Generic EPS file? Because the coordinate system used in FreeHand's EPS is based on the lower-left corner of the pasteboard—not on the lower-left corner of the page (see Figure 8-17). This makes absolutely no difference to applications importing or printing the EPS, but makes it more diY-cult to use this technique. Illustrator format keeps things simple, which is just what we want, in this case.

FIGURE 8-17
Which would you
rather work with?

FreeHand version	Illustrator version
1735.3014 1559 m	43.3014 -25 m
1692 1533.9998 L	0 -50.0002 L
1648.6986 1558.9998 L	-43.3014 -25.0002 L
1648.6986 1609 L	-43.3014 25 L
1692 1634.0002 L	0 50.0002 L
1735.3014 1609.0002 L	43.3014 25.0002 L
1735.3014 1559 L	43.3014 -25 L

1. Open the file with your word processor.

2. Delete everything preceding the first line ending with an "m" ("moveto") instruction.

3. Delete everything from the end of the last line ending with an "L" or a "C" to the end of the file.

4. Delete any occurrence of "vmrs", "vmr", "vms", "u", or "U" remaining in the file.

At this point, the file contains only the commands for drawing the shape (or shapes) you drew.

Once you've got the line pattern, you can plug it into a couple of PostScript routines. Type the code shown below, replacing the variables shown in italics with the names you want your routines to use and with the line pattern you extracted from the EPS graphic in the previous procedure.

```
ropedict begin %FreeHand's set of stroke effect procedures
/linePatternName %Enter the name for your custom line here
{cnt 0 eq
{q blw w Q} if incrcnt
 blocksetup
```

```
drawingCommands %%paste your drawing commands here
f Q} def %%enter "s" instead of "f" to stroke the path,
rather than fill it
end
```

Here's an example line pattern.

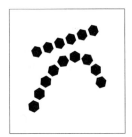

Printed example of the Hexagon custom stroke

```
ropedict begin
/~Hexagon
{cnt 0 eq
{q blw w Q} if incrcnt
 blocksetup
.01 .01 scale
43.3014 -25 m
0 -50.0002 L
-43.3014 -25.0002 L
-43.3014 25 L
0 50.0002 L
43.3014 25.0002 L
43.3014 -25 L
f Q} def
end
```
Make sure you add a space or a return here!

Creating a Post resource. Now that we've gotten the code we need, it's time to create a Post resource (see Figure 8-18).

1. If you're not still in ResEdit, start ResEdit and open the external resource file you've been working on.

2. Press Command-K and add a new Post resource.

3. Open the Post resource you created and paste the code from your word processor into the resource.

4. Set the Post resource ID to the last ID you entered in the GnEF (in our earlier example, you'd use ID 2200). Give the Post resource the same name as you've entered in the User name field of the GnEf (in our example, "~Hexagon").

5. Save the resource file.

Adding an Xvrs Resource. The last thing you need to do, before you launch FreeHand and test your new custom stroke effect, is to add an Xvrs resource to your external resource file. If your external resource file contains an Xvrs resource, FreeHand won't complain about the file during startup (see Figure 8-19).

FIGURE 8-18
Creating a Post
resource

*Press Command-K to
create a new resource.
ResEdit displays
the Select New Type
dialog box.*

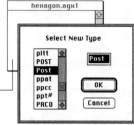

*Choose Post from the
list of resource types, or
type "Post" in the field.*

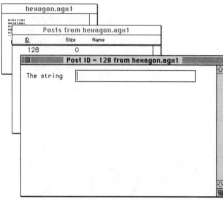

ResEdit displays a new Post template.

*Copy text out of your word
processor and paste it into the
Post resource.*

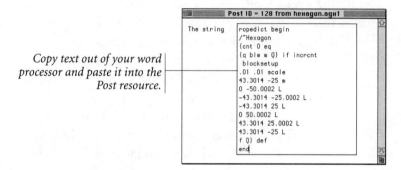

FIGURE 8-19
Creating an
Xvrs resource

*Press Command-K to
create a new resource.
ResEdit displays the
Select New Type dialog
box.*

*Choose Xvrs from the list of
resource templates, or type
"Xvrs" in the field.*

ResEdit creates a new Xvrs resource.

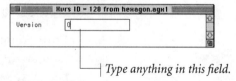

Type anything in this field.

*Press Command-I to
display the Info window
for the Xvrs Resource.*

Type 9999 in this field.

1. Open the resource file you added the GnEf and Post resources to.

2. Create a new resource of type Xvrs.

3. Enter "0" (or anything, for that matter) in the Xvrs resource.

4. Give the Xvrs resource an ID of 9999.

5. Save your file.

Tip:
Omitting Xvrs
Resources on
Purpose

In some cases, you might want to omit Xvrs resources from your external resource files because you might want to choose which external resource files FreeHand loads. To keep the resource from loading, click the Cancel button when FreeHand displays the "earlier version" message. If you do this, you won't have to move files around in the Finder to keep FreeHand from loading them.

Setting the resource file's type and creator. If an external resource file doesn't have the correct file type and creator, FreeHand ignores it. Here's how to add those key bits of information (see Figure 8-20).

1. Choose Get Info for *filename* (where *filename* is the name you gave the file when you created it) from the File menu. ResEdit displays the Info dialog box for the file.

2. In the Type field, type "AGX1". In the Creator field, type "FH40".

3. Press Command-W to close the dialog box. ResEdit asks if you want to save the changes to your file. You do, so click Yes.

4. Quit ResEdit.

Testing your new external resource file. Test your new external resource file by opening FreeHand, drawing a path, and pressing Command-Option-L to display the Stroke Inspector. Choose Custom from the Stroke Type popup menu. Can you see your example stroke effect on the Effect popup menu? If so, select it. If not, run through the procedures above and try to see where you made an

FIGURE 8-20
Setting the file
type and creator

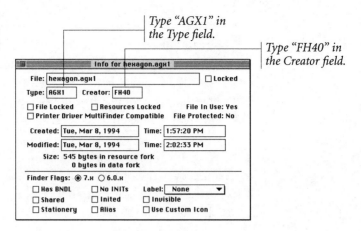

Type "AGX1" in
the Type field.

Type "FH40" in
the Creator field.

error (I got tired of getting errors because of mismatches between the PostScript procedure name, the "User name," and the "Internal name," so I started using the same name for all three purposes).

Apply the stroke effect to a path and try printing the file. If it prints, congratulations! You've just added a stroke effect to your copy of FreeHand. If it doesn't print, it's most likely you've either typed something wrong or have made an incorrect entry in the Post resource containing the drawing commands (suspect this first if you get an "undefined" PostScript error).

This is where LaserTalk comes in handy; you can troubleshoot your PostScript by stepping through it, line by line, while in direct communication with your printer.

Adding a preview of your stroke effect. As far as I know, you won't be able to add a preview image of your custom stroke effect, as FreeHand does for its built-in effects. At this point, I can get *something* to appear in the preview window, but it's never what I want. If you figure it out, please give me a call!

| Tip:
Space Out | Make sure that you add a space or a carriage return following the last character of your PostScript code. If you don't, characters Free-Hand sends following your effect might get appended to one of your procedure names, resulting in PostScript files that won't print. This is especially true for the PostScript you enter in the GnEf—FreeHand's going to put a "Q" right at the end of it. If there's no space, you're going to be in trouble. |

Creating Custom Fill Effects

Because you can create tiled fills inside FreeHand, there's not much need to create fill effects that simply repeat one pattern over and over again. If you want a fill effect that randomly resizes, scales, or skews a pattern inside a filled object or if you want to create a tiled effect where each tile rotates around its center point, however, custom fills are just the ticket.

Creating a UIrz resource for a custom fill. The contents of the UIrz resources are the buttons, fields, and static text you see in the Fill Inspector. Your custom fill effect can use as many controls as you can shoehorn into the Inspector (not many!).

Creating UIrz resources is a complex process, and the only way I can think of to make it easier is to show you how to create an example custom PostScript fill. I'll try to explain what we're doing as we work through the process.

Start ResEdit and create a new resource file in your FreeHand folder. Set the file's type to AGX0 and its creator to FH40 (if you've forgotten how to do this, refer back to the procedure for creating external resource files, earlier in this chapter). Create a new UIrz resource and fill it in as shown in Table 8-5.

TABLE 8-5
Example
UIrz Resource

Item	Field	Enter	What it does
Number of items		18	Sets the number of user interface items displayed by this fill effect.
1	Type	Frame	"Frame" is the area of the Inspector that the effect's controls take up. Every UIrz resource starts with a frame.
	Frame	0 0 121 161*	This rectangle takes up (more or less) all of the available space in the Inspector (that is, everything but the Inspector buttons and the Fill Type popup menu).

* FreeHand's rectangles—whether they're for a Frame, a TextView, a BtnView, or a ColorWell, are measured, PostScript-style, from their lower-left corners. The lower-left corner of the Inspector, therefore, is 0,0. The measurements are in pixels.

Item	Field	Enter	What it does
1 (continued)	ID	0	Leave this at zero for the UIrz resources you create.
	Flags	00000000	See Table 8-6 for a description.
	Title		If the control has a title, enter it here. Otherwise, leave this field blank.
	Tag	0	Leave this set to zero for the UIrz resources you create.
2	Type	ColorWell	Creates a FreeHand color well.
	Frame	7 140 115 160	Defines a frame for the color well. Note that this frame is wide enough to display the name of any color you drop into it.
	ID		0
	Flags	000B0002	
	Title		
	Tag	0	
3	Type	TextView	Creates both static text (labels) and text edit fields.
	Frame	76 106 108 122	
	ID	0	
	Flags	00030002	
	Title		
	Tag	0	
4	Type	TextView	
	Frame	42 106 74 122	
	ID	0	
	Flags	00030002	
	Title		
	Tag	0	

Item	Field	Enter	What it does
5	Type	TextView	
	Frame	76 87 108 103	
	ID	0	
	Flags	00030002	
	Title		
	Tag	0	
6	Type	TextView	
	Frame	76 68 108 84	
	ID	0	
	Flags	00030002	
	Title		
	Tag	0	
7	Type	BtnView	Creates buttons—check-boxes, radio buttons, and icon buttons.
	Frame	6 49 116 63	
	ID	0	
	Flags	00050002	
	Title	Random rotation	
	Tag	0	
8	Type	BtnView	
	Frame	6 36 116 48	
	ID	0	
	Flags	00050002	
	Title	Random skewing	
	Tag	0	
9	Type	TextView	
	Frame	1 106 40 122	
	ID	0	
	Flags	00800002	
	Title	Size:	
	Tag	0	

Item	Field	Enter	What it does
TABLE 8-5 Example UIrz Resource (continued)			
10	Type	TextView	
	Frame	1 87 74 103	
	ID	0	
	Flags	00800002	
	Title	Spacing:	
	Tag	0	
11	Type	TextView	
	Frame	1 68 74 84	
	ID	0	
	Flags	00800002	
	Title	Angle:	
	Tag	0	
12	Type	TextView	
	Frame	108 68 120 84	
	ID	0	
	Flags	00000002	
	Title	°	
	Tag	0	
13	Type	MUView	Draws a dotted line across the Inspector, separating different sections.
	Frame	0 136 121 137	
	ID	0	
	Flags	00002002	
	Title		
	Tag	0	
14	Type	MUView	
	Frame	0 65 121 66	
	ID	0	
	Flags	00002002	
	Title		
	Tag	0	

TABLE 8-5
Example
UIrz Resource
(continued)

Item	Field	Enter	What it does
15	Type	MUView	
	Frame	0 32 121 33	
	ID	0	
	Flags	00002002	
	Title		
	Tag	0	
16	Type	TextView	
	Frame	1 3 121 15	
	ID	0	
	Flags	00040002	
	Title	Real World FreeHand 4	Your message here
	Tag	0	
17	Type	TextView	
	Frame	40 125 76 138	
	ID	0	
	Flags	00040002	
	Tag	0	
18	Type	TextView	
	Frame	74 125 110 138	
	ID	0	
	Flags	00040002	
	Title	max:	
	Tag	0	

The Flags field in the UIrz resource tells FreeHand how to format and how to interpret the control. Table 8-6 shows what the different flags mean.

Different flags can be added together. To produce a color well you can drag color swatches out of (00020000) or drop color swatches into (00010000), which also displays the name of the color to the right of the color well (00080000), and displays that name in nine-point Geneva (00000002), you'd enter 000B0002 ("B" because 8 + 2 + 1 = B in the hexadecimal universe—where you count 0, 1, 2, 3, 4, 5, 6, 7, 8, 9, A, B, C, D, E, F).

TABLE 8-6
Selected UIrz flags
and what they mean

Item	Flag	What it means
Any	00000002	Display text in nine-point Geneva
MUView	00002000	Draw a gray line on either side of the text
ColorWell	00010000	Color swatches can be dropped in
	00020000	Color swatches can be dragged out
	00080000	Display the color name to the right of the color well
TextView	00008000	Left-align text
	00040000	Center text
	00800000	Right-align text
	00010000	Draw a border around the text
	00020000	Editable field
	00400000	Italicize text
	00080000	Make text bold
BtnView	00010000	Button toggles when clicked (like a checkbox)
	00040000	Button is a checkbox
	00080000	Button is a radio button
	00100000	Button is an icon button

Creating a GnEf resource for a custom fill. You create GnEf resources for custom fills exactly as you would for a custom stroke effect (see "Creating a GnEf Resource," earlier in this chapter). For our example custom fill, enter the values shown in Table 8-7.

TABLE 8-7
Example GnEf

Field	What you enter
Version	1
Type	2
Number of parameters	7
Name	boldXfilled
User name	boldXfilled
PostScript resource 1	145
PostScript resource 2	1101
PostScript to invoke effect	^1 ^2 ^3 ^4 ^5 ^6 ^0 boldXfilled
UIrz ID	27061

Field	Label	What you enter
UIrz item 1*	Type	0
	Minimum	0
	Maximum	0
	Default	1
UIrz item 2	Type	3
	Minimum	65535
	Maximum	6553500
	Default	786432
UIrz item 3	Type	3
	Minimum	65535
	Maximum	6553500
	Default	786432

* The GnEf resource refers to the UIrz controls in order and starts counting following the Frame item in the UIrz. In this case, the color well is UIrz item #1, UIrz items 2 and 3 set the minimum and maximum size of the "X," and UIrz items 5 and 6 are the checkboxes controlling random rotation and random skewing, respectively. When FreeHand uses the values from these items in the PostScript it sends to the printer (as directed by the GnEf), everything shifts down by one—the value in UIrz item 1 is plugged in for variable "^0", the value for UIrz item 2 is entered for "^1", and so on.

	Field	Label	What you enter
TABLE 8-7 Example GnEf (continued)	UIrz item 4	Type	4
		Minimum	-23592960
		Maximum	23592960
		Default	1966080
	UIrz item 5	Type	7
		Minimum	0
		Maximum	1
		Default	0
	UIrz Item 6	Type	7
		Minimum	0
		Maximum	1
		Default	0

Creating a Post resource for a custom fill. I drew the "X" shape using the FreeHand grid file we created (see "Getting the Post-Script Code You Need," earlier in this chapter), exported it as an Illustrator 1.1 file, and extracted the drawing commands from the Illustrator file using Microsoft Word. I then pasted the drawing commands into a fill procedure (which I derived from FreeHand's own Squares custom fill). Figure 8-21 shows examples of this fill effect.

Enter the text shown below in your word processor.

```
%%boldXfilled tiled fill effect
%%from Real World FreeHand 4
%%by Olav Martin Kvern
%%on stack: minSize,
%%maxSize, spacing, angle,
%%randRotate?, randomSkew?,
%%color
%%example:10 12 45 true
%%[0 0 0 1] boldXfilled
supdict begin
/boldXfilledLoop
{ystart spacing ystart abs
{/ycur xdf
xstart spacing xstart abs
{q ycur m
```

```
currentpoint translate
%%random rotation?
randomRotate true eq
{360 randint rotate} if
%%random skewing?
randomSkew true eq
{
/xSkew 360 randint def
/ySkew 360 randint def
[1 xSkew sin ySkew sin neg 1 0 0] concat} if
%random scaling?
randomScale true eq
{maxSize minSize sub randint minSize add /size xdf} if
%%scale the tile
size 100 div dup scale
q
%%start drawing commands
-25 -50 m
-50 -25 L
-25 0 L
-50 25 L
-25 50 L
0 25 L
25 50 L
50 25 L
25 0 L
50 -25 L
25 -50 L
0 -25 L
-25 -50 L
%%end drawing commands
f
Q
Q
} for
} for
}
def
end
/boldXfilled
{
supdict begin
q newinside
/color xdf
colorchoice
/randomSkew xdf
/randomRotate xdf
/angle xdf
/spacing xdf
/maxSize xdf
/minSize xdf
minSize maxSize eq
```

```
{/randomScale false def minSize /size xdf} {/randomScale true
def} ifelse
/xstart x1 x2 add 2 div neg spacing sub def
/ystart y1 y2 add 2 div neg spacing sub def
dx 2 div dy 2 div translate
angle rotate boldXfilledLoop
Q end
} def
```

Now that we've got the code we need, it's time to create a new Post resource.

1. Start ResEdit (if it's not already running) and open the external resource file you've been working on (if it's not already open).

2. Add a new Post resource.

3. Paste the code from your word processor into the Post resource.

4. Press Command-I to display the Info dialog box for the resource. Set the resource's ID to 2101 (remember, it's 1000 higher than the number you entered in the GnEf). Name the Post resource "boldXfilled".

5. Save the resource file.

FIGURE 8-21
Your new custom
fill effect

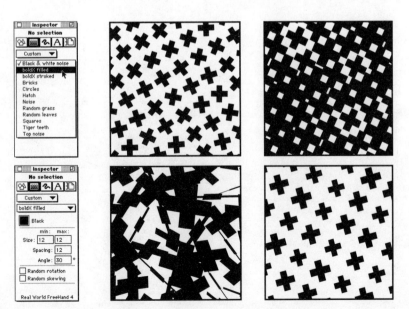

Add an Xvrs resource to the file (see "Adding an Xvrs Resource," earlier in this chapter) and save the file. The next time you start FreeHand, you should see a new menu item "boldXfilled" on FreeHand's list of custom fills in the Fill Inspector. When you choose this item from the popup menu, FreeHand should display the controls for your new effect in the Inspector.

PostScript Postscript

This has been the hardest chapter in the book to write, and I feel I've only scratched the surface of what you can do with FreeHand and PostScript. Once I figure out how to do text effects, I may even have to create an addendum to this book. Or, this being a book by Peachpit Press, maybe we can do *The Little FreeHand PostScript Fills Book*. Now there's an idea!

Appendices

Index

Like other desktop publishing tools, FreeHand does not exist in a vacuum. Sure, you can can create great-looking publications without using a single other program—but the power and usefulness of FreeHand can be multiplied many times by having an array of utilities and System resources available.

Sometimes these additional tools perform just one, limited function; sometimes they're entire applications in their own right. In either case, having them around either improves your FreeHand productivity or (essentially) adds capabilities to FreeHand.

The first thing you need is a system configuration that is both reliable and that fits you like a glove. Your Macintosh should respond to your directions exactly the way you want it to, without crashing in mid-operation or doing anything you didn't expect.

In this chapter (indeed, in the rest of the book), I'm assuming that you're using System 7.0 or higher, and all the illustrations and explanations are based on that assumption.

System

Your Macintosh system is made up of the System file itself and your extensions, control panel devices (which I'll refer to as "cdevs"), Apple Menu items, and fonts. Extensions contain supplements and changes to the system software that get loaded when you start your Macintosh. Control panel devices are utilities that let you change characteristics of your system or extensions (like the background screen pattern, or what network type you're using). Cdevs sometimes contain extension-like material as well that gets loaded at startup. Part of an extension (or cdev with code) is in RAM all the time, waiting for you to do whatever it is that activates it.

Apple Menu items are small utility programs that get put in the Apple Menu Items folder in the System Folder. (Actually, anything you put in this folder automatically shows up on the Apple menu; it's just that Apple Menu items are put here by default.)

Fonts are resources which, when dragged onto the System Folder icon, are placed in the System file (in System 7.0.x) or Fonts folder (in System 7.1). Or, you can use a font-management utility like MasterJuggler or Suitcase to tell the system where the fonts are. Once fonts are installed on your system, applications (such as Free-Hand) can call on and use them.

The following are a few more of my "golden rules."

◆ Have only one System file per Macintosh.

You can use a utility to "bless" one of several Systems on a Macintosh, but I've never seen it work well. The only reason to try this is if you're working with a KanjiTalk or Chinese System and need to switch back and forth between localized Systems. Otherwise, don't. If you need to store unused fonts somewhere, store them in suitcase files, not in an unused System file.

◆ Don't switch to the most current System version until it's been around for a couple of months.

Some System versions are buggy—some are even withdrawn by Apple after they've been in circulation for awhile. What you really need is an idiot friend who always installs the newest System version as soon as it's available—even before they're released (I'm this way, actually). Let them lose work because of incompatibilities and bugs. Then ask them about the new System software. Once their level of bitching and whining declines, you know it's safe to upgrade (by this time they're on to a new version, anyway).

◆ When you update your System, check all of your extensions and control panels for compatibility.

Check your applications, too, but you'll generally have more problems with the items that live inside the system folder. Most of the problems I had when I updated from System 6 to System 7 revolved around the extensions and cdevs I use (although the worst problems actually had to do with the ROMs in my video board).

If you suspect your extensions and cdevs are causing your problems, turn them off. To do this, restart your Macintosh and hold down Shift before you see the "happy Mac" icon.

◆ Don't work on a live System file with ResEdit.

I lose work all the time doing this. It's a stupid thing to do.

◆ When you update your System, make sure that you use the Installer application, don't drag items over.

Apple's Installer application (used by most developers and Apple itself to install new software) sometimes needs to install low-level system resources which can't be simply dragged over. Many of the system updaters have these resources. Note that for applications that don't use the Apple Installer—such as FreeHand—many items that you need aren't automatically copied and aren't available by clicking the Customize button. In this case, you need to look at the disks, find the items you need, and copy them over manually. Do this as a last resort, however.

◆ Less is not more, but can be less trouble.

Every extension and cdev you use takes up RAM, and the more extensions and cdevs you have, the more likely it is that they'll conflict with each other or with your applications. Do you really need to have a rainbow-colored cursor? Or a rotating globe instead of a watch? Like the tree in the garden of Eden, the Macintosh gives us the ability to make our systems as weird and stupid as we want. Rule of thumb: If you're running more than 10 extensions/cdevs on a Macintosh with eight megabytes of RAM, it's time to exercise some restraint. Tell the snake you're not interested.

◆ Before you blame the application, check your System.
As far as I can tell, 50 percent of the technical support calls to Macintosh application developers are about funky Systems, multiple Systems, corrupted font files, etc.

◆ Your system is more than your System.
As wonderful as the Macintosh system is, a real desktop-publishing system includes other applications: word processors, other page-layout tools, font-editing software, utilities, and image-editing programs. The whole of the software on your Macintosh should be greater than the sum of its parts.

Extensions and Control Panels

As I mentioned earlier, extensions and (some) cdevs are little applications that are loaded when your system starts up. Part of an extension or cdev is always active in your Macintosh's memory, waiting for you to do something it needs to respond to.

ATM and TrueType. In the early days of Macintosh, you had to have a screen font for every size of type you used—unless you didn't mind your type looking jagged on screen. These days, Adobe Type Manager (ATM) produces smooth-looking characters on your screen (as smooth as they can be at your screen's resolution) from your Type 1 PostScript printer fonts. If you don't have the printer fonts, ATM won't produce better-looking type. Apple's TrueType fonts, which are included with System 7, also produce smooth type on screen.

Should you buy lots of TrueType fonts? Or should you get ATM and use PostScript Type 1 fonts? Which font format is better from FreeHand's point of view? While FreeHand supports TrueType, ATM and PostScript Type 1 fonts are your best bet. For me, the deciding factor is that PostScript Type 1 fonts print well on PostScript imagesetters. And—there's no nice way to say it: True-Type fonts don't.

MasterJuggler and Suitcase. These two extensions make everything about working with fonts easier and quicker, because you can add fonts to your system without opening the Font/DA Mover (pre-System 7) dragging them onto your System icon (System 7.0.x), or dragging them into the Fonts folder in your System Folder (System 7.1 or newer). With either MasterJuggler or Suitcase, you can load and unload fonts in seconds, without having to claw your way through folders in the Finder. System 7 was supposed to make these extensions obsolete. It didn't.

That said, these two extensions do about the same things. I like MasterJuggler better, because it's got a better user interface and a great application launcher (so I don't have to claw my way through folders to find an application to launch—or clutter my desktop with aliases), but Suitcase is marketed by a larger company and gets updated (to keep up with system changes) more often.

Tip:
Where You
Should Put
Your Fonts

If you're using a font-management utilty (such as MasterJuggler or Suitcase), keep your outline (or printer) fonts in the same folder as the suitcase containing the bitmap (or screen) fonts.

If you're not using a font-management utility, store your bitmap fonts in the System file itself; or, in System 7.1, in the Fonts folder.

Tip:
When FreeHand
Can't Find
Your Fonts

If you're using MasterJuggler or Suitcase and FreeHand is having trouble finding your outline fonts, put them into the correct location in the System Folder: the Extensions folder in System 7.0.x, or the Fonts folder in System 7.1. Then restart your Macintosh.

Can FreeHand find the fonts now? If not, you're probably using an outdated version of your font management program (at the time of this writing, the current version of MasterJuggler is 1.59, and the current version of Suitcase is 2.1.4)—or an old version of ATM (the current version is 3.6).

Until you can update these utilities, you'll need to keep your fonts in your Fonts folder (under System 7.1; if you're using System 7.0.x, put the bitmaps in the System file and put the outlines in the Extensions folder). I understand that this is an inconvenience for people who like to keep their fonts in other folders, in other places. But this is the real world, and reality encompasses certain unpleasant facts. What's more important—keeping the fonts in another folder, or being able to use them? You choose.

ATR. Adobe Type Reunion (ATR) combines your font families into groups on your font menus (see Figure A-1). Instead of having separate menu choices for Minion and Minion Black, ATR shows you a menu item for "Minion," and lists "Regular" and "Black" on a submenu attached to the font family's name.

Previous versions of ATR didn't work very well with FreeHand (FreeHand would lose track of its filters while ATR was running), but the most current version (1.1) works just fine.

FIGURE A-1
Adobe Type Reunion

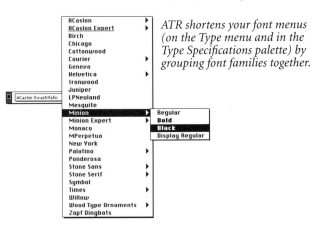

ATR shortens your font menus (on the Type menu and in the Type Specifications palette) by grouping font families together.

Super Boomerang. Super Boomerang, from the Now Utilities package, is a cdev that is active only when you're in a "standard file" dialog box (these are the dialog boxes where you see a listing of files you can open, save, or place). When Super Boomerang's running, a menu appears across the top of those dialog boxes (you can see it in many of the screen shots in this book). The File and Folder menus show you files and folders you've been working with recently. You can use this menu to switch from file to file, folder to folder, and volume to volume quickly, or you can use Boomerang's keyboard shortcuts to move even more quickly (see Figure A-2). You can also permanently add files and folders to these menus.

Do you frequently go to an Open or a Place dialog box and forget what file name you wanted—or where you left the file? If

FIGURE A-2
Super Boomerang

Super Boomerang displays a menu across the top of standard Open, Save, and Place dialog boxes.

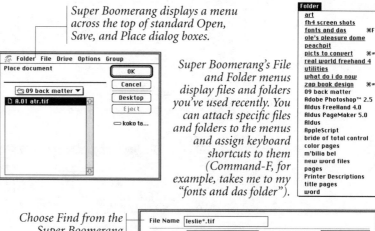

Super Boomerang's File and Folder menus display files and folders you've used recently. You can attach specific files and folders to the menus and assign keyboard shortcuts to them (Command-F, for example, takes me to my "fonts and das folder").

Choose Find from the Super Boomerang Options menu, and you can direct Super Boomerang to search your system for a files (or even for text inside files).

you do, you'll love Super Boomerang's Where Is feature. Choose Where Is from Super Boomerang's Options menu (or press Command-?), and Super Boomerang displays a nifty little dialog box that'll help you find your file. Whatever you named it. Wherever it is (see Figure A-3). Super Boomerang can even search the contents of files for text—and it does so with frightening speed.

QuicKeys. QuicKeys (version 2.1 or higher), from CE Software, is an extension that you use to create keyboard shortcuts and macros (a macro is a series of tasks performed in a sequence). If you find yourself wishing for more keyboard shortcuts in FreeHand (like a shortcut for the Move palette, to name only the most needed), get yourself a copy of QuicKeys and add them.

Tip:
Apply and close

As much as I love FreeHand's palettes, I find it's too easy to forget to close them when I don't need them—especially the Transform palette and the Align palette. The result? Sometimes, I lose sight of my publication. Figure A-3 shows how to create a QuicKey that applies the changes you've made in a palette, then closes the palette.

FIGURE A-3
Apply and
close QuicKey

*Display the QuicKeys
control panel (unless
you've changed
the default, you can
press Command-
Option-Return).*

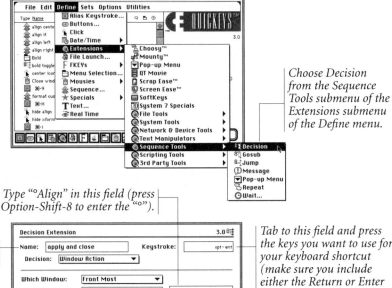

*Choose Decision
from the Sequence
Tools submenu of the
Extensions submenu
of the Define menu.*

*Type "°Align" in this field (press
Option-Shift-8 to enter the "°").*

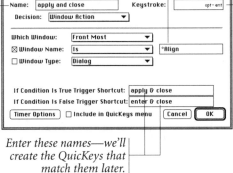

*Type a name for the
QuicKey here.*

*Choose Window Action
from the Decision
popup menu.*

*Tab to this field and press
the keys you want to use for
your keyboard shortcut
(make sure you include
either the Return or Enter
key for this QuicKey).*

*We have to use a
Decision QuicKey,
because the Align
palette (alone of all the
palettes) doesn't apply
its changes when you
press Return (or Enter).*

*Enter these names—we'll
create the QuicKeys that
match them later.*

*Choose Sequence from
the Define menu
to create a new
Sequence QuicKey.*

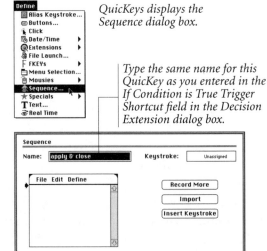

*QuicKeys displays the
Sequence dialog box.*

*Type the same name for this
QuicKey as you entered in the
If Condition is True Trigger
Shortcut field in the Decision
Extension dialog box.*

*Choose Buttons from
the Define menu to
create a new Button
QuicKey.*

FIGURE A-3
Apply and
close QuicKey
(continued)

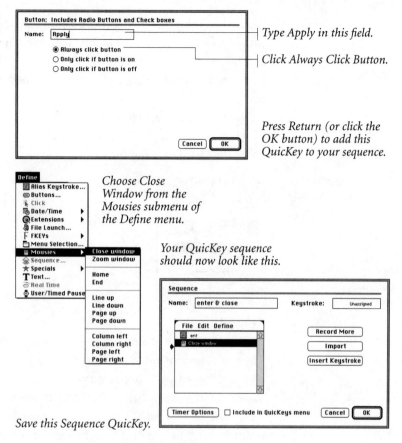

Type Apply in this field.

Click Always Click Button.

Press Return (or click the OK button) to add this QuicKey to your sequence.

Choose Close Window from the Mousies submenu of the Define menu.

Your QuicKey sequence should now look like this.

Save this Sequence QuicKey.

Using the techniques shown earlier in this figure, create another Sequence QuicKey.

Click Insert Keystroke and press Enter (or Return) to create the first item in this sequence.

Choose Close Window from the Mousies submenu of the Define menu to create this sequence item.

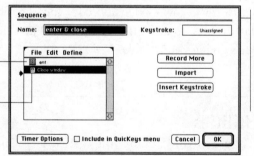

Type a name for the second Sequence QuicKey here. This name should match the name you entered in the If Condition is False Trigger Shortcut field in the Decision Extension dialog box.

Close QuicKeys. Next, test the QuicKey. Select some objects and press Command-Shift-A to display the Align palette. Choose an alignment and press Option-Enter (or whatever keystroke you've assigned to the QuicKey). If everything's working, FreeHand will apply the alignment and close the Align palette. This QuicKey works well with every palette but the Type Specifications palette.

Extension managers. If you use extensions and cdevs to add features to your Macintosh system, you need an extension manager,
such as Startup Manager from the Now Utilities package, or the
freeware Extension Manager (where do they get these crazy product names?). Usually, extension managers are cdevs that set themselves up to load before any other cdevs or extensions, and control
which other extensions and cdevs load, and (in some cases) in what
order they load (see Figure A-4).

FIGURE A-4
Extensions Manager

What's the use of this? I have a pressure-sensitve drawing tablet.
The tablet is controlled by a cdev. I don't like having the tablet on
all the time—mostly because the cdev conflicts with the cdev that
makes my modem work. So, using Extension Manager, I keep two
"sets" (or lists of which extensions and cdevs to load)—one for
when I want to use the tablet; one for when I want to use the
modem.

Extension managers also come in very handy when you're trying to track down extension/cdev incompatibilities—you can turn
startup files on and off, one (or more) at a time, to find out which
one's giving you trouble.

Utilities
While I might caution you against large numbers of extensions
and cdevs, utilities are another thing. You can never have too many
utilities.

ResEdit. Simply put, you cannot do without this utility if you want
to customize your programs to better fit the ways that you work.

And if you want to create external resources for FreeHand it's essential (technically speaking, you can also use the Think C utility SARez, or similar resource compilers for other programming environments).

In the old days, ResEdit was a terrifying and unstable product—more prone to demolish any file it touched than make it more useful. These days, ResEdit is still a little rough around the edges, but it's safe enough for your kids to play with.

FreeHand's resources are set up beautifully from ResEdit point of view—usually each resource does only one thing. Heck, some of them are even labelled. Get yourself a copy of ResEdit and start investigating a copy of FreeHand.

File-compression utilities Like work expanding to fill the time available for it, your files expand to fill the amount of space you have on your hard drive. StuffIt, DiskDoubler, and (my favorite) Compact Pro compress files so that they take up less space on your disk (now if I could only find a work compression utility!).

All these programs compress FreeHand PostScript files to less than a third of their original size (the degree of compression varies depending on the file's contents), which is a great thing to do when you're taking your file to an imagesetting service bureau or sending files to someone using a modem. Your service bureau may even prefer getting compressed files—ask them.

Torquemada the Inquisitor. So you want to search through a text file for every occurrence of "<B>" and change it to "\b"? That's pretty easy—just about any word processor can do that. But what if you want to find "<B>", followed by an indeterminate amount of text ending with "<P>" and change it to "\b", followed by the same, unspecified text and replace the "<P>" with "\plain"? This is hard for most word processors, but it's easy for Torquemada the Inquisitor, an incredible search and replace (or, as the youngsters say, "find and change"—never having seen WordStar) utility. Torquemada can only search text-only files—but that covers both text-only and RTF, the two text formats FreeHand can import. Think about it—you've got to be able to do search and replace to clean up text files, and Torquemada's free (see Figure A-5).

FIGURE A-5
Torquemada
the Inquisitor

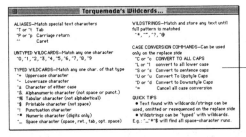

Torquemada's Case Conversion Commands are just the thing for cleaning up text typed in ALL CAPS.

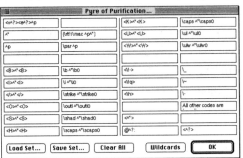

Unlike the search-and-replace functions of your word processor, Torquemada can do multiple searches on a single pass through a file. This set converts XPress Tags to RTF.

3-D Rendering Applications

I love taking paths I've drawn in FreeHand to 3-D applications, such as Adobe Dimensions, Ray Dream's addDepth and Ray Dream Designer 3.0 (I'd mention other products—but I can't afford them). Once I've imported the paths, I can extrude them, or rotate them around a central axis, or rotate them in 3-D space. It's hours of fun—and, once you get into rendering the objects, I do mean *hours*!

Adobe Dimensions. At around $100, Dimensions is a good way to get into 3-D—and it's sometimes bundled with other Adobe products by mail-order outfits (which means it's free, if you're already planning to buy the Adobe product). Dimensions has an edge over addDepth in one area—wrapping paths around a curved surface (though it can't wrap a TIFF or other bitmap image around a surface generated from a FreeHand path).

To get FreeHand paths into Adobe Dimensions, you'll have to export the paths in the Aldus FreeHand 3 file format—Dimensions can't yet open FreeHand 4 files.

Dimensions can export files as FreeHand 3 files, so you can bring the results of your 3-D experiments back into FreeHand and add them to your layouts

See Figure A-6 for an example of a FreeHand path extruded and altered in Dimensions.

FIGURE A-6
FreeHand paths and
Adobe Dimensions

Create a path in FreeHand and save it as a FreeHand 3 file.

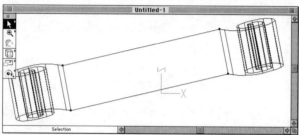

Import the path into Dimensions and use the Extrude command to add depth to the path.

Create some text in FreeHand. Convert the text to paths and export it as a FreeHand 3 file.

In Dimensions, select the extruded path and choose Artwork Mapping from the Appearance menu. Click the Import button and import the text you exported from FreeHand.

Render the artwork in Dimensions, and export it as a FreeHand 3 file. You can then open and edit the FreeHand 3 file in FreeHand.

Ray Dream addDepth. AddDepth can't, at the time of this writing, open FreeHand 4.0 files or EPSs. This doesn't mean you're out of luck, however—addDepth can read and write FreeHand 3 files. This makes it, of the three programs mentioned here, the most convenient to use. Export your files as FreeHand 3, open and edit them in addDepth, and then save them as FreeHand 3 files (which you can open in FreeHand 4). addDepth doesn't support everything you can create in FreeHand, as noted below.

◆ Graduated and radial fills you've created in your FreeHand publication don't transfer to addDepth (paths with these fill types applied show up in addDepth without their fills). Blends, however, are supported by addDepth. If you want a graduated fill, you can always fill the path using addDepth's Gradation fill.

◆ Patterned fills, textured fills, PostScript fills, and custom fills are not supported by addDepth.

FIGURE A-7
FreeHand paths and
Ray Dream addDepth

Create some text in FreeHand. Convert the text to paths and export it as a FreeHand 3 file.

Import the FreeHand file into addDepth. Rotate and extrude the paths, then click on a shader you want to use in the Shaders window or create your own (in this example, I've chosen the Metallic Shader). Save the file in the FreeHand 3 format, and you can open and edit it in FreeHand.

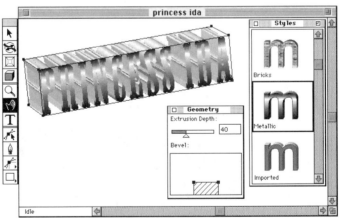

Printed example.

◆ addDepth supports only solid basic strokes—no dashed strokes, patterned strokes, custom strokes, or PostScript strokes.

◆ Any imported artwork in the FreeHand 3 file is not included when you open the file in addDepth.

◆ addDepth can't handle text that's been bound to a path. Convert the text to paths, however, and you'll have no problem.

◆ addDepth doesn't support FreeHand's text effects (Zoom, Inline, and Shadow).

For an example of the 3-D effects you can achieve with addDepth, see Figure A-7.

Ray Dream Designer. I have to admit it—I like this program (even though the documentation is skimpy in the extreme). Designer is a very capable 3-D drawing and rendering program—and it costs a third of what similar programs (such as the excellent Alias Sketch) cost. As far as I can tell, this is because Designer (as of version 3.02, anyway) doesn't contain any animation features.

While Designer can open FreeHand 3 files, getting FreeHand paths into Designer isn't as easy as getting them into addDepth or Dimensions. At the time of this writing, Designer couldn't import FreeHand 4 files. Designer can, however, export rendered scenes as TIFF (or—ugh!—bitmap PICT) you can place in FreeHand. Getting a FreeHand path into Designer for the first time isn't at all easy, so I'll show you how in the following steps (see Figure A-8).

1. In FreeHand, export the objects you want to import into designer as a FreeHand 3 document.

2. Switch to Designer and choose FreeForm from the Objects menu. Designer's Perspective window changes to show you a cross-section (cross-sections are the basic building blocks of 3-D scenes in Designer).

3. Choose Import Artwork from the Sections menu (at the top of the Perspective window, not on the main menu bar).

FIGURE A-8
FreeHand paths and
Ray Dream Designer

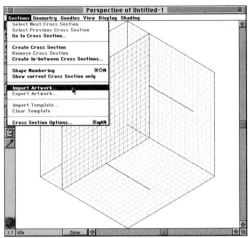

*Draw some objects
in FreeHand and
export them as a
FreeHand 3 file.*

*In Ray Dream Designer, display the FreeForm window
and Choose Import Artwork from the Sections menu.
Apply Shaders and textures to the imported paths…*

*…and render them
(rendering at high
resolution takes
time, so you might
want to schedule
all your rendering
for times you're not
planning to use your
Macintosh—like when
you're sleeping).*

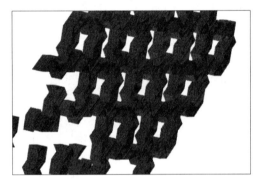

*Paths rendered with Ray
Dream Desinger's Stone
Wall Shader.*

Designer displays the Import Artwork dialog box. Pick a file
name and press Return (or click OK).

4. Designer imports the artwork and places it on the selected
    cross section. Designer converts any text in the FreeHand
    publication to paths. At this point, you can work with the
    paths in the converted FreeHand file as you would any other
    object in Designer.

Image Tools

Desktop design, illustration, and page layout rely on three things:
type, line drawing, and images. FreeHand covers the first two
items well. Photoshop handles the last item better than anything

else (I have heard good things about a Macintosh version of Aldus PhotoStyler, and Fractal Design's Painter is also good).

Adobe Photoshop. If you can buy only one other application (in addition to FreeHand), it should be Photoshop. When you want to work with bitmaps—be they scanned photographs or freeform paintings, Photoshop is the place to do it.

There's no way I can cover an application the size of Photoshop in this appendix, but I can throw in a favorite tip.

Tip:
Smoother graduated fills with Photoshop

When you create a graduated fill that goes a long distance—say, 25 inches or so—the bands between the gray steps in the graduated fill become very obvious. Even if you're working with a 256 shades of gray, there just aren't enough different gray shades available to make a smooth graduation. What can you do?

To create a smooth blend using Photoshop, follow these steps (see Figure A-9).

1. Create a blend in FreeHand.

2. Export the blend in the Adobe Illustrator 3.0 format.

3. Open the Illustrator file with Photoshop. As Photoshop opens the file, it displays the EPS Options dialog box. Enter the resolution and size you want and press Return. Photoshop opens the file, converting the blend to a bitmap as it does so.

4. Choose Add Noise from the Noise submenu of the Filters menu. Photoshop displays the Add Noise dialog box.

5. Type a number in the Amount field. You'll have to experiment to see what works best for you—I like to enter "3", "5", or "7". Press Return, and Photoshop adds a little bit of noise to the image. When you print, this noise smooths the optical transitions between gray bands.

6. Place the TIFF in FreeHand, replacing the original blend in your publication.

FIGURE A-9
Smoother blends
with Photoshop

FreeHand blend from 40 to 60 percent gray. Some banding should be visible.

Open the blend in Photoshop and add some noise to smooth the transitions between gray bands (in this case, I entered "3" in the Amount field in Photoshop's Add Noise dialog box).

DeBabelizer. DeBabelizer is a file conversion utility for images. If you want to change an image from one image format to another—especially if you've got lots of files to convert or are working with an exotic file type (such as an Apple II color image), DeBabelizer is for you (see Figure A-10).

When you've got hundreds of PICT screen shots you want to convert to TIFFs—a situation I've faced several times as I produce books for other people—DeBabelizer can save the day. Instead of opening each PICT file (cursing the person who created it) in an Photoshop and then saving the file as a TIFF (cursing some more as I do so), I can give DeBabelizer a list of files to convert and go home for the evening. While I'm away, DeBabelizer converts the PICTs to TIFFs, and has them waiting for me in the morning. Thanks to DeBabelizer, I am a better, more tolerant person.

FIGURE A-10
DeBabelizer

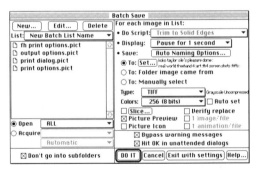

PostScript Tools

If you're creating your own PostScript dictionaries or external resource files for stroke and fill effects, or if you're just trying to find out why your last publication didn't print, you need some tools for working with PostScript. Here are a few of my favorites.

LaserTalk. LaserTalk is the essential PostScript utility. With Laser-Talk, you can communicate directly with the PostScript interpreter in your printer, and, better yet, *you can see what's going on* (see Figure A-11). If you're serious about creating PostScript effects for FreeHand, you've got to get LaserTalk.

FIGURE A-11
LaserTalk

LaserTalk puts you in direct contact with the PostScript interpreter in your printer.

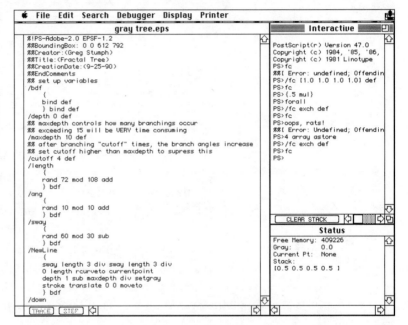

LaserStatus. LaserStatus is an Apple Menu Item PostScript down-loader from PrairieSoft. It's not big, but it's better than many other the PostScript downloading applications (such as Apple's Laser-Writer Font Utility). The great thing about LaserStatus is that you can create sets—lists of files you want downloaded. When you want to send a series of files to your printer, just choose the set you've created with those file names in it (see Figure A-12).

NeXT machine. Stop laughing, I'm serious. The black boxes made by NeXT, Inc., before they got out of the hardware business to go head-to-head with Microsoft in the operating system business (it's OK to laugh again, at this point) are worth having even if all you

FIGURE A-12
LaserStatus

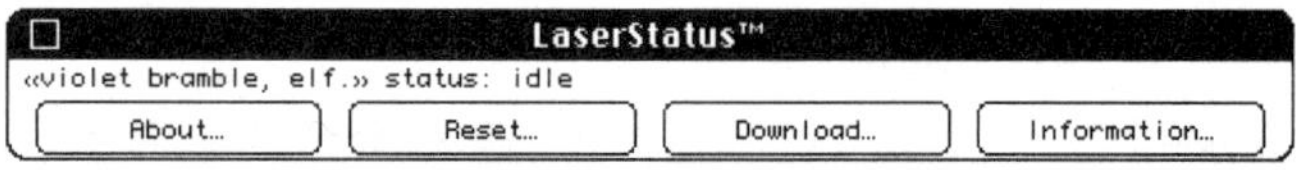

Use LaserStatus to download PostScript files without leaving your current application.

Use LaserStatus sets to download groups of PostScript files (including fonts, as shown in this example).

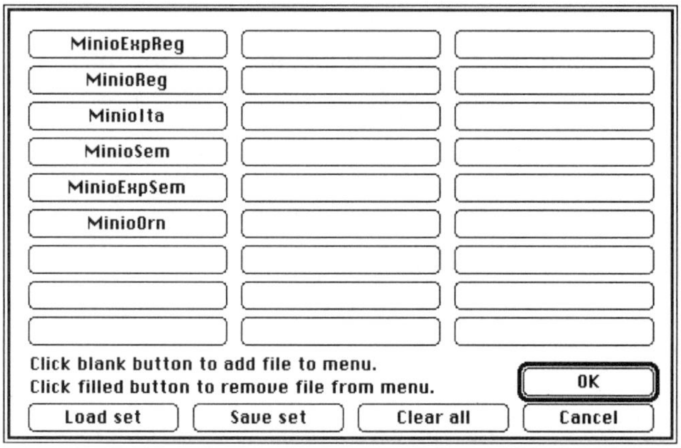

do with them is develop PostScript code. It's because they use PostScript to control their screen display—you can actually see your PostScript effects on screen (see Figure A-13). Because the NeXT is perceived as an "orphaned" machine, you can pick them up fairly cheaply. I don't know if PC-compatible 80486 machines running Nextstep work as well—I haven't tried them.

You might also be interested in Virtuoso, a version of FreeHand (marketed by Altsys) that runs on machines running the Nextstep operating system (and on Sun Workstations).

FIGURE A-13
The Nextstep operating system uses PostScript to drive its screen display

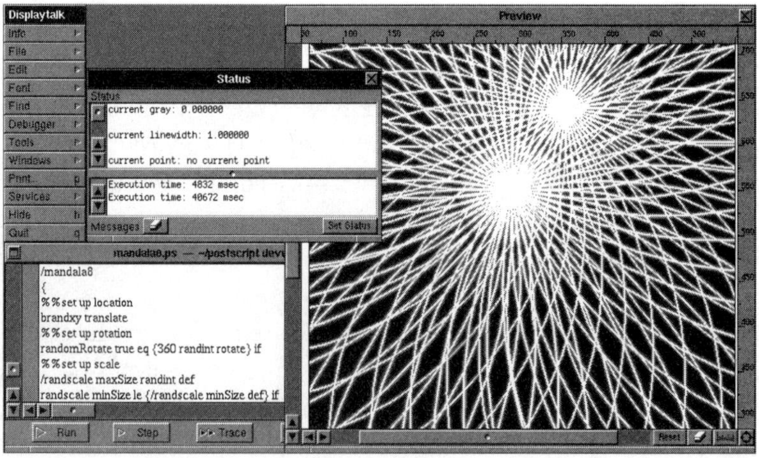

FreeHand

comes with several disks' worth of subsidiary files, most of which end up on your hard drive when you install FreeHand. What is all of this stuff? Where does it all go? Table A–1 shows you what's where, and why, for a standard Free-Hand installation. If you change folder names, or drag files around after you've installed them, things will look different.

Tip:
Use the Default
Installation

Why ask for trouble? Leave your FreeHand files where FreeHand's installer thinks they should go. Ideally, of course, FreeHand could find the files wherever you put them, with whatever names you cared to give them—ideally. We don't live in an ideal world, how-ever. and neither does FreeHand. FreeHand looks for specific files in specific folders. If it can't find them, it can't use them.

Always install your copy of FreeHand from copies of the origi-nal product disks, rather than by dragging the files off another drive or fileserver. It's too easy to miss all of the subsidiary files that aren't inside the application folder.

In spite of this admonition, it's okay to change the name of your FreeHand folder and put it anywhere you want.

FreeHand
Preferences

FreeHand stores the current settings of the Preferences dialog boxes, the location and state of all the palettes, and a variety of other, esoteric information in the FreeHand Preferences file, which you'll find in your Aldus folder in your System Folder.

TABLE B−1		What's installed when you install FreeHand
Folder	**File**	**What it is**
System:Extensions*	QuickTime	This extension makes it possible for your Macintosh to play onscreen "movies" saved in the QuickTime format. You need this file if you've installed the Features at a Glance online demonstration program.
	LaserWriter 8	PostScript printer driver file. Check the version number of the file—if it's not version 8.1.1 or newer, use a newer version of the driver and throw this file away.
System:Extensions: Printer Descriptions	Various PPDs	PostScript Printer Description files, which customize printing for a specific printer model. These are the printer models that appear in the Open PPD dialog box when you click Select PPD in the Print Options dialog box. If you don't have, and don't intend to use printers for which you have PPDs (including imagesetters at your service bureau), you can throw away those PPD files.
System:Aldus*	Aldus FreeHand Defaults	FreeHand defaults template file. You can open this file and change FreeHand's defaults, or add your own default colors layers, and styles.
	FreeHand Preferences	A text file containing your FreeHand preference settings (see "FreeHand Preferences," in this appendix for a description of the file's contents).
	FreeHand 4.0 Help	FreeHand's online help file. FreeHand has a very good context-sensitive online help system, so you might want to save this file. If you never use online help, you can throw this file away.
	FreeHand 4.0 Help.note	Notes you've taken while using FreeHand's online help. If you don't use online help, you can throw this file away.
System:Aldus:Utilities	Aldus Installer/Utility	The program you used to install FreeHand. If you want to use any of the diagnostic checks it performs (fonts, system version, etc.), or if you want to decompress any of the FreeHand files you didn't install, keep this around. If you don't, you can throw it away.

*In this table, I'll use the Macintosh's own shorthand for referring to folder locations. Instead of saying "In the Proximity folder in the Aldus folder in the system folder," I'll say "System:Aldus:Proximity."

TABLE B–1 (continued)   What's installed when you install FreeHand

Folder	File	What it is
System:Aldus:Utilities	TeachText	Like every other Installer in the world, FreeHand's gives you a copy of TeachText, Apple's simple text-viewing utility. You probably already have 20 or 30 of these, so you can throw this one away.
System:Aldus:Colors	Various color libraries (files labeled with the file extension .BCF or .ACF)	FreeHand's color libraries. Don't delete these unless you really have no intention of using a color from a specific color library. You can, however, shorten the Color List's popup menu by moving some of these files to another folder. You can import colors from color libraries in any folder.
System:Aldus:Proximity	AldUsn.bpx ALDUSN.NFO AldUsn00.vpx	FreeHand's hyphenation dictionaries. Don't throw these away. If you have hyphenation dictionaries for other languages installed, you'll see them in the Proximity folder, as well.
Aldus FreeHand 4.0**	Aldus FreeHand 4.0	You know, FreeHand.
	Aldus Installer Diagnostics	A text file created by the installer during installation. If you weren't watching the installer screens, and something went wrong, you can find it in this file. It's a log of the installation. If you ever plan to call Aldus Technical Support, keep this file. They'll be able to use it to help you troubleshoot your system. Otherwise, throw it away.
	Aldus Installer History	A text file created by the Installer during installation. You can throw this file away.
	ReadMe	A text file containing late-breaking information about FreeHand. Do read this file— there's often good stuff in it. I printed the file and threw it away, what you do with it is up to you (provided you read it, first).
	Shortcuts	A FreeHand publication containing tables of FreeHand's keyboard shortcuts and miscellaneous tips. Print this file out and keep it next to your machine until you find you're not referring to it anymore, then throw it away.
	FH 4.0 Balloon Help	Ballon Help files for FreeHand. I always turn Balloon Help off, so I throw these away.

**Wherever you put it, whatever you named it.

TABLE B-1 (continued)	What's installed when you install FreeHand	
Folder	**File**	**What it is**
Aldus FreeHand 4.0	Features at a Glance	An online demonstration program that shows you FreeHand's features by playing QuickTime movies. Once you've used FreeHand for a few days, you can throw this file away.
	FH4.QT1, FH4.QT2 FH4.QT3, FH4.QT4 FH4.QT5, FH4.QT6 FH4.QT7, FH4.QT8	QuickTime moves played by the Features at a Glance demonstration program. Throw these away when you throw Features at a Glance away.
Aldus FreeHand 4.0: Type 1 PostScript Fonts	128 Type 1 PostScript font files	You can use these fonts in any application—though you'll have to install them, first. You won't see these files unless you check Type 1 PostScript Fonts in the Aldus Installer Main Window. It's worth installing the lot to get Stone Print.
	UnStuffit	FreeHand's Type 1 PostScript font files are saved in compressed Stuffit archives. To decompress them, you need this application. If you already have Stuffit, you can delete this file.
Aldus FreeHand 4.0: Sample Illustrations	Various FreeHand publications	Sample FreeHand publication files (mostly the ones you see in printed form in the first section of the *Aldus FreeHand User Manual*). Install these files if you want to take a look at the way they're built—but you should be aware that they don't always demonstrate the best way to do things in FreeHand (they're better than previous samples, however). These files take up quite a bit of disk space, so you might want to delete them once you've finished examining them.

You can edit this file to change your preferences, but you've got to remember it's a "live" file—FreeHand writes changes to the file every time you quit the program (if not more frequently). Figure B-1 shows the contents of the FreeHand Preferences file, as well as a few tips (with each tip following the line it refers to) I've been able to figure out.

All of the coordinates in the FreeHand Preferences file are in pixels, and are measured from the lower-left corner of your screen (PostScript-style).

FIGURE B-1
Inside the FreeHand
Preferences file

```
% Aldus FreeHand Preferences File v4.0
(Modal21040Pos) (106 310 364 522)
```
All of the lines beginning with "(Modal" are the default positions of FreeHand's dialog boxes (such as the Add Pages dialog box or the Output Options dialog box).

```
(Modal21020Pos) (118 332 328 500)
(Modal24030Pos) (101 171 381 661)
(Modal21011Pos) (121 316 321 516)
(Modal27010Pos) (132 323 288 509)
(Modal20390Pos) (112 316 348 516)
(Modal21030Pos) (257 114 464 358)
(Modal24210Pos) (240 141 304 395)
(Modal24230Pos) (94 304 399 528)
(Modal24264Pos) (77 205 307 435)
(Modal24260Pos) (65 163 345 477)
(DataTypeAGD1ToClip) (Yes)
```
"Yes" to put data in FreeHand's native format on the Clipboard when you Cut or Copy FreeHand objects.

```
(DataTypeRTFToClip) (Yes)
```
"Yes" to put RTF data on the Clipboard when you Cut or Copy FreeHand text.

```
(DataTypeASCIIToClip) (Yes)
```
"Yes" to put ASCII data on the Clipboard when you Cut or Copy FreeHand text.

```
(DataTypeMacPICTToClip) (Yes)
```
"Yes" to put object PICT format data on the Clipboard when you Cut or Copy FreeHand objects.

```
(Modal27040Pos) (132 323 287 510)
(Modal27055Pos) (133 330 284 503)
(Modal27050Pos) (139 330 264 503)
(Modal21012Pos) (121 316 321 516)
(Modal24215Pos) (150 289 234 543)
(Modal24220Pos) (149 340 237 492)
(Modal21005Pos) (116 316 336 516)
(XformSwitchZoom) (No)
```
"Yes" to minimize the Transform palette (if it's visible).

```
(XformSwitchVis) (No)
```
"Yes" to make the Transform palette visible.

```
(XformSwitchPos) (301 519 523 658)
```
Location of the Transform palette (if it's visible).

```
(AlignMgrZoom) (No)
```
"Yes" to minimize the Align palette (if it's visible).

```
(AlignMgrVis) (No)
```
"Yes" to make the Align palette visible.

```
(AlignMgrPos) (125 79 325 199)
```
Location of the Align palette (if it's visible).

```
(HtoneEdZoom) (No)
```
"Yes" to minimize the Halftone palette (if it's visible).

```
(HtoneEdVis) (No)
```
"Yes" to make the Halftone palette visible.

FIGURE B-1
Inside the FreeHand
Preferences file
(continued)

(HtoneEdPos) (278 95 400 215)
Location of the Halftone palette (if it's visible).

(StyleLPZoom) (No)
"Yes" to minimize the Styles palette (if it's visible).

(StyleLPVis) (No)
"Yes" to display the Styles palette.

(StyleLPPos) (314 488 421 606)
Location of the Styles palette (if it's visible).

(TintMgrZoom) (No)
"Yes" to minimize the Tints palette (if it's visible).

(TintMgrVis) (No)
"Yes" to display the Tints palette.

(TintMgrPos) (451 -12 551 108)
Location of the Tints palette (if it's visible).

(FHLayerMgrZoom) (No)
"Yes" to minimize the Layers palette (if it's visible).

(FHLayerMgrVis) (No)
"Yes" to display the Layers palette.

(FHLayerMgrPos) (317 179 411 299)
Location of the Layers palette (if it's visible).

(FontMgrZoom) (No)
"Yes" to minimize the Type Specifications palette (if it's visible).

(FontMgrVis) (Yes)
"Yes" to display the Type Specifications palette.

(FontMgrPos) (230 455 253 711)
Location of the Type Specifications (if it's visible).

(ColorLPZoom) (No)
"Yes" to minimize the Color List (if it's visible).

(ColorLPVis) (No)
"Yes" to display the Color List .

(ColorLPPos) (119 668 235 794)
Location of the Color List (if it's visible).

(ColorMakerZoom) (No)
"Yes" to minimize the Color Mixer (if it's visible).

(ColorMakerVis) (No)
"Yes" to display the Color Mixer.

(ColorMakerPos) (147 241 281 361)
Location of the Color Mixer (if it's visible).

(InspMgrZoom) (No)
"Yes" to minimize the Inspector (if it's visible).

(InspMgrVis) (No)
"Yes" to display the Inspector.

FIGURE B-1
Inside the FreeHand
Preferences file
(continued)

```
(InspMgrPos) (121 458 361 578)
```
Location of the Inspector (if it's visible).

```
(ToolMgrZoom) (No)
```
"Yes" to minimize the Toolbox (if it's visible).

```
(ToolMgrVis) (Yes)
```
"Yes" to display the Toolbox.

```
(ToolMgrPos) (387 239 530 290)
```
Toolbox location.

```
(QTCompressType) (smc )
(QTCompressQuality) (512)
(UseQTCompression) (No)
(ThrashOMeter) (No)
```
Beats me!

```
(ExpandMiter) (3.8636932373)
```
Default Miter Limit.

```
(ExpandCap) (0)
```
*Sets the default Cap style 0 = Butt cap, 1 = Square cap,
2 = Round cap (see page 134)*

```
(ExpandJoin) (0)
```
*Sets the default Join style. 0 = Miter join, 1 = Round join,
2 = Beveled join (see page 135)*

```
(ExpandWidth) (3)
```
Sets the default distance for Expand Stroke (see page 128)

```
(InsetMiter) (3.8636932373)
```
Sets the default Miter Limit for Expand Stroke and Inset Path.

```
(InsetJoin) (0)
```
*Sets the default join style for the Expand Stroke and Inset Path
(see "(Expand Join)", above).*

```
(InsetWidth) (6)
```
Sets the default distance for Inset Path (see page 129)

```
(HypLangName) (US English)
(SaveWindowSizeNLoc) (Yes)
```

*The following entries correspond to the fields and checkboxes in the
Preferences dialog boxes (unless otherwise noted).*
```
(HiResTIFF) (Yes)
(FetchPreviewSize) (100)
(AddFetchPreview) (No)
(Dither8BitColors) (No)
(BitmapPICTPreviews) (No)
(GridColor) (1.0 0.0 0.0)
(DynamicScrollBarThumbs) (Yes)
(BufferedDrawing) (No)
(ConvertPICTPatsToGrays) (Yes)
(ColorAdjustBlack) (0.0 0.0 0.0)
(ColorAdjustBlue) (0.075 0.006 0.488)
(ColorAdjustGreen) (0.002 0.531 0.217)
```

FIGURE B-1
Inside the FreeHand
Preferences file
(continued)

```
(ColorAdjustRed)  (1.0 0.0 0.0)
(ColorAdjustYellow)  (1.0 1.0 0.0)
(ColorAdjustMagenta)  (0.937 0.016 0.499)
(ColorAdjustCyan)  (0.007 0.626 0.775)
(AdjustColors)  (Yes)
(IncludeEPSFonts)  (No)
```
"Yes" to include downloadable fonts in exported EPS files.

```
(GroupTransformsAsUnit)  (No)
(TransformLines)  (No)
(TransformFills)  (No)
(TransformContents)  (Yes)
(ViewingSetsActivePage)  (Yes)
(UserPSIncludeFile)  (UserPrep)
```
*If you want to call the file containing your custom PostScript routines
something other than "UserPrep", enter the filename here.*

```
(UndoCount)  (10)
(TraceToolTightFit)  (Yes)
```
"No" to turn off Tight Fit in the Tracing Tool dialog box (see page 132).

```
(TraceForegroundElements)  (Yes)
```
*"No" to turn off Trace Foreground Elements in the Tracing Tool
dialog box (see page 132).*

```
(TraceBackgroundElements)  (Yes)
```
*"No" to turn off Trace Background Elements in the Tracing Tool
dialog box (see page 132).*

```
(ToolsSetActivePage)  (Yes)
(TiffModePrintOverride)  (1)
(GreekTextBelow)  (8)
(StockLineWeights)  (0.25 0.5 1 1.5 2 4 6 8 12)
```
*Enter (or delete) stroke widths here to change the stroke widths displayed on the
Stroke Widths submenu of the Arrange menu (see page 29).*

```
(SnapDistance)  (3)
(SnapToVGuideSound)  (Wild Eep)
(SnapToPointSound)  (Sosumi)
(SnapToHGuideSound)  (Indigo)
(SnapToGridSound)  (Droplet)
(SnapSoundsWithMouseUp)  (No)
(SnapSoundsEnabled)  (No)
(RememberLayers)  (Yes)
(RememberDocumentView)  (Yes)
(RectangleCornerRoundness)  (0.0)
(PickDistance)  (3)
(NGonToolStarPointSharpness)  (0.4899902344)
```
*Sets the position of the slider in the Star Points section
of the Polygon Tool dialog box (see page 47).*

```
(NGonToolNumberOfSides)  (8)
```
Sets the number of sides in the Polygon Tool dialog box (see page 47).

```
(NGonToolMakeStars)  (No)
```
"Yes" to make the Polygon tool to draw stars (see page 47).

FIGURE B-1
Inside the FreeHand
Preferences file
(continued)

```
(NewStylesTakeCurProps) (Yes)
(NewStylesAutoApply) (Yes)
(HighQualityGrads) (No)
(GuideColor) (0.5188067445 0.5188067445 0.5188067445)
(FHToolVariableWidth) (No)
```
*"Yes" to turn the FreeHand tool into the Variable Stroke tool
by default (see page 49).*

```
(FHToolCalligraphic) (No)
```
*"Yes" to turn the FreeHand tool into the Calligraphic Pen tool
by default (see page 50).*

```
(FHToolTightFit) (Yes)
```
*"Yes" to turn on the Tight Fit checkbox in the FreeHand Tool
dialog box (see page 49).*

```
(FHToolMinWidth) (1)
```
*Sets the Min field in the FreeHand Tool dialog box when you choose
Variable Stroke (see page 49).*

```
(FHToolMaxWidth) (12)
```
*Sets the Max field in the FreeHand Tool dialog box when you choose
Variable Stroke (see page 49).*

```
(FHToolConnectDots) (Yes)
```
*"Yes" to turn off the Draw Dotted Line checkbox in the FreeHand Tool
dialog box (see page 49).*

```
(FHToolCalligraphicWidth) (16)
```
*Sets the Min field in the FreeHand Tool dialog box when you choose
Calligraphic Pen (see page 49).*

```
(FHToolCalligraphicAngle) (45)
```
*Sets the Max field in the FreeHand tool dialog box
when you choose Calligraphic Pen (see page 49).*

```
(EmbedDocInEps) (Yes)
```
*"Yes" to include a copy of the FreeHand document in
EPS files when you export EPS.*

```
(DrawWhileScrolling) (No)
(PreviewDragLimit) (1)
(DrawTextEffects) (Yes)
(DeleteEmptyTextContainers) (Yes)
(InspectorPanel) (0)
(NewDocumentTemplate) (Aldus FreeHand Defaults)
(CursorKeyDistance) (1)
(CrackPlacedEPS) (No)
(EditsChangeDefaults) (Yes)
(AlwaysJoinPaths) (Yes)
(AlwaysEmbedImports) (No)
```

Your FreeHand Preferences file might look a little different (that is, some keywords might appear in different places in your file). Don't worry about this—sometimes FreeHand writes things in a different order than the one shown here.

Confetti or Worms

When you hold down Option and click in picture in the About FreeHand dialog box, FreeHand displays an animated squiggle that runs around inside the confines of the dialog box. I've been told these squiggles are supposed to look like confetti, but they look more like hyperactive worms to me. Exhaustive research shows that you can have up to 20 worms active at time (see Figure B-2).

FIGURE B-2
Confetti (Worms)

Hold down Option as you click on the picture in the About FreeHand dialog box, and you'll see confetti streamers (or worms) celebrating the release of Aldus FreeHand 4.

FernHead

Is Altsys at work on the ultimate anagram generator? Try this: hold down Command-Control as you choose About FreeHand from the Apple menu, and then type "beavis". FreeHand displays the dialog box shown in Figure B-3.

FIGURE B-2
Anagrammatical fun

This appendix tells you where to get the things mentioned in this book. First of all, you can write to me or send me a message on Compuserve. I'd love to know what you thought of the book (even if you didn't like it—I took my best shot, but I can't correct my aim unless I know I've missed). I'd also love to hear about any fabulous FreeHand tips and tricks you've come up with (so I can steal them for the next editon).

Olav Martin Kvern
1619 Eighth Avenue North
Seattle, Washington 98109-3007
(206) 285-0308 (fax)
Compuserve: 76636,2535
internet: olavkvern@igc.apc.com

Adobe Systems, Incorporated
Adobe Illustrator, Adobe Dimensions, Adobe Photoshop,
Adobe Type Manager, Adobe Type Reunion,
Adobe PostScript, LaserTalk
1585 Charleston Road
Mountain View, California 94039
(415) 961-4400

Aladdin Systems, Incorporated
StuffIt Deluxe
Deer Park Center, Suite 23A-171
Aptos, California 95003
(408) 685-9175

Aldus Corporation
Aldus PageMaker, Aldus FreeHand, Aldus Persuasion,
Aldus PrePrint, Aldus TrapWise, Aldus ChartMaker
411 1st Avenue South
Seattle, Washington 98104
(206) 622-5500

AlSoft
MasterJuggler
P.O. Box 927
Spring, Texas 77383
(800) 257-6381
(713) 353-9868 (fax)

Altsys Corporation
EPS Exchange, Fontographer, Metamorphosis Pro, Virtuoso
269 West Renner Road
Richardson, Texas 75080
(214) 680-2060

ANPA
Newspaper Association of America
11600 Sunrise Valley Drive
Reston, Virginia 22091
(703) 648-1367

Apple Computer
MacDraw, ResEdit
20525 Mariani Avenue
Cupertino, California 95014
(408) 996-1010

CE Software
QuicKeys
1801 Industrial Circle
West Des Moines, Iowa 50265
(515) 224-1995

Focoltone
Springwater House
Taffs Well, Cardiff   CF4 7QR
United Kingdom
(44) 222-810-962

Microsoft Corporation
Microsoft Word, Microsoft Excel, RTF Specification
One Microsoft Way
Redmond, Washington 98052
(206) 882-8080

Now Software
Now Utilities (including *Super Boomerang)*
520 S.W. Harrison Street, Suite 435
Portland, Oregon 97201
(503) 274-2800
(503) 274-0670 (fax)

Pantone
55 Knickerbock Road
Moonachie, New Jersey 07074
(201) 935-5500

Peachpit Press
Lots of great books, especially—from this book's point of view—
Learning PostScirpt; A Visual Approach, by Ross Smith.
2414 Sixth Street
Berkeley, California 94710
(800) 283-9444

PrairieSoft
MockPackage (including *LaserStatus*), *DiskTop*
1650 Fuller Road
P.O. Box 65820
West Des Moines, Iowa 50265

Salient Software
DiskDoubler
124 University Avenue
Palo Alto, California 94301
(415) 321-5375

Seattle Gilbert & Sullivan Society
*Thespis, Trial by Jury, The Sorcerer, H.M.S. Pinafore, The Pirates of
Penzance, Patience, Iolanthe, Princess Ida, The Mikado, Ruddigore,
The Yeomen of the Guard, The Gondoliers, Utopia Limited, The
Grand Duke,* and, yes, even Sullivan & Burnand's *Cox and Box*
P.O. Box 15314
Seattle, Washington 98115

Symantec
Suitcase
175 West Broadway
Eugene, Oregon 97401
(800) 441-7234

TechPool Software, Inc.
1463 Warrensville Center Road
Cleveland, Ohio 44121-2676
(216) 291-1922

Toyo Ink Manufacturing Company Ltd.
3-13, 2-chome Kyobashi
Chuo-ku, Tokyo 10
Japan
(481) 3-2722-5721

TruMatch
25 West 43rd St., Suite 802
New York, New York 10036
(212) 302-9100

REAL WORLD FREEHAND 4 & THE DISK

Fold here

Peachpit Press
2414 Sixth Street
Berkeley, California
94710

place
stamp
here

REAL WORLD FREEHAND 4 § THE DISK

If you'd like to get your hands on a disk full of FreeHand fun, here's your chance. *Real World FreeHand 4 § The Disk* contains all of the PostScript lines and fills shown in this book, plus more lines and fills I didn't have space to show you (plus a few I've only just thought of). Besides that, you'll find AGX1 files for supercharging your copy of FreeHand, several useful color libraries, ResEdit templates for creating your own AGX1 files, .r files for building resources in C programming environments, FreeHand templates containing tiling and latticework patterns seen in this book, and even more FreeHand tips and tricks.

ORDERING INFORMATION

COPIES		PRICE	TOTAL
	REAL WORLD FREEHAND 4 § THE DISK	$20.00	

You can order by phone by calling Peachpit Press at (510) 548-4393 (In the United States, you can call toll-free: (800) 283-9444); or by faxing an order to (510) 548-5991.	SHIPPING *To anywhere in the world (including Finland)*	$4.00
	California residents please add 8.25% sales tax ($1.65)	
	TOTAL	

NAME

ADDRESS

CITY & STATE/PROVINCE	COUNTRY	ZIP/POSTAL CODE

CHECK ENCLOSED ☐	VISA ☐	MASTERCARD ☐	COMPANY PURCHASE ORDER

CREDIT CARD NUMBER	EXPIRATION DATE

Satisfaction unconditionally guaranteed or your money cheerfully refunded!